Enforcement of Transnational Regulation

PRIVATE REGULATION

Series Editor: Fabrizio Cafaggi, *European University Institute, Italy*

Under the general editorship of Fabrizio Cafaggi, and the guidance of a small, international advisory board including leading figures David Levi Faur, Katharina Pistor and Colin Scott, this *Private Regulation* series is a forum for monographs and collaborative, interdisciplinary volumes on private regulation through the lenses of law, economics, political science, sociology and philosophy. The role of transnational regulation and global governance is reshaping the distribution of power and opportunities across the world, calling for a radical conceptual transformation. Each of the books in the series will appeal not only to an academic audience but will also engage policy makers and practitioners involved in designing, implementing and enforcing regulatory policies.

Enforcement of Transnational Regulation

Ensuring Compliance in a Global World

Edited by

Fabrizio Cafaggi

Professor of Comparative Law and Director of the Centre for Judicial Cooperation, European University Institute, Italy (on leave from the University of Trento)

PRIVATE REGULATION

Edward Elgar

Cheltenham, UK • Northampton, MA, USA

Published by
Edward Elgar Publishing Limited
The Lypiatts
15 Lansdown Road
Cheltenham
Glos GL50 2JA
UK

Edward Elgar Publishing, Inc.
William Pratt House
9 Dewey Court
Northampton
Massachusetts 01060
USA

A catalogue record for this book is available from the British Library

Library of Congress Control Number: 2012930620

FSC www.fsc.org MIX Paper from responsible sources FSC® C018575

ISBN 978 1 78100 372 5 (cased)

Typeset by Columns Design XML Ltd, Reading
Printed and bound by MPG Books Group, UK

Contents

PART III TRANSNATIONAL PRIVATE REGIMES: CONTRASTING JUDICIAL AND NON-JUDICIAL ENFORCEMENT ACROSS SECTORS

PART IV CONCLUSION

Figures and tables

FIGURES

TABLES

Contributors

Eyal Benvenisti is Anny and Paul Yanowicz Professor of Human Rights, Tel Aviv University Faculty of Law. He is an Editorial Board member of the *American Journal of International* Law, and Member Associe of the Institut de Droit International. His areas of teaching and research include international law, constitutional law and administrative law. His publications include *Sharing Transboundary Resources: International Law and Optimal Resource Use* (2002) and *The International Law of Occupation* (second edition 2012).

Fabrizio Cafaggi is Professor of Comparative Law at the European University Institute on leave from Trento University. He is a member of the Executive Committee of the European Law Institute and coordinates the HiiL project on transnational private regulation. He is the Director of the Centre for Judicial Cooperation at EUI. His recent publications include *Contractual Networks, Inter-firm Cooperation and Economic Growth* (editor), *New Foundations of Transnational Private Regulation*, and *Transnational Governance by Contract: Private Regulation and Contractual Networks in Food Safety*.

Federica Casarosa is a research assistant at the European University Institute, Department of Law. She graduated in Private Comparative Law at the University of Pisa and obtained a Master of Research in Law from the European University Institute (2003). In 2008, she successfully defended her PhD thesis on the role of information in online contracting, in particular analysing the protection provided to consumers in the pre-contractual phase. She has worked as a consultant for FAO and as a Jean Monnet Fellow at the Robert Schuman Centre for Advanced Studies. Her research interests focus on new media law and regulation, and on child protection in the media sector. Her work appears in several Italian and international journals, such as the *European Review of Private Law*, the *Journal of Internet Law*, and *Diritto dell'Informazione e dell'Informatica*.

Sabino Cassese is Judge of the Italian Constitutional Court. Having graduated *summa cum laude* in law in 1956, from the University of Pisa, since 1961 he has served as Professor of Administrative Law at the Universities of Urbino, Naples and Rome. He has been a member of many governmental committees and, in 1993–94, was a member of the Italian Government. He currently teaches History and Theory of the State at the 'Scuola Normale Superiore', in Pisa and Global Regulation for the Master of Public Affairs at Sciences Po, Paris. He taught Administrative Law at the Faculty of Law of the University of Rome 'La Sapienza' from 1985 to 2005.

He has received a *doctor honoris causa* degree from seven Universities: Aix-en-Provence, Cordoba, Paris II, Castilla-La Mancha, Athens, Macerata and the European University Institute.

He was President of the European Group of Public Administration (International Institute of Administrative Sciences) from 1987 to 1991, and visiting professor at the NYU Hauser Global Law School (2004 and 2010). In 2006 he founded the Institute for Research on Public Administration (IRPA). His most recent works include: *Il mondo nuovo del diritto* (2008, Laterza), *Il diritto globale* (2009, Einaudi), *Massimo Severo Giannini* (2010, Laterza) and *Il diritto amministrativo: storia e prospettive* (2010, Giuffrè), *Lo Stato fascista* (2010, Il Mulino), *When Legal Orders Collide: the Role of Courts* (2010, Global Law Press), *L'Italia una società senza Stato* (2011, Il Mulino).

Elisa D'Alterio, PhD (Administrative Law), and lawyer, is research fellow at the University of Rome 'Sapienza'. She won several scholarships on administrative law topics, and participated as discussant in prestigious seminars on global administrative law. Her major areas of research are: relations among legal orders, the regulatory function of courts, transparency and performance of public administrations, and outsourcing of public activities. Her most recent publications include the book, *La funzione di regolazione delle corti nello spazio amministrativo globale* (*The Regulatory Function of Courts in the Global Administrative Space*) (Giuffrè, 2010) and several articles, in particular: 'From judicial comity to legal comity: a judicial solution to global disorder?' in *International Journal of Constitutional Law* (*I·CON*) (2011), and 'Tecniche giudiziarie di regolazione dei rapporti tra diritto europeo e diritto globale' ('Judicial techniques of regulation of relations between European law and global law'), in *Sistemi regolatori globali e diritto europeo* (*Global Regulatory Systems and European Law*) (Giuffrè, 2011).

Kevin E. Davis is Beller Family Professor of Business Law at New York University School of Law. His research and teaching interests include contracts, commercial law, economic crime, and the relationship between law and economic development.

Maurizia De Bellis is tenured Assistant Professor in Administrative Law at the University of Rome 'Tor Vergata'. She is also clerk at the Italian Constitutional Court. She has been Global Research Fellow at New York University School of Law and Jemolo Fellow at Nuffield College, Oxford University. She co-authored the book *Global Administrative Law and EU Administrative Law* (edited by B.G. Mattarella and E. Chiti.), writing the chapter 'EU and global private regulatory regimes: the accounting and auditing sectors'. Among her recent publications are also 'Public law and private regulators in the global legal space', in *International Journal of Constitutional Law*, **9**(2) (2011) and 'Global standards for sovereign wealth funds: the quest for transparency', in *Asian Journal of International Law*, **1**(2) (2011). Currently, her research interests focus on financial regulation and climate finance.

George W. Downs is Professor of Politics and the former Dean for Social Sciences at NYU. Prior to coming to NYU 1998, he was Boswell Professor of Peace and War at Princeton University. His areas of specialization are international institutions and international cooperation, and his current research focuses on the changing role of the judiciary in the international global regulatory system and the impact of failed states on human rights outcomes. Publications include the books *Bureaucracy, Innovation, and Public Policy*; *The Search for Government Efficiency*; *Tacit Bargaining, Arms Races and Arms Control*; *Collective Security After the Cold War* and *Optimal Imperfection? Domestic Uncertainty and Institutions in International Relations*, as well as articles in political science, international law, and for statistics journals.

Cynthia Estlund is the Catherine A. Rein Professor of Law at the New York University School of Law. She has written extensively on labour and employment law, and is the author of *Regoverning the Workplace: From Self-Regulation to Co-Regulation* (Yale University Press, 2010).

Francesco Francioni, Dr. Jur. (Florence and LL.M Harvard), is Professor of International Law and Human Rights and Co-Director of the Academy of European Law at the European University Institute in Florence. Prior to moving to the European University Institute, he was the Director of the International Peace Studies Center and Jean Monnet Chair in European Law (Professore Ordinario) at the Faculty of Law, University of Siena. He is a member of the Institut de Droit international and of the American Law Institute. He was the chairman of the World Heritage Committee of UNESCO and the Italian delegate of many diplomatic negotiations for the adoption of treaties and other normative instruments on the protection of cultural property, including the UNIDROIT Convention and the Second Protocol to the 1954 Convention. He is a member of the Editorial Board of the *European Journal of International Law* and general editor of the Italian *Yearbook of International Law*. He has written and edited many books, most recently *War by Contract* (with Ronzitti, OUP, 2011), *The 1972 World Heritage Convention: A Commentary* (OUP, 2008), *Access to Justice as a Human Right* (OUP, 2007) and *La Dimension pluridisciplinaire de la responsabilité sociale de l'entreprise* (with M.A. Moreau, Aix-en Provence, 2007). Recent articles in peer reviewed journals include: 'International human rights in an environmental horizon', *EJIL* (2010); 'Au-delà des traités: l'émergence d'un nouveau droit coutumier pour la protection du patrimoine culturel', *Revue Générale de droit international public* (2007) and 'From cultural property to cultural heritage: the dynamic evolution of a concept and scope', *L'action normative de l'UNESCO* (2007).

Geoffrey P. Miller, the Stuyvesant P. Comfort Professor at New York University Law School, is a nationally recognized expert on banking and financial institution regulation, law and economics, and complex litigation. Professor Miller attended Columbia University Law School, where he was Editor-in-Chief of the Law Review, served as a judicial clerk to Judge Carl McGowan of the U.S. Court of Appeals for the District of Columbia Circuit and to Justice Byron White of the United States Supreme Court, and worked as an attorney in the United States Department of Justice Office of Legal Counsel and at a private firm before entering law teaching. Miller is the Director of NYU Law School's Center for Financial Institutions and a founder and former co-president of the Society for Empirical Legal Studies. A recent inductee in the American Academy of Arts and Sciences, Miller has been a visiting professor or visiting scholar at institutions around the world. He is author of five books and nearly two hundred scholarly articles in the fields of banking law, civil procedure, corporate law, legal ethics, and law and economics.

Ernst-Ulrich Petersmann is Emeritus Professor and former Head of the Law Department of the European University Institute at Florence, Italy. He has published more than 25 books on international economic law and was a former legal advisor in the German Ministry of Economic Affairs, GATT and the World Trade Organization.

Colin Scott is Dean of Law and Professor of EU Regulation & Governance at University College Dublin. His main research interests are concerned with the design and operation of regulation regimes, accountability of regulation and non-state regulation.

Richard Stewart is University Professor at New York University, where he serves as Faculty Director of the Hauser Global Law School Program, and Director of the Guarini Center on Environmental and Land Use Law. He teaches and writes on environmental law and policy, administrative law and regulation, and law and global governance. His current research interests include global administrative law, international and domestic climate finance and regulation, and nuclear waste issues.

Paul Verbruggen is a PhD researcher at the European University Institute. He writes on the design and operation of non-stage, private regulation and its interplay with public regulatory frameworks, focusing on questions of legitimacy, accountability and enforcement. His current research interests include EU regulatory policy, risk regulation and consumer protection issues. One of his publications is entitled 'Does co-regulation strengthen EU legitimacy?', which appeared in the *European Law Journal*.

Preface

THE CONTENT OF THE BOOK AND THE WIDER PROJECT

This book focuses on the enforcement of transnational regulation. It is part of a broader research project concerning different aspects of transnational private regulation (for further information on the project please see http://privateregulation.eu/). It can be located within the debate on legal aspects of globalization.

Transnational private regulation is a new research project that wants to open up a new field focusing upon regulatory regimes that are not exclusively State based, but include private actors. Within the private sphere the research highlights the different roles of firms and NGOS in rule-making, monitoring compliance and enforcing transnational rules. These regimes have emerged for different reasons and pose serious challenges to State sovereignty. They have been criticized for lack of accountability, conflict with democratic principles and compliance with rules of law. An even more serious criticism is related to the enforceability of the rules. Often the commitments made by single firms or trade organizations are considered not legally enforceable and not binding, thereby reducing their effectiveness. Enforcement, thus, becomes a key question to examine the private–public divide.

Transnational Private Regulation and *Lex Mercatoria*

Transnational private regulation (TPR) emerges as a different phenomenon from conventional transnational private regimes like *lex mercatoria* and commercial arbitration. The regulatory dimension assumes a preponderant role in the mission and activity of private regulators. They respond to market and governmental failures at the global level, manage systemic risks, and govern global commons. The new private regulatory regimes are often multiple, frequently competing, and sometimes overlapping in different regional areas. They reflect preferences of developed and developing countries and may imply different distributional consequences. The most evident case is the one on food safety regimes, where retailers and distributors have designed different but overlapping regimes, imposing heavy compliance burdens on producers in developing countries.

Harmonization of Legal Rules at Global Level

One of the main goals of transnational private regulation is to harmonize standards and principles and make them compliant with fundamental rights, as in the case of private securities companies, where putting a stop to human rights abuses is the main objective of transnational private regulatory regimes. Legislative divergences between developed and developing countries are profound, but often practices among developed countries differ significantly. Lack of political consensus prevents the enactment of international treaties or implementing them in a consistent manner. Often private regulatory regimes provide vehicles for harmonization or instruments to implement soft international law principles.

The Public–Private Divide

Private regulatory regimes emerge to fill gaps created by weaknesses of the public sphere at the global level. However, they consolidate not as an alternative to public regulation, but as a complement that needs to rely on strong public institutions, especially at the domestic level. The advertising sector, for instance, has a layered system where international private regulations are administered and enforced by national self-regulatory organizations; however, in the accounting sector, global private governance relies on domestic public authorities. Also, from the point of view of enforcement, there is often a combination of domestic courts and global private enforcers, including arbitrators. The case of online trading platforms provides another illustration, as the enforcement systems are differentiated in relation to the type of actors involved in the conflicts, for instance in regulator versus regulatees or regulatees versus third parties.

Enforcement of TPR

How different are the enforcement mechanisms in private regimes in comparison with those adopted by international organizations and intergovernmental organizations? What happens when hybrids including public and private organizations collaborate to define rules and enforcement?

These regimes are often multilevel, involving different types of dispute resolution systems, ranging from internal mediation, where the solution to the conflict can be achieved through mere collaboration of the interested parties, to arbitration, where third parties, previously selected by the regulator, provide the solution to the conflict, applying either general principles of law (e.g. in the case of ICANN) or specific rules defined in the TPR (e.g. in food safety regimes such as GlobalGap). Rule making takes place globally, while enforcement occurs locally, either by way of judicial intervention or the use of private enforcers including arbitration. This can be seen in the case of ICANN, where *ex ante* approved arbitrators and domestic courts can solve the disputes between domain name users and third parties, depending on the choice left to the latter.

This dynamic makes domestic courts key players of the enforcement mechanisms. However, domestic courts act upon their domestic principles and may reach very different results concerning both the enforceability of transnational private regulation and the available remedies in case of violations. Divergences pose problems of coordination and governance of the effects of judicial review on the regimes. Furthermore, often enforceability is granted by private enforcers which operate either within the overall regime or as independent enforcers. In particular, this can be perceivable in the already mentioned case of advertising, where national self-regulatory organizations apply international rules through the lenses of national consumers' expectations, but are at the same time trying to converge in their interpretation, at least at European level, through participation in the European Advertising Standards Alliance.

The aim of the book is to bring together different disciplinary perspectives on the enforcement of transnational regulation. The goal is, on the one hand, to open up the field of transnational private regulation, with the contribution of private lawyers whose expertise is related to contract and tort, and, on the other hand, to engage with current research projects on legal globalization associated with public international law and global administrative law.

Fabrizio Cafaggi

Acknowledgments

This book was designed within the HiiL project on the role of private actors. It is part of a wider research project that addresses legitimacy, quality, effectiveness and enforcement of transnational private regulation. It is the first book in the private regulation series, which will host contributions coming from different disciplines including law, economics, political science and sociology.

I am deeply grateful to Rebecca Schmidt and Federica Casarosa for their extremely valuable contributions to the editorial work and coordination. Without their commitment and ability, the book could not have been published. I am also very grateful to Rebecca Hastie, Kate Pearce and Laura Seward for their very effective editorial assistance to the manuscript. Finally, my deep gratitude to those who have travelled with me through the difficult period I have been living in.

To my EUI students, 2002–2012, with gratitude.

Introduction: The transformation of transnational private regulation: enforcement gaps and governance design[1]

Fabrizio Cafaggi

Transnational private regulation (TPR) is growing, giving rise to numerous regimes at the global level which interplay with public, international and domestic regimes. TPR encompasses regimes that primarily, but not exclusively, regulate firms operating in markets that extend beyond States' boundaries. The scope ranges from trade (electronic platforms to trade goods, services and shares) to human rights, from food safety to financial and banking, from professional (accounting, legal, medical) to technical (telecom, aviation, electricity) standards, from environmental to employment standards, and from advertising to data protection. Within each sector, global supply chains have become relevant global regulators, developing contractual regulatory tools which are applied to some or all participants.[2] TPRs are frequently embedded within independent private orders, often pursuing conflicting policies; their normative foundations are primarily based on private autonomy, freedom of contract and association limited by constitutional and international laws. Thence, they are primarily regulated by their relevant constitutional contracts and/or organizational charters; gaps are filled by reference to domestic private law regimes, whereby

[1] This introduction has strongly benefited from deep and rich discussions with the EUI Casebook working group. My thanks go also to Rebecca Schmidt and Federica Casarosa for editorial and research assistance. Responsibility for the text is mine.

[2] See on the relationship between private regulation and supply chains, S. Henson and J. Humphrey, 'The impact of private food safety standards on the food chain and on public standard setting processes', paper prepared for FAO/WHO, May 2009, available at www.fao.org (last visited April 2011). (Hereafter, 'The impact of private food safety standards'.) For a taxonomy of global value chains in relation to different power relationships see G. Gereffi, J. Humphrey and T. Sturgeon, 'The governance of global value chain', *Review of International Political Economy*, 2005, 78–104.

the rules applicable are determined by conflict of law rules.[3] Their scope is sector specific and they lack a general legal framework but for the one provided by applicable public international law and common constitutional principles.[4] Growing recognition of the necessity to coordinate and avoid conflicts has begun to generate private meta-regulators, organizations whose goal is to produce general transnational rules that private organizations, across sectors, can freely adopt.[5] However this trend is in its infancy.

TPR often consolidates as a result of combined governmental and market failures. However, it emerges not only as a consequence of the weaknesses and shortcomings of States and global public regulatory regimes, but also for technological reasons which require fast and effective decision-making processes, allowing rules to be adapted in line with both industry and human rights evolution.

The consolidation of TPR, complementary to international regulation enacted by States through treaties or other legally binding instruments, poses daunting challenges to market governance but also to the implementation of fundamental rights and rule of law principles.[6] It shifts power and responsibility from public to private entities. It redistributes rule-making powers among actors, within the private sphere, and across markets between northern and southern players. Those challenges pertain to its legitimacy and effectiveness vis-à-vis other forms of public global regulation based on States' direct or delegated exercise of rule-making power at the international level.[7] They stand at the core of the scope of global democracy and transnational legal pluralism.

Unlike many forms of *lex mercatoria*, which predominantly apply only to the members of the regulatory 'club', these regimes produce global collective goods or '*bads*', having effects beyond the members of the

---

[3] See F. Cafaggi, 'New foundations of transnational private regulation', in C. Scott, F. Cafaggi and L. Senden (eds), *The Challenges of Transnational Private Regulation: Conceptual and Constitutional Debates*, Blackwell, 2011, pp. 20ff. (hereafter, 'New foundations').

[4] On the application of public international law to TPR see Chapters 5 and 6, this volume.

[5] An example is that of ISEAL whose codes are meant to apply to its members but can also reach a much wider community of 'users'. See the Codes available at http://www.isealalliance.org/ (last visited June 2011).

[6] See 'Introduction', in C. Scott, F. Cafaggi and L. Senden (eds), *The Challenges of Transnational Private Regulation: Conceptual and Constitutional Debates*, Blackwell, 2011.

[7] See B. Kingsbury, N. Krisch and R. Stewart, 'The emergence of global administrative law', 68 *Law and Contemporary Problems*, 15 (2005) and S. Cassese, 'Global standards for national administrative procedure', 68 *Law and Contemporary Problems*, 109 (2005).

regulatory bodies that govern the rule-making process. Unlike international commercial law, the standards have regulatory purposes in addressing both market and governmental failures. They deploy various standard setting instruments, ranging from principles and guidelines to codes of conduct, regulatory contracts, and master agreements. These are primarily voluntary tools to which regulated entities subscribe in different forms: from acquiring membership to becoming a signatory of the regulatory contracts or by choosing to become a regulated entity, making reference to the regulator's master agreement and incorporating its terms in their executory contracts.[8]

In fact, regulated entities, which voluntarily subscribe to a regime, undertake contractual or organizational commitments to abide by the rules and to comply with sanctions when infringements occur. Violations of these commitments are, in theory, subject to ordinary domestic laws of contract or association and company laws.

Enforcement represents a strategic juncture for the effectiveness and legitimacy of TPR. For the purpose of this book, legal enforcement encompasses administrative, judicial and non-judicial private enforcement. Within private non-judicial enforcement we include different types of legal mechanisms characterized by the existence of an enforcer (first, second or third party) using some type of adjudicating procedure, which may include also self-enforcing contracts subject to *ex post* scrutiny.[9] Accordingly we oppose the idea that private non-judicial enforcement belongs only to the social rather than also to the legal sphere. Litigation is part of the enforcement mechanisms and the distinction between individual and aggregate litigation has been at the core of the recent debate in the domain of transnational litigation.[10] Such a distinction is relevant for TPR but the

---

[8] Global private standards become binding also by way of tort law when courts refer to them in defining rules of conduct like the duty of care or negligence. In the contributions both contractual and tort-based enforcement are considered.

[9] Self-enforcement should be distinguished from spontaneous enforcement through market or community mechanisms. The former is part of the legal toolbox, the latter do not deploy legal mechanisms. Even in self-enforcement, parties are limited by legal constraints linked with due process and other general principles. See for a general overview applied to self-enforcing contracts: S.E. Masten and J. Prufer, 'On the evolution of collective enforcement institutions: communities and courts', TILEC Discussion Paper, DP 2011–017, pp. 1ff. (available at SSRN: http://papers.ssrn.com/sol3/papers.cfm?abstract_id=1773486); A. Katz, 'Taking private ordering seriously', 144 *University of Pennsylvania Law Review* (1995–1996), 1745ff. See also generally: I. Ayres and J. Braithwaite, *Responsive Regulation: Transcending the Deregulation Debate*, OUP, 1995.

[10] See S. Issacharoff, R.H. Klonoff, R.A. Nagareda and C. Silver, *Principles of the Law of Aggregate Litigation*, ALI, 2010.

aggregate dimension is significantly underdeveloped both in the judicial and non-judicial domain.

While the analysis concerning enforcement of international public regimes is quite advanced, enforcement of transnational private regimes has not yet been adequately investigated.[11] Enforcement, including judicial, administrative and non-judicial enforcement, performs manifold functions in ensuring the effectiveness and evolution of TPRs: (1) it defines the boundaries of private regimes, allocating regulatory power among transnational regulators; (2) it produces and/or corrects (un)desirable distributional effects; (3) it contributes to the architecture of transnational legal pluralism, transcending inter-governmentalism; and (4) it fills gaps when regimes are based on incomplete 'contracts' or private legislation.

Domestic courts, administrative agencies and private enforcers could play a significant role to ensure TPR's effectiveness by policing the regulatory agreements, by monitoring the commitments of regulated entities and by ensuring regulatory compliance. However, important differences exist among them and choice of forum may have strategic implications. Often conflict of laws rules designate developing countries with weak and inadequate judicial systems as competent jurisdictions, while nevertheless being alert to the extraterritorial effects of Western jurisdictions. An institutional design dilemma underlies the alternatives of empowering developing countries' courts or granting extraterritorial effects to developed countries' enforcers.[12] Currently the responses vary from sector to sector, and from country to country.

Courts, administrative agencies and private enforcers are not the only policing institutions of TPRs; markets and communities contribute a great deal to secure compliance through non-legal devices, giving rise to an apparent paradox. While, formally, private regulations are voluntary

---

11 See in this volume F. Francioni, Chapter 5. For a general discussion from different perspectives see S. Cassese, *Il diritto globale, Giustizia e democrazia oltre lo Stato*, Einaudi, 2009, esp. pp. 133ff. See also B. Kingsbury, 'Weighing global regulatory rules and decisions in national court', *Acta Juridica*, 90, 2009; E. Benvenisti and G. Downs, 'Will national court cooperation promote global accountability? The judicial review of international organizations' (hereinafter 'National court cooperation'), unpublished manuscript on file with the author; R. Teitel and R. Howse, 'Cross-judging tribunalization in a connected but fragmented global order', 41 *International Law and Politics* 2009; A. von Bogdandy and I. Venzke, 'In whose name? An investigation of international courts' public authority and its democratic justification', 2010, available at SSRN: http://papers.ssrn.com/sol3/papers.cfm?abstract_id=1593543

12 Enforcers should be understood as both courts and private enforcers to the extent that they operate in territorial rather than functional jurisdictions.

instruments, to which parties are free to subscribe or alternatively, abstain, their adoption has often come to be understood as the precondition for access to global markets or other regulatory spaces. Frequently then, these transnational private regimes are legally voluntary but socially or economically binding.

Legal enforcement constitutes only one mechanism to achieve compliance, a fundamental goal to meet basic 'rule of law' requirements. It primarily operates *ex post* while traditionally compliance mechanisms tend to operate *ex ante*. Compliance, like enforcement mechanisms are context and sector-dependent.[13] They vary across sectors, but, more importantly, they vary in relation to the specifically adopted regulatory strategy. In TPR, we can identify different approaches ranging from command and control, to responsive or market-based regulation, each one calling for specific instruments.[14] In particular, the combination of *ex ante* and *ex post* devices constitutes a crucial turning point in the design of the mix of compliance and enforcement tools: when a regime opts for strong *ex ante* requirements, associated, for example, with certification or licensing, the role of *ex post* legal enforcement decreases. When access to the regulatory regime by the regulated is free or it is simply linked to membership requirements, the role of legal enforcement increases.

While rule-making is ever more transnational, enforcement is still predominantly decentralized at the local level. Decentralization in TPR is not only territorial but also functional, as it is the case in the field of corporate social responsibility (CSR) for enforcement in supply-chain based regulatory systems that cut across State boundaries.[15] However, the institutional allocation between transnational and local does not follow for the classical partition within international law between primary and secondary rules.[16]

---

[13] See for example the evaluation of compliance in relation to international soft law agreement; E. Brown Weiss, 'Rethinking compliance with international law', in E. Benvenisti and M. Hirsch, *The Impact of International Law in International Cooperation*, CUP, 2004, pp. 134ff.

[14] The use of categories developed in domestic public regulation should be accompanied by a word of caution about mechanic transfers. Clearly the private dimension calls for a reconceptualization, which considers the different normative foundations of TPR.

[15] As we shall see in supply-chain-based private regulation, compliance mechanisms are designed by the multinational corporations (MNCs) to be applied along the chain with some adaptations to the national legal system where the dispute arises.

[16] On the actual role of this distinction and more broadly the actual direction of the debate between monism and pluralism see Francioni, Chapter 5 in this volume.

Often the private standard setter defines both the substantive and procedural rules, with the exception of judicial enforcement, where the definition of the latter is usually provided by national legal systems. Compared with public regimes, especially in non-judicial enforcement, TPR displays a wider variety of institutional arrangements existing among different levels, and giving rise to different types of architectures. Institutional complementarity between public and private standards has thence relevant effects on enforcement strategy.[17]

ENFORCEMENT GAPS AND INSTITUTIONAL DESIGN

Compliance and enforcement have become central issues for the credibility and legitimacy of TPR.[18] The multiplication of legal regimes at the transnational level has so far not been accompanied by effective enforcement mechanisms, as a result of which enforcement gaps that undermine their legitimacy and credibility have arisen. These gaps have both an institutional and a substantive dimension.

Institutionally, specialized private enforcement bodies still tend to focus primarily on internal disputes within regimes, neglecting conflicts among them. This asymmetry partly depends on a lack of jurisdiction over inter-organizational disputes and partly on the willingness to reinforce separateness among different global legal orders.[19] For example, the dispute settlement body (DSB) of a transnational private regulator has jurisdiction over disputes between its members or between them and the regulator, while it has limited ability to adjudicate over conflicts concerning the interpretation of a code of conduct enacted by another organization to which 'its' members have committed to comply. Suppose, for instance, that a CSR organization has a clause in its bylaws imposing compliance with a code of conduct concerning employment standards enacted by another private organization. If conflicting interpretations arise over the nature of those employment standards, it would not be possible for each DSB to give

---

[17] See on these questions Cassese, D'Alterio and De Bellis, Chapter 12 in this volume.

[18] The question of compliance has become central in public international law and international relations in the last 20 years. See D. Shelton (ed.), *Commitment and Compliance*, OUP, 2000, and E. Benvenisti and M. Hirsch, *The Impact of International Law in International Cooperation*, CUP, 2004.

[19] See F. Cafaggi, 'The architecture of transnational private regulation' (May 1, 2011). EUI Law working paper, available at SSRN: http://ssrn.com/abstract=1899555

the final word because no DSB has conclusive or exclusive jurisdiction over the dispute among instruments enacted by different regulators. Their jurisdiction would probably be limited to the effects of the interpretation of the code over their members. The conflicting interpretations of multiple private enforcers will have to co-exist. Cooperative joint enforcement is highly underdeveloped among transnational private organizations; however, new forms of coordination have recently emerged through Memorandum of understanding (MoU) and functional equivalents.[20] Jurisdictional conflicts arise not only among private enforcers but also between them, administrative agencies and domestic courts. The coordination between international and domestic courts and between courts, administrative agencies and private enforcers is not sufficiently developed and there is limited room for voluntary measures aimed at coordinating contractually established dispute settlements.

Substantively, the enforcement power of these bodies is limited and compliance with sanctions by the infringers may be relatively low. Sanctions issued by private enforcers may be not respected, requiring, as a result, courts' intervention to enforce contractual obligations in order to execute sanctions. Domestic public regulators are also increasingly engaged with the enforcement of TPR to warrant its effectiveness.

Both institutional and substantive gaps require new solutions; accordingly, there is a need for devising better coordination among existing enforcement regimes, both in detecting infringements and in effectively sanctioning violations. The institutional challenges ahead point to the improvement of coordination mechanisms both within and among enforcement mechanisms, even when competition rather than cooperation is the distinctive feature.

This book tries to map enforcement mechanisms by considering four fundamental questions:

1. The identity and the power of the enforcers: *who are the enforcers?*
2. *The means of enforcement*: what are the boundaries between adjudication and administration?
3. *The effects of the enforcement and the scope of jurisdiction*, comparing judicial, private non-judicial and administrative enforcement: who can be involved in litigation and who is affected by private, judicial and administrative judgments?
4. *The specificity of remedies connected to the regulatory functions of the private regimes*: how does enforcement of private regulation differ

[20] See Chapter 12 in this volume and F. Cafaggi, 'The architecture of transnational private regulation', op. cit.

from enforcement of conventional contracts and organizational undertakings?

To frame these questions, a functional approach is useful. Enforcement of TPR has a double regulatory function. It affects the regulatory process because the solution arising from the controversy can highlight gaps in the regulation that need be filled; it thus engages rule makers in a 'regulatory dialogue' with the enforcers that may transform the (content of the) rules over time. A second related dialogue takes place between enforcers and infringers and feeds that with rule-makers. In this context, the reasons underlying the infringement perform a compelling function. Enforcement responses do and should vary according to violations' causes.[21] Violations can occur either for reasons of regulatory incapacity or on the basis of rational calculations.[22] Enforcement mechanisms should be tailored accordingly. In particular, the combination of cooperation and hierarchy in enforcement will vary depending on the reasons inducing the violation, i.e. its motivations. When the violation is caused by regulatees' incapacity, cooperative enforcement is likely to be more effective. When it is consciously directed at infringing the standards, despite there being an ability to meet the requirements, more hierarchy is needed. The orthodox distinction between hierarchical and adversarial enforcement versus cooperative compliance does not reflect the current approaches to TPR enforcement.[23] By way of enforcement rule-makers and the addressees of the regulatory regimes can engage in a learning relationship which can eventually improve regulatory effectiveness.

The second function of enforcement is the re-distribution of regulatory power. Enforcers of TPR, primarily domestic courts, may redistribute regulatory power within private actors or between private and public actors.[24] When enforcers decide how social standards apply to multinational corporations (MNCs) or the degree of privacy protection to which users are entitled when engaging in e-commerce, they reallocate regulatory

---

[21] See R. Baldwin and J. Black, 'Really responsive regulation', 71 *The Modern Law Review*, 1 (2008), 59–94; Scott in this volume, Chapter 4.

[22] See for a wider discussion in this volume Colin Scott's chapter in this volume, Chapter 4.

[23] For a thoughtful introduction to the relationship between enforcement and compliance see N. Gunningham, 'Enforcement and compliance strategies', in R. Baldwin, M. Cave and M. Lodge (eds), *The Oxford Handbook of Regulation*, OUP, 2010, pp. 120ff, esp. 121ff.

[24] Private enforcers often lack jurisdiction over inter-regimes disputes. They can only indirectly redistribute regulatory power by defining the scope and boundaries of the regime whose rules they can enforce.

powers between industries or between industry and NGOs. The recognition of the regulatory function implies that adjudication can result in the reallocation of regulatory power from one regulator to another or from one regime (free trade, e-commerce) to another (fair trade, data-protection). When, for example, courts apply the principle of conforming interpretation, imposing an outcome which dictates that one regime has to conform to another one (free trade and human rights or CSR), they allocate regulatory power by creating a hierarchy between the two regimes. Another clear example of the regulatory function of enforcement is represented by the liability of private regulators and the scrutiny of the validity of disclaimers that private regulators often include in their charters and bylaws to immunize themselves from liability towards regulated and/or third parties. Disclaimers of private regulators and enforcers constitute a tool for the allocation of regulatory power between regulators and third parties and between regimes when, for example, the challenge concerning the regulator's liability comes from NGOs representing interests conflicting with those protected by the regulator.[25] What are the limits of this function? In particular, how are the limits based on private autonomy reconciled with those grounded on democratic principles?

This book addresses some of the enforcement challenges and gaps in transnational regulation, offering some proposals to improve its effectiveness, in a manner consistent with justice and global democracy.

HOW GOVERNANCE MODELS OF PRIVATE REGULATORS CAN AFFECT TPR ENFORCEMENT STRATEGIES

TPR differs from international regulation since it refers primarily to standards designed and/or implemented by private actors.[26] This said, it also includes hybrid forms like the delegation of rule-making power by public to private entities and various forms of co-regulation operating within the framework of institutional complementarity.[27] TPR often emerges as a response to the limitations of public international law. It complements

---

[25] See Cafaggi, Chapter 2 in this volume.

[26] F. Cafaggi, 'New foundations of transnational private regulation', op. cit., pp. 1ff; T. Büthe, 'Private regulation in the global economy: a (p)review', 12 *Business and Politics*, 3, 2010, 1.

[27] For a map of different forms see K. Abbot and D. Snidal, 'Governance triangle', in W. Mattli and N. Woods (eds), *The Politics of Global Regulation*, Princeton University Press, 2009, p. 46. Taking a different perspective see T. Büthe,

transnational public regulation and frequently intertwines with it.[28] Even more, TPR and its enforcement mechanisms constitute an avenue to provide private parties with access to redress that they would not have had under public international law. This is, for instance, the case when private regulatory contracts incorporate, by reference, soft law provisions related to the respect of fundamental rights, making them binding and enforceable before national courts (NCs), and/or even before private enforcers. However contract law is not the only mechanism that can be employed to 'harden' soft law.[29] Extra-contractual liability also provides an enforcement avenue for soft law rules when they integrate the content of liability standards such as the duty of care. By rendering international public soft law rules enforceable via both transnational contracts and domestic private law, TPR not only increases the effectiveness of public international law but it also lends it legitimacy.[30] Furthermore, in specific cases public international law might also be integrated into private regimes. This can be particularly observed when the private regulator is vested with a high degree of regulatory power. In these scenarios general principles of international law such as good faith, etc. would be applicable to a private regulator's enforcement processes.[31] We therefore observe an evolving interaction between the public and the private regulatory instruments at the transnational level, where relationships may take competitive or cooperative forms, mutually reinforcing, especially in the latter case, their legitimacy.

'Private regulation in the global economy: a (p)review', op. cit. 2010, 1; G. Shaffer, 'How business shapes law: a socio-legal framework', 42 *Connecticut Law Review*, 147, 2009.

[28] See R. Stewart, Chapter 2 in this volume suggesting that transnational public regimes can be interpreted as responses to the failures of TPR.

[29] See for a general overview G. Shaffer and M. Pollack, 'Hard vs. soft law: alternatives, complements, and antagonists in international governance', 94 *University of Minnesota Law Review*, 706, 2010.

[30] See F. Cafaggi, 'New foundations', op. cit., pp. 20ff.

[31] International Centre for Dispute Resolution, *ICM Registry, LLC* v *Internet Corporation for Assigned Names and Numbers*, Declaration of the Independent Review Panel, ICDR Case No. 50 117 T 00224 08, February 19, 2010, pp. 62ff. The Panel in this case interpreted Article 4 Bylaws which make reference to international law as including general principles as mentioned in Article 38 of the ICJ Statute. The rationale for this conclusion was based on ICANN's 'governance of an intrinsically international resource of immense importance to global communications and economies'.

TPR concerns the whole private sphere, encompassing firms and NGOs, with coinciding or conflicting interests.[32] Conflicts of interest may occur within the same regime or across private regimes when they are aimed at regulating different market failures.[33] Conflicting interests are not only those between businesses and consumers but also concern business interests like those which emerge in conflicts between small suppliers of developing economies and big retailers of developed economies.[34] Thence within the private spheres, conflicts concern the regulated and the beneficiaries, both of whose interests are protected by the regulatory process.

The relationship between private non-judicial enforcers and infringers encompasses different features from that of (domestic) courts and litigants. The common feature across private non-judicial enforcement schemes is the repeat nature of the relationships between enforcers and potential infringers, permitting the enforcer to devise escalating systems which could hardly be used in judicial enforcement where repeat interaction between enforcer and infringers only rarely occurs.[35] The nature of the relationship however is not necessarily homogeneous across regulated entities. Private enforcers need to adapt their strategy to the (dis)homogeneity of regulated entities and their attitudes towards risks in order to engage in effective enforcement practices. The selection of strategies and their effectiveness therefore depends on the characteristics of the infringers and their respective responsiveness, which varies according to size, market power, and the relevant internal organizational model.

---

[32] See D. Vogel, 'Private global business regulation', *Annual Review of Political Science* (2008), 261ff; D. Vogel, 'The private regulation of global corporate conduct', in W. Mattli and N. Woods (eds.), *The Politics of Global Regulation*, Princeton University Press, 2009, esp. p. 156; T. Büthe and W. Mattli, *New Global Rulers: The Privatization of Regulation in the World Economy*, Princeton University Press, 2011.

[33] See F. Cafaggi, 'The architecture of transnational private regualtion', op. cit.

[34] See Edward Rubin, 'Images of organizations and consequences of regulation', *Theoretical Inquiries in Law*, 2005, Vol. 6, No. 2, Article 4. Available at: http://www.bepress.com/til/default/vol6/iss2/art4

[35] For repeat interaction to occur in judicial enforcement the 'constitutional' contract or bylaws have to introduce a choice of forum clause, identifying one single court as competent to resolve disputes concerning the private regime. For a critical assessment of the enforcement pyramid in relation to repeat interaction concerning public regulators, see C. Scott, 'Regulation in the age of governance: the rise of the post-regulatory state', in J. Jordana and D. Levi-Faur, *The Politics of Regulation: Institutions and Regulatory Reforms in the Age of Governance*, Edward Elgar, 2004, pp. 145ff.

Many contributions to this book emphasize the importance of governance for private enforcers and the correlation between legal forms of governance and enforcement strategies. This is certainly an important difference from judicial enforcement where courts' governance across legal systems is not conceived as a significant variable, perhaps mistakenly so. In particular, enforcement mechanisms vary between contractual and organizational forms of private enforcers.[36] Within organizational forms, particular significance rests on the distinction between for-profit and non-profit organizations, partially linked to that between first and third-party enforcers.[37]

Contractual forms, especially those organized around supply chains, adopt primarily first-party enforcement approaches, sometimes developing staged procedures along the management ladder, depending on the complexity of the dispute. One party in the contractual chain operates as a direct (with its contractual partner) or indirect (with contractual partners along the chain) enforcer. Organizational models increasingly take the form of third-party enforcement under the growing pressure of separation among different regulatory functions. The choice of enforcement mechanisms is not entirely free, even within the private domain; meta-public regulation influences the regulatory approach, the selection of the governance model and that of procedural rules.[38] Availability of different enforcement forms is growing. Especially with regard to third-party enforcement, there is increasing competition between arbitral institutions and mechanisms existing beyond arbitration.[39]

The link between governance and enforcement can be illustrated by analyzing some of the most diffused models, which certainly could not reflect the extraordinary variety of the present regimes:

(1) The simplest enforcement model is that of a multinational corporation (MNC), regulating the relationships with its employees, consumers and environmental organizations through the self-enforcement of its own

---

[36] See for a broader analysis concerning standard setting F. Cafaggi, 'New foundations of transnational private regulation', op. cit., pp. 1ff.

[37] For the comparison between for-profit, non-profit and public institution see the contribution of Kevin Davis, Chapter 7, this volume.

[38] See C. Parker, *The Open Corporation: Effective Self-regulation and Democracy*, CUP, 2002; C. Coglianese and E. Mendelson, 'Meta-regulation and self-regulation', in R. Baldwin, M. Cave and M. Lodge (eds), *The Oxford Handbook of Regulation*, OUP, pp. 146ff.

[39] See J. Dammann and H. Hansmann, 'Globalizing commercial litigation', 94 *Cornell Law Review* 1 (2008).

rules.[40] The MNC can enact one or more codes of conduct and/or guidelines, define unilaterally the nature of commitments, whether and how these are binding and over which actors they can produce effects.[41] Increasingly, these codes are associated with compliance programs required by domestic statutes, concerning the conduct of employees and managers and relationships with third parties (for example, suppliers in procurement policies).[42] In these schemes, the role of non-legal enforcement and that of compliance systems, based on hierarchy, are rather strong, whereas judicial enforcement is usually weak. Even if the MNC is involved in global supply chains it does not perform enforcement functions which are left to bilateral contracting. In this model enforcement is limited to the most immediate stakeholders of the MNC.

(2) A more sophisticated variant emerges when the regulatory body is the supply chain, where, together with the MNC, the up- and downstream participants of the chain are involved in regulating matters dealing with the production of goods and services. Commercial contracts here become regulatory instruments, regulating in combination with corporate and labor law.[43] MNCs exercise enforcement functions in this model as well, but their regulatory activity produces effects all along the chain, beyond the

---

40 Somewhat specific features come with providers of financial services where the activity and its impact on the financial market modify the MNC's regulatory model and its enforcement features. For example the relevance of compliance programs is much stronger in the financial market entity than in other sectors. Geoffrey Miller's chapter in this volume (Chapter 9) is dedicated to this topic.

41 See for an overview of the theme: J. Ruggie, *Business and Human Rights: Mapping International Standards of Responsibility and Accountability for Corporate Acts*, Report of the Special Representative of the Secretary General on the issue of human rights and transnational corporations and other business enterprises, A/HRC/4–35, 19 February 2007.

42 Compliance with the codes thus performs different functions: due diligence, exempting from criminal/administrative liability, and performance of undertakings in contracts with different stakeholders. Codes' violations symmetrically bring about different simultaneous consequences: they can trigger at the same time criminal and civil liabilities often evaluated by multiple enforcers (public and private). The boundaries between compliance programs and enforcement are rather thin in this model. Enforcement of these rules is often exercised via internal bodies, for example the ethical committee, with a limited degree of independence from the board of directors and the standard setting body. The level of centralization and hierarchy in the enforcement model often reflects the specific business model adopted by the MNC. For example compliance programs against fraudulent behavior or anti-money laundering as in the USA Patriot Act, as discussed in Chapter 9, this volume, p. 269.

43 There is an unexplored link between TPR, regulatory practices and enforcement strategies.

small group of stakeholders closely involved in the previous model. The relationship between enforcers and infringers, based on repeated interaction, is stable.[44] The use of commercial contracts as vehicles of transnational private regulation raises important questions from the enforcement perspective. On the one hand, they ensure rapid and fast monitoring of suppliers' compliance; on the other hand, they may often fail to protect the public interest or even the collective interest dimension. There is a risk of being instrumentalized in order to serve, exclusively, the market interests of the leading firm. Even if regulation is incorporated into bilateral commercial contracts, the enforcement of regulatory clauses has particular importance for the whole chain, going beyond the bilateral relationship in the context of which the breach has occurred. Privity of contract and the *de jure* inability of the lead enforcer to enforce third parties' obligations can increase the implementation costs of this model. The use of network contracts could mitigate these problems by enabling the lead firm to directly enforce obligations of all the participants and, at the same time, promote collaboration and peer monitoring among suppliers.[45] As many contributions show, this interdependence of relationships along the chain affects contractual enforcement of regulatory provisions.[46] NCs are divided over codes' enforceability when the codes stand alone, and even when their provisions are included in commercial contracts by reference.[47]

The difference with the previous model is that the MNC here not only operates as a standard setter for the whole supply chain but also as a monitor and enforcer. It has (limited enforceable) duties to monitor and enforce suppliers' regulatory obligations for which it is made (at least partially) accountable to the final consumers via 'independent' audit and litigation. Limitations come from principles of contract law which reduce the possibility of enforcing third parties' obligations undertaken by second or third tier suppliers. Regulatory provisions in commercial contracts refer to MNCs' direct or third-party auditing to ensure compliance, and, in case

---

44 Not every regulatory supply chain is identical and changes are taking place, shortening their length and promoting the creation of suppliers' groups and coalitions to pursue common regulatory objectives.

45 See. F. Cafaggi (ed.), *Contractual Networks, Inter-firm Cooperation and Economic Growth*, Edward Elgar, p. 201.

46 See in this volume, Estlund, Chapter 8, and Scott, Chapter 4, p. 147ff.

47 In Estlund's contribution to this volume (Chapter 8) the US courts' position over enforceability of labor standard codes is examined. She analyzes the litigation over codes' enforceability in the US and underlines how courts have subscribed to the idea that codes' monitoring and enforcement is a right rather than a duty. Thence when suppliers violate codes' provisions MNCs cannot be made liable for failure to monitor and enforce codes' provisions. See Chapter 8, p. 237ff.

of violations, they provide potential leeway for unilateral termination of the contractual relationship. Often, however, contractual termination constitutes the last resort, deployed only after cooperative enforcement has been tried without success.[48]

More broadly, the structure of the supply chain affects standard setting and enforcement. But the opposite is also true: private regulation and the enforcement model influence the length and form of the supply chain. Changes in the supply chain are driven by several concurring regulatory regimes, from product safety to environmental protection, and from labor to privacy standards, often integrated within one single model. These models have been adopted in the food safety sector and, to a limited extent, in the field of CSR and have subsequently been applied within other regulatory fields.[49] The supply chain, therefore, often constitutes a vehicle for regulatory transfers from one regulatory field to another, which may affect enforcement strategies. For example, one regulatory model is adopted in the field of product safety, and is later applied within other fields like labor or consumer protection. The MNC in the supply chain model often monitors compliance with regulatory clauses in similar ways regardless of whether they relate to safety, quality, labor or environmental protection. As a result, the supply chain regulatory model tends to integrate monitoring standards arising from within different private regimes, generating more harmonized enforcement strategies across sectors than other governance models.

What is the relationship between the two enforcement models just outlined? Do MNCs have a choice? The adoption of the supply chain model becomes necessary when private regulation concerns process or quality management, more than product standard, for in the former instance, suppliers' activities need to be monitored continuously to ensure regulatory compliance. Here, the regulatory chain is wider and includes several suppliers' tiers. The private regulatory toolbox adds to the company and labor law, commercial contracts between the MNC and suppliers and

---

[48] See the Walmart approach reported in Chapter 8: 'When violations are found our priority is to work with our suppliers to ensure that factories achieve compliance. We are confident that this collaborative approach is the best way to help our suppliers understand the business benefits of operating factories meeting labor, environmental, and health and safety standards' (Estlund, Chapter 8, p. 242).

[49] In food safety the subscription to the supply chain approach by public regulation has been applied also to private regulation shifting costs of monitoring, and, to some extent, enforcement onto MNCs which have then passed it on partly to the suppliers and partly to the final consumers. See Henson and Humphrey, 'The impact of private food safety standards', op. cit. pp. 1–14; T. Havinga, 'Private regulation of food safety by supermarkets', 28 *Law & Policy* (2006), 515 at pp. 522ff.

between the first, second and additional tiers. The effectiveness of the supply chain enforcement model, far more so than the simple MNC, is dependent upon the efficient interaction between the leader firm and independent auditors combining consensual and hierarchical components in enforcement policies.

(3) More complex governance models which reflect different enforcement mechanisms include: (a) single or multi-stakeholder agreements (firms and consumer organizations, or retailers and suppliers along the supply chain, for example); or (b) organizational models like associations, foundations, and 'for-profit' companies regulating the activities of their members, often by setting standards.[50]

(i) Within the family of regulatory contracts relevant differences between enforcement mechanisms currently exist, depending on whether the regulatory provisions are designed as independent tools or are included in commercial contracts along the supply chain. In the former case, an agreement concerning transnational private standards can be made between a group of firms and consumer organizations, trade unions, environmental protection organizations or all of the above.[51] This agreement can define the standards or design the architecture of the implementation of standards defined in codes of conduct or international soft law declarations. The contractual arrangement regulates the relationship among the signatories but it also produces effects on third parties; its validity and enforceability are subject to domestic or transnational contract law, depending on the choice of *lex loci* and *lex fori*. Regulatory contracts of this type are quite common in the field of CSR but have also developed in other sectors like Internet regulation (ICANN), financial private regulation (ISDA) and environmental protection (EMAS).[52] In relation to financial regulation, they often take the form of master agreements to be applied

---

[50] In some instances the agreement is transformed into an organization. See the example of the Business Social Compliance Initiative, a network of retailers, industry and importing companies, which has formed a strategic alliance with SA8000 (the global social accountability standard) to create a Global Reporting Initiative (GRI) which develops 'sustainability reporting guidelines' for the global business community.

[51] For a detailed examination of this model in the field of labor standards see C. Estlund, this volume, Chapter 8, p. 243.

[52] See Human Rights Council, Report of the Special Representative of the Secretary-General on the issue of human rights and transnational corporations and other business enterprises, John Ruggie, 'Guiding principles on business and human

in individual transactions (SEPA or IPF in the payment system).[53] They are generally supported by private grievance mechanisms; however, judicial enforcement is also deployed to complement them.[54]

A different model, already mentioned, is that of commercial contracts between firms along the supply chain, which may include clauses regulating safety, environmental protection, labor and occupational health and safety. Often these contracts have self-enforcing mechanisms and are rarely litigated before courts, given the significant power asymmetry between the parties and the strong use of reputational mechanisms. However, the relevance of regulatory provisions for the other participants to the supply chain may undermine the effectiveness of self-enforcement and might call for new responses.[55]

(ii) In the latter case (b) an organization is created with a membership that may include different types of stakeholders, be they individual members or organizations.[56] Three different families exist within the organizational model. The first two are sector-specific; the third is a general model deployed across sectors.

The first family is sector-specific and is represented by the traditional professional and trade associations.[57] At a transnational level they are federations, composed of national professional or trade associations. Enforcers are generally part of the organization and their independence from standard setters is rather limited.

---

rights: implementing the United Nations "Protect, Respect and Remedy" framework', A/HRC/17/31, 21 March 2011, available at: http://www.business-humanrights.org/media/documents/ruggie/ruggie-guiding-principles-21-mar-2011.pdf (hereafter Ruggie 'Guiding principles'). Examples concerning environmental protection are in Stewart's contribution to this volume (Chapter 1), for financial markets, see the taxonomy in Miller's contribution (Chapter 9), while for the Internet, see the analysis in Casarosa's contribution (Chapter 10).

[53] This is the case for swaps regulated by ISDA master agreement and for payments in EURO regulated by SEPA. For a broader analysis see A. Riles, *Collateral Knowledge*, University of Chicago Press, 2011.

[54] See Ruggie 'Guiding principles', op. cit., art. 31.

[55] In commercial contracts the exercise of the power to terminate in the hands of the MNC is not made conditional upon examination of the interests of the full chain. When regulatory matters are considered, the interests of the participants may not be perfectly aligned when a violation is committed. Some could prefer injunctive relief, others termination and the current structure of international commercial contracts does not often include collective interests considerations.

[56] For example contrast IATA (single stakeholder) with the Forest Stewardship Council (multi-stakeholder with a multiple chamber structure).

[57] Some of these models are described in Cassese, D'Alterio and De Bellis, Chapter 12, this volume.

Another family is based on new industry alliances often cutting across sectors or encompassing multiple stakeholders. They regulate members' conduct (generally business enterprises) and often their relationship with third parties (i.e. consumers, suppliers, banks), in relation to the scope of the regime. Unlike the traditional trade/professional association self-regulatory model, these organizations design new enforcement mechanisms drawing on different sources, and, further, the degree of independence is higher even when enforcers are technically within the boundaries of the organization.[58]

In all of these models, both the validity and enforceability of the rules are subject to domestic or transnational private laws, associated with the law of the place of incorporation of the private regulator, unless the enforcer is a fully independent entity incorporated elsewhere. Disputes over the rules' interpretation and application is governed primarily by the law of association, and when applicable by company law, which offers a much higher level of insulation from judicial intervention, applying the business judgment rule or its functional equivalents. The limits of the law of association, in legal systems that recognize it, regulating global standard setting, emerge quite clearly in many contributions although legal systems permit some degree of innovation. These drawbacks are often solved by recourse to administrative regulation. In areas like sports, environment, e-commerce and advertising, litigation and administrative enforcement by way of domestic regulators have played a very significant role.

Within private non-judicial enforcement, the organizational model so far described presents specific functional features, drawing on membership of a collective entity. Functionally, enforcement is based on deterrence through signaling rather than via direct punishment. Two complementary aims are pursued by these private enforcers: general deterrence, to discourage other members from engaging in unlawful behavior, and specific deterrence, to reduce the incentives of repeat infringements by the same regulated entity. Punishment often constitutes the last resort, which arises when the threat to the collective reputation calls for exclusion from the organization or for contractual termination. Corrective measures, and to a

---

[58] Sources of these codes are multiple. Ever more they are the outcome of multilateral initiatives led by MNCs within a negotiating framework with NGOs and trade unions. Estlund in her contribution to this volume (Chapter 8) points out that often within the third party auditing systems (including SAI, ETI, FLA), additional requirements like freedom of association become part of the regulatory scheme. She concludes by analyzing the relationship between enforcers and infringers. See Cynthia Estlund, Chapter 8 this volume, p. 241ff.

limited extent fines, are generally deployed, in association with a reputational mechanism based on community or market incentives.

A third, alternative model, is that of third-party enforcer; these are independent organizations that do not participate in standard setting. They tend to be not sector-specific but general transnational enforcers. This model, developed in arbitration, has subsequently spread over different enforcement techniques. Rules are designed by each organization (for example different arbitral institutions) but tend to converge on the core, which is also the case for the important role of international treaties and conventions. The hybrid sources of the rules, especially when there is a strong international public law component, constitute a driver towards uniformity. These organizations are often electing the not-for-profit form for their enforcement function, producing public goods more similar to those generated by courts than those arising from for-profit commercial enforcers.[59] Unlike the previous models, including the supply chain – where even in the case of structural separation the enforcers are part of the same group and come from the regulated or the beneficiaries' community – in this model enforcers are professionals.

The professionalization of transnational private justice with the combination of consolidated forms like arbitration and new forms arising from a private meta-regulator constitutes an important trend worth underlining.

Governance of enforcers affects the selection of enforcement instruments. A different combination of private and judicial enforcement emerges between contractual and organizational regulatory models. This is: (a) partly due to the legal framework, for contractual agreements – except for self-enforcing contracts – relying, to a greater extent than organizational models, on both judicial and non-judicial external enforcers; and (b) partly due to the differences among domestic private legal regimes, which govern the features of transnational regulatory bodies. Even within organizational models, the complementarity between judicial enforcement and professional third-party private enforcers (for instance, arbitral or mediation institutions) reflects a different dynamic from the nature of complementarity existing between courts and supply chains models. In the first case, complementarity can become a form of alternative dispute resolution and private justice can replace judicial enforcement; in the case of supply chains, and other forms of regulatory contracts, the role of domestic courts is much stronger and it would be inappropriate to speak of non-judicial enforcement as an alternative dispute resolution mechanism to courts.

---

[59] See for a full discussion Kevin Davis, Chapter 7, this volume.

THE LINK BETWEEN THE NATURE OF DISPUTES, THE IDENTITY OF THE LITIGANTS AND THE ENFORCEMENT MODELS

Models of enforcement vary not only across sectors but also within each field.[60] As mentioned we observe at least three concurring enforcement mechanisms concerning disputes arising within TPR: (1) the increasing role of domestic courts in enforcing and reviewing transnational private regimes; (2) the complementary development of transnational private dispute resolution mechanisms, including both first and third-party enforcers; and (3) the oversight and direct enforcement by both domestic and international public regulators.[61]

Judicial, administrative and non-judicial private enforcement are often combined with the intervention of gatekeepers. These are private bodies with formal or informal links to private regulators and/or the regulated firms. Gatekeepers vary from field to field and tend to be sector-specific but contribute significantly to effective enforcement within TPR. They range from the media in advertising, to banks in CSR, to credit rating agencies in financial markets. In the first case, media bodies have powers arising from contracts with advertisers and from legislation to stop and remove deceptive or injurious advertisements. In the case of CSR, banks can make access to credit conditional upon the respect of fundamental rights or social standards by firms in the supply chain. Often they have promoted supply chain regulation by requiring the lead firm to monitor suppliers' compliance with fair and equitable labor standards. There is also a development of general, cross-sectorial techniques like auditing and certification, increasingly deployed in combination with direct TPR, giving rise to new forms of private meta-regulation.

---

[60] Differences exist not only among but also within regimes. Even within the same regime enforcement strategies may be tailored to different classes of regulated entities. In the case of firms, responsiveness to an enforcement strategy may vary according to size, market power, and the regulatory capacities of regulatees.

[61] Domestic administrative regulators come to oversee and enforce TPR through different avenues. The most common is when domestic statutory laws endorse private standards in legislation and confer on them the power to enforce the standards. This is clearly the case for financial accounting, for advertising, for certification in the field of timber, forestry just to name a few. A different path is when international organizations (FSB, World Bank, BIS, ILO, FAO, WHO) endorse or refer to transnational private standards in soft law instruments to be enforced at the domestic level by way of administrative acts.

Important questions emerge about their interaction: how do the enforcement regimes interplay?[62] Is there any manifestation of hierarchy among them? Is the interaction reflected in different sequencing (i.e. first private, then administrative, then judicial)? Can parties decide which sequence should occur? What are the consequences of the adoption of a decentralized review system, encompassing all the systems, for transnational private rule-making?

The book explores these questions from various disciplinary perspectives and methodological approaches, looking at which coordinating and which conflict-avoiding systems are in place among the three types of enforcers and the gatekeepers, given that often they operate at both transnational and domestic levels.

In order to compare the various enforcement mechanisms, it is useful to distinguish among different types of disputes according to the litigants' identity, building on the notion of regulatory relationship developed in earlier work:[63]

(a) disputes between the regulator and the regulated;[64]

---

[62] On the complementarity of judicial and private responses to violation of human rights by non-state actors see J. Ruggie, *Promotion and Protection of all Human Rights, Civil, Political, Economic, Social and Cultural Rights, including the Right to Development. Protect, Respect and Remedy: a Framework for Business and Human Rights*, Report of the Special Representative of the Secretary-General on the issue of human rights and transnational corporations and other business enterprises, John Ruggie, 7 April 2008, in particular points 82ff. (hereafter Ruggie, *Protect, Respect and Remedy*). The reporter states (p. 9): 'The framework rests on differentiated but complementary responsibilities. It comprises three core principles: the State duty to protect against human rights abuses by third parties, including business; the corporate responsibility to respect human rights; and the need for more effective access to remedies'. For an analysis of the different modes of interaction between private and administrative enforcement see Cassese, D'Alterio, De Bellis, Chapter 12, this volume. For the complementarity between judicial and private non-judicial enforcement see Cafaggi, Chapter 2, this volume.

[63] F. Cafaggi, 'New foundations of transnational private regulation', 38 *Journal of Law and Society* (2011), 20, pp. 31ff.

[64] These disputes may arise both for nonfeasance and misfeasance. They concern the relationship between MNCs and suppliers, the associations and its members or third parties engaged in contractual relationships with them. The private regulator has a contractual or an organizational right/duty to regulate. It follows that inaction or violations can be subject to judicial scrutiny. The regulator has to comply with substantive (non-discrimination) and procedural duties (information, reason giving) which may also give rise to judicial claims or regulatory intervention when oversight is allowed.

(b) disputes among the regulated;[65]
(c) disputes between the regulator and third parties;[66]
(d) disputes between the regulated and third parties.[67]

The distinction highlights the differences between judicial and private non-judicial enforcement mechanisms as to how they solve these classes of disputes. Furthermore, there is an implicit, albeit conscious, division of labor between the two.

Private non-judicial enforcement tends to focus on the first two classes of disputes, often denying or making access to third parties very selective.[68] Access for NGOs to industry-led regulatory regimes is rather limited. Limitations are stronger for participation in enforcement than in standard setting. This is unlike transnational public regulation where, having overcome the traditional obstacles posed by public international law, the rights of NGOs before domestic courts and agencies have been recently more widely granted to secure compliance, and sometimes (i.e. in relation to the

---

[65] These disputes arise for instance when all the members of a standard setting body have committed to a certain standard and one of them deviates from that standard to gain competitive advantage over the other members. A different type of dispute is that of a regime that generates a collective reputation with, for example, a certification system, and certified members violate the rules that secure compliance with the collective goals.

[66] A third party is not a member of the organization or a signatory of the contract depending upon which instrument has been used to govern the transnational regime. For example a consumer or a consumer organization is a third party of a regime which is regulated by industry members. Third parties can be negatively or positively affected by the regulatory activity. They are often the beneficiaries of the regulatory process and are granted rights to ensure that the benefits really accrue.

[67] This is, for example, the case when workers want to enforce provisions of the code enacted by the MNC concerning obligations of suppliers; similarly if product safety regulations imposed on suppliers by an MNC give rise to a claim by consumers. These disputes may be brought under a tort claim when there is no relationship between the regulated and the third party who has been negatively affected by the violation. They can be brought under contract if the regulated has committed itself contractually to comply with the standards set by the private regulator like in a sale contract where the food safety standards become part of the warranty or an employment contract where the provisions of the CSR code of conduct are incorporated into the contract. A third avenue is that of a contract for the benefit of a third party when the claimant is the intended beneficiary of the relationship between regulator and regulated.

[68] See Scott, Chapter 4, this volume. This might not always be the case, however. In the field of advertising, for example, the majority of claims come from individual consumers or their organizations, not from competitors.

World Bank panel) to participate in the negotiations concerning remedies.[69] Increasingly however, important exceptions can be identified, where private enforcement mechanisms have been made accessible to third parties, as in the field of advertising, CSR and e-commerce. In advertising, individual and consumer organizations can bring claims before SROs (self-regulating organizations) and seek remedies to correct or to eliminate misleading or indecent advertisements.[70] In CSR, workers of the suppliers are given access to compliance committees composed of representatives of trade unions and the enterprises.[71] However, access is not the only explanatory variable for the allocation of dispute resolution among different enforcement mechanisms. Exit can certainly contribute to explaining the division of labor between the three modes of enforcement. Private enforcers dispose of organizational sanctions through which they have control over membership, since they can order expulsion or terminate the contract. These sanctions typically apply to disputes between regulator and regulatees, or among the latter. They do not apply by definition to those with third parties. Thence different sanctioning techniques can explain the division of tasks.

Private non-judicial enforcement is used in the first two cases, where disputes concern regulators and regulatees in compliance with the principle of forbearance.[72] Judicial enforcement often limits its intervention to the last two cases; that is, those in which third parties are involved.

In fact, as exemplified in the field of corporate law, the first two sets of disputes are often considered internal affairs of the organization and left to their internal rules, but for listed public corporations where a higher level of monitoring, both by internal members (minority shareholders) and by the regulator, is required. On the contrary, judicial enforcement often grants wider access to third parties, who are negatively affected by the private regimes, be they competitors of the regulated or their customers.

Enforcement of these four types of disputes plays a very different role within the context of the regulatory regime and, consequently, its link with legitimacy differs. In order to examine the different mechanisms and compare them, it is useful to distinguish between: (1) *internal legitimacy*, concerning the relationships and disputes between regulators and the regulated or among the latter; and (2) *external legitimacy*, concerning the

---

[69] See the examples provided by Richard Stewart, Chapter 1, this volume. For a more general overview see A. Peters (ed.), *Non-state Standard Setters*, CUP, 2009.

[70] See Paul Verbruggen, Chapter 11, this volume.

[71] See Estlund, Chapter 8, this volume, p. 237ff.

[72] In the domain of international organizations this is the area where litigation before domestic courts has developed.

relationship between the regulator and the regulated on the one hand, and third parties, on the other hand. Access to and definition of jurisdiction by private enforcers reflect different combinations of internal and external legitimacy to be achieved via enforcement.

A more complex set of issues, beyond the scope of this paper, concerns regimes' interdependences and their effects on enforcement.[73] Conflicts are understood to exist among regimes even if they take the form of disputes between the regulated and beneficiaries or between two classes of regulated entities, which have subscribed to different, competing regulatory regimes. These conflicts, and the subsequent disputes, occur between different private regimes but also between public and private regimes.[74] One example is provided by regimes making rules in violation of other regimes. The enforcement of rights, grounded on one TPR and violated by another TPR, occurs when, for example, a technical standard setting body defines standards in violation of environmental or consumer rights conferred by a different private regime. Disputes among regimes are often settled by way of negotiation rather than adjudication. When they repeatedly arise, a governance response beyond simple negotiation is provided.

THE AIM OF THE BOOK AND ITS CONTRIBUTIONS

Enforcement of TPR is manifested in a large variety of forms, which have emerged over time as a result of sector-specific dynamics associated with different market and governmental failures and distributional effects. Therefore, addressing enforcement mechanisms implies factoring sector-specificity into the general scheme of transnational adjudication, which makes generalization rather hard. The contributions show that no single answer to the question of TPR's enforcement can be given: adjudication of disputes in transnational private regimes reflects a very diverse set of rules and principles, partly associated with the specificity of sectors, and partly with divergent national legal systems supplying substantive and procedural rules, elected according to the *lex fori* and the applicable law when private enforcers are created. Nonetheless, it may be useful to try to identify a

[73] In the domain of transnational public regulation an ever more frequent example is that of financial conditionality deployed by the World Bank and the IMF to impose on firms the adoption of standards concerning employment, safety or environmental standards. See on these issues Stewart, Chapter 2, this volume and Francioni, Chapter 5, this volume.

[74] See Stewart, Chapter 2, this volume.

common frame to explain the high degree of differentiation among enforcement regimes in different fields.

Enforcement in TPR operates to ensure compliance with privately produced rules, which are often conflicting. It influences the process of transnational legal harmonization and the creation of regulatory practices, which could give rise to private regulatory customary law. Unlike public international law, where a common framework exists, it operates in the background of different, at times conflicting, procedural and substantive domestic laws, which may result in privileging private rather than judicial enforcement to the extent that parties have a choice between the two regimes, or at least, can sequence access to them. Voluntary sequencing occurs when disputant parties, or the organizations to which members have subscribed, introduce a mandatory provision imposing the preliminary use of private non-judicial enforcement and only after unsuccessful attempts at non-judicial enforcement permits access to courts.

Research both within TPR and comparative research on the interplay between TPR and public regimes, specifically focusing on enforcement, is still very preliminary. The contributions to this book aim to fill this gap by providing a conceptual framework to be complemented by further empirical research which will shed light on rules and practices. In the first section, framing chapters provide a general overview of public and private transnational enforcement models; the second section looks at enforcement models of public international law, primarily in terms of public enforcers, while the third, in contrast, is specifically devoted to enforcement of private regimes. The fourth part contains a final concluding chapter which offers a broader view of hybrids and how public and private enforcement systems are linked.

Richard Stewart (Chapter 1) focuses on the enforcement of transnational public regulation. He subscribes to a broad definition of enforcement, which includes administrative orders, requiring or prohibiting conducts, imposition of penalties, criminal prosecutions and civil actions brought by governmental officials. The chapter begins from the premise that credible and effective enforcement is essential to those transnational regimes which promote the protection of regulatory beneficiaries. Stewart distinguishes between enforcement and review, and, within the latter, between the review of administrative domestic bodies, implementing transnational rules, and the direct review of transnational rules by administrative and judicial bodies. He emphasizes the role of liability as a monitoring device to secure compliance by the regulated, with both private rights of initiation and private enforcement rights. In relation to judicial review, he distinguishes three approaches adopted by domestic courts: one applies the same test for domestic and transnational norms, another gives more deference to transnational norms, while the third denies the applicability of transnational norms altogether, asserting their political rather than legal status. Stewart provides a conceptual framework for enforcing transnational public law, identifying four sets of related variables: applicable laws; targets of remedy; courts or tribunals providing the remedies; and types of remedy. He emphasizes that there has been a growing trend towards extending the rights of the regulated against the regulators to regulatory beneficiaries. The empowerment of beneficiaries derives primarily from transnational norms, giving NGOs rights to enforce compliance before national administrative bodies or courts. He specifies however that this trend is uneven across jurisdictions, and even where it is more pronounced (i.e. the USA) regulatory beneficiaries have not yet gained an equivalent position to that of the regulated. Stewart suggests that the rationales – harmonization and enhanced protection of regulatory beneficiaries – for this expansion of rights, might differ in relation to transnational regulation as compared to domestic regulation.

Fabrizio Cafaggi (Chapter 2) provides a framework for examining the enforcement of TPR, focusing primarily on the relationship between judicial and non-judicial private enforcement. The former occurs primarily via domestic courts engaged in enforcing, interpreting, and, to a limited extent, reviewing transnational private regulation. The latter follows very different patterns and is much less homogeneous than judicial enforcement, even internalizing divergent interpretations. It goes from first-party to third-party enforcement via professional, specialized institutional bodies such as arbitral institutions. Cafaggi first identifies the main differences between the two sets of mechanisms along the same variables, focusing on the nature of the dispute and the identity of litigants, the power of the enforcer, the adversarial or inquisitorial nature of the proceedings, the relationship between the enforcer and litigants, the type of sanctions and their enforcement, and the degree of procedural due process. He comes to the conclusion that they operate as complementary devices, both horizontally and vertically (at the international and domestic level). Complementarity however is spontaneous rather than designed and often the interaction is not optimal and does not achieve the expected results, consequently giving rise to divergences and resulting in a situation lacking coordination and sequencing. He concludes with some policy recommendations for better coordination mechanisms, both within and across jurisdictional mechanisms, designed to ensure effective compliance with transnational regulatory policies.

Eyal Benvenisti and George Downs (Chapter 3) discuss the role of NCs in regulating TPR, examining substantive and procedural doctrines in the light of the values of economic efficiency, democracy and equality. Among the former, they indicate those concerning the limits and constraints of delegating rule-making power, the role of competition law, the *Drittwirkung* and the principle of proportionality. These examples illustrate how NCs have been trying to ensure compliance with (some) public values, thereby reducing the risk of self-interested private regulation. Benvenisti and Downs then examine procedural norms, starting from the premise that private law litigation, within which TPR disputes are decided, is generally less open to participation than public law litigation. Standing is based on different requirements: that is, showing a legally protected interest versus establishing the infringement of a right. On the other hand, private litigation does not face territorial boundaries to the same extent as public law litigation, especially when the regulator is protected by immunity. Given the functional rather than the territorial dimension of TPR, NCs can subject private regimes to judicial scrutiny on the basis of their (adverse) effects. They then analyze NCs' incentives to intervene and police TPR, suggesting that collective action problems arise in relation to two different issues: (1) the adverse or beneficial effects produced by TPR; and (2) considering potentially conflicting incentives they allude to how the NCs can coordinate or avoid divergent interpretation of the same TPR.

Colin Scott (Chapter 4) firstly addresses the boundaries between compliance and enforcement, suggesting that they should be examined contextually. Scott analyzes and contrasts public, private and hybrid enforcement regimes, asking in particular whether and how the enforcement of TPR differs from public enforcement in the domestic realm. On the basis of the debate triggered by Ayres and Braithwaite's enforcement pyramid, Scott concludes that the distinction between public enforcement, based on formal legal instruments, and private enforcement, based on soft, informal features, is inaccurate. The effectiveness of soft and informal measures is often ensured by the reinforcement (potentially) provided by formal sanctions. Within the private domain, he focuses on non-judicial enforcement, pointing out that the reach of these regimes is at the same time narrower, because of contract law limitations on third-party effects, and wider, because it crosses States' boundaries to a much greater extent than public enforcement. He then examines the different private models, including organizations, supply chains and contracts, underlining the importance of non-judicial enforcement and their interaction with compliance-securing devices in relation to the courts' intervention. Scott finally moves on to consider hybrid forms of enforcement where public, including judicial, and private enforcement mechanisms co-exist. He identifies three sets of reasons why such hybrids might emerge: incomplete regulatory capacity, demand by national legal systems to make enforcement binding and lack of organizational capacity and expertise.

Francesco Francioni begins the second section, which is devoted to public international law. His contribution focuses on the role of national courts in enforcing international law and thus serving international justice, complementing the contributions of both international courts and diplomatic means. After glossing over the influence of the monist/dualist debate on domestic enforcement and suggesting that the subject has gained new insights, Francioni examines the different functions of domestic courts. He distinguishes between the production of customary law and treaties' applications. In relation to the former, he draws attention to the necessity for domestic courts to engage in comparative evaluation and international practices in order to avoid diverging interpretations. In relation to the latter, he focuses on enforcement, interpretation, and then, in relation to treaty application, touches upon invalidity and termination. He then moves on to consider the relationship between domestic courts and national executives, subscribing to Conforti's thesis of judicial independence, and contends the desirability of limiting the executive's power to 'breach' international law by adopting new practices, thereby deviating from current treaty-based law. According to Francioni, NCs are asked to play a more active role in 'governing' the interaction among international and domestic legal orders. Three challenges stand before them: (1) the removal or minimization of doctrinal obstacles to the effective implementation of international law in the domestic sphere (judicial deference to the executive, incorrect application of immunity); (2) the infusion of international law concepts in domestic laws in order to contribute further to legalizing international relations; and (3) the widening of the sphere of justice beyond the boundaries of nation states.

Ernst-Ulrich Petersmann's chapter locates TPR within the broader context of international economic law and its constitutional foundations. TPR, with its multilevel judicial review and enforcement, constitutes a response to the constitutional Westphalian failures of international law in supplying global public goods in a manner similar to an efficient world trading system, promoting the adequate protection of fundamental rights and the rule of law. However this response is not boundless. Limitations of both governmental and market failures require constitutional restraints of abuses, of both public and private powers; the same is true within TPR. Compliance with the rule of law can serve to minimize risks of abuses; however it is a highly contested concept, both from a disciplinary and an institutional perspective. Petersmann analyzes different disciplinary and institutional perspectives of the concept, reaching the conclusion that only an integrated view could satisfactorily address the governance failures that give rise to the underproduction of global public goods. In particular he defends a constitutional approach to economic international law based on citizens' fundamental rights. The international rule of law that emerges should, in Petersmann's view, prevent abuses of foreign policy powers and promote a moral duty of justice.

Kevin Davis' chapter opens the third section. He compares different legal forms of transnational enforcement institutions. In particular he addresses for-profit, non-profit and public international organizations, evaluating the advantages and disadvantages of each form in relation to both incentives and resources. He firstly critically addresses the literature on for-profit/commercial providers, and then describes the real world of transnational arbitral institutions, and shows that an interesting mix might exist between for-profit and non-profit forms, with a significant relevance attached to the latter. Davis suggests that for-profit enforcement providers may be at a disadvantage in terms of access to labor, capital and information vis-à-vis non-profit enforcers. Furthermore, they may be less responsive to public interest and third-party externalities and to demand for high quality services. In the following section, he identifies the benefits of using non-profit forms among which, the following stand out: the ability to internalize third-party effects and the provision of procedural incentives to widen access; the willingness to consider distributional effects; the incentives to promote legal innovation; and the possibility to rely on professional volunteerism. From the perspective of incentives, the non-profit forms show remarkable advantages, which partly explain the choice made by arbitral institutions, on which the discussion is primarily based. However, he concludes that the analysis is too preliminary to draw final conclusions on the optimal organizational forms of transnational enforcement, but for the claim that they are relevant in relation to efficiency.

The focus of Cynthia Estlund's chapter is supply chain enforcement of labor standards. Cynthia Estlund concentrates on the MNCs' role in monitoring and enforcing codes of conduct concerning suppliers' compliance with labor standards. The chapter is divided into two parts; the first describes the field's most recent evolution while the second addresses the main issues arising in relation to codes' enforcement. She suggests that the structure of the supply chain is changing due to the adoption of new monitoring practices, confirming the general view that there is a dual causal correlation between private regulation and the supply chain features. She identifies two potential trade-offs framed as policy dilemmas: (1) increasing enforceability raises costs and may create disincentives to buy into CSR programs; and (2) the use of CSR programs may crowd out public norms or at least decrease their effectiveness. Estlund explores the different types of relationships involving labor standards' implementation and the various available enforceability instruments. She reaches the conclusion that current doctrines, especially in the US, and the institutional weaknesses of judicial systems in developing economies, make judicial enforcement a relatively poor response, and thus she examines the potential of non-judicial mechanisms as more effective alternatives. After briefly touching on the possibility of creating a global tribunal for enforcing privately designed labor standards, she focuses on arbitration and the core principles that should guide labor arbitration as the enforcement mechanism for transnational disputes. She concludes that, building on the Fair Labor Association's party complaint procedures, the inclusion of arbitration provisions could increase the level of lead firms' accountability for compliance with CSR standards.

Geoffrey Miller (Chapter 9) considers different types of regulations actively involving private actors: house rules, cartels, contracts, internal compliance, private standard setting bodies, and private litigation management-based regulation. In some cases they are limited to standard setting, leaving enforcement to public bodies, as is the case for the accounting standard system, primarily implemented and enforced by public or private but state-created bodies. The extent of the involvement of the public varies; it is minimal in the first three (house rules, contracts, cartels), it induces private regulation in the other three (internal compliance, private standard setting bodies and private litigation), while it is rather more relevant in the case of management-based regulation. The chapter identifies seven factors that determine the pattern of public/private interaction and ultimately the mode of enforcement: (1) minimization of transaction costs; (2) access to information; (3) expertise; (4) political power of the regulated industry; (5) contests over regulatory turf; (6) regulatory budget constraints; and (7) history or path dependence. It is the different combination of these variables that can explain the current forms of enforcement and their evolutionary pattern.

The chapter by Federica Casarosa (Chapter 10) deals with Internet regulation, with particular emphasis on private regulation. The analysis focuses on two peculiar cases of private regulation: one, already addressed within the academic debate, concerning the ICANN regulation; and the other, more recent but amassing interest, concerning the online auction website regulation, taking as an example, the eBay website. The two cases provide distinct examples of private regulation where the enforcement systems are organized differently, due both to the governance structure adopted and to the type of actor that is subject to the regulation. While the ICANN model is focused on the management of the technical architecture of the Internet network, providing a transnational private regime based on a chain of contracts, the eBay model is focused on the regulation of commercial exchanges through an online auction system, where the parties accept the rules of behavior defined therein without involving the latter in the commercial exchange. The comparison between the two cases shows that the level of formality of the enforcement system is higher where the technical infrastructure of the Internet is involved and the rules are to be included in linked contracts, to the extent that such a framework requires not only clear-cut rules concerning procedures but also specific rules about the proceedings, thereby ensuring some degree of procedural fairness.

Paul Verbruggen (Chapter 11) examines enforcement in advertising. While standard setting follows a multilevel pattern, enforcement is highly decentralized with some efforts made to harmonize by reference to best practices defined by the European Advertising Standards Alliance (EASA). After describing the regulatory chain and emphasizing the importance of the International Chamber of Commerce (ICC) and EASA, and the discretion of national SROs in designing their codes, Verbruggen focuses on the five key variables concerning decentralized enforcement systems in order to answer the more general question of the potential costs to which decentralization gives rise. The first variable is timing: the relationship between *ex ante* and *ex post* control. Within the discussion of *ex ante* control, copy advice (voluntary) and pre-clearance (when there is a duty on the enforcer to act) are considered. Here, variations of the *ex ante* and *ex post* combination among private enforcers are significant. The second variable is the composition of the enforcing body, and in particular the participation of non-industry members. The third is related to procedural features. The fourth variable is concerned with differences in remedies and sanctions and the fifth concerns the type of media involved. In the conclusion of his chapter, Verbruggen examines the degree of procedural fairness in SROs' proceedings. The reason for the variation observed across private enforcers is that the occurrence of this variation depends on whether the SRO (is considered to) exercise(s) a public function. Where this is the case, jurisdiction over third parties, recognition of a duty to give reasons, and an open hearing are generally granted, with some differences existing across jurisdictions. In the negative case, where the SRO is not considered to exercise a public function, a much lower threshold of procedural fairness is required. Verbruggen concludes that while common standards of procedural fairness are not applied in their entirety, nevertheless, a common principle recognizing due process rights applies to private and judicial enforcement. Further empirical research is required to explore private regulation in action.

In their concluding chapter, Cassese, D'Alterio and De Bellis describe enforcement mechanisms in TPR. They start by asking definitional questions, concerning both the nature of private regulation and its enforcement mechanisms, and specifically whether enforcement of TPR should be considered to be an oxymoron. In particular, they examine whether TPR enforcement is limited to self-enforcement mechanisms, usually deployed by conventional self-regulatory regimes, or whether it is based on a combination of private and administrative enforcers that jointly collaborate to enforce transnational private rules. After considering ten examples in various sectors, building on the Leebron linkages approach among different regimes, they identify three different sets of mechanisms in relation to which this hybridity materializes, according to the various degrees of effectiveness exhibited therein. A first model, with soft effectiveness, is based on monitoring by administrative bodies within private regulators. A second model, with medium effectiveness, encompasses arbitration and quasi-judicial remedies. A third model, with hard effectiveness, operates when public actors participate directly in enforcing the standards, primarily through decentralized mechanisms that include direct sanctioning power. According to the authors, linkages among public and private enforcement regimes can reach the point of interchangeability, thence creating overlapping jurisdictions. Regimes' linkages are grounded on various rationales: they improve effectiveness, they avoid or solve overlapping problems, and they facilitate the interchangeability of enforcement mechanisms. Cassese, D'Alterio and De Bellis conclude that the enforcement of TPR is not a fictitious oxymoron since 'first, it is not always self-enforcement, but often third party (public or private) enforcement; second, it is not always private, but increasingly hybrid, regulation' (p. 365).

LOOKING FORWARD: A RESEARCH AGENDA FOR TPR ENFORCEMENT

TPR regimes vary significantly across organizations, sectors and territories. Their enforcement results from different combinations of judicial, administrative and private non-judicial enforcers. They deploy different instruments to solve disputes, and review and interpret private regulations. The current diversity suggests that different TPRs call for related enforcement schemes and that a one-size-fits-all model would not adequately reflect normative regulatory pluralism.

An important distinction emerges from the public/private divide. The jurisdiction of public enforcement regimes, including both administrative agencies and domestic courts, tends to be general and territorially-based; while private non-judicial regimes are sector-specific and functionally-based, with jurisdictions overcoming states boundaries. This has not always been the case but it goes back to the move, in the public domain, from personal to territorial jurisdiction. The public/private distinction today remains, even if, especially within judicial enforcement, a tendency towards extraterritorial effects of judgments and specialized global international courts is becoming consolidated, albeit with important differences among states. Clearly the public/private divide is reduced when TPR is directly enforced by international organizations whose 'jurisdiction' tends to be both functional and territorial. The second difference concerns the existence of general principles in public international law and global administrative law, while within the private field, no general framework exists and domestic jurisdictions differ both institutionally and substantively (especially in relation to procedural laws). These differences pose additional problems when, as it is often the case, the enforcement regimes co-exist and overlap, thereby making coordination at transnational level a necessity. Coordination is necessary not only within the public (between courts and agencies) and the private spheres, but also between them.

While the book provides a new conceptual framework to integrate diverse methodological approaches, given the preliminary stage of the research it poses more questions than it is able to answer. The following list summarizes some of the main findings while refining open research questions to be further investigated.

1. In transnational regulation, and particularly in TPR, enforcement cannot be disjoined from standard setting and compliance. There is a significant functional interdependence among the different stages of each regulatory process, far stronger than that observable in other areas of transnational private law, that is commercial transactions. Such interdependence is linked to the governance structure of private regulators, and, in particular, to the degree of functional separation between standard setting and enforcement. The need for independent private enforcers has characterized the evolution of TPR over the last 20 years; impartiality and other due process guarantees are correlated to independence. Less independence corresponds to lower procedural due process. Structural separation between rule-makers and enforcers depends also on the choice between first and third-party enforcement. When lead firms are direct enforcers, it is achieved by devising internal separation within the corporate form. When associations of firms or multi-stakeholders are the enforcers, the separation is realized through the creation of groups or independent bodies coordinated via regulatory agreements or memoranda of understanding. Clearly, the degree of functional separation, and consequently of impartiality, is lower than that potentially achievable through third-party enforcement, where professional and 'independent' organizations operate. However within third-party enforcement, there exist numerous models exhibiting different degrees of impartiality depending on the for-profit/non-profit nature of the organization, the 'for

sale' or 'for free' performance of enforcement services, and the professional or voluntary identity of the enforcer.

The efforts to achieve separation have been quite successful in some sectors, like sports, advertising and CSR, and less so in others, such as e-commerce and data protection. They vary according to the number of standard setters and the level of market concentration of regulated entities. Clearly, the necessity for functional separation within the private regulatory entity is linked to the role of public, domestic and transnational regulators and that of courts. Effective public enforcement renders less dramatic the need for structural separation in the private domain. However, it does not eliminate the desirability of functional separation between standard setters and enforcers in order to grant impartiality, accountability and legal innovation.

There is no necessary conflict between: (i) the need to separate private standard setters and enforcers to avoid conflicts of interest and to ensure effective compliance; and (ii) the necessity to govern interdependence among different stages of the regulatory process. However, the simultaneous pursuit of structural separation and functional integration requires the careful governance design of transnational private regulators. More empirical research is needed to verify how effective structural separation has been and how the trade-offs between impartiality and effectiveness operate.

2. The specific correlation between standard setting and enforcement is highly relevant. Enforcement tools and institutions are linked to the choice of the specific regulatory model and the composition of the private regulatory body. Command and control requires enforcement mechanisms quite different from responsive or market-based regulation.[75] Different relationships between regulators, regulatees and beneficiaries, reflected in each regulatory option, give rise to various combinations of legal and non-legal enforcement, and, within legal instruments, between judicial and non-judicial ones. The attempt to provide a general framework for TPR enforcement has to meet the challenge of distinguishing among different rule-making techniques and sector-specificity. The framework developed in CSR differs from that deployed in environmental or data protection because private regulators have to address different market failures, and in doing so, address different incentives to infringe rules within the same regime, let alone among diverse regulatory regimes.

---

[75] See Stewart, Chapter 1, in this volume.

Often, when these are industry-driven standards, firms are both the regulators and the regulated, but having different incentives across sectors. The regulation of data protection developed by IT firms will be applied to environmentally-friendly firms that enact environmental standards to be applied to other manufacturing enterprises. The regulatory cascade is sometimes entirely within the industry components but with divergent regulatory objectives. The scope of regulation for these three categories may differ significantly and bring about the misalignment of incentives, a result that has to be addressed in the enforcement design.

The picture becomes more complex when private regulators include, in their governing bodies, several potentially conflicting components both within industry and between industry and NGOs. An even higher degree of complexity occurs when the interplay with international organizations is added. More empirical research is needed to identify the differences that private regulatory autonomy has developed when devising the correlation between standard setting, monitoring and enforcement. What needs to be tested is, for example, whether private regulators, with a high degree of NGOs present in their governing bodies, will set up different enforcement mechanisms which open up to third parties to a greater extent than those established by industry-led regulators, in relation to which NGOs act only as external claimants.

3. The link between governance and regulation influences enforcement options and their effectiveness. This is clear for private non-judicial enforcement but to some extent might be true for courts and administrative bodies as well. The regulatory strategy depends also on the models of private regulators' governance. In particular, it is relevant whether the choice between contractual or organizational forms and, within them, between for-profit and non-profit, will affect the selection of enforcement mechanisms and the degree of (domestic) judicial intervention. In the case of contractual transnational regulation, as represented, for example, by supply chains, the regulator, generally the lead MNC, acts as an enforcer vis-à-vis the regulatees (the suppliers), using its market power to threaten contract termination in the case of non-compliance along the chain. Contractual arrangements generally call for a higher degree of judicial enforcement, but in relation to self-enforcing contracts, courts generally only intervene *ex post*. When in place, regulatory contracts may increase the effectiveness of regulatees' compliance, but will have very limited access to third-party beneficiaries. Hence they do not enhance protection of regulatory beneficiaries and fail to capture the losses suffered,

through regulatory infringements, by the whole chain. When organizational models are chosen, especially multi-stakeholder bodies, dispute resolution and enforcement mechanisms tend to be more proceduralized and combined with peer monitoring, supplemented by social and market accountability systems. Clearly, there is a correlation between the degree of internal hierarchy of the organization and the combination of legal and non-legal enforcement.[76] Non-legal enforcement often increases with the growing degree of hierarchy in the governance of the regulator.[77]

4. Enforcement, effectiveness and legitimacy are strongly linked. Effective enforcement provides legitimacy to the regulatory process. Depending on the identity of the litigants and the nature of the disputes, different effects on legitimacy emerge. When access to the dispute resolution is limited to the members of the regulatory body, internal legitimacy may be preserved, but external legitimacy towards third parties and the public is limited.
5. A fifth question concerns the relationship between judicial and non-judicial enforcement and the manifold role of domestic courts in enforcing transnational regulation. The implementation and enforcement of TPR are still decentralized, creating coordination failures both within and between enforcement mechanisms.[78] A general transnational legal framework concerning principles of implementation and enforcement could help to address some of these failures. Some indications come from private meta-regulators, which have started to propose common rules for quality and effectiveness. Enforcers can freely adopt these rules or refer to them in the case that a specific dispute arises. The rate of adhesion by private regulators to these rules is quite impressive given the short time they have been in place; it suggests that when the goal is bottom-up harmonization the regulatory failures generated by the absence of common rules are rather significant.

---

[76] However there is no necessary causal correlation between the choice of organizational form and the degree of internal hierarchy. In some organizations hierarchy is very low and compliance is secured through peer control rather than authority.

[77] Hierarchy is not a substitute for enforcement, but it affects the ratio between legal and non-legal tools.

[78] In relation to transnational public regulation, Stewart identifies three causes of enforcement failures: lack of coordination among enforcement bodies; lack of legal capacity; and inaction. (See Chapter 1, this volume.)

6. A related issue is that of jurisdiction over inter-regime disputes. The development of regulatory instruments that apply across sectors is raising important jurisdictional questions about the identity of the competent enforcer and how far its powers can go.[79] Private enforcers have limited jurisdiction and are often unable to settle inter-jurisdictional disputes. Which bodies can solve conflicts among transnational regimes? Domestic courts have often provided solutions, but the rendering of divergent interpretations has reduced certainty and caused implementation problems. Increasing judicial cooperation on transnational disputes constitutes a partial answer to this problem, but, ultimately, any solution should also include the vertical dimension between national and international courts.[80]
7. The widespread use of TPR poses daunting challenges to the principle of state-sovereignty and democracy.[81] Domestic courts can exercise a powerful role by accepting or denying the effects of private regulation. They can incorporate transnational private standards into domestic systems or oppose their entry into national legal orders. How legitimate is their role? Which institutions should contribute to the evaluation of whether and how TPR should have access to domestic orders? How useful is the scheme developed by public international law?
8. Enforcing TPR implies references to domestic private laws since most of the constitutional contracts and charters are incomplete. Traditional domestic private and procedural laws, developed primarily within States' boundaries, provide the basis for the governance of these transnational regimes, but show their weaknesses in respect of the foregoing challenges. Transformations of private law instruments are taking place in contract, property and tort law. As a result, a combination of private and public law instruments, the former mainly related to governance, the latter to the activity, has been designed by regulators or imposed by enforcers, in particular by

---

[79] For example, when the members of one organization have committed to comply with those undertakings contained in a code of conduct enacted by a different organization. The DSB would have jurisdiction only for violations of those undertakings committed by regulated entities but not over the interpretation of the code enacted by a different regulator, if this is conflicting with that provided by the drafting organization.

[80] See on both vertical cooperation and competition, Y. Shany, *Regulating Jurisdictional Relations between National and International Courts*, OUP, 2007.

[81] Many contributions to this volume refer to these challenges and the role of enforcement. See in particular Benvenisti and Downs, Chapter 3, this volume, p. 00, and Cassese, D'Alterio and De Bellis, Chapter 12, this volume, p. 238.

> domestic courts, to meet accountability and effectiveness requirements.[82] The GAL project has contributed to a better and innovative understanding of these instruments and their operation across sectors. This combination, however, requires that a fresh look is taken of the private and public divide in the transnational context. The distinction remains important but it requires that hybrid features, combining public and private enforcement mechanisms, be accommodated. Internal reforms of both substantive and procedural private laws to adapt the regulatory nature are necessary.

This book's contributions address these challenges both to scholarly and practitioners' communities.

[82] See e.g. Swiss Federal Tribunal decision of November 24th 2010, BGE 132 III 389 SC.2 2 pp. 392ff; Federal Tribunal decision of January 5th 2007, 4P 240/2006; Federal Tribunal decision of September 28th 2010, 4A_144/2010 of September 28, 2010; Swiss Federal Court 15 March 1993 *Gundel* v *Federation Equestre Internationale*, BGE 119 II, S. 271ff.; *Club Atlético de Madrid SAD gegen Sport Lisboa E Benfica – Futebol SAD*, Federal Court, 136 III 345/4A_490/2009, 13 April 2010.

PART I

Rethinking the public–private divide

1. Enforcement of transnational public regulation

Richard Stewart[1]

I. INTRODUCTION

Enforcement of transnational public regulation is a vast topic. This chapter deals with selected aspects of the subject to focus on issues that are instructive, by way of comparison and potential synergy, with the issues of private transnational regulation that are the central concern of this volume. It addresses transnational regimes established by treaties among states, by agreements among international organizations (e.g. Codex Alimentarius), or by agreements among networks of government agencies and officials, aimed, directly or mediately, at coordinated regulation of private market actors' conduct.[2] It also considers the important role in enforcement of transnational regulatory administrative authorities established pursuant to such arrangements and the role of Global Administrative Law (GAL).

Examples of the fields covered by transnational public regulation include environmental health and safety ('EHS'), consumer protection, investment, financial products and services, intellectual property, and competition. Generalizing across such a wide variety of regimes and fields of regulation, presenting very different circumstances and considerations, is hazardous, but I will endeavor to provide a general framework. Because I am most familiar with EHS regimes and US law, many of the examples discussed herein will be drawn from them.

The chapter does not deal with arrangements among domestic or transnational agencies for mutual recognition or recognition of regulatory

[1] The excellent research assistance of Kiri Mattes and helpful suggestions by Sabino Cassese and Lorenzo Casini are gratefully acknowledged.

[2] While these various regimes often have different names, such as 'international', 'intergovernmental', etc., I term them all transnational in accordance with the terminology of this volume.

equivalence. Because of the EC's distinctive supranational legal and administrative structure, it does not treat the EC as a transnational regulatory regime. It does not deal with transnational liability regimes providing compensation for harms caused by private actors, although these may certainly have strong regulative effects.[3] The chapter also does not address transnational application of one country's regulatory or liability laws (including laws that may be based or are claimed to be based on global regulatory norms) to activities or actors abroad.[4] Further, the chapter does not systematically address relations between transnational public regulation and transnational private regulation, including co-regulation and hybrid, nested, or coordinated public and private regimes, and the various ways in which they may be regarded as complements or substitutes.

Regulatory Enforcement

This chapter focuses on systems of regulation involving enforcement actions brought by public authorities or private plaintiffs against actors subject to public regulatory requirements. These include administrative orders requiring or prohibiting specified conduct, administrative imposition of penalties, criminal prosecutions, and civil actions brought by governmental officials for specific relief or civil penalties – in all cases backed by the coercive power of the state. In the era of the regulatory welfare state, enforcement can also include governmental denial or revocation of permits or licenses to carry on productive activities or denial or withdrawal of state-provided grants and other forms of financial assistance for failure to meet specified requirements or conditions. Such conditions have become a highly important regulatory tool. Domestic systems of constitutional and administrative law increasingly provide legal protections analogous to those provided in cases of coercive sanctions to persons

---

[3] International agreements increasingly provide for strict liability, often on private actors, for environmental harm to other states or the global commons. Examples include agreements relating to marine oil pollution, carriage at sea of hazardous and noxious substances, interstate impacts from nuclear power accidents, and transboundary shipments of hazardous wastes. Negotiations are pending to establish liability systems for transboundary shipments of genetically modified organisms (GMOs) under the Cartagena Protocol. Common characteristics of such regimes include strict liability, liability channeling, liability limits, and compulsory insurance.

[4] See Hannah Buxbaum, 'Transnational regulatory litigation', 46 *Va. J. Int'l L.* 252 (2006); Christopher Whytock, 'Domestic courts and global governance', 84 *Tulane L. Rev* 67 (2009).

denied such advantageous opportunities because of failure to meet regulatory conditions. Enforcement also includes civil actions, sometimes termed 'citizen suits,' or 'private attorney general' actions, by private plaintiffs against regulated actors to enforce regulatory compliance or sanction violations.

In defining regulation as involving enforcement of conduct requirements or prohibitions, this chapter follows what Neil Walker has identified as the narrow view of regulation – one shared by most lawyers – as distinguished from a broader view of regulation that encompasses other norm-based practices and institutions that shape conduct in regular patterns, including much network regulation and elements of new governance.[5]

In addition to enforcement, this chapter discusses 'upstream' legislative and administrative measures to implement regulatory programs and help assure compliance by market actors, including programs for monitoring, record keeping, and reporting. It also briefly considers collateral incentives for compliance by regulated actors with public regulatory norms, such as avoidance of tort liability or the demands of supply chain partners. Also highly relevant, but not systematically addressed herein, is the suite of 'responsive regulation' tools other than enforcement that public authorities, transnational or domestic, may apply to promote compliance.[6]

A core (but perhaps contestable) premise of this chapter is that credible and effective enforcement, as defined above, is essential to many and probably most public regulatory regimes, including transnational regimes. Enforcement also carries an epistemological premise, namely that the legal system is capable of distinguishing whether a regulated actor is or is not in compliance with regulatory requirements, which in turn implies that applicable regulatory norms have a suitably hard-edged character that will support such distinctions.[7] Thus, I do not regard regulatory systems that rely *solely* on 'soft' norms, peer review mechanisms, and other reputational incentives as involving enforcement, even if effective in promoting compliance, although enforcement-based regulatory systems may also include or be supplemented by such arrangements.

---

[5] Neil Walker, 'On regulating the regulation of regulation', in Fabrizio Cafaggi (ed.) *Reframing Self-regulation in European Private Law* (Kluwer, 2006), pp. 347–357.

[6] See, for example, John Braithwaite, *Regulatory Capitalism: How it Works, Ideas for Making it Work Better* (Edward Elgar, 2008) (hereafter, *Regulatory Capitalism*).

[7] I am indebted to Bill Simon for this point.

Transnational Regulatory Administration and Global Administrative Law

A striking feature of contemporary transnational public regulation, in common with many other elements of global governance, is the powerful decision-making role of transnational administrative bodies, including the management and staff of international organizations, network institutions, various committees and councils, and other expert and specialized groups. States and agencies party to transnational regulatory regimes have delegated responsibility to such bodies to particularize and revise regulatory norms, and take steps to promote and oversee their implementation and enforcement. These administrative bodies respond to the need to continuously monitor and manage regulatory implementation and make necessary adjustments to improve performance and respond to changing circumstances and demands, all of which require organizational specialization, initiative, flexibility, and dispatch. The old international law model of treaties, interpreted and applied on a wholly decentralized basis by signatory states, is not capable of meeting contemporary regulatory demands, which require coordinated and consistent regulation of actors operating in global markets in order to redress market failures and secure collective goals.

Increasingly, global regulatory administrative bodies determine the detailed content of the *primary regulatory norms* defining the conduct prescribed or recommended, as well as the *secondary norms* governing arrangements and procedures for implementation and enforcement. The growth of these extra-statal administrative authorities, operating below or beyond the reach of treaty-based consent by states, raises profound and unresolved challenges of legitimacy and accountability. The premise of GAL is that these challenges can be addressed, in part, through the application of administrative law tools of transparency, participation, reason-giving and review to many elements of regulatory decision-making by the new global administrative bodies. These GAL principles and practices are increasingly being recognized and followed by transnational administrative bodies and tribunals.[8]

---

[8] An overview of GAL is found in Benedict Kingsbury, Nico Krisch and Richard B. Stewart, 'The emergence of global administrative law', 68 *Law and Contemp. Probs* 15 (2005). See also S. Cassese, B. Carotti, L. Casini, M. Macchia, E. McDonald and M. Savino (eds), *Global Administrative Law: Cases, Materials, and Issues* (2nd edn, 2008) (http://www.iilj.org/GAL/GALCasebook.asp) (hereafter *Global Administrative Law*). Information on the activities including conferences and publications of the Global Administrative Law research project at NYU Law

A focus of this chapter is the availability of legal remedies and other mechanisms to promote effective implementation and enforcement of transnational regulatory programs, and thereby enhance protection of regulatory beneficiaries, including tools to address failures by either transnational or domestic administrative authorities to effectively or appropriately implement and enforce regulatory norms. These measures include the GAL procedural norms and remedies that regulatory beneficiaries may assert against regulatory agencies, domestic or transnational, for regulatory failures and derelictions. They also include private enforcement or damages actions brought by regulatory beneficiaries as 'private attorneys general' against regulated actors pursuant to public regulatory regimes. Remedies may be established under domestic or transnational law, and may be enforced by either domestic or international administrative bodies or courts. The relation among these remedies, including the extent to which they are substitutes or complements, as well as their implications for collateral compliance incentives, must also be considered. A key issue is the interplay between public enforcement, private actions and collateral compliance incentives.

II. TRANSNATIONAL TREATY OR NETWORK REGULATORY REGIMES

For Addressing Market and Decentralization Failures

Transnational regulatory regimes are (ideally, in theory) established to address twin institutional failures: (1) market failures; and (2) decentralization failures resulting from the inability of states acting independently though purely domestic measures to adequately or properly regulate market actors in circumstances of global economic regulation and transnational externalities. They may also (again ideally) be understood as responses to failures or limitations of transnational private regulation.[9]

The various elements and dimensions of market failures cannot be rehearsed here, except to note that classical analyses of public regulation generally ignores the potential for, and possible roles of, private regulation and co-regulation.

School, conducted with partners in many other countries, can be found at: http://www.iilj.org/GAL/

[9] Transnational private regulation may be similarly understood as a response to market and decentralization failures and the failures or limitations of transnational public regulation. Sustainable forestry certification regimes are an example.

In the case of products, decentralization failures often take the form of transactions costs and impediments to scale economies resulting from differing and potentially conflicting national standards. The response is a transnational regime, public, private, or hybrid, to establish uniform or approximated product regulatory standards, and, often, implementing arrangements. Informational asymmetries and domestic regulatory failures in developing countries may also account for product regulatory regimes such as the Cartagena Protocol on Biosafety to the Convention on Biological Diversity or the Basel Convention on the Control of Transboundary Movements of Hazardous Wastes and their Disposal. Regulation of production and process measures (PPMs) is justified by various forms of transnational non-pecuniary externalities (global or regional pollution, biodiversity loss), or, much more doubtfully, the risk of a 'race to the bottom' in domestic regulation resulting from international competitiveness factors and pecuniary externalities. Transnational regulation of financial and other services (e.g. banking regulation) often represents an intermediate case with characteristics of both product and PPM regulation. Other factors, including the desirability of tailoring regulation to differing local circumstances and preferences, or the potential desirability of competition among diverse regulatory systems, may limit regulatory harmonization.

While functional considerations derived from mutually beneficial opportunities for regulatory coordination or cooperation among states, as well as constructivist factors, play both an explanatory and justificatory role in transnational regulatory regimes, interest-based political economy drivers are also critical. These may be modest and manageable in situations having the characteristics of coordination games, where all participants have an interest in uniform 'rules of the road' for transactions and other activities, and the choice of rule does not have significant distributional consequences. Technical standards for products and services often approximate this situation. Situations having the character of cooperation games involving the need for concerted action to achieve collective goods under conditions that invite free riding, especially in circumstances where defining the terms of cooperation generates major conflicts over the distribution of burdens and benefits, present much greater difficulties in a global setting in which each participating state or domestic or global agency must voluntarily assent to a cooperation scheme, and domestic interests exert significant power.

In circumstances of free trade in goods and services and capital mobility, industries in heavily regulated jurisdictions often favor extension of stronger regulation to other jurisdictions with less stringent regulation in order to avoid competitive disadvantage, while firms in those jurisdictions correspondingly resist harmonization. If the former fail to achieve 'harmonization up', regulatory competition among jurisdictions may, in some cases, depress the overall level of regulation. Under other circumstances, 'race to the top' incentives for technological or product quality leadership may result in regulation at a high level in many jurisdictions as a result of competition among firms and regulating states. Regulatory beneficiaries in a given jurisdiction sometimes oppose transnational regulation as involving 'leveling down', but in other circumstances view it as an opportunity to enhance the level of domestic regulatory protection. International and transnational NGOs often support regulatory harmonization to increase the level of protection globally or in certain nations, such as developing countries. Harmonization may also be resisted or distorted by a variety of other local political and institutional factors. Transnational regulatory harmonization may be partial, addressing some elements while leaving others, or it may secure a degree of convergence falling short of uniformity, for example by setting minimum standards while allowing states discretion to adopt more demanding standards, either generally or in specified circumstances.

III. IMPLEMENTATION AND ENFORCEMENT OF TRANSNATIONAL PUBLIC REGULATION

The objectives of transnational regulation, including harmonization and enhanced regulatory protection, will not be achieved unless the regulatory norms adopted – whether by agreement among states, international organizations, or networks of government officials or by decisions of transnational administrative bodies – are effectively implemented and enforced against market actors operating in and across different jurisdictions. Otherwise only 'Potemkin harmonization' will be achieved. In a *vertical perspective*, public transnational regulation, whether established by treaty or network accord, traditionally operates at two levels: regulatory norms are adopted at the transnational level, while responsibility for implementation and enforcement is allocated to states and domestic agencies. Although instances of direct regulation of private actors by transnational administrative authorities are beginning to appear, transnational enforcement remains relatively rare. In a *horizontal perspective*, unless enforcement and other arrangements secure fairly consistent compliance by all market actors, the benefits anticipated from coordinated or cooperative measures to address market/decentralization failures and 'harmonize up' will not be realized. Accordingly, adoption at the global level of more or less uniform secondary norms and measures to harmonize and promote effective implementation and enforcement by different states and domestic agencies of primary global regulatory norms may be needed to secure regulatory goals. Further, there must be adequate global arrangements to ensure that states and domestic agencies comply with these secondary norms and measures.

Decentralized domestic implementation and enforcement of transnational regulatory norms may fail for several basic reasons. First, governments or agencies may fail to agree on specific primary or secondary norms, either because of disagreement or uncertainty over norms, bargaining failures, or the need for flexibility to deal with future changes in political and economic circumstances and information. Subsequently, different domestic agencies and courts in different jurisdictions may interpret the agreed but general or ambiguous norms in different ways.[10] Second, governments or agencies may decide for a variety of political and policy reasons not to carry out their undertakings. They may wish to avoid imposing regulatory burdens on, or otherwise favor, domestic producers and prefer to free ride on other states' efforts. New information or changing circumstances may lead them (influenced by powerful domestic constituencies) to regard the agreed requirements as imprudent, impracticable, or of lesser priority.[11] Third, states or agencies may lack legal and administrative capacity to effectively implement the agreed norms. Fourth, the agreed regulatory instruments and strategies may have intrinsic efficacy limitations.

Transnational public regulatory regimes undertake measures to address these several sources of implementation and enforcement failure, including the creation of transnational regulatory administrative bodies. These bodies develop and adopt more specific primary regulatory norms in the form of regulations, standards and guidelines, and periodically revise them in light of evolving conditions and accumulating experience. They may include centralized dispute settlement mechanisms to interpret, clarify and thereby promote more consistent application of regulatory norms. Many regimes include administrative bodies for compliance review, compliance

---

[10] Catherine Redgewell, 'National implementation', in Ellen Hay, Jutta Brunée and Daniel Bodansky (eds), *The Oxford Handbook of International Environmental Law* (OUP, 2007), 936–937 (hereafter *Oxford Handbook*).

[11] Pierre-Hugues Verdier, 'Transnational regulatory networks and their limits', 34 *Yale J. Int'l L.* 113 (2009); Kenneth Abbott and Duncan Sindal, 'Strengthening international regulation through transnational new governance: overcoming the orchestration deficit', 42 *Vand. J. Transnat'l L.* 501 (2009) (analyzing breakdown of implementation and enforcement of Basel Committee regulation of banks because of divergences in interests among major economy banks due to changing circumstances).

assistance, and sanctioning. They may adopt incentives for state compliance such as trade sanctions and subsidies overseen by administrative bodies; carry out capacity building programs through administrative bodies; and adopt more effective regulatory instruments and strategies. Further, transitional regulatory regimes increasingly establish, very often by administrative decisions, secondary norms specifying implementation (and sometimes enforcement) procedures and measures that participating states and agencies must follow. Transnational administrative bodies orchestrate networks of domestic agencies to share experience and best practices, promote peer review, receive and compile reports from participants, and track performance. The administrative bodies that devise and manage these systems of implementation information and review can then undertake needed adjustments to the regime to improve regulatory efficacy and recommend changes to the founding parties.[12] Bilateral aid programs and multilateral development banks play an important complementary role through programs to strengthen legal and administrative capacities in developing countries, thereby enhancing their ability to implement global regulatory norms.

In addition, where powerful states like the US place a high priority on global regulatory efficacy in specific areas, they exercise political and economic leverage to push other states to implement and enforce regulatory controls, as illustrated by the Financial Action Task Force (FATF) anti-money laundering regime.[13] Under trade-based and transactions-based regulatory regimes, such as CITES, the Basel Convention on Transboundary Movements of Hazardous Wastes and their Disposal, the Cartagena Biosafety Protocol, and the FATF, compliance with global regulatory norms can be policed by both of the states involved in a transnational transfer or transaction.

It is increasingly recognized that public access to information and participation at the level of domestic decision-making can make a vital contribution to effective implementation and enforcement of transnational public regulation, especially in fields such as environmental and consumer

---

12 Kal Raustiala, 'Compliance and effectiveness in regulatory cooperation', 32 *Case West. Res. J. Int'l L.* 387 (2000), at 415–422. The OECD network regime for mutual assurance of non-clinical chemical safety test data illustrates many of these strategies. See James Salzman, 'Decentralized administrative law in the Organization for Economic Cooperation and Development', 68 *Law & Contemp. Probs* 189 (2005), at 200–206 (hereafter 'Decentralized administrative law').

13 See Kal Raustiala, 'The architecture of international cooperation: transgovernmental networks and the future of international law', 43 *Va. J. Int'l L.* 1 (2002), at 73–74 (hereafter, 'The architecture of international cooperation').

protection, and human rights. The Aarhus Convention establishes a transnational system of secondary regulatory norms for public information, participation, and access to justice in environmental cases. These arrangements strengthen the domestic political influence of regulatory beneficiary NGOs and also provide a platform for their assertion of administrative and judicial enforcement remedies, as discussed below. They also facilitate organization and mobilization of transnational NGO networks to promote regulatory initiatives and implementation, both at the level of the transnational regime and at the domestic level.

Mechanisms that operate to harmonize domestic regulation in the absence of any agreements among states or domestic agencies should be noted. Regulatory competition among states, coupled with the ability of regulated firms or persons to relocate or otherwise choose to be governed by the regulation of a given state may promote harmonization in certain regulatory fields. Network effects may also produce common standards for products or services without any transnational agreements. The WTO regime may generate incentives for states to adopt applicable international standards in order to defend against challenges to their domestic regulations under the Agreements on Sanitary and Phytosanitary Measures and on Technical Barriers to Trade. Emulation and other constructivist influences may also promote regulatory convergence. These mechanisms, however, lack transnational governance arrangements, and as a result may often fail to secure harmonized or effective implementation and enforcement.

IV. REGULATORY INSTRUMENTS AND COMPLIANCE MECHANISMS

An important component in the design and performance of transnational public regulatory regimes is the type of regulatory instrument used for securing compliance with regulatory requirements.[14]

Command and Control Instruments

Generally, transnational public regulatory regimes either define regulatory norms in general terms that allow states discretion as to which regulatory instruments to use, or call for the use of command and control measures that prohibit or mandate specified conduct by regulated actors. Where

---

14 For discussion in the field of environmental regulation, see Richard Stewart, 'Instrument choice', in *Oxford Handbook*, at 936–937.

discretion is afforded, states and domestic agencies have generally used command instruments. In effective command regulatory systems, domestic authorities specify more detailed conduct requirements through administrative rule-making or adjudication (including conditions in licenses and on grants and other forms of government assistance) and enforce them against regulated actors in case of violation. A notable recent development is the rise of transnational regulatory regimes that call on domestic agencies to regulate conduct through financial conditionality. An example is the OECD programme that calls on domestic export credit agencies to apply social and environmental conditions on assistance to domestic firms.[15] Financial conditionality can also be used by transnational administrative bodies to promote enforcement by domestic agencies. For example, the World Bank and IMF give financial assistance to governments on the condition that they follow and enforce Basel regulatory norms on their banks.

Under many systems of domestic constitutional and administrative law, regulated actors can invoke procedural and judicial review in defense of government enforcement actions. In some systems these rights attach to upstream administrative actions (such as rule-making or licensing) to specify and apply regulatory norms prior to the enforcement stage. Increasingly, in many jurisdictions domestic constitutional and administrative law has extended procedural and judicial review rights to regulatory beneficiaries to promote their interests in regulatory decision-making by domestic agencies. In certain cases, beneficiaries may also have rights under domestic regulatory law to enforce or maintain liability actions against regulated firms for damages caused by regulatory violations. Private treble damages actions under the US antitrust laws are a prominent example.

While global regulatory regimes generally leave a fair amount of discretion to states and agencies regarding enforcement, there are some recent examples of a far more directive approach. Notable examples are found in the international security field, which powerful states regard as imperative. The Security Council and its 1267 Committee have mandated that UN member states freeze the assets of, and deny entry to, persons listed by the Committee as financing terrorism. The Financial Action Task Force has developed a stringent regime requiring participating governments to police money laundering by regulating domestic financial institutions and their transactions. The Montreal Protocol is an example in the environmental field of a transnational regulatory regime where major developed countries

---

[15] The OECD 'Common Approaches' is discussed further in James Salzman, 'Decentralized administrative law', op. cit., at 206–212.

regarded stratospheric ozone protection as a paramount global objective, warranting use of trade sanctions, side payments to developing countries, and a strong transnational administrative compliance system to ensure that all states comply with restrictions on the production and use of ozone-depleting chemicals.

Market-based and Information-based Regulatory Instruments

Because of the dysfunctions encountered by governments in attempting to extend and intensify command and control requirements to meet increasingly ambitious regulatory goals, many developed and some developing countries have adopted market-based and information-based regulatory instruments as a supplement or alternative to traditional approaches. Rather than dictating conduct, these tools steer the conduct of regulated firms in the desired direction by directly imposing a price on disfavored conduct or mobilizing consumers, investors, and the public generally, to reward firms and products with superior regulatory performance and shun those with inferior records.

Although the modern regulatory state, at least in developed countries, enjoys ample power, a virtually unrelenting reliance on command regulation has made the state an increasingly maladroit and arbitrary regulator. In the global setting, on the other hand, the problem is the relative weakness of institutions. Market-based and information-based programs can potentially address both types of problems. An important issue for transnational regulation is whether economic and information-based instruments can, through their mobilization of the price and market system and non-governmental interests and incentives, better compensate for those weaknesses than command-and-control regulation. Here, a key consideration, much debated in the regulatory context of climate, is the relative institutional demands, including demands for monitoring, verification, and enforcement capacities, of emissions taxes and quota-trading programs relative to command instruments

Although they allow regulated firms flexibility in the means of achieving regulatory objectives, the new tools generally involve requirements on the regulated that must be enforceable through methods ultimately based on government coercion. Thus, in emissions trading or tax systems firms must hold quotas or credits or pay taxes equal to their true emissions. In information systems, they must accurately report and disclose the information required. Compliance by regulated firms with the requirements of market incentives (e.g. payment of taxes on emissions) and information disclosure must be enforced, but because these forms of regulation do not involve detailed conduct requirements there may be less scope for legal remedies by regulatory beneficiaries in the implementation and enforcement of the regulatory program.

The development of innovative regulatory instruments in the public transnational context is still at an early stage. The most notable example of market-based instruments is the use of tradable emissions quotas and credits under the Kyoto Protocol to the United Nations Framework Convention on Climate Change, including Joint Implementation (JI) and the Clean Development Mechanism (CDM). The CDM and similar transnational emissions trading systems will play a major role in mobilizing private investment from developed countries to achieve greenhouse gas emissions reductions in developing countries and mitigate climate change.[16] Enforcement requires tracking of quota or credit holdings, accurate emissions monitoring and reporting, and sanctions for failure by sources to hold quota/credits equal to their emissions. Another emerging market-based regulatory approach is the use of Individual Transferable Quotas (ITQs) for regional high seas fishery management. A significant feature of these instruments is that the regulatory markets operate transnationally, with purchases and sales occurring across jurisdictions as well as within participating jurisdictions. This necessitates effective transnational administrative authorities to ensure the uniform and proper functioning of transnational markets and, with them, of the component domestic markets.

Market-based regulatory mechanisms create powerful incentives for effective transnational monitoring and enforcement assurances because cheating undermines the financial integrity of the market as well as its environmental performance. The Executive Board of the CDM, a transnational administrative authority, has developed an elaborate system of review, verification and enforcement to meet these requisites. Non-state actors, including NGOs, play an important role in the processes of monitoring and determining compliance. Market-based transnational regulatory systems can also mobilize market mechanisms to promote compliance by, for example, adopting buyer liability for excess emissions under emissions trading regimes. Under buyer liability, emissions quotas or credits sold by a non-complying source with excess emissions are invalidated or discounted based on the violation. This prospect will lead credit and quota buyers to demand compliance assurances through contractual provisions or otherwise, that will, in turn, promote compliance.

---

[16] Richard Stewart, Benedict Kingsbury and Bryce Rudyk (eds), *Climate Finance: Regulatory and Funding Strategies for Climate Change and Sustainable Development* (NYUP, 2009).

Information-based systems can mobilize consumers, socially responsible investors, and other regulatory beneficiaries to favor products, services and firms with high levels of regulatory performance and avoid those with inferior performance. They can do so through the use of product labels, or publication and dissemination of information on performance. Public transnational examples of such programs that effectively regulate private actors include the OECD anti-bribery program, the World Bank's anti-corruption program, and the requirements in the Biosafety Protocol for GMO labeling and disclosure of risk assessment information. While the Biosafety Protocol information regime is aimed in part at assisting states considering whether or not to consent to importation of GMOs (states can be regarded as regulatory beneficiaries in these circumstances), it is also accessible and used by other regulatory beneficiaries, including consumers and NGOs. Transgovernmental bodies such as the World Bank are increasingly using indicators to rank the performance of governments in achieving development and other goals, and base development assistance grants on their performance.[17] It is likely that indicators will be used in the future as a means for global regulation of private economic actors.

Network Regulatory Strategies

In response to the limitations of command regulation, governments have also adopted various forms of networked regulation, making extensive use of private and hybrid public–private institutions, including arrangements for co-regulation. These arrangements seek to economize on the role of enforcement, which inevitably implies an adversarial relationship between regulator and the regulated, in favor of non-hierarchical institutional strategies that emphasize cooperation, experimentation, and horizontal information sharing.[18] They are not addressed in this chapter, which is focused on public regulatory enforcement. Where domestic governments use networked strategies, however, their implementation and enforcement of public transnational regulatory norms may employ these strategies, along with more traditional regulatory mechanisms.

---

[17] Kevin Davis, Benedict Kingsbury and Sally Engle Merry, 'Indicators as a technology of global governance', *GAL Working Paper 2010/2*, available at the GAL Project website, at: http://www.iilj.org/publications/2010–2.Davis-Kingsbury-Merry.asp

[18] See John Braithwaite, *Regulatory Capitalism*, op. cit.; Charles Sabel and Jonathan Zeitlin (eds), *Experimentalist Governance in the European Union, Towards A New Architecture* (OUP, 2010).

Collateral Compliance Mechanisms Mobilized by Public Regulation

In addition to being enforced by domestic governments, transnational public regulation can also trigger a number of collateral incentives and mechanisms that serve to promote compliance by regulated market actors. Examples (many of which are also applicable to private transnational regulatory regimes) include the following:

- In some fields, transnational standards, notably 'technical' standards for product or service identity or quality, can solve coordination problems for firms in the global marketplace, and, as a result, become widely adopted without the need for enforcement actions by public authorities.
- Firms may face market incentives to adhere to transnational public regulatory norms in order to provide credible assurances of quality to supply chain partners, consumers or investors.
- Insurers and third-party certifiers may demand compliance with applicable transnational public regulatory standards, such as the standards for preventing oil pollution from ocean vessels.[19]
- In order to ensure their own compliance and reputations, regulated firms often require other firms with whom they contract to certify their compliance with relevant public regulatory standards. These arrangements may extend the effective reach of a transnational regulatory regime beyond the states that have agreed to it, as exemplified by the extension of Basel I bank regulations and Financial Action Task Force anti-money laundering regulations through the market leverage exercised by financial institutions in the major economies.
- Courts or arbitrators can look to compliance with transnational public regulatory norms when determining liability in contract or tort actions among private parties.
- The information generated in the course of implementing and enforcing transnational public regulatory norms, including information collected and distributed and indicators constructed by transnational regulatory administrative bodies, may lead business partners, consumers and investors to avoid firms with inferior regulatory performance or prefer those with superior performance, and thereby promote compliance by the regulated. Transnational NGOs or associations of socially responsible investors as well as the media may organize and

---

[19] See Kal Raustiala, 'The architecture of international cooperation', op.cit., at 413–415.

disseminate this information. The compliance push of public regulatory regimes can thereby be extended and enhanced.

As these examples show, transnational public regulatory standards are often enforced against regulated economic actors by other economic actors.

Direct Enforcement by Transnational Authorities

Global administrative bodies in public transnational regulatory regimes not only take steps to promote implementation and enforcement by states against regulated actors, but in some instances themselves wield enforcement powers based on their authority to grant or deny market actors regulatory authorizations which are recognized by states domestically or otherwise have important economic consequences, or to condition financial benefits on compliance with regulatory requirements.

The Kyoto Protocol CDM provides a notable example. The CDM Executive Board establishes and administers rules and procedures for registering projects in developing countries to reduce greenhouse gas emissions, and issuing certified emissions reduction credits (CERs) based on reductions achieved. CERs are internationally traded and commercially valuable because they can be used by firms to help meet their climate regulatory obligations in European countries or are purchased by some developed countries to meet their own Kyoto obligations. CERs provide a significant part of the economic return to CDM project developers and investors. Denial by the CDM of registration or issuance of CERs for failure to meet regulatory requirements is a form of regulatory enforcement against these private economic actors. On the other hand, overgenerous registration or CER certification results in higher emissions, to the detriment of environmental beneficiaries.

Multilateral financial institutions such as the World Bank (including its Prototype Carbon Fund), the International Finance Corporation, the IMF, and the regional development banks also engage in regulatory enforcement through financial conditionality. They deny funding or other financial assistance to projects that fail to meet conditions established pursuant to their social and environmental guidelines. In the case of the International Finance Corporation (IFC), enforcement operates directly against private firms seeking financial assistance from it.[20] The Multilateral Investment Guarantee Agency (MIGA) directly regulates the conduct of

---

[20] See IFC, 'International Finance Corporation's performance standards on social & environmental sustainability', April 30, 2006. Performance Standards

private firms undertaking foreign investment, with the grant of its political risk insurance conditional on project compliance with various conditions, such as the requirement to undertake environmental impact assessments.[21] The International Bank for Reconstruction and Development (World Bank) and the regional development banks impose conditions regarding financial assistance to developing country governments for development projects and programs. Because private creditors and investors 'piggyback' on Bank assistance for projects or operate under Bank-assisted programs, the conditions effectively regulate these private actors as well. Furthermore, private financial regulatory bodies, such as the Equator Principles Association, adopt the regulatory norms of the IFC and other multilateral institutions, and thereby extend their regulatory effect.

Limits to Harmonized Transnational Public Regulation

While transnational harmonization of secondary norms and institutions for domestic implementation and enforcement can make important contributions to substantive regulatory harmonization and efficacy, there are significant limits to such efforts. These limits may be attributable to the desire of states and domestic agencies to maintain future regulatory flexibility, differences in domestic circumstances including legal and administrative systems and traditions, and resistance to dictation of what are regarded as internal matters, especially with respect to administrative and judicial procedures and remedies. This discretion can, in turn, spawn implementation and enforcement failures that leave regulatory beneficiaries without protection, as well as undermining global regulatory consistency.

Because of the vast differences in the many different types of transnational regulatory regimes, no useful generalizations regarding their performance can be made. The degree of harmonization achieved and the extent to which regimes achieve their stated objectives vary enormously. The field of regulation; the regulatory objective; the identity of the regulated and the conduct regulated; the number, identity, and interests of the states, domestic agencies, and global administrative bodies participating;

---

define clients' roles and responsibilities for managing projects as well as the requirements for receiving and retaining IFC support in the areas of: social and environmental assessment and management; labor and working conditions; pollution prevention and abatement; community health, safety and security; land acquisition and involuntary resettlement; biodiversity conservation and sustainable natural resource management; indigenous peoples; and cultural heritage.

[21] See MIGA, 'Multilateral Investment Guarantee Agency's performance standards on social & environmental sustainability', October 1, 2007.

the design of the regulatory regime, including the instruments used; and transnational implementation and enforcement arrangements are all relevant. The varying priorities of the larger and more powerful states and the diverse configurations of affected economic, NGO, and other organized interests are among the more important factors. Uniformity is never fully achieved, nor would it be desirable in most cases.

Regulatory beneficiaries, organized through domestic and transnational NGOs, have begun in the past two decades to play an important role in promoting more effective implementation and enforcement of transnational regulatory regimes through a variety of advocacy efforts. Many of these efforts build on the implementation and enforcement arrangements developed by transnational regulatory administrative bodies, often in cooperation with them. Regulatory beneficiaries often have a greater interest in stronger regulation than in harmonization as such, but their efforts to promote implementation and enforcement in weaker states may tend to promote a degree of convergence.

V. REMEDIES AND MECHANISMS FOR PROTECTION OF REGULATORY BENEFICIARIES

This section focuses on the ability of regulatory beneficiaries to invoke legal procedures and remedies, including administrative law rights of transparency, participation, reason giving and review as well as civil remedies, at both the domestic and transnational levels in order to promote implementation and enforcement of transnational regulatory norms. The basic legal and institutional taxonomy of regulatory beneficiary remedies can be summarized as follows:

Applicable law

- Domestic
- Transnational

Target of remedy

- Domestic administration
- Regulated actor
- Transnational administration

Court or tribunal providing remedy

- Domestic
- Transnational or international

Type of remedy

- Government/administrative adherence to procedures for transparency, participation, reason-giving and review
- Government/administrative initiation of implementation and enforcement measures against regulated firms
- Beneficiary recovery of damages against administrative bodies for regulatory failures
- Beneficiary recovery of damages against regulatory violators
- Beneficiary injunctive relief against regulatory violators
- Beneficiary imposition of penalties against regulatory violators.

This section first discusses the availability, under domestic law, to regulatory beneficiaries of procedural and remedial rights with respect to domestic administrative implementation of transnational regulatory norms. Next, it examines domestic implementation and enforcement rights conferred on regulatory beneficiaries by transnational law. Finally, it considers such rights, whether conferred by domestic or transnational law, with respect to transnational regulatory bodies and officials. All of these different types of rights, insofar as they run against domestic or transnational administrators, include rights within the province of global administrative law, but they can also include rights assertable by regulatory beneficiaries directly against regulated actors.

Rights of Regulatory Beneficiaries under Domestic Administrative Law with Respect to Domestic Administrative Implementation of Transnational Public Regulatory Norms

Remedies afforded under general principles of administrative procedure and judicial review

Although there are some differences among jurisdictions, domestic administrative law generally governs implementation and enforcement of transnational regulatory norms on the same basis as that of domestic norms. Indeed, in very many cases it is not possible to distinguish the two, because domestic officials often use authority already conferred under pre-existing domestic statutes to carry out transnational regulatory undertakings, and may not specifically identify the transnational origin of the norm being applied. Only in relatively few cases (generally in the context of new treaty-based undertakings) is new domestic legislation required such that a regulatory norm's transnational origins are clearly identified. In other cases, the influence on domestic administration decisions of transnational regulatory norms and of decisions by global administrative bodies and tribunals tends to be opaque and difficult to trace.[22]

Under general domestic constitutional and administrative law, regulated actors typically enjoy rights of defense at the stage of government enforcement, including rights to a hearing (either before the agency or in a court or tribunal), and judicial review of legality. These rights may, however, not be available in cases where agencies enjoy broad discretion in the award of funds or other advantageous opportunities. Depending on the domestic legal system, regulated actors may also enjoy procedural rights and rights to review at pre-enforcement stages in the administrative decision-making process, such as agency rule-making or the issuance of authoritative interpretations of applicable law. These various domestic law procedural and review rights may generally be invoked by regulated actors contesting domestic enforcement of transnational regulatory law, thereby contributing to the development of global administrative law. One example from Europe is provided by French *Conseil d'Etat* decisions, granting relief to third-country nationals denied visas on the basis of notifications made to the Schengen Information System (SIS).[23] *Kadi*[24] and other cases arising

---

22 See Catherine Redgewell, 'National implementation', in *Oxford Handbook*, op. cit. (influence of transnational tribunals' decisions on domestic decision-making). For the problems that this circumstance creates for reviewing courts attempting to review the delegation of regulatory decision-making powers to transnational bodies, see Richard Stewart, 'The global regulatory challenge to U.S. administrative law', 37 *NYU J.Int'l L. & Pol.* 695 (2005) (hereafter, 'The global regulatory challenge').

23 The June 1999 cases of *Madame Hamssaoui* and *Madame Forabosco* are discussed in M. Benedetti, 'The *Conseil d'Etat* and Schengen', in Cassese et al. (eds), *Global Administrative Law*, op. cit., at 208. The fact that the applicant in one case could not even determine which state had reported her to the SIS led the court to conclude that the decision was insufficiently reasoned, and therefore ought to be annulled. In another case, the court found that German authorities had made a legal error in reporting the applicant to the SIS.

24 *Kadi* v *Council of the European Union and Commission of the European Communities* Case T-315/01 (2005) (Court of First Instance), and Case C-402/05 P (2008) before the European Court of Justice. Other prominent examples relating to the domestic implementation of international sanctions include *Bosphorus Hava Yollari Turzim ve Ticaret AS* v *Minister of Transport, Energy and Communications and Others* 1996 ECR I-3953 ('*Bosphorus*') and *Segi, Araitz Zubimendi Izaga, Aritza*

out of the Security Council 1267 Committee anti-terrorism regulatory regime pose important issues of the extent to which transnational regulatory law can override rights of enforcement defense under domestic law.

Under the traditional model of constitutional and administrative law in the United States and many other jurisdictions, rights to an administrative hearing and judicial review were generally limited to regulated actors whose liberty or property was the target of government enforcement. Such rights were generally not available to regulatory beneficiaries or other indirectly affected persons, including competitors, although specific statutes might provide such rights in defined circumstances. Over the past 40 years, an interest representation model of administrative law has emerged in the United States, Europe, and many developed countries elsewhere through judicial innovations in doctrines of standing, intervention, reviewability of statutory interpretation, and, in some cases, rulings based on constitutional norms or international human rights. As a result of these innovations, the law has extended to regulatory beneficiaries, and other indirectly affected interests, many rights of participation and judicial review formerly restricted to regulated actors. General systems of public access to government information have also been established. Further, reviewing courts have increasingly recognized that regulatory beneficiaries and other indirectly affected persons, as well as the regulated, have the right to require regulatory administrative bodies to provide reasoned justifications for their decisions.[25]

Although there are exceptions, government officials generally have the sole authority (and in many jurisdictions, extremely wide discretion) to decide whether or not to initiate administrative or civil or criminal judicial proceedings for regulatory enforcement. Third parties, including regulatory beneficiaries, generally do not have the right to intervene in such proceedings or obtain judicial review of officials' prosecutive decisions. However, regulatory beneficiaries often have rights of participation and review with respect to administrative decisions upstream of the enforcement stage, including with respect to the interpretation and implementation of regulatory norms and aspects of the arrangements for implementation, including licensing and monitoring, reporting, and other information requirements. Moreover, regulatory beneficiaries often enjoy some rights of participation

Galarraga v *Council of the European Union* 2007 ECR I-01657 ('*Segi*'), both of which are discussed, along with *Kadi* in Erika de Wet, 'Holding international institutions accountable: the complementary role of non-judicial oversight mechanisms and judicial review', 9 *German LJ* 1987 (2008).

25 Richard Stewart, 'The reformation of American administrative law', 88 *Harv. L. Rev.* 1669 (1975).

and judicial review with respect to administrative proceedings to issue or renew or even to revoke the grants of licenses, permits, registrations, etc. to regulated firms. In such proceedings, beneficiaries can advance their views as to the governing regulatory norms as well as the adequacy of administrative arrangements to ensure compliance. Regulatory beneficiaries may enjoy similar rights with respect to the regulatory conditions that administrators are obliged by law to impose on grants to private actors of financial or other assistance. For example, many jurisdictions require administrators, licensees or grantees to prepare environmental impact statements with respect to projects or activities with significant environmental consequences. In some instances such requirements have explicit transnational sources, such as the Convention on Environmental Impact Assessment in a Transboundary Context (Espoo Convention). When these beneficiary rights and remedies are deployed in the context of transnational or global regulation, they represent a significant contribution to the development of GAL.

In form, these rights on the part of regulatory beneficiaries run against government agencies and officials, and the remedy generally available is to nullify unlawful agency action. But their effect is often to regulate private economic actors undertaking or involved in projects or activities undertaken, authorized or funded by governments.

Specific statutory remedies for administrative failure to regulate and enforce

In addition to procedural and review rights applicable to administrative decision-making generally, regulatory beneficiaries may have *private rights of initiation*, in the form of judicially enforceable rights to prod, or require, administrators to implement and enforce regulatory requirements.[26] Such rights are, for example, conferred by 'citizen suit' provisions in US environmental statutes authorizing 'any person' (subject to satisfying constitutional requirements of standing) to bring actions to force administrators to carry out duties imposed by statute, including the initiation of specific regulatory programs or the issuance of implementing regulations in accordance with statutory deadlines.[27] Even in the absence of such provisions, courts may effectively require initiation of regulatory controls under general principles of administrative law and statutory interpretation. A dramatic example is the recent US Supreme Court decision in *Massachusetts* v *EPA*, overturning the EPA' s refusal to initiate regulation of carbon

---

[26] Richard Stewart and Cass Sunstein, 'Public programs and private rights', 95 *Harv. L. Rev.* 1193 (1982).

[27] See, for example, Clean Air Act, section 404.

dioxide emissions from motor vehicles.[28] The Court did so by rejecting the policy reasons given by the agency for not regulating carbon dioxide as inadmissible under the Clean Air Act, and holding that the Act requires such regulation if scientific evidence shows that vehicle emissions endanger public health and welfare. The requirement that agencies give reasons for decisions, including those traditionally regarded as discretionary, has become a potent judicial tool.[29]

A second innovative remedy for regulatory beneficiaries consists of *private enforcement rights* against regulated actors. Such rights are also conferred by citizen suit provisions in US environmental regulatory statutes authorizing 'any person' (again, subject to meeting standing requirements) to bring suit against regulated actors for failure to comply with specific regulatory requirements. Courts may award injunctive relief and impose civil penalties on violators. Successful plaintiffs are entitled to recover attorney fees and litigation costs. It is conceivable that, even in the absence of express statutory authorization, courts might entertain private actions against regulated actors for injunctive relief against regulatory violations.

Private initiation and enforcement rights mobilize private resources and initiative and can remedy gaps and deficiencies in public enforcement. But they are inconsistent with the tradition in many jurisdictions of vesting discretion as to whether or not to initiate enforcement actions in executive or judicial officials, and have potential drawbacks. Private rights of initiation may impair responsible officials' ability to set priorities in deploying limited resources, and override prosecutive decisions to decline enforcement in cases where it would be inequitable or counterproductive. Private enforcement actions also create risks of overbroad enforcement and divergent interpretations of the same regulatory statute by enforcing officials and courts in private actions.

---

[28] 549 U.S. 497 (2007).

[29] Other examples of under-protective regulatory regimes that have been successfully challenged since *Massachusetts* v *EPA*, include *Center for Biological Diversity* v *National Highway Traffic & Safety Administration* 538 F. 3d 1172 (2008) (in which the Ninth Circuit Court of Appeal required the NHTSA to reconsider its fuel efficiency standards for light trucks) and *Natural Resources Defence Council* v *Kempthorne* 506 F Supp 2d 322 (2007) (in which the District Court held that the Fish and Wildlife Services erred by failing to consider the impact of climate change in a biological opinion concluding that water diversion planned for the California Bay Delta would not jeopardize a listed species). These cases, along with *Massachussetts* v *EPA* are discussed in Andrew Long, 'Standing and consensus: globalism in *Massachusetts v EPA*', 23 *J. Envtl L. & Litig.* 73 (2008) and Andrew Long, 'International consensus and US climate change litigation', 33 *Wm & Mary Envtl L. & Pol'y Rev.* 177 (2008).

Civil liability actions against public regulatory agencies or officials for regulatory enforcement failures are another potential remedy for regulatory beneficiaries. Such remedies are generally not available in the US but may be available in other jurisdictions, for example against EU member state authorities pursuant to the *Frankovich* principle.[30]

Liability actions against regulated actors for damages caused by regulatory violations

Statutory actions for damages caused by regulatory violations, brought by government officials or private plaintiffs, can also be regarded as a form of regulatory enforcement because the threat of liability often provides a powerful incentive for compliance by regulated actors. In the US, some federal and state statutes, including antitrust and consumer protection statutes, authorize private rights of action for damages by injured parties, including consumers and competitors. In some cases, for example under the federal securities laws, courts have implied private rights of action for damages in the absence of any statutory provision authorizing them. In addition, regulatory beneficiaries may use violations by regulated firms as a basis for imposing liability and recovering damages under contract or tort law. Class actions provide a vehicle for imposing collective liability in situations involving large numbers of injured consumers or others with individually small losses; here deterrence goals predominate over compensatory ones. These methods for imposing civil liability based on regulatory violations tap the considerable energies and skills of plaintiffs' lawyers (primarily in the US, but now to some extent elsewhere) and consumer organizations, mobilizing significant private resources for implementation enforcement.

Special issues presented by judicial review of domestic administrative decisions involving transnational regulatory norms

As noted above, domestic administrators generally implement and enforce transnational regulatory norms under pre-existing statutory and administrative authorities for implementation and enforcement of domestic regulatory norms. In such a context, reviewing courts generally do not treat cases involving transnational norms differently than those involving purely domestic norms. Decisions are beginning to emerge, however, which focus on the distinction between the two types of situations and the possibility of distinctive treatment by reviewing courts of administrative decisions

---

[30] As enunciated by the European Court of Justice in *Andrea Frankovich* v *Italian Republic*, Joined Cases C-6/90 and C-9/90 [1991] ECRI-5357.

involving transnational regulatory norms, including those adopted by transnational regulatory bodies.

Putting aside important questions of how domestic courts should interpret domestic statutes in cases where transnational norms may apply, and the principles of deference that courts should follow with respect to interpretations of those statutes and norms by domestic agencies and by transnational administrative bodies, domestic courts, as exemplified by US practice, can adopt three basic approaches in reviewing domestic administrative decisions involving transnational regulatory norms. First, courts can review agency decisions applying or refusing to apply transnational norms on the same basis, and apply the same procedural requirements, as in cases involving only domestic law (the 'parity' approach). Alternatively, they can hold administrative decisions involving transnational norms to less demanding procedural requirements and apply a more deferential standard of review in cases, in recognition of the Executive's role in foreign affairs (the 'parity minus' approach). Finally, they can follow a more demanding approach in cases involving transnational norms, because of concerns over the effective delegation of lawmaking power to the external authorities that adopted the norms in question. In the US experience, the courts have generally followed the first approach or the second.[31]

A fourth option, reflected in the decision of the US DC Circuit decision in *NRDC* v *EPA*, is not to recognize transnational regulatory norms at all.[32] The court rejected a challenge by an environmental NGO to a domestic environmental regulation which, they asserted, allowed farmers to use the fungicide methyl bromide, an ozone-depleting chemical, in greater amounts than authorized under a decision by the Conference of the Parties (COP) to the Montreal Protocol, which established quantitative limits on use of the substance in the US. The court held that the COP decision was a political commitment only and not legally enforceable; in making this ruling it invoked concerns about delegation of regulatory authority to global bodies such as the COP. NRDC subsequently attempted to challenge the EPA's decision on a different ground, namely that it was arbitrary and capricious

---

31 See Richard Stewart, 'The global regulatory challenge', op. cit.

32 *NRDC* v *EPA* 464 F.3d 1 (D.C. Cir 2006). The concerns with delegation of regulatory authority to extra-statal bodies reflected in the court's opinion parallels those discussed explicitly in the German Constitutional Court's decision in the Lisbon Treaty Judgment (June 30, 2009) regarding the validity under the German Constitution of powers delegated to the European Union.

in light of US agreements with other nations regarding the use of methyl bromide. This challenge was dismissed on the basis that the matter was *res judicata.*[33]

There are, contrary to *NRDC*, examples outside the US of decisions rejecting legal challenges to direct domestic enforcement of transnational regulatory norms. For instance, the Dutch Crown, on the advice of the Council of State, upheld a decision by the Governor-General of the Netherlands-Antilles to nullify the issue of a lease and building permit to construct a resort immediately adjacent to a Ramsar territory, based on decisions of the COP to the Ramsar Convention that an environmental impact assessment was required in such circumstances.[34]

Holding domestic administrations to international human rights standards
Regulatory beneficiaries have recently had some success in challenging domestic administrative decisions on the basis of non-compliance with international human rights norms – another GAL development. In *Mazibuko* v *City of Johannesburg*, the Constitutional Court of South Africa found that a decision by the City to limit the free supply of water to residents to 25 liters per person per day (or 6 kl per household per month) breached the constitutional right to access to adequate water. In determining what would constitute 'sufficient water' for the purpose of the Constitution, the Court considered the right to a standard of living adequate for health and well-being under the Universal Declaration of Human Rights and various UN resolutions, the International Covenant on Economic, Social and Cultural Rights, and guidelines of the World Health Organization.[35] In *Gbemre* v *Shell Petroleum Development Company of*

---

[33] 513 F 3d 257 (2008).

[34] The Governor-General of Netherlands-Antilles annulled the lease and permit on the basis that they were contrary to the Ramsar Convention, primarily due to the lack of an environmental impact assessment (EIA) in accordance with Ramsar guidelines. Notably, the Convention does not explicitly require EIAs, but resolutions and recommendations of the COP include such an obligation. The Crown rejected an appeal by the local authorities, accepting advice from the Council of State that resolutions, decisions and guidelines accepted unanimously by the COP should be considered part of the Netherlands' obligation under the Convention: E.C. Newton, 'Annulment of decisions for building near Ramsar site on Bonaire was justified' 12 November 2007, available at: http://www.ramsar.org/cda/en/ramsar-news-archives-2009-a-ramsar-site-wins-its/main/ramsar/1-26-45-84%5E18583_4000_0__ (news archives on the official website of the Ramsar Convention on Wetlands).

[35] *Mazibuko* v *City of Johannesburg* [2009] ZACC 28. The Court set aside the City's decision, made declarations as to what would constitute sufficient water for the terms of s. 27(1) of the Constitution, and ordered the City to reconsider and reformulate its free water policy in light of these declarations.

Nigeria,[36] the Nigerian Federal High Court found that the gas-flaring activities of Shell violated the rights to life and dignity guaranteed by the Nigerian Constitution and reinforced by the African Charter on Human and Peoples' Rights, that the failure of Shell to carry out an environmental impact assessment contributed to this violation, and that domestic legislation allowing gas-flaring in Nigeria was invalid.[37]

Rights Conferred by Transnational Public Regulatory Regimes on Regulatory Beneficiaries with Respect to Domestic Administration

Transnational public regulatory regimes are also beginning to generate global administrative law requirements and norms that regulatory beneficiaries can invoke in domestic proceedings against government officials to promote or secure implementation and enforcement against regulated actors of substantive transnational regulatory norms. A dramatic example is the TRIPS Agreement, which is a global regulatory regime for the protection of holders of intellectual property rights. TRIPS requires WTO member states to provide intellectual property rights (IPR) holders with a detailed set of informational, procedural and review rights to prevent and redress violations of their rights. WTO member states can invoke the powerful WTO dispute settlement procedures and remedies to promote

---

[36] *Gbemre* v *Shell Petroleum Development Company of Nigeria* B/CS/53/05, Federal High Court, Benin Judicial Divison, 14 November 2005, reported in *Oxford Reports on International Law, International Law in Domestic Courts*. See also discussion in Olufemi O. Amao, 'Corporate social responsibility, multinational corporations and the law in Nigeria: Controlling multinationals in host states', 52 *Journal of African Law* 89 (2008), at 102; and Amy Sinden, 'The emerging human right to security from climate change: the case against gas flaring in Nigeria', in William C.G. Burns and Hari M. Osofsky (eds), *Adjudicating Climate Change* (CUP, 2009), at 173.

[37] The applicant acted both for himself and as a representative of the Iwherekan Community in Delta State, to seek orders enforcing the fundamental rights to life and dignity as provided by sections 33 and 34 of the Constitution of the Federal Republic of Nigeria, and articles 4, 16 and 24 of the African Charter on Human and Peoples' Rights. The Court found that Shell's gas flaring actions constituted a gross violation of these rights. It also found that Shell's failure to carry out an environmental impact assessment was in clear violation of domestic legislation, and, furthermore, contributed to a further violation of the fundamental rights in question. While no specific government decision was challenged, the Court found that relevant provisions of domestic legislation permitting gas flaring were inconsistent with the rights to life and dignity, and were thus unconstitutional, null and void. On the basis of these findings, the Court made orders restraining Shell from further flaring of gas in the applicant's community.

compliance with these requirements for the benefit of their IPR holders. These and similar, if less far reaching, global administrative law requirements in other WTO agreements, such as the Agreements on Sanitary and Phytosanitary Measures and on Technical Barriers to Trade, have had broad impacts on domestic regulatory administration in China and other countries, furthering the protection, not only of IPR holders, but foreign economic actors more generally.[38]

Another prominent example is the Aarhus Convention, which requires state parties to guarantee environmental groups and individuals access to government environmental information, participation in environmentally-related government administrative proceedings, and rights to review. Rights to information and participation in environmental impact assessment such as those conferred by the Espoo Convention, are another example of global administrative law in the environmental context. While such rights can generally be asserted only against government authorities, they can be used to help block or secure modifications in private projects licensed or funded by domestic agencies, including by giving NGOs procedure-based bargaining chips. Further, the Aarhus Compliance Committee has ruled that Aarhus procedural norms apply to a private firm carrying out public functions.[39]

The North American Agreement on Environmental Cooperation (NAAEC) establishes an innovative process under which NGOs in any of the three states party to the North American Free Trade Agreement (NAFTA) may file Citizen Submissions on Enforcement Matters with the Secretariat, asserting that a party is failing to effectively enforce its environmental law. This process can produce an independent review by a NAFTA body of enforcement by the administrative authorities in an NGO's own state or in another NAFTA jurisdiction, which can in turn create publicity and other pressures for correction.[40] A similar mechanism to promote

---

[38] Richard Stewart and Michelle Ratton-Sanchez, 'The World Trade Organization and global administrative law', in Christian Joerges and E-U. Petersmann (eds), *Constitutionalism, Multilevel Trade Governance and International Economic Law* (Hart Publishing, 2011).

[39] Marco Macchia, 'Legality: The Aarhus Convention and the Compliance Committee', in Cassese et al. (eds), *Global Administrative Law*, op. cit., at 71.

[40] A similar framework has also been established by the Canada–Chile Agreement on Environmental Cooperation. For discussion of the NAFTA citizen submission process see Kal Raustiala, 'International "enforcement of enforcement" under the North American Agreement on Environmental Cooperation', 36 *Va. J. Int'l L.* 721, 723 (1996); Marirose J. Pratt, 'The citizen submission process of the NAAEC: filling the gap in judicial review of federal agency failures to enforce environmental laws', 20 *Emory Int'l L. Rev.* 741 (2008); and for evaluation of the

compliance with labor laws by the NAFTA states is established under the Northern American Agreement on Labor Cooperation (NAALC). A still different mechanism is illustrated by the intervention, prompted by NGO lobbying, of the World Heritage Organization into a domestic US controversy over licensing a private gold mining project near Yellowstone National Park, by designating the Park as a World Heritage site, which ultimately led the project sponsor to abandon it.[41]

Further examples are provided by the following. The International Centre for Settlement of Investment Disputes (ICSID) regime provides remedies for foreign investors against domestic governments asserting expropriation of their investments in violation of bilateral investment treaty provisions; claims of expropriation may include challenges to domestic administrative procedures as well as substantive decisions. In a quite different field, athletes subject to disciplinary sanctions may invoke hearing rights against domestic authorities pursuant to the World Anti-Doping Code adopted by the World Anti-Doping Agency and referenced by the UNESCO International Convention against Doping in Sport. Disciplinary decisions by domestic sports authorities are subject to review by the global Court of Arbitration for Sport.[42] The International Labor Organization (ILO) provides several review mechanisms under which ILO bodies hear complaints filed by trade unions or employer associations that member governments have failed to comply with ILO Conventions.

Another potential avenue for transnational review of domestic regulatory action is through the admission of *amici curiae* briefs in WTO dispute settlement proceedings, although this possibility is yet to produce any significant outcomes. The Appellate Body confirmed in *United States – Import Prohibition of Certain Shrimp and Shrimp Products (US Shrimp)* (1998) that panels are entitled to accept *amicus* briefs as part of their general right to seek information, and adopted a procedure for seeking leave to file such briefs in *European Communities – Measures Affecting Asbestos and Asbestos-Containing Products (EC–Asbestos)* (2000). However, the ability of panels to admit unsolicited submissions from third

effectiveness of the process under the NAAEC since its inception see David L. Markell, 'The role of spotlighting procedures in promoting citizen participation, transparency and accountability', 45 *Wake Forest L. Rev.* 425 (2010).

41 Benedetto Cimini, 'Global bodies reviewing national decisions: the *Yellowstone* case', in Cassese et al. (eds), *Global Administrative Law*, op. cit., at 192.

42 See Lorenzo Casini, *Il Diritto Globale dello Sport* (Giuffrè Editore, 2010).

parties remains contentious among developing country WTO members,[43] and while panels continue to accept *amicus* briefs (and emphasize their right to do so), they usually refuse to consider them substantively.[44]

The proliferation of transnational regulatory mechanisms for review of domestic decisions has created situations where more than one mechanism is applicable to a given case. An example is the Vlora Thermal Power Plant in Albania, where regulatory beneficiaries succeeded in mobilizing both the World Bank Inspection Panel[45] and the Aarhus Compliance Mechanism,[46] creating a need for the two institutions to coordinate and sequence their reviews.

---

[43] See General Council, Minutes of the Meeting of 22 November 2000, WT/GC/M/60; and WTO, 'Participation in dispute settlement proceedings' in *Dispute Settlement System Training Module,* at 9.3.

[44] See, for example, *US – Imposition of Countervailing Duties on Certain Hot-Rolled Lead and Bismuth Carbon Steel* (May 2000), at paras 39–42 and *US – Final Countervailing Duty Determination with Respect to Certain Softwood Lumber from Canada* (January 2004) AB-2003–6, at para. 9; discussion in Peter Van den Bossche, 'NGO involvement in the WTO: a comparative perspective', 11 *J. Intl Econ. L.* 717 (2008), at 738–741; and Yves Bonzon, 'Institutionalizing public participation in WTO decision making: some conceptual hurdles and avenues', 11 *J. Intl Econ. L.* 751 (2008), at 758.

[45] The applicant in both the Inspection Panel and Aarhus processes was a local NGO, representing residents of Vlora affected by the project. The request for investigation made to the Inspection Panel argued that the project was based on a material misrepresentation of the site, that the environmental impact assessment upon which the Bank's loan was based was misleading and wrong, and that the Bank's procedures were in violation of Albanian and EU laws relating to the environment, public participation, cultural heritage and EIAs. The Panel ultimately recommended an investigation of several of the matters raised: see World Bank Inspection Panel, 'Report and recommendations, Albania: power sector generation and restructuring project (IDA Credit No. 3872-ALB)', July 2, 2007, Report 40213-AL.

[46] The Aarhus Compliance Committee found that Albania contravened the Convention by failing to provide adequate opportunities for public participation in decision-making relating to the project, and in its failure to establish a clear, transparent and consistent framework implementing the provisions of the Convention in Albanian legislation: see 'Meeting of the parties to the convention on access to information, public participation in decision-making and access to justice in environmental matters', Report by the Compliance Committee, 'Compliance by Albania with its obligations under the Convention', ECE/MP.pp/2008/5/Add 1, 2 April 2008.

Rights of Regulatory Beneficiaries Regarding Decisions of Transnational Regulatory Administrative Bodies

The rapid growth of transnational regulatory administrative bodies has begun to trigger recognition of the need for GAL mechanisms to secure their accountability and responsiveness to affected private actors and interests, including regulated actors and regulatory beneficiaries. Such mechanisms are indeed beginning to emerge. They can provide regulatory beneficiary NGOs with tools to stimulate enforcement by transnational administrative bodies directly against private regulated actors, and to mobilize these bodies to promote implementation and enforcement by domestic authorities.

One type of mechanism is provided by the arrangements adopted by the World Bank, IFC and other multilateral development institutions to ensure compliance by projects receiving financial assistance with the donor institutions' environmental and social guidelines. These requirements include both procedural requirements, for example to conduct social and environmental impact assessments,[47] and substantive norms requiring avoidance or mitigation of adverse environmental and social impacts. The World Bank's Inspection Panel, for example, has evolved into a mechanism by which affected residents and environmental and social NGOs in developing countries hosting such projects can promote compliance by participating in the Panel's assessment and review procedures, raising claims of non-compliance, and sometimes by participating in the process of revising projects to promote compliance. Regulatory beneficiaries have procedural rights to participate in the Panel's assessment of compliance, which they can use to create pressures and publicity to obtain modifications of projects or even termination of funding.[48] The Panel's reports are formally directed at the conduct of the Bank management, and affect funding to developing

[47] See David Collins, 'Environmental impact statements and public participation in international investment law', 7 *Manchester J. Int'l Econ. L.* 4 (2010) for an overview of World Bank and regional development bank policies that, in particular, impose requirements on private firms to assess the environmental impacts of projects and facilitate public participation and stakeholder consultation.

[48] For further discussion of the Inspection Panel, see Daniel D. Bradlow and David B. Hunter (eds), *International Financial Institutions and International Law* (Kluwer, 2010), especially Bradlow 'International law and the operations of the international financial institutions', Ch. 1 at 27–28, and Chimni, 'International financial institutions and international law: a third world perspective', Ch. 2 at 48–52; also Dana Clark, Jonathan Fox and Kay Treakle (eds), *Demanding Accountability: Civil Society Claims and the World Bank Inspection Panel* (Rowman & Littlefield, 2003).

country governments, but the effect is to secure regulatory compliance by projects which are undertaken or financed in substantial part by private economic actors. The IFC, which provides financial assistance directly to private firms, provides regulatory beneficiaries with similar rights, which they have successfully exercised, for example in the case of a Guatemalan gold mining venture financed by the IFC.[49] Here the connection to private economic actors is more direct.

The Aarhus regime has a non-compliance system that authorizes environmental NGOs to raise claims of non-compliance by state parties with Convention obligations with the Compliance Committee. NGOs also have a right to representation on the committee itself. Thus, the Aarhus regime represents a striking application of GAL mechanisms in favor of regulatory beneficiaries at two levels, domestic administration and transnational administration.

A number of transnational regulatory regimes, such as the Codex Alimentarius, provide significant opportunities for participation by NGOs representing beneficiary interests in the adoption of transnational regulatory norms, including, in some cases, secondary norms relating to implementation and other steps by participating states or agencies to secure compliance by regulated actors. While these decisions are upstream of enforcement actions by domestic authorities, they have the potential to significantly promote regulatory beneficiary protection.

The Executive Board of the CDM is an example of a global administrative body that exercises direct enforcement authority against private actors, but has no established GAL procedures or judicial review mechanisms to protect the interests of either regulated actors (here, project developers and investors) or regulatory beneficiaries. Two types of proposals have been advanced for review of Executive Board decisions, the first for review by domestic courts, and the second for review by a transnational review body

---

49 In June 2004, the IFC granted $45 million in financing to Glamis Ltd in connection with large-scale excavation activities in Guatemala. In January 2005, Colectivo ecologista Madreselva, an NGO representing the interests of the local indigenous peoples, lodged a complaint with the Compliance Advisor Ombudsman (CAO) (the independent recourse mechanism for the private sector arm of the World Bank) regarding negative impacts of the project on the environment and inadequate procedures for consultation with indigenous people. The CAO upheld the latter claim, finding the consultation proceedings were inadequate. In subsequent public consultation with the Sikapapa population, organized by the Guatemalan government, 11 out of the 13 voting districts voted against the continuation of mining activities, a result that was subsequently confirmed by the Constitutional Court: Gianluca Sgueo, 'Participation of indigenous people: the Guatemala Marlin Gold Mine', in Cassese et al. (eds), *Global Administrative Law*, op. cit., at 133.

established within the Kyoto/CDM regime.[50] It seems unlikely that this lacuna will persist: the CDM Subsidiary Body for Implementation (SBI) has recently been tasked with developing recommendations for appeal procedures, with a view to the CMP adopting a decision on this issue at its seventh session in 2011.[51]

VI. CONCLUDING OBSERVATIONS

This chapter has sought to provide a taxonomy of the various types of procedures and remedies available to regulatory beneficiaries under transnational public regulatory regimes. Although it has found substantial adoption of GAL procedures and remedies in a variety of institutional settings, the chapter has not sought to identify or account for any functional or other pattern in the availability of different remedies under different regimes, nor has it sought to develop a systemic analysis of the relative advantages and disadvantages of the different procedures and remedies, their interrelations, and their ultimate contributions to regulatory performance or legitimacy. Nor has any sustained analysis of these questions been found elsewhere in the literature. In these respects, the field of transnational public regulation is far behind that of transnational private regulation, in which much progress has been made, thanks to the work of Professor Cafaggi and his colleagues. The deficit on the public regulatory side may, to some extent, be accounted for by the greater range and diversity of public regulation, and the fact that the public authorities that constitute it are also quite diverse. Moreover, the private actors that play such an important role in the constitution and operation of transnational private regulation enjoy, by virtue of private contract and the freedom to create and link various special-purpose private regulatory organizations, much greater institutional flexibility than comparable public actors. This

---

50 Ernestine Meijer, 'The international institutions of the clean development mechanism brought before national courts: limiting jurisdictional immunity to achieve access to justice', 39 *NYU J. Int'l L. & Pol.* 877 (2007).

51 Decision -/CMP.6 'Further guidance relating to the clean development mechanism', para. 18. The SBI has been directed to take into account the EB's 2010 Annual Report which sets out detailed recommendations for procedures to appeal EB rulings to an 'appellate body': see 'Annual report of the Executive Board of the clean development mechanism to the Conference of the Parties serving as the meeting of the Parties to the Kyoto Protocol', FCCC/KP/CMP/2010/10, Annex II 'Recommendations on the procedure for appeals against rulings by the Executive Board of the clean development mechanism regarding requests for registration or issuance'.

transactional and organizational flexibility may make it easier to develop greater consistency, coherence, and functionality with respect to private regulatory remedies than is possible in the case of public regulation. Courts play an important role in both regimes, but the roles that they play vis-à-vis the private actors and the public authorities that constitute the respective regulatory regimes are very different.

A further matter for future research is the role played by regulatory beneficiary NGOs. The political economy of NGOs is such that they play a far more active role in some areas of regulation, including environmental, labor, and certain types of consumer regulation, than in others. Even in consumer regulation, there is far more NGO interest and activity in, for example, GMO regulation than, for example, the entire fields of financial regulation or competition policy, although the latter has huge consequences for the welfare of consumers. The drivers of these differences in NGO focus, and their implications for the development of private and of public regulation in different fields of regulation, invite examination in order to develop a more complete and systemic account of transnational public regulation and the role of law in its governance.

2. Enforcing transnational private regulation: models and patterns

Fabrizio Cafaggi[1]

1. INTRODUCTION

In this chapter, the analysis focuses on transnational private regulation's (TPR) enforcement and its influence on governance choices by private regulators. Enforcement of transnational regimes can refer to transnational and, to a limited extent, even to domestic litigation, where two or more disputants belong to the same jurisdiction.[2]

Transnational enforcement is related to three different classes of conflicts: (1) within the regulatory body; (2) among organizations performing regulatory functions in the same field; and (3) among regulators across fields.[3] The focus of this book is on conflicts 'within' rather than 'among' organizations, but references to regimes' conflicts are occasionally made.

In this chapter, a relative broad functional definition of enforcement is assumed, due to its manifold functions. Enforcement of TPR contributes: (1) to designing the boundaries between different transnational regulatory regimes and their rule-making power; (2) to defining the domain and the

[1] An earlier version of this chapter was originally circulated as a framing paper for the conference held at EUI in May 2010 within the HiiL project on transnational private regulation. The structure still preserves the character of issues mapping. I thank Eyal Benvenisti, Kevin Davis, Cindy Estlund and Dick Stewart for useful discussions at NYU when I visited the law school in 2009. Research and editorial assistance by Federica Casarosa and Rebecca Schmidt is gratefully acknowledged. Responsibility for the text is mine.

[2] There is a growing debate on transnational litigation and how it differs from national litigation. For the purpose of this chapter, a broad notion of enforcement is adopted, encompassing both transnational and domestic litigation; thereby, hypothetically, where a transnational regime is litigated between two disputants belonging to the same jurisdiction.

[3] See on these three levels F. Cafaggi, 'The Architecture of Transnational Private Regulation', EUI W.P. 2011/12.

scope of each regime; (3) to allocating rights and responsibilities, within and across regimes, among different stakeholders; and (4) to filling gaps by completing *ex post* the constitutive regulatory contracts when, as it is often the case, they are *ex ante* incomplete.

The chapter builds on the premise that enforcement can be analyzed across sectors, despite the specificity of regulatory strategies; for example, whether command and control or responsive regulation is used in one regime. Clearly enforcement mechanisms vary across fields and depend on the regulatory strategy. A command and control enforcement strategy will, or at least should, strongly differ from those deployed in a market-based or responsive regime. A market-based regulatory scheme in environmental regulation may differ from one in food safety and lead to different enforcement choices. That said it is important to identify the macro-variables that should be deployed to define enforcement in transnational private regulation. At a deeper level the specificity of the regulatory strategy should be taken into account.

To pursue this objective I build on the notion of regulatory relationship, which encompasses regulators, regulatees and beneficiaries to distinguish among classes of disputes and the choice of enforcers. Regulators are private entities in terms of legal forms and the nature of regulatory instruments; regulatees are generally firms. Beneficiaries of the regulatory process are those who would benefit from compliance and be harmed by infringements. In the field of food safety, beneficiaries are, for example, consumers whose safety increases if standards are complied with or decreases if violations occur. In the field of financial regulation, regulatees are banks and financial institutions; beneficiaries can be firms (listed firms) or investors. In the field of corporate social responsibility (CSR), different classes of beneficiaries are involved in relation to compliance with codes of conduct ranging from employees to consumers, and from environmental to human rights organizations. Beneficiaries may or may not have direct legal protection via enforcement. Even if they do not have direct access to justice, effective enforcement of private rules does affect their positions in the regulatory process, increasing or decreasing their voice and exit opportunities.

TPR is often deemed to be ineffective, due to the low enforcement rate, frequently associated with lack of enforcers' independence compared to the rule-makers.[4] Rather than regulatory gaps or fallacies in the rule-making

---

[4] See K. Abbot & D. Snidal, 'The Governance Triangle', in: W. Mattli & N. Woods, *The Politics of Global Regulation*, Princeton University Press, 2009, p. 46. For a more detailed analysis across sectors see D. Vogel, 'The Private Regulation of

process, enforcement by private bodies has thence become the key factor in measuring the effectiveness and legitimacy of TPR.[5]

The links between effectiveness and legitimacy are complex and, at a preliminary stage, the obvious can be stated: more effective enforcement provides greater legitimacy. However, as will be shown, legitimacy and effectiveness may also conflict and trade-offs exist.[6] There are instances where enhancing legitimacy by, for example, widening participation may decrease effectiveness, and vice versa. The distinction, however, is often within legitimacy and lies in the relationship between procedural and substantive legitimacy.[7]

The chapter proceeds as follows. After briefly addressing the framework within which multiple enforcement mechanisms can co-exist, identifying the potential conflicts between them and how they can be solved, the chapter proceeds to a separate examination of each mechanism, both judicial and private non-judicial enforcement. The nature of this relationship is addressed, asking whether the two types of enforcement (judicial and non-judicial) should be considered alternative or complementary. As a practical matter, complementarity occurs more frequently than alternativity, pursued by means of mandatory arbitration or compulsory mediation, either contractually agreed or imposed by legislation. After separately examining each regime and sub-regime, the relationship is addressed in order to identify differences and similarities between them. Concluding remarks highlight the main features of complementarity and the changes necessary to improve institutional design in order to increase the effectiveness of private regulation.

Global Corporate Conduct', in: W. Mattli & N. Woods, *The Politics of Global Regulation*, Princeton University Press, 2009, pp. 151ff.

5 The link is well illustrated in the recent Guidelines drafted by UN Representative J. Ruggie and approved by the UN in June 2011. According to point 30, '[i]ndustry, multistakeholder and other collaborative initiatives that are based on respect for human rights related standards should ensure that effective grievance mechanisms are available'. See J. Ruggie, 'Guiding Principles on Business and Human Rights: Implementing the United Nations "Protect, Respect and Remedy" Framework', March 2011, available at: http://www.business-humanrights.org/media/documents/ruggie/ruggie-guiding-principles-21-mar-2011.pdf (hereinafter: Ruggie, 'Guiding Principles').

6 See below text and notes at p. 93.

7 See F. Cafaggi, 'Rethinking Effectiveness of Private Regulation and its Links with Legitimacy', on file with the author.

2. ON THE RELATIONSHIPS BETWEEN ENFORCEMENT MECHANISMS IN TPR: TRANSCENDING THE PRIVATIZATION OF JUSTICE DEBATE

In order to provide a general framework for the scope of enforcement in TPR, it is useful to distinguish between families of enforcement mechanisms and the nature of disputes.

Three main mechanisms have developed in relation to TPR:

1. judicial, mainly at the national level, through domestic courts;
2. administrative, primarily through independent domestic and international public regulatory bodies, including international organizations, performing quasi-adjudicatory functions;[8] and
3. private non-judicial, primarily at transnational level based on a combination of governance devices and dispute settlement bodies.[9]

The focus in this chapter is on the relationship between judicial and private non-judicial enforcement, leaving aside administrative enforcement of private regulation.[10] Within the two mechanisms, four main classes of disputes will be considered:

(a) disputes between the regulator and the regulated;
(b) disputes among the regulatees;

[8] Examples of administrative enforcement of private regulation can be found in those instances where the regulatory agency enforces codes of conducts or other forms of private regulation to which firms have committed.

[9] A general definition of non-private non-judicial mechanisms is now provided by the 'Guiding Principles'. According to the Commentary of Principle 28 Non-State-Based Grievance Mechanisms, '[o]ne category of non-State-based grievance mechanisms encompasses those administered by a business enterprise alone or with stakeholders, by an industry association or a multi-stakeholder group. They are non-judicial, but may use adjudicative, dialogue-based or other culturally appropriate and rights compatible processes. These mechanisms may offer particular benefits such as speed of access and remediation, reduced costs and/or transnational reach ...'.

[10] It should be pointed out that the focus is on the narrow question of complementarity of enforcement mechanisms concerning a single private regulatory regime. In many of the cases examined below, complementarity exists also between public and private regulations. The public–private complementarity poses wider problems, including enforcement questions by public international and domestic actors going beyond the scope of this chapter.

(c) disputes between the regulator and third parties; and
(d) disputes between regulatees and third parties.

In comparing judicial and non-judicial enforcement mechanisms we shall analyze which class of disputes concern which enforcement mechanisms and why.

A second preliminary clarification concerns the difference between this question and the more conventional comparative institutional analysis of different enforcement mechanisms, in particular between judicial and alternative dispute resolution systems. Many of the factors that have promoted the growth of such systems and private justice at the domestic level do not apply to TPR, where enforcement is often part of the regulatory regime itself, rather than a response to the shortcomings of international and domestic 'public' justice.

What is the relationship between judicial and private non-judicial enforcement of TPR?

From a normative perspective, they stem from different sources and different principles are applied. Judicial enforcement is regulated by law; private non-judicial enforcement is primarily based on private autonomy and freedom of association. The balance between public and private interests, including community interest, is different. However, some common principles are emerging due to the innovative approach of some international and domestic courts. Accordingly, constitutional principles do constrain private enforcers and force them to comply with due process, thereby contributing to a common legal framework which should be further developed. The contribution of the European Court of Human Rights in relation to the right of fair trial (Article 6 and Article 13) represents a path for potential development. Article 47 of the European Charter also defines common principles that could contribute to the endeavor. The Strasbourg Court has recognized the applicability of Article 6 to professional bodies and has subsequently allowed different applications to the judicial and the non-judicial systems to further efficiency and flexibility.[11] To date review mechanisms of private enforcement complying

---

[11] The ECtHR regards as falling within the scope of Article 6 § 1 proceedings which, in domestic law, come under 'public law' and whose result is decisive for private rights and obligations. In other words the notion of 'tribunal' according to the case law of the court includes also the professional organizations adjudicating on disciplinary offences, if they satisfy at least one of the following requirements: either the jurisdictional organs themselves comply with the requirements of Article 6 § 1, or they do not so comply but are subject to subsequent control by a judicial body that has full jurisdiction and does provide the guarantees of Article 6 § 1 (see

to a large extent with the fair trial prerequisites as set out in human rights treaties and constitutional provisions are becoming more and more common.[12]

Three potential functional relationships between judicial and private non-judicial enforcement can be identified:

(a) enforcement systems are mutually reinforcing;
(b) systems are neutral, that is, they do not influence each other; and
(c) the existence of one system undermines the 'credibility' of the other,

---

Albert and le Compte v *Belgium*, judgment of 10 February 1983, Application no. 7299/75; 7496/76, para. 29). The court has also recognized *Le Compte in Van Leuven and De Meyere* v *Belgium*, judgment of 23 June 1981, Series A No. 43, p. 20.

[12] The quotation for ICANN bylaws includes the following text:

'Section 3:
Independent Review of Board Actions
1. In addition to the reconsideration process described in Section 2 of this Article, ICANN shall have in place a separate process for independent third-party review of Board actions alleged by an affected party to be inconsistent with the Articles of Incorporation or Bylaws.
2. Any person materially affected by a decision or action by the Board that he or she asserts is inconsistent with the Articles of Incorporation or Bylaws may submit a request for independent review of that decision or action'.

Whereas the quotation from the Forest Stewardship Council's (FSC) Dispute Resolution System includes the following text:

'The FSC Dispute Resolution System provides a framework by which FSC members, certification bodies and stakeholders may resolve disputes that they may have with the FSC Board of Directors, the FSC and/or its affiliates or with FSC accredited certification bodies or their FSC certificate holders. The framework consists of procedures which detail the process according to the nature of the dispute and the respective roles of the different parties involved in the process. Any dispute related to the FSC Certification Scheme, including the FSC Accreditation Program, shall be treated with procedural fairness and incorporate the following guidelines:
- A person or organisation, who is the subject of a complaint or a appeal, should be given adequate notice about the proceedings.
- A person making a decision should declare any personal interest they may have in the proceedings.
- A person who makes a decision should be unbiased and act in good faith. He/she therefore can not be one of the parties in the case, or have an interest in the outcome.
- Proceedings should be conducted so they are fair to all the parties.
- Each party to a proceeding is entitled to ask questions and contradict the evidence of the opposing party.
- A decision-maker should take into account relevant considerations and mitigating circumstances, and ignore irrelevant considerations'.

showing some degree of disruptive competition and decreasing the overall legitimacy of TPR.

This chapter makes two general claims, both related to the features of complementarity between enforcement mechanisms.

Firstly, in general, judicial and private enforcement are functionally mutually reinforcing; when they operate effectively, they increase the overall legitimacy of the transnational private regime. According to the current regimes, private non-judicial enforcement (arbitration, dispute settlement mechanisms, etc.) still primarily affects internal legitimacy, whereas judicial enforcement mainly concerns external legitimacy, incorporating only some aspects of internal legitimacy.[13]

The second claim concerns the content of complementarity in relation to remedies and procedural matters. The adoption of this perspective requires a change of approach; currently, these enforcement mechanisms are described as alternative dispute resolutions (ADR), and have characterized the scholarly and policy-making debate at the domestic level. Private dispute resolution mechanisms are generally not alternative but primarily complementary to adjudication by domestic courts. They become alternative when the law gives private enforcement priority, constraining the scope of subsequent judicial review, as the example of commercial arbitration illustrates.

3. JUDICIAL ENFORCEMENT OF TPR

Four questions are addressed in relation to judicial enforcement of TPR:

1. What are the functions of TPR judicial enforcement?
2. Who are the judicial enforcers?
3. Where does judicial enforcement take place?
4. What are the effects of judicial enforcement on global regulatory regimes?

3.1 What are the Functions of TPR Judicial Enforcement?

Judicial enforcement can perform various functions:

(a) securing/inducing regulatory compliance;

[13] On the distinction between internal and external legitimacy, see below.

(b) allocating regulatory power within and among constituencies and in particular, between regulatees and beneficiaries;
(c) empowering stakeholders: sometimes at the expense of one class of regulated entities, sometimes at the expense of third parties;
(d) (re)distributing institutional and financial resources between the public and the private sphere and, within the latter, among different actors.

Before engaging in a more detailed description of the four functions, it is important to highlight that courts have increasingly contributed to defining the boundaries among global private regulatory regimes when conflicts have arisen, and have used procedural devices to ensure protection of collective interests. In the absence of a common system of rules to define conflicts regulation among TPRs, domestic courts have often faced litigants' requests to solve disputes concerning overlapping transnational regimes with conflicting goals. The function of enforcement here is predominantly regulatory. Judicial doctrines concerning comity, counterlimits, margins of appreciation, conforming interpretations, and loyal cooperation, have contributed to define a body of rules similar to that played by sources of law in domestic state-centric regimes.[14] Enforcement of TPR is therefore related to drawing regulatory boundaries, defining the scope of overlapping regimes and solving conflicts of interests among different participants to the same regulatory process.

In these conflicts, the collective interest of the regulator is combined with the disputants' individual interests. Interestingly, even when the disputes arise among regulated entities, the private regulator intervenes in the proceedings because often the outcome of the single dispute can affect the entire regulatory regime.[15] The standard setter's intervention contributes to defining both the dispute's scope and outcome. This further illustrates the regulatory nature of these disputes, unlike the more traditional commercial

[14] See. S. Cassese, *I tribunali di Babele, I guidici alla ricerca di un nuovo ordine globale*, Donzelli, Roma, 2009, pp. 1–105; and S. Cassese, E. D'Alterio and M. De Bellis, in this volume, Chapter 12.

[15] For example in the field of financial contracts, particularly derivatives, the International Swaps and Derivatives Association (ISDA) intervenes in the proceedings with the aim of explaining and interpreting the Master Agreement that is incorporated in the specific swap transactions which are litigated. The objective is to ensure that the regulatory function and its correlated objectives are preserved in the litigation that includes the Master Agreement incorporated by reference. See *Lomas et al.* v *JFB et al.* 2010 [EWHC] 3372 (CH).

disputes, where, for example, the supplier of standard contract forms rarely intervenes in litigation concerning the terms he supplies.[16]

The most obvious function of enforcement is securing compliance with the rules by solving individual disputes concerning infringements.

Secondly and, perhaps more importantly, judicial enforcement of TPR defines and allocates the regulatory power between and within the regime, among the different actors (i.e. different market players) and its effects on third parties (i.e. consumers). This occurs not only in conflicts among regulated firms along the supply chain, but also when disputes between regulatees and NGOs arise.

Thirdly: the empowerment's function. Disputes at the transnational level may be 'strategic'; they emerge to empower some constituencies at the expense of others. They are often deployed by NGOs to facilitate negotiations with the industry, directly influencing private rule-making. Litigants, particularly NGOs, try gaining voice *ex post*, via judicial enforcement. Sometimes, the remedy sought may provide NGOs with a voice in the regulatory process; this occurs when litigation concerns not only substantive matters but also procedural requirements like transparency, participation or review.[17] Through litigation, stakeholders gain negotiating power with the organization and can influence rule-making more effectively. Bargaining between beneficiaries and regulators can occur either under the threat of litigation or after litigation has begun, at the settlement stage. Judicial enforcement may thence constitute a form of stakeholders' empowerment for those not selected at the initial rule-making stage to participate in standard setting.[18]

---

[16] See for example the role of ICC when Incoterms are litigated by parties.

[17] See in the ICANN regime the many critiques to the Uniform Dispute Resolution Policy (UDRP) focused on the low level of fairness of the proceeding: L.A. Walker, 'ICANN's Uniform Domain Name Dispute Resolution Policy', 15 *Berk. Tech. L. J.* 289 (2000); M. Froomkin, 'ICANN's "Uniform Dispute Resolution Policy" – Causes and (Partial) Cures', 67 *Brook L. Rev.* 605 (2002); N. Chatterjee, 'Arbitration Proceedings Under ICANN's Uniform Domain Name Dispute Resolution Policy – a Myth of Reality', *Int'l Bus. L.J.*, 728 (2006); J. Hörnle, *Cross-Border Internet Dispute Resolution*, Cambridge University Press, 2009. The major flaw of the system depends on the lack of specific remedies for a breach of such rules, albeit the inclusion of several clauses to provide procedural protection. The same is true for appeals based on substantive matters, as there is no procedure to review the decision on the factual findings, and no appeal on points of law. E.G. Thornburg, 'Fast, Cheap, and Out of Control: Lessons from the ICANN Dispute Resolution Process', 6 *J. Small & Emerging Bus. L.* 191 (2002).

[18] On the relationship between empowerment and responsiveness of the law see P. Selznick, *The Moral Commonwealth, Social Theory and the Promise of Community*, University of California Press, 1992, p. 465.

Fourthly, the distributional effects of judicial enforcement are also relevant: not only monetary resources, but also political power and institutional capabilities are allocated while enforcing transnational private regulation across markets and states.[19]

3.2 Who are the Judicial Enforcers?

Judicial enforcement of TPR is carried out by domestic and, to a limited extent, by international courts.[20] It has now become rather conventional to speak of an intertwined international judicial system with continuous interaction, not always cooperative, between domestic and international courts.[21]

International courts are composed of two main categories: general and specialized courts. The former deploy primarily voluntary jurisdictions; the latter are usually empowered with compulsory jurisdictions.[22] They interact in different ways with domestic courts.[23] Their jurisdiction is primarily concerned with international public law and private regulation is normally only considered if provided for within the regime's normative framework. A clear illustration of this point is the jurisdiction of the International Court of Justice (ICJ).[24]

The role of domestic courts in transnational global governance has attracted attention for some time, which has stimulated the effort to identify

---

[19] In deciding modes of implementation of a food safety standard, designed by retailers and affecting the production process of suppliers, domestic courts affect the distribution of liabilities and capabilities along the supply chain. When the chain is international they redistribute wealth and institutional capabilities between developed and developing economies. See F. Cafaggi & K. Pistor, 'The Distributional Effects of Transnational Private Regulation', unpublished manuscript.

[20] The exceptions are represented by the ECJ. The ECJ has often been confronted with transnational private standards. The ECJ has considered technical standards set by the European Committee for Standardization (CEN), where these standards have been published in the Official Journal of the European Union. See: Case C-470/03 *AGM-Cosmet SRl* [2007] ECR I-2749.

[21] See e.g. A.M. Slaughter, *A New World Order*, Princeton University Press, 2005; H. Buxbaum, 'Transnational Regulatory Litigation', 46 *Va. J. Int'l L.* 251 (2006).

[22] See Y. Shany, 'No Longer a Weak Department of Power? Reflections on the Emergence of a New International Judiciary', 20 *EJIL* 73 (2009).

[23] See Y. Shany, *Regulating Jurisdictional Relations between National and International Courts*, Oxford University Press, 2007, particularly pp. 33ff.

[24] See e.g. *Fragmentation in International Law: Difficulties Arising from the Diversification and Expansion of International Law*, Report of the Study Group of the International Law Commission, finalized by M. Koskenniemi, A/CN.4/L.682, 2006.

common principles.[25] A number of difficult questions arise: Have domestic courts become agents of private global regulation? How does the relationship between enforcement and legitimacy change when domestic enforcement applies to transnational private rule-making? To what extent are domestic courts empowered to review these regimes? How does the review power change according to the private/hybrid nature of the regime and its constitutional foundations at the domestic level? What happens when multiple jurisdictions can intervene in the same dispute? In particular, what are the consequences on the scope and goals of the regime of divergent/conflicting judgments issued by national courts? What if one court strikes down part of the regulatory regime for violation of their domestic legal principles while others do not? Thus far, what are the responses of these regimes to domestic judicial oversight?

Enforcement by national courts is well established in public international law, where their role has long been recognized.[26] It has not been widely investigated in transnational private law and even less in TPR, with some exceptions.[27] The importance of domestic courts has, for example, been

---

[25] See H. Koh, 'Transnational Public Law Litigation', 100 *Yale L.J.* 2347 (1991); H. Buxbaum, 'Transnational Regulatory Litigation', 46 *Va. J. Int'l L.* 251 (2006), B. Kingsbury, 'The Concept of Law in Global Administrative Law', IILJ Working Paper 2009/1, Global Administrative Law Series. A. von Bogdandy & I. Venzke, 'In Whose Name? An Investigation of International Courts' Public Authority and its Democratic Justification', available at: http://papers.ssrn.com/sol3/papers.cfm?abstract_id=1593543

[26] See R. Falk, *The Role of Domestic Courts in the International Legal Order*, Syracuse University Press, 1964; B. Conforti, *International Law and the Role of Domestic Legal Systems*, Martinus Nijhoff Publishers, 1993; A. Reinisch, *International Organizations before National Courts*, Cambridge University Press, 2000. More recently, from a different perspective, E. Benvenisti, 'Reclaiming Democracy: The Strategic Uses of Foreign and International Law by National Courts', 102 *Am. J. Int'l L.* 241 (2008); B. Kingsbury, 'Weighing Global Regulatory Rules and Decisions in National Courts', *Acta Juridica* 90 (2009); and C. Whytock, 'Domestic Courts and Global Governance', 84 *Tulane L.R.* 67 (2009). See F. Francioni, in this volume, Chapter 5.

[27] See G. Teubner, 'Global Private Regimes: Neo-Spontaneous Law and Dual Constitution of Autonomous Sectors?', in: K. Ladeur (ed.) *Public Governance in the Age of Globalization*, Nomos Verlagsgesellschaft, 2004, p. 71; C. Scott & R. Wai, 'Transnational Governance of Corporate Conduct through the Migration of Human Rights Norms: The Potential Contribution of Transnational Private Litigation', in: C. Joerges, J. Sand & G. Teubner (eds) *Transnational Governance and Constitutionalism*, Hart, 2004, p. 287; R. Wai, 'Transnational Private Law and Private Ordering in a Contested Global Society', 46 *Harvard Int'l L.J.* 471 (2005). See also E. Benvenisti and G. Downs, in this volume, Chapter 3.

widely acknowledged in the area of transnational commercial arbitration.[28] Unlike international courts, domestic courts have jurisdiction over TPR by virtue of private international law rules. Different rules concerning *lex fori* apply depending on whether the regime is regulated through contracts or associations/foundations. Courts apply their domestic procedural rules and often their domestic private law, potentially leading to divergent interpretations of the same issue when multiple jurisdictions are competent over the same or similar disputes.[29]

3.3 Where Does Judicial Enforcement Take Place?

Judicial enforcement of TPR by domestic courts is *decentralized*. This has costs and benefits for transnational regulation.

State courts differ in their capacity to enforce global regimes.[30] Their independence from political and economic powers varies across countries and these divergences may contribute to conflicting judgments.[31] Yet, even aside the different institutional settings, judicial interpretations may vary according to each legal tradition.[32] This divergence may pose problems for rule-making, if courts' reviews provide conflicting indications. The problem of conflicting case law has emerged, for example in financial markets, in relation to credit rating agencies, ISDA and accounting standards and in e-commerce, in relation to some trading platforms (e-Bay, Craigslist) or to search engines.[33]

---

[28] See T. Carbonneau, 'The Ballad of Transborder Arbitration', 56 *U. Miami L.R.* 773 (2002). In relation to the US, see C.A. Whytock, 'The Litigation–Arbitration Relationship in Transnational Dispute Resolution: Empirical Insights from the US Federal Courts', 2 *World Arbitration and Mediation Review*, 39 (2009).

[29] In relation to regulatory regimes divergent solutions are problematic, even when the disputants are different but the subject matter of the dispute is the same.

[30] The distinctions between developed and developing countries and those between home and host States capture some of the taxonomies that explain the effects of decentralized enforcement often facilitating forum shopping.

[31] See E. Benvenisti & G. W. Downs, 'National Courts Review of Transnational Private Regulation', available at SSRN: http://papers.ssrn.com/sol3/papers.cfm?abstract_id=1742452

[32] See J. Bell, *Judiciaries Within Europe: A Comparative Review*, Cambridge University Press, 2006.

[33] The differences between domestic courts applying public international law, and those enforcing transnational private regulation are significant, due primarily to rules of interpretation but also to the identity of litigants and the nature of the disputes. While in the case of 'hard international law' the rules are those of statutory interpretation, primarily provided by the Vienna Convention on the Law of Treaties (VCLT), in the case of transnational regulatory contracts, the applicable rules are

Decentralized enforcement can also have beneficial effects, fostering regulatory innovation and increasing accountability. Some countries have designed rules to promote access to courts for human rights litigation, others have been less open. Decentralized adjudication can foster regulatory innovation where domestic courts have the ability and the expertise to introduce innovative solutions that can subsequently be followed by other courts in different states, if they prove to be effective. Perhaps the strongest driver for decentralized enforcement at the state level is respect for national sovereignty. Domestic courts exercise control over global private powers and prevent them from exercising their rule-making power outside or within rule of law principles. They try regulating the effects of private regulatory power on democratic decision-making processes at the state level.

The existence of costs and benefits for decentralized judicial enforcement suggests that it is a necessary – yet often an insufficient – mechanism to ensure effective compliance; it also needs to be complemented by more centralized mechanisms in the realm of non-judicial enforcement, and by coordination devices.[34]

---

those of contractual interpretation where the will of the parties and private autonomy dominate. For example in the area of derivatives, the use of ISDA Master Agreement refers to rules of contract interpretation of English and (notice!) New York contract law. Clearly, differences exist even within each field when considering the application of international soft law and tort or property, instead of contract. But even within the realm of contract law, employment contracts have different rules of interpretation from those deployed in regulatory contracts among different enterprises, as in the case of food safety, banking or the internet.

[34] A powerful illustration of a centralized private non-judicial enforcer is provided in the sports system by the CAS-TAS, a centralized Court of arbitration created in 1984 and reformed after a judgment by the Swiss Federal Tribunal in 1993 (Swiss Federal Court 15 March 1993, *Gundel* v *Federation Equestre Internationale*, BGE 119 II, p. 271ff.) to ensure independence and impartiality. The necessity of a central enforcer was perceived by the IOC as a vehicle to harmonize interpretations of rules concerning the Olympic Charter and later the anti-doping rules. It is now codified in Article 59 of the Olympic Charter where exclusivity is granted. With the Paris Agreement of 1994 International Federations have committed to integrate their statutes and bylaws accordingly. The effects of centralization are reinforced by the choice of the Swiss Federal Tribunal as the only Court empowered to review CAS judgments.

A different approach is that of ICANN where the Uniform Domain Name Dispute Resolution Policy (UDRP) adopts a pluralistic and relatively decentralized approach to dispute resolution. In Article 4 para. (d) the option to choose a provider to administer the dispute proceedings (those registered with ICANN) is stipulated. Para. (h) holds: 'Our Involvement in Administrative Proceedings. We do not, and will not, participate in the administration or conduct of any proceeding

3.4 What are the Effects of Judicial Enforcement on Global Regulatory Regimes?

Two very important effects of TPR judicial enforcement should be highlighted: gap-filling and dialogue within the regulatory process:

(a) Gap-filling: When domestic courts enforce transnational regulatory contracts, master agreements or codes of conducts between private actors, they must apply their domestic contract law to interpret the rules of the transnational regime and to fill gaps. For example, in a regulatory contract between the regulator and regulated firms (i.e. a code of conduct) when a breach by a regulated entity occurs, the available sanctions are often those defined by the domestic applicable law, in addition to those specified in the code.[35] This enforcement mechanism creates a strong complementarity between applicable national private laws and the transnational regulatory regime, but it also introduces a high level of variation, since, for example, remedies for breach of contract differ in each legal system.[36] Similarly, when contracts have to be interpreted, divergences among national courts may emerge due to different rules of interpretation in contract laws.

---

before an Administrative Panel. In addition, we will not be liable as a result of any decisions rendered by the Administrative Panel.' Furthermore the availability of court proceedings is provided for in para. (k). Article 5 leaves the opportunity to resolve '[a]ny other dispute or litigation' in any way possible or available.

[35] In most private regimes a clause concerning applicable law to the disputes is introduced. These clauses provide a common basis for interpretation. Often the choice of applicable law corresponds to that of *lex fori* but sometimes they diverge. An example where procedural and substantive law coincides is provided by the ICC Code on Advertising: the code holds that it must be applied against the background of applicable law (thus implying both procedural and substantive law).

[36] In the area of e-commerce differences concern the qualification of the contract between eBay and users. In the US, eBay's user agreement was interpreted as not constituting a contract of adhesion, since it was held that users have the opportunity to carefully evaluate its content and reject the provisions it contains. The agreement was simply considered as opening the possibility to engage in a certain marketplace that presents additional business opportunities. Individual terms were not further examined upon their validity and terms not scrutinized under the unconscionablility doctrine (*United States District Court, E.D. Pennsylvania* v *eBay, Inc., et al.*, 2009 WL 3365873, Oct. 19, 2009). In contrast European law sets stricter standards concerning the validity of terms when concerning consumers (Directive 93/13/EEC of 5 April 1993 on unfair terms in consumer contracts). Furthermore there seems to be less doubt that terms constitute a contract of adhesion and courts generally assess the validity of certain provisions within their decisions. LG Köln, decision of May 4, 2005, 9 S 17/05, BeckRS 2005, 10688.

The same is true for tort law when an environmental or a product safety transnational regime is applied by a domestic court, which has to fill the meaning of duty of care, negligence or causation. Thence a product may be considered safe under one jurisdiction and dangerous under another, undermining legal certainty and generating instability in the regulatory process. When domestic courts evaluate whether the violations of private standards might constitute a tort of negligence, they apply domestic national laws to the transnational regime. Since the differences among domestic civil liability are significant, different outcomes may occur, affecting the uniformity of safety, environmental or CSR standards designed by the transnational regulation.

Judicial enforcement of TPR reinforces *vertical complementarity* between national, procedural and substantive private laws (mainly contract and tort, but also property and IPR) and transnational private regulation, but encounters the danger of fragmentation.[37]

(b) Dialogue with rule-makers: Often judgments by domestic courts, especially when they review the (validity of) rules, engage the rule-makers. Some domestic courts, like the Swiss Federal Supreme Court or the Belgian Cour de Cassation, have played a prominent role given that many of the private organizations are incorporated in those two countries, thereby conferring jurisdiction on the court of the place of incorporation, according to private international law.

4. DISTINGUISHING BETWEEN ENFORCEMENT, REVIEW AND INTERPRETATION

Domestic courts enforce private regimes, review them and clarify the meaning of the regulatory agreements by virtue of interpretation. While enforcement is widely accepted, judicial review is much more limited in its scope.[38] Nonetheless, there are examples worth considering since they have contributed to the subsequent modifications in the private regulatory regimes.

---

[37] For a very general proposition well beyond private law, see International Standard Organization (ISO) Bylaws Article 22.1, 'The law of the country in which the organization has its seat shall apply in any or all cases not specifically provided for in the Statutes or in the rules of procedure'.

[38] In general, scope and domains of judicial review of private regimes vary across states. The limitations of review power are grounded on different rationales. Some rely on the public–private distinction, others on the delegation to private parties, others on the deference to the principle of forbearance. See, in relation to

The differences between enforcement and judicial review are significant. The former is linked to a dispute, unconcerned with the validity of the rules. The latter is primarily directed at examining the validity of rules and their compliance with general principles without engaging in a liability inquiry.[39] Domestic courts review sports federations' rules to ensure their compliance with freedom of movement and non-discrimination; they review electronic trading platforms users' agreements to warrant freedom of choices by traders, or environmental agreements to grant participation and transparency to the rule-making process by NGOs. Courts have engaged in judicial review affecting not only the rule-making power but also the oversight and enforcement powers of private regulators; they have scrutinized in particular the level of discretionary power to detect and to punish violations of contractual obligations undertaken by members.[40]

At the domestic level, while the regulatory function of judicial review is widely recognized, that of enforcement is not. At transnational level, both perform strong but different regulatory functions, due to different standing rules.[41]

the UK, J. Black, 'Constitutionalising Self-regulation', 59(1) *Modern Law Review* 24 (1996), and for a more detailed comparative analysis at EU level, F. Cafaggi (ed.) *Reframing Self-Regulation in European Private Law*, Kluwer Law International, 2006, pp. 16–18.

[39] See Peter Cane, 'Review of Executive Action', in: P. Cane & M. Tushnet (eds) *The Oxford Handbook of Legal Studies*, Oxford University Press, 2003, p. 146; id., 'Judicial Review and Merits Review: Comparing Administrative Adjudication by Courts and Tribunals', in: S. Rose Ackerman & P. Lindseth, *Comparative Administrative Law* (Research Handbooks in Comparative Law), Edward Elgar, 2010, p. 426; P. Craig, *Administrative Law*, 5th edn, Sweet and Maxwell, 2003; id., 'Judicial Review of Question of Law: a Comparative Perspective', in S. Rose Ackerman & P. Lindseth, *Comparative Administrative Law* (Research Handbooks in Comparative Law), Edward Elgar, 2010, p. 449; A. Turk, *Judicial Review of EU Law*, Edward Elgar, 2009.

[40] See in the area of e-commerce, *Durick* v *eBay*, 2006 WL 2672795 (Ohio Ct. App. Sept. 11, 2006), where the court supported the enforcement of a sanction towards a member given that it was not complying with the contract clauses.

[41] As pointed out by Richard Stewart in relation to the US, while judicial review used to be available only to regulated entities when their life, liberty or property interests were harmed, in the last 40 years beneficiaries have been granted access to judicial review thereby reducing the differences between the two categories. See R. Stewart, in this volume, Chapter 1. Access to third parties in transnational private regulation is much less frequent even when review is granted to the regulated entities.

Private regimes are frequently immunized from fully-fledged judicial review.[42] Only rarely do domestic courts scrutinize the validity of transnational private regimes to decide whether or not rules should be set aside (validity control).[43] The European Court of Justice (ECJ) has examined the validity of private rules in various fields, setting aside rules violating freedom of movement or fundamental rights.[44] Domestic courts, while reviewing parties' contractual agreements on procedural rules show more deference than they do with their own procedural rules.[45]

Generally, when transnational private regulation is scrutinized by courts only invalidity sanctions are available, while remedies like acceptance, acquiescence or estoppel are outside the scope of judicial intervention. It will be for the regulators, in particular those entrusted with rule-making power, to react to the invalidity declared by domestic courts and enact a new regulation or modify the old one; courts are generally not allowed to

---

[42] For example in the field of sports, Swiss law limits the judicial review of decisions by the Arbitral Tribunal and subjects them to strict conditions: 'Le recours de droit public n'est ouvert contre la sentence du TAS qu'à la double condition que ce prononcé soit effectivement une sentence arbitrale international, au sense des art. 176 ss LDIP, et qu'il porte sur des points de droit, partant qu'il n'ait pas pour unique objet des règles de jeu dont l'application échappe en principe à tout contrôle juridique ...', Swiss Federal Court 15 March 1993, *Gundel* v *Federation Equestre Internationale*, BGE 119 II, p. 271ff, at 275.

[43] In the field of social policy, the European trade association for SMEs, UEAPME, brought a claim before the ECJ against its exclusion from the conclusion of a pan-European industry agreement on parental leave. Despite the fact that UEAPME represented the interests of millions of employers, the European Commission had not granted UEAPME the status of 'representative', which was required for trade associations in order to participate in the conclusion of social partner agreements. After the Council of Ministers had codified the European social partner agreement in a separate Directive UEAPME challenged its exclusion by bringing an action for annulment (review of legality of acts) before the ECJ. The action was dismissed, however. See Case T-135/96, *Union Européenne de l'Artisanat et des Petites et Moyennes Enterprises (UEAPME)* v *Council of the European Union* [1998] ECR II-2335. See, for a discussion, P. Verbruggen, 'Does Co-Regulation Strengthen EU Legitimacy?', 15 *European Law Journal* 425 (2009).

[44] In *Walrave* v *UCI* C-36/74 the ECJ held that the prohibition of discrimination based on nationality applies not only to public authorities but also to private organizations, like sports federations. In the *Bosman* case (*Union Royale Belge des Sociétés de Football Association ASBL* v *Jean-Marc Bosman* (1995) C-415/93) the ECJ held that restrictions relating to the nationality of professional players who were nationals of other EU member states and the participation in competition between different football clubs or associations were prohibited.

[45] Decisions by US courts on the forum selection clauses of the eBay User Agreement: *Nazaruk* v *eBay Inc.*, 2006 WL 2666429 (D. Utah Sept. 14, 2006); US District Court, *Domenic Tricome* v *eBay, Inc.*, 2009 WL 3365873, Oct. 19, 2009.

substitute invalid with valid private rules. Compared to the very limited role of courts in relation to judicial review of International Organization (IO) rule-making, they perform a more significant function in reviewing TPR; nevertheless, they can only indirectly indicate what the rules should look like.

While limited, the 'dialogue' between transnational rule-makers and domestic courts has been one of the most powerful drivers of organizational innovation, increasing transparency and accountability of the rule-making process.

Judicial review concerning private regulation has had a strong impact, particularly on the organizational features of private regulators. It has played a significant role in furthering the separation of functions, particularly between rule-making and enforcement.[46] Domestic courts reviewing decisions issued by private enforcers have often scrutinized due process principles and voided or reformed them on the basis of insufficient impartiality based on inadequate independence of the private enforcer from the rule-maker.[47] The power to have an independent private enforcer with sanctioning authority over members is made conditional upon meeting basic due process requirements. One of the most famous and illustrative examples is the decision taken by the Swiss Federal Court concerning the lack of independence of the body created by the International Olympic Committee (IOC) to adjudicate disputes (TAS/CAS: Tribunal Arbitral du Sport/Court of Arbitration for Sport).[48] The Swiss Federal Court suggested that TAS was not sufficiently independent from the IOC and 'stimulated reform process that led to the current regime'. It should be underlined that the Swiss Federal Court operates as the single Court of

---

46 This conclusion is stated by a later judgment issued by the Federal Swiss Supreme Tribunal : 'Dans un arrêt rendu en 1993, le Tribunal Fédéral a formulé des réserves quant a l'Independence du TAS par rapport au CIO, en raison des liens organiques et économiques existant entre le deux institutions. Selon lui, il était souhaitable que l'on assurait une indépendance accrue du TAS à l'égard du CIO (ATE 119 II 271 conidie 3B BGE 129 II 445 p. 451) p. 280. Cet arrêt a entrainé une importante réforme du TAS. Les principales nouveautés on consisté dans la création à Paris, le 22 juin 1994, du Conseil de l'arbitrage en matière de sport (CIAS) et dans la rédaction du Code de l'arbitrage en matière de sport'. BGE III 445, 27 May 2003.

47 See in particular the role of the Swiss Federal Tribunal exercising jurisdictional power over several regimes. In the area of sport see the famous judgment, Swiss Federal Court 15 March 1993, *Gundel* v *Federation Equestre Internationale*, BGE 119 II, p. 271ff.; as well as *Club Atlético de Madrid SAD gegen Sport Lisboa E Benfica – Futebol SAD*, Federal Court, 136 III 345/4A_490/2009, 13 April 2010.

48 See Swiss Federal Court 15 March 1993, *Gundel* v *Federation Equestre Internationale*, BGE 119 II, p. 271ff.

last resort in the domain of Olympic sports, quite a unique position, to ensure uniformity and compliance with rule of law principles in the area of *lex sportiva*. In other instances, courts have scrutinized private regulation introducing mandatory arbitration clauses and forced them to re-write clauses deemed unconscionable.[49]

Domestic courts engage more frequently in *indirect* judicial review by solving disputes while at the same time assessing the legitimacy and effectiveness of private standards.[50] For instance, if a contract defines obligations concerning product safety or quality, based on a code of conduct enacted by a self-regulatory organization (SRO), courts may solve disputes related to the code's application and 'indirectly' scrutinize its legitimacy, when, for example, a breach of contract is grounded on the violation of the code standards incorporated by reference within the contract.[51] If they accept the private standard as an indicator in deciding whether a breach has occurred, recognition and, by extension, legitimacy is attached to the private standard. If they don't, they implicitly decrease its authority, denying its legitimacy. Similarly, in the case of professional malpractice or environmental harm, if the standard of care is, at least in part, defined by the professional rules contained in a code of conduct, courts may scrutinize the code and its drafting procedure when deciding if and how it applies to the standard of care in negligence. They may consider not only the substantive content of the standard, but also the procedural rules established for the approval and implementation of the standard.[52]

---

[49] See e.g. *Craig Comb* v *PayPal* N.D. California, 30 August 2002, holding the PayPal User Agreement unconscionable in relation to the arbitration clause which forced PayPal to rewrite the clause.

[50] See F. Cafaggi, 'New Foundations of Transnational Private Regulation', 38 *J. L. & Soc.* 20, 29ff. (2011).

[51] See *Hazelwood Grocery Ltd* v *Lion Foods Ltd* [2007] EWHC B5 (QB), [2007] EWHC B5 (QB) where the judge acknowledged the breach of contract between a supplier and a final producer, also taking into account the absence of the most updated certification system.

For the e-commerce case, see *Bergraft* v *eBay* (N.J. Super. Ct. Oct. 1, 2003), where the court interpreted eBay's user agreement so as to clarify that the clauses implied in it also include the 'non-binding bid policy' applicable to the sale of estates.

[52] See R. Stewart, 'Accountability, Participation, and the Problem of Disregard in Global Regulatory Governance', IILJ International Legal Theory Colloquium Discussion Paper, 2008, available at: http://www.iilj.org/courses/documents/2008Colloquium.Session4.Stewart.pdf. In the US, the review of procedural rules concerning the negotiating procedures is more common than in continental Europe.

Several implications derive from domestic 'indirect' review of transnational private regulatory regimes: some are circumscribed to the domestic environment where the reviewing court operates, others extend to the nature of the regimes themselves. In particular, one implication, more limited than cases of review of public and hybrid regimes, is related to the domestic allocation of power between courts and the executive; another is related to the effects of national review on the transnational private regimes.[53]

An intermediate function, between enforcement and review, is performed by judicial interpretation. This function is best illustrated by the advisory opinions rendered in the field of public international law by the ICJ and other courts like the ECJ.[54] By providing advisory opinions, courts try to prevent disputes from arising when an issue of interpretation emerges. The controversy may be settled by rendering an advisory opinion with or without binding effect.[55] Similar functions can be found in the field of private enforcement, where, for example, in the field of sports CAS can issue non-binding advisory opinions to IOC, WADA, international sports federations and other bodies.[56] In the field of advertising, the International

---

[53] See E. Benvenisti & G.W. Downs, 2009, note 31 above.

[54] See for an overview, J. Klabbers, *International Institutional Law*, 2nd edn, Cambridge University Press, 2009, pp. 231ff.

[55] On the use of advisory opinions by ICJ and their functions, see R. Ago, '"Binding" Advisory Opinions of the International Court of Justice', 85 *Am. J. Int. L.*, 439 (1991). For a very detailed overview see, H. Thirlway, 'Advisory Opinions', in *Max Planck Encyclopedia of Public International Law*, 2006, available at: http://www.mpepil.com/subscriber_article?script=yes&id=/epil/entries/law-9780199231690-e4&recno=6&searchType=Quick&query=advisory+opinions; K. Oellers, 'Article 96 UN Charter', in: A. Zimmermann, C. Tomuschat & K. Oellers-Frahm (eds) *The Statute of the International Court of Justice: A Commentary*, Oxford University Press, 2006.

[56] Rule 60 of the CAS Statutes of the Bodies Working for the Settlement of Sports-Related Disputes provides for the possibility of requesting an opinion: 'The IOC, the IFs, the NOCs, WADA and the organizations recognized by the IOC and the OCOGs, may request an advisory opinion from the CAS about any legal issue with respect to the practice or development of sport or any activity related to sport. The request for an opinion shall be addressed to the CAS and accompanied by any document likely to assist the Panel entrusted with giving the opinion'. See e.g. CAS Advisory Opinion on FIFA compliance with the World Anti-Doping Code, April 21st, 2006, CAS 2005/C/976&986, FIFA & WADA, available at: http://www.wada-ama.org/Documents/World_Anti-Doping_Program/WADP-Legal_Library/Advisory_and_Legal_Opinions/CAS_Opinion_FIFA.pdf; or: CAS Advisory Opinion upon the request by the Comitato Olimpico Nazionale Italiano (CONI), CAS 2005/C/841 CONI, April 26th, 2005, available at: http://www.rdes.it/TAS opinion.pdf

Chamber of Commerce (ICC) interpretation panel performs a distinct interpretive function, while proper enforcement is decentralized at the SRO level.[57] Finally, the Independent Review Panel, providing reviews of the Internet Corporation for Assigned Names and Numbers (ICANN) Board, also held that its decisions have to be considered as advising rather than binding.[58]

Domestic courts therefore not only ensure compliance, but also play an active role in defining the limits and boundaries of private authority at transnational level.

5. NON-JUDICIAL ENFORCEMENT BY PRIVATE BODIES

Transnational private enforcement (TPE) refers in this context to the specific modes of enforcement of regulatory regimes rather than the broader phenomenon of transnational private justice.

By non-judicial private enforcement we refer to a set of mechanisms, premised on the existence of an independent body, adjudicating disputes between the regulator, regulatees and third parties. Clearly such a body can be part of an integrated wider organization that also encompasses rule-making and monitoring but it has to be entrusted with sufficient independence and impartiality. For private enforcement, functional separation within the regulatory process must translate into some degree of structural separation between standard-setting, monitoring and enforcement, with sufficient guarantees of independence within a unitary regulatory framework. The delicate institutional design question which transnational private regulators face therefore concerns the correlation between structural separation and functional integration among different regulatory stages.[59]

---

[57] See P. Verbruggen, in this volume, Chapter 11.

[58] *International Centre for Dispute Resolution, ICM Registry, LLC* v *Internet Corporation for Assigned Names and Numbers, Declaration of the Independent Review Panel*, ICDR Case No. 50 117 T 00224 08, February 19, 2010, p. 61.

[59] For an example of internal enforcement see ICANN, or eBay (at least to the degree that it sanctions or suspends user accounts). With regard to GLOBALGAP, FSC, MSC, ISO or CEN, enforcement takes place externally either through certifiers or by means of implementation of national members. Another example of external enforcement is the International Financial Reporting Standards (IFRS) that are mainly enforced by implementation in national legislation. For a good overview see the country case study on IFRS conducted by UNCTAD, *Practical Implementation of International Financial Reporting Standards: Lessons Learned*, 2008, available at: http://www.unctad.org/en/docs/diaeed20081_en.pdf

The choice among enforcement mechanisms, and, even before, the choice of including an enforcement body within the regulatory process, is normatively based on freedom of contract and/or association. The source of enforcement power hence lies primarily in freedom of contract: authority is based on autonomy.

Parties, regulators and regulated decide procedural rules and sanctions themselves via contracts or bylaws. The dominance of private autonomy as an organizational principle constitutes a major difference from judicial enforcement, where, in many legal systems, the source of the enforcement power is the law; procedural rules are mandatory, and parties cannot contract them out.[60] That said, constitutional principles, both at domestic and international level, apply to both judicial and private non-judicial enforcement.[61]

In the last 20 years, external pressures, deriving from beneficiaries' organizations and public bodies together with important courts' judgments, have modified non-judicial private enforcement and the balance between private autonomy and general principles.[62] These changes have influenced the choice concerning both if and how enforcement should be integrated within TPR.

TPE develops primarily:

---

[60] But see K.E. Davis & H. Hershkoff, 'Contracting for Procedure', 53 *William and Mary L. Rev.* (2011) forthcoming, available also at SSRN: http://papers.ssrn.com/sol3/papers.cfm?abstract_id=1892914

[61] In Europe the ECtHR has held Article 6 on fair trial applicable to private enforcers. In particular the case law has addressed arbitration. In relation to impartiality see, for example, what was stated in the European Court of Human Rights in *Findlay* v *United Kingdom* [1997] 24 E.H.R.R. 221: 'in order to establish whether a tribunal can be considered as "independent", regard must be had inter alia to the manner of appointment of its members and the term of office, the existence of guarantees against outside pressures and the question of whether the party presents an appearance of independence. As to the question of "impartiality", there are two aspects to this requirement. First, the tribunal must be subjectively free from judicial bias. Secondly, it must also be impartial from an objective view point, that is, it must offer sufficient guarantees to exclude any legitimate doubt in this respect'.

[62] These transformations have certainly improved private enforcement's effectiveness towards regulated and third parties. Yet this improvement has hardly touched on the enforcers' liability for complying with the rules failing to increase their accountability. Enforcement of rules concerning the obligations of the enforcer (i.e. compliance with due process) is still rather limited. In particular to what extent the regulator's obligations can be sanctioned, especially on the basis of complaints brought by third parties, is an open question. Ultimately compliance rests on the control exercised by courts over enforcers' liability.

1. to increase effectiveness, speeding the solution of disputes among interested parties in the regulatory process;
2. to 'secure' the independence of the regulatory regime from outside interferences, coming not only from political actors but also from other regimes; and
3. to ensure consistency along the regulatory cycle.[63]

6. THE FEATURES OF NON-JUDICIAL PRIVATE ENFORCEMENT

Enforcement by private non-judicial bodies differs across regimes. Relevant variables for examining these differences in private non-judicial enforcement regimes include:

1. the identity of the private regulator: whether a single firm, NGO, a whole sector or a federation of different NGOs;
2. the nature of the dispute and the identity of litigants;
3. the relationship between the enforcer and the litigants;
4. access and due process;
5. sanctions;
6. the link with non-legal enforcement mechanisms, like those deploying market and community sanctions; and
7. the choice between a centralized or decentralized system: i.e., a global transnational private enforcer or various local enforcers not necessarily identified with states.

6.1 The Identity of the Private Regulator

Private regulation is characterized by multiple models, encompassing both contractual and organizational forms,[64] the legal form of which may impinge on the choice among enforcement mechanisms. There are differences between individual enterprises exercising regulatory functions via codes of conduct, and complex organizations, whether single or multi-stakeholder, enacting guidelines or principles to be applied by members, often organizations themselves. There is a correlation worth exploring between the 'regulatory business model' and the choice of enforcement strategies.

---

[63] For an analysis of the reasons to transnationalize enforcement regimes see R. Stewart, in this volume, Chapter 1.

[64] See F. Cafaggi, 'New Foundations', note 50 above.

When the private regime is governed by a single multinational corporation (MNC), monitoring of compliance and enforcement is generally provided within the organization by inside 'independent' committees, reporting directly to the governing body (i.e. the board of directors or the CEO).[65] Enforcement in this hypothesis coincides with tools deploying company and/or labor law, as is the case for many MNC codes of conduct.[66] Insulating the enforcer from the organizational corporate hierarchy ensures independence; however, the results so far have been rather limited and more independence is needed. When private regulation extends beyond the MNC to encompass the whole supply chain, enforcement is more complex; it goes beyond compliance or ethical internal committees, often including multiple participants in the chain.

When TPR is governed by an association, foundation or a corporation, the key feature is membership. The enforcer is often a separate yet not fully independent body: ranging from a simple committee to a fully-staffed entity with independent enforcing power.[67] Compliance is highly dependent on the advantages of membership. Organizational sanctions are highly effective when the private regulator is a monopolist and the regulatory regime is a precondition of market access. Their effectiveness decreases if exit is not costly and participation in the regime does not constitute a requirement for trading.

In contractual forms of private regulation, permanent dispute resolution bodies are rare; conflicts are often referred to institutional arbitration, which varies depending on the nature of the dispute.[68] When the TPR is governed by a contract with many signatories, the enforcement body may either be external or internal, with some degree of independence concerning appointment, procedural rules and liability.[69] In the former case,

---

[65] Recent developments in the field of CSR show that MNCs have engaged in governance reform to ensure independence of compliance and ethical committees and have made them directly accountable to the Board.

Similar developments are taking place in international organizations: see for example the World Bank Dispute Settlement Panel.

[66] For a comprehensive proposal concerning guidelines on grievance mechanisms linked with CSR but subject to a wider application see Ruggie, 'Guiding Principles'.

[67] Enforcement power can come directly from the bylaws and the charter or can be delegated by the governing body in general or ad hoc modes.

[68] The competence of the dispute resolution body is generally associated with disputes among members concerning interpretation of internal rules. Arbitration is deployed primarily for litigation with third parties, although its use for internal disputes is frequent; see the cases of eBay and ICANN.

[69] See, for examples, note 60 above.

adjudication can be performed by an affiliated organization or outsourced to a third party in order to ensure higher independence and impartiality.

6.2 The Nature of the Dispute and the Identity of Litigants

Different disputes over the same regime may be brought before different enforcers depending on standing, types of infringement and nature of remedies.

Disputes, as mentioned earlier, can occur:

(a) between the regulator and the regulated;
(b) among the regulated;
(c) between the regulator and third parties; and
(d) between regulated and third parties.

In some cases there is a single enforcer with jurisdiction over all kinds of disputes; in others, disputes are dealt with by different non-judicial enforcement mechanisms. While the first category – disputes between regulator and regulated – is partly administered by arbitration and partly by the private enforcer, the second – disputes among regulated – is generally managed with the internal rules of the organization, since the regulated are often, though not always, members.[70] The last two categories of disputes are sometimes regulated by organizational rules (i.e. company or associational law), and sometimes by arbitration, but mostly by judicial enforcement, since usually no full standing is granted to non-members for breach of internal rules by the regulated entities let alone by the regulator itself.[71] While direct participation to the adjudicatory process and the request for a remedy by a third party is limited, much more common is the possibility to file a complaint, informing the private enforcer of a violation; such a

---

[70] The case of advertising shows the opposite, however. Disputes between the regulated and third parties (e.g. consumers) are generally solved via non-judicial enforcement. In France, for example, the SRO body enforcing the ICC code has so far not been used to settle disputes between competitors (i.e. the regulated) and operates only in disputes between businesses and consumers (i.e. the regulated against third parties). Here, the regulated have preferred to address their disputes via judicial enforcement.

[71] See case *Abc Real Estate Services, Inc., and Santos Realty, Inc., Plaintiffs* v *American Plaza Corp., City Rooms, Inc., et al.*, 2009 WL 1158829 (S.D.N.Y.), April 28, 2009, where the court denied the possibility of interpreting the terms of use of the auction website Craigslist as a contract for the benefit of third parties, affirming that the clauses included in the terms are only applicable to the contractual relationship between the auction website and the member.

violation is generally prosecuted *ex officio*, independently from the direct participation of the complainant to the proceedings.[72] More recently, private regulatory bodies have been forced to give reasons to the complainant concerning the actions or inaction, following the complaint. These changes have been correlated by an increasing accessibility to third parties of dispute resolution mechanisms.

These differences are partly the consequence of the contractual origins of the enforcement activity. In the domain of TPR, freedom of contract concerning the choice of enforcement plays a different role according to the nature of the dispute: this is very strong in relation to the first two classes, and quite limited in relation to the third. Third parties do not usually participate in the codes' drafting and hence have no say in determining procedural and substantive rules. There are, however, areas where the internal dispute resolution mechanism is open also to third parties. This feature represents a departure from traditional self-regulation where third party access was generally unavailable and reflects the complexity of non-judicial enforcement across different sectors.

Freedom of contract is not evenly distributed among the members. When parties subscribe to a private regime by virtue of adhesion contracts, they have very limited freedom to choose enforcement mechanisms. For this reason, contractual rules concerning arbitration and other dispute resolution mechanisms have been scrutinized under unconscionability or unfairness doctrines, in order to evaluate their validity and applicability.

6.3 The Relationship between the Enforcer and the Litigants

Variations also feature in relation to the procedural model. They concern the power to commence the proceeding, the definition of the scope of litigation and the choice of remedies.[73] Both the start of the proceeding and its structure confer on the parties the power to define the scope of litigation and its objectives (i.e. which remedies are sought).

Some subscribe to an inquisitorial regime where the enforcer has the power to start the proceedings *ex officio*, with the authority to prosecute the

---

[72] See e.g. in the case of forestry, the rule set by the FSC providing that '[a]ny individual or organization may file a complaint against the FSC Certification Scheme (incl. the FSC Accreditation Program)' (e.g. 'Processing Complaints in the FSC Certification Scheme, FSC-PRO-01–008 (V1–0) EN', available at: http://www.fsc.org/fileadmin/web-data/public/document_center/international_FSC_policies/procedures/FSC-PRO-01–008_V1–0_EN_Processing_complaints.pdf).

[73] On remedies and sanctions see below, text and notes, p. 103ff.

violation and impose sanctions on the infringers.[74] Often these enforcement regimes allow both the regulator and the potential litigants to initiate the proceedings. Others, more akin to judicial enforcement, endorse an adversarial approach, preclude *ex officio* proceedings and defer the initiative to the parties. This difference can be partially explained by the variable weight of the collective and individual interests pursued by the regulatory regime. In theory, the stronger the collective interest, the more likely the enforcer is to be entrusted with hierarchical power, while the adversarial feature prevails when protection of individual interests is the primary goal.

The judgments issued by the private enforcer are often binding on all the members, and not only the litigants. This feature increases the regulatory function of private litigation compared to that of judicial enforcement. The resolution of the dispute produces effects beyond the sphere of the litigants, since the judgment defines a rule applicable to all members of the organization.

6.4 Procedural Fairness and Due Process

Two important shortcomings are often related to the use of private non-judicial enforcement: weaker due process and limited access/standing.

Procedural due process has different connotations in relation to public adjudication and private non-judicial enforcement.[75] The analysis here is limited to the private sector and assumes the applicability of the principle but does not imply mere transposition from the context of public law to private dispute resolution mechanisms.[76] Clearly due process here must be balanced with freedom of contract and private autonomy.[77]

Procedural due process includes many rights, among which are: the right to be heard, the right to an impartial, independent tribunal, the right to a fair trial, to a reasoned decision, and the right to appeal.

Independence and impartiality, transparency and openness are limited and in some circumstances, totally lacking. Clearly, they have different

---

74 In the case of advertising, most private enforcement institutions have this right. Belgium is an exception in this respect. See: *Le Reglement Jury d'Ethique Publicitaire*, available at: http://www.jep.be/media/pdf/reglement_jep/reglement_jep__fr.pdf

75 For a comparative analysis of due process see D. Galligan, *Due Process and Fair Procedures*, Oxford University Press, 1996.

76 These differences emerge in the case law of the European Court of Human Rights in relation to the application of Article 6 of the European Convention on Human Rights regarding private enforcers, in particular professional bodies.

77 The link between the two is explored in relation to arbitrability of agreements concerning labor standards by C. Estlund, in this volume, Chapter 8.

importance in relation to the class of disputes: whether between regulator and regulatee or regulator and third parties.[78] In particular, compliance with due process principles has promoted independence and impartiality of enforcement. While in the past, the same entity would set the rules and adjudicate disputes over them, nowadays, functional separation between setting and enforcing standards, similar to the separation of powers in the public domain, is becoming the dominant feature.[79] The creation of an independent and separate enforcer has become the rule rather than the exception in multi-stakeholder private regulators.[80] However, independence is not the only dimension. Recent elaborations in the field of CSR provide comprehensive definitions of the main features of non-state grievance mechanisms. Accordingly they should be: legitimate, accessible, predictable, equitable, transparent, rights-compatible and a source of continuous learning.[81]

The balance between these principles and private autonomy also differs in relation to the identity of disputants. Due process or procedural fairness in relation to dispute resolution is fundamental to ensuring credibility of the regime when the regulatory effects extend beyond the members.[82] Many private regimes recognize its importance. For example, in the field of sports, due process guarantees concerning disputes before CAS are explicitly recognized.[83]

---

78 On the different types of disputes and their impact on private non-judicial enforcement, see text and notes above, p. 99.

79 See e.g. pp. 7 and 8 of *EASA Best Practice Self-regulatory Model*, 2004, available at: http://www.easa-alliance.org/page.aspx/162

80 See e.g. Article 31 of Ruggie, 'Guiding Principles', where in the commentary it is stated: '... Since a business enterprise cannot, with legitimacy, both be the subject of complaints and unilaterally determine their outcome, these mechanisms should focus on reaching agreed solutions through dialogue. Where adjudication is needed, this should be provided by a legitimate, independent third-party mechanism.'

81 See commentary to Point 31 of the Ruggie, 'Guiding Principles'.

82 See in the field of CSR the recommendations made by the UN reporter John Ruggie, *Protect, Respect and Remedy: a Framework for Business and Human Rights, Report of the Special Representative of the Secretary-General on the Issue of Human Rights and Transnational Corporations and Other Business Enterprises*, A/HRC/8/5, 7 April 2008 (hereafter: Ruggie Report) – p. 24, para. 92 lists a number of prerequisites for non-judicial mechanisms to address alleged breaches of human rights: legitimacy, accessibility, predictability, equitability, rights-compatibility, and transparency. They are now in Article 31 of the Ruggie, 'Guiding Principles'.

83 See CAS 2008/A/1545 *Andrea Anderson et al.* v *IOC*, decided on16 July 2010 available at: http://jurisprudence.tas-cas.org/sites/CaseLaw/Shared%20Documents/1545.pdf. While the award confirms the existence of due process rights it also confirms the principle stated in the case law whereby violations of due process by

In addressing these drawbacks, dispute resolution bodies have adopted, in many regimes, an independent status and consequently the power to establish their own procedural rules according to due process.

Openness and transparency are also limited. In some cases like commercial arbitration, even the awards are not public. In other cases, the judgments are available but the access to proceedings is limited.[84]

6.5 Sanctions

Within legal sanctions, non-judicial enforcement is characterized by: (1) a wide use of organizational sanctions that rely on membership; (2) relatively scarce use of compensatory sanctions; (3) moderate use of fines and other types of monetary penalties; and (4) significant deployment of injunctive relief in the form of cease and desist orders.

What are the sources of private enforcers' sanctioning power? Sanctioning power is grounded on freedom of contract and freedom of association. Unlike judicial enforcement, where the judicial and administrative sanctioning power derives from law, here the primary sources of authority are private autonomy and consent. Such power is conferred to protect the collective interest of the regulator and the community of regulatees, in addition to their individual interests. Sanctioning power of private enforcers is therefore regulated primarily by contract or organizational charters and bylaws, with significant limitations differing across jurisdictions.

What are the foundations and limits of these powers? In many legal systems, the state monopoly of procedural rules has affected the power of private parties to design new remedies. Particularly in relation to punitive remedies and those concerning invalidity of the rules, the state's monopoly significantly limits freedom of contract and freedom of association in

sports organizations can be fully cured by the appeal before CAS and therefore they do not lead to the annulment of the act in violation of due process.

[84] Lack of openness and transparency in arbitration is strongly interlinked with the principle of confidentiality of arbitration processes. Even if there is a general tendency towards mere publication of arbitral awards, the general access to arbitral awards is still limited. See C.A. Rogers, 'Transparency in International Commercial Arbitration', *Kansas Law Review*, 2006 available at SSRN: http://papers.ssrn.com/sol3/papers.cfm?abstract_id=888485. Moreover, the access to arbitral proceedings of third parties and 'persons not involved in the proceedings' is strictly determined by the arbitrators' discretionary powers. See Article 21(3) of the ICC Arbitration Rules. See also: M. Hwang & K. Chung, 'Protecting Confidentiality and its Exceptions – The Way Forward?', in: ICC's Court of Arbitration Special Supplement 2009: *Confidentiality in Arbitration: Commentaries on Rules, Statutes, Case Law and Practice* (2009).

designing procedural rules and remedies.[85] Given that domestic laws regulate transnational private regimes, these limitations hold also for TPR. Furthermore, procedural fairness influences both the foundations and limits of enforcement power, and, specifically, sanctioning. Limitations of private sanctioning power concern both the type of remedies and their correlation with the gravity of the infringement. For example, disproportionate sanctions, imposed by private enforcers on the basis of rules agreed upon by the parties, either within an organization or a contract, can be scrutinized under the principle of proportionality, concerning compliance with procedural due process.[86] For example, the discretion of an organization to define escalating sanctions, depending on the gravity of the violations, is limited by procedural due process constraints.[87]

Private enforcement power is also limited in relation to enforcing sanctions and it often requires judicial intervention. Contract and association laws constitute the main regulatory toolbox to monitor and deter non-compliance with sanctions by either the regulators or the regulatee. A violation is a breach of contract or associational law.[88] Non-compliance also constitutes a breach that can be sanctioned firstly before a private enforcer and then, if the violation persists, before a court, since regulated parties undertake the obligation to comply with the sanction when they voluntarily join the regime.

---

[85] The debate has mainly focused on penal clauses and punitive damages and the limits private parties face in contractually defining new remedies. The discussion developed between contract and procedural lawyers similarly applies to remedies in the context of transnational private regulation.

[86] See below p. 107.

[87] The approach of escalating sanctions was deployed by I. Ayres & J. Braithwaite, *Responsive Regulation*, Oxford University Press, 1992, and then refined by N. Gunningham, P. Grabosky & D. Sinclair, *Smart Regulation*, Oxford University Press, 1998.

[88] In e-commerce, breach can be sanctioned directly by the regulator (eBay for example), which disposes of a wide array of sanctions ranging from warning, to deletion of the offer, to exclusion of the user from the trading platform. The User Agreement states that 'Without limiting other remedies, we may limit, suspend, or terminate our service and user accounts, prohibit access to our sites and their content, services, and tools, delay or remove hosted content, and take technical and legal steps to keep users off the sites if we think that they are creating problems or possible legal liabilities, infringing the intellectual property rights of third parties, or acting inconsistently with the letter or spirit of our policies. We also reserve the right to cancel unconfirmed accounts or accounts that have been inactive for a long time, or to modify or discontinue eBay sites, services, or tools'. See http://pages.ebay.com/help/policies/user-agreement.html

Given the consensual source of the enforcement authority, the use of private sanctioning power is subject to limited judicial review.[89] Courts do not engage in a full but rather a more limited review concerning the fairness of the terms that empower the regulator.[90]

Sometimes, parties employ direct sanctions, such that private enforcers or courts intervene only *ex post*. When regulatory regimes are contractual, self-enforcement is often deployed. Many of the regulatory contracts between the regulator and regulated include termination clauses (exclusion in the context of organization) concerning violations committed by the regulated. In this case, the sanction is directly imposed on the regulated, in the absence of any proceeding, with serious concerns for due process. The party whose contract is terminated can thereafter resort to internal dispute mechanisms or to courts, claiming wrongful termination.

The nature and seriousness of the violation affects the choice of sanctions

Organizational sanctions range from warning, to temporary suspension, termination or expulsion. Organizational sanctions concerning membership and activity, like expulsion or temporary suspension, prevail over pecuniary sanctions, to ensure deterrence and protect the common interest. Their role is strictly linked to the historical roots of private regulation and to the protection of collective reputation. Private regulation was previously based on regulating access for 'close' bodies operating as clubs. Regulating access and exit through sanctioning constituted a powerful control mechanism. Today, transnational private regimes have lost the club feature and often represent the private production of a public or at least a semi-public good. Still, however, the credibility and legitimacy of private regulators requires that organizational sanctions concerned with forced exit of regulated entities be deployed. Their effectiveness is linked with the importance of membership and the degree of regulatory concentration. If the regulator

---

[89] See e.g. in the context of the ECJ C-519/04, *Meca Medina* v *Commission*, p. 47 where the Court has stated: 'It must be acknowledged that the penal nature of the anti-doping rules at issue and the magnitude of the penalties applicable if they are breached are capable of producing adverse effects on competition because they could, if penalties were ultimately to prove unjustified, result in an athlete's unwarranted exclusion from sporting events, and thus in impairment of the conditions under which the activity at issue is engaged in. *It follows that, in order not to be covered by the prohibition laid down in Article 81(1) EC, the restrictions thus imposed by those rules must be limited to what is necessary to ensure the proper conduct of competitive sport (see, to this effect,* DLG, *paragraph 35)*' (emphasis added).

[90] See, *Durick* v *eBay*, 2006 WL 2672795 (Ohio Ct. App. Sept. 11, 2006); *Bragg* v *Linden Research*, Inc., 487 F. Supp. 2d 593 (E.D.Penn. 2007).

is a monopolist and compliance is a prerequisite to market access, organizational sanctions are highly effective. If exit is cheap, they must be complemented by other sanctions to effectively deter wrongful behavior by the regulated.

Often the sanctioning scheme reflects an escalating architecture that correlates the sanction to the frequency and seriousness of the violation.[91] This is possible because the interaction between enforcers and litigants is repeated, unlike in judicial enforcement where the general pattern reflects spot interactions between classes of litigants and multiple courts.[92] The first violation is sanctioned mildly, aiming to ensure further cooperation. The subsequent violations are sanctioned more harshly, the deterrent function increasing with the repetition of the infringements over time.

In non-judicial enforcement, the seriousness and frequency of the violation therefore significantly impacts the choice of sanctions. In the field of e-commerce, we find repeat infringers policies.[93] Within these policies there is often a correlation between the severity of the sanction and the frequency

---

[91] E.g. the food safety regime of GLOBALGAP provides for such forms of sanctions vis-à-vis the producer: warning, product suspension and cancellation. Furthermore, such escalating sanctions also exist with regard to the third-party certifiers active within the GLOBALGAP system. Here sanctions are the cancellation of the license agreement, request of additional integrity assessments, fines (up to 5000 EUR), reimbursement of costs linked to investigations and sanctions, cancellation of contract with the certification body, and mandatory education measures of the inspectors concerned.

Similarly in the case of the auction website Craigslist, where reputational sanctions are coupled with an estimation of possible pecuniary damages to be paid to the auction platform where breaches are confirmed, see Article 19 of Craigslist's Terms of Use.

[92] On the link between escalating and interaction see Ayres & Braithwaite, above at note 87. Only when information is available about the identity of the infringer and the causes of violations, are escalating techniques likely to be effective. See N. Gunningham, 'Enforcement and Compliance Strategies', in: D. Bodansky, J. Brunnee & E. Hey (eds), *The Oxford Handbook of International Environmental Law*, Oxford University Press, 2006, pp. 128–129 emphasizing the role of information flow between enforcers and infringers.

[93] See the EU *Memorandum of Understanding* 4 May 2011 between internet platforms and copyright owners, Section 6 'Repeat infringers', states: 'Internet Platforms and Rights Owners commit to cooperate in the detection of repeat infringers, especially but not limited to, those selling high volumes, dangerous, pre-release or obvious Counterfeit Goods ... Internet Platforms commit to implement and enforce repeat infringer policies, according to their internal guidelines', paras 34, 35 (http://ec.europa.eu/internal_market/iprenforcement/docs/memorandum_04052011_en.pdf).

and repetition of the violation.[94] Similarly, in sports, the WADA Code regulates multiple violations with specific sanctioning policies.[95] These sanctions, unlike those traditionally associated with breach of contract or violation of unfair trade practices, are related to the wrongdoer's behavior before the particular violation under scrutiny.

Correlation of the sanction with the frequency of wrongdoing indicates that private non-judicial enforcement combines the protection of the victim with that of the collective interest in the regulatory process.

The private autonomy of regulators and enforcers is constrained by general principles like proportionality. Both the general definition of the sanctioning scheme, and more specifically the implementation of escalating sanctions, should conform to proportionality. Remedial proportionality requires a functional correlation between the gravity of the sanction and the seriousness of the violation. The lack of proportionality in the scheme may be challenged under due process or even under unconscionability, if the procedural rule allows too wide a discretion (constituting arbitrariness) when conferring sanctioning power onto the private enforcer.

6.6 The Combination of Legal and Informal Enforcement

A distinguishing feature of private enforcement is the greater reliance on the correlation with non-legal mechanisms. Both provide incentives to monitor and administer effective sanctions, and, often, private enforcement mechanisms rely upon community and market sanctions, in addition to legal remedies.[96] For example, reporting violations and making them public

---

[94] See *L'Oreal and eBay International* 2009 EWHC 1094 (CH), para. 88: 'eBay applies a variety of sanctions to users, and in particular to sellers, who breach their policies. The sanction increases in severity depending on the nature, number and frequency of the breaches.'

[95] For escalating sanctions vis-à-vis the certifiers of GLOBALGAP see note 91 above. Concerning the FSC, sanctions depend on whether the violation is considered a minor or a major non-compliance. Depending on this a timeframe will be set up to remove the violation (more time for minor violations less for major). Ultimately, minor violations will be considered major ones if not removed and major violations will lead to a suspension of the certification. For an overview see http://www.fsc.org/fileadmin/web-data/public/document_center/accreditation_documents/certification_bodies/FSC_STD_20_011_V1_1_EN_Chain_of_Custody_Evaluations.pdf at p. 4. See also in the sport sector Article 10.7 on multiple violations of WADA Code 2009.

[96] A distinction is emerging between reputational and non-reputational enforcement mechanisms. When reputational mechanisms exist often they are open to third parties who have entered into some relationship with the regulated party. In this case, complaints about non-compliance by a third party are generally accepted.

may trigger blaming, naming and shaming, severely diminishing the breaching entity's reputation. The Global Reporting Initiative (GRI) is one example of a monitoring scheme that, combined with non-judicial enforcement, provides a new enforcement strategy in the field of TPR. Similarly, ISEAL Codes are based on the premise of working combinations between legal and non-legal mechanisms.

In addition to the contribution of monitoring by independent organizations, peer-monitoring has proven to generate strong deterrence effects on incentives to violate private regulatory regimes. The use of peer-monitoring in e-commerce platforms constitutes a clear example of the link with enforcement and the different weight of non-legal mechanisms.[97] Transnational private regulators rely on the threat that peers can pose to the members who breach. These mechanisms range from refusal to deal, to exclusion from the business community. Consumers can also impose market sanctions, when their organizations promote boycotts of products. In the field of CSR, the link between legal and social responsibility, based on community and market sanctions, can be strong, rendering difficult the determination of what pertains to the social and the legal sphere.[98]

Peer-monitoring and the associated reputational sanctions often transform the scope and the function of enforcement by private bodies, from deterrence to reflexive governance. Even when the enforcer, for independence reasons, is autonomous from the ruler, the functions of non-judicial enforcement in private regulatory regimes reflect an expectation of responsiveness higher than that of judicial enforcement. As will be outlined below, this is a distinctive feature of private non-judicial enforcement.

6.7 The Degree of Centralization of Enforcement

Within transnational private regimes, we observe different models of non-judicial enforcement: some rather centralized, in order to ensure wider uniformity, others decentralized in order to reflect institutional diversity. Private enforcement mechanisms may have different degrees of centralization: they range from a single centralized body to moderate decentralized bodies, when for example many national SROs operate as adjudicatory

---

On the contrary it is highly unlikely that a non-member can bring a claim before the private body claiming that a regulated entity has violated the rules.

[97] A very prominent example in this regard is eBay's feedback system (for further information see: http://pages.ebay.com/help/feedback/allaboutfeedback.html), as well as numerous other electronic marketplaces that use similar systems, see e.g. Amazon.

[98] See Ruggie, 'Guiding Principles'.

bodies in the context of common guidelines provided by the transnational organization(s).[99]

When enforcement is centralized, the same dispute resolution regime will decide the claims regardless of national regimes.[100] In addition, centralized systems often use direct and indirect oversight, relying on compliance committees to control local regulators and the compliance by the regulated entities.

Decentralized enforcement, even with common rules, may generate different outcomes, considering different institutional approaches; some are focused on dispute resolution, others on facilitating bargaining among litigants for agreement negotiation.[101] As the case of advertising illustrates, while rule-making occurs both at the international (ICC code and various European-wide codes) and national level, enforcement is primarily administered by national SROs, guided by regional organizations.[102]

Frequently, centralized and decentralized systems are combined, depending on the nature of the dispute. For example, in e-commerce, organizations have internal dispute resolution mechanisms, and reference to arbitration for disputes concerning transactions taking place within the platforms.[103] In the field of technical standardization, the ISO has a

---

99 This is the case in advertising; see P. Verbruggen, in this volume, Chapter 11.

100 As the example of CAS-TAS in the sports field shows, the arbitrators sitting in the courts apply the law of the parties but have tried to generate a common body of principles commonly called *lex sportiva*. One of the main goals of the creation of CAS-TAS was that of reducing divergences generated by domestic courts in the litigation arising out of the application of the Olympic Charter. See L. Casini, *Il Diritto Globale Dello Sport*, Giuffrè Editore, 2010, pp. 215ff.

101 The highest degree of decentralization occurs when the transnational regime deploys arbitration and arbitrators are given wide discretion about both procedural and substantive rules. It is an open question whether references to arbitration in these disputes imply the application of commercial arbitration or whether the regulatory nature of the dispute and the field specificity require a different set of principles. In other regimes, like advertising, enforcement is highly decentralized for reasons related to the amount of claims and the necessity to consider local factors.

102 This model has developed in European advertising where the EASA operates as a coordinator and enacts 'Best Practice Recommendations' for national SROs, which act as the enforcers. These recommendations concern issues such as complaint handling, jury composition, monitoring, and appeal (available at http://www.easa-alliance.org/page.aspx/162). However, differences in procedural and substantive rules are still quite significant despite the coordination role played by the EASA.

103 For example when ICANN established a new framework for registering domain names, it also authorized a new process for the resolution of disputes arising out of domain names. Currently, the ICANN system for disputes over domain name registrations under the Uniform Dispute Resolution Policy (UDRP)

centralized dispute resolution system for disputes concerning members and an arbitration system for disputes arising out of standards application between purchasers of the standards and the organization.[104]

Both options have pros and cons. Centralized systems have the advantages of ensuring a higher degree of consistency, and easier, more effective dialogue with rule-makers and monitors but are subject to higher risks of capture and conflicts of interests. The accumulation of case law in a centralized system can contribute to the definition of a common set of rules that integrate the rule-making processes. When a centralized system exists, the advantages are mainly related to the uniformity it generates. When decentralization prevails, innovation and mutual learning can occur at the expense of stability and uniformity.

7. ON THE DIFFERENCES BETWEEN JUDICIAL AND PRIVATE NON-JUDICIAL ENFORCEMENT

The foregoing analysis suggests the existence of important differences between the two modes of enforcement. Some of them are worth examining further.

7.1 The Relationship Between Monitoring, Compliance and Enforcement

In judicial enforcement, monitoring is left either to the potentially injured parties or to an independent body, as it is often the case when certification is deployed. Monitoring compliance with TPR is therefore based on the incentives of parties who generally bring claims only after the fact. Private regulators infrequently use judicial enforcement to solve disputes with their members.

In private non-judicial enforcement monitoring, burdens are at least shared between the regulator and the parties. Incentives to monitor are driven not only by the seriousness of the potential harm and the probability of being granted the remedies, but also by the potential effects of litigation on the legitimacy of the regime. Parties may bring a claim to question or increase the legitimacy of private regulation.

---

is administered by a number of online dispute resolution (ODR) providers, all of which are required to arbitrate disputes.

[104] See Article 5.10 ISO Rules of Procedure, in particular the procedures concerning appeals and the power of the Council to solve disputes concerning action or inaction on the basis of a proposal by the Technical Management Board.

In private non-judicial enforcement, monitoring and enforcement are generally more strictly intertwined. Monitoring may be decentralized (by peers, i.e. the regulatees and the beneficiaries) and/or centralized (by a specific body). Often peer and hierarchical monitoring co-exist.[105] They link with enforcement in different ways, depending on the priorities selected by the regulator. Monitoring is also undertaken by specialized private intermediaries, driven by strategic considerations. In TPR, transnational and domestic NGOs have developed effective monitoring systems in order to bring claims before 'friendly' domestic courts.

In sum, the two enforcement models are grounded on different monitoring systems over the same rules, which may increase overall effectiveness, if effectively combined.

7.2 The Adversarial Nature of Judicial Enforcement Versus the Cooperative Nature of Private Enforcement

Judicial enforcement is conventionally characterized by the adversarial nature of the proceedings.[106] Injurers and victims are often seen as conflicting parties, each seeking to maximize their interests at the expense of the others. Conventionally, the higher the degree of multiple constituencies

---

[105] See the case for e-commerce in auction websites, where in order to safeguard users' interests and to facilitate the transparency of negotiations, eBay appoints its own users to perform such monitoring activity. Each party is asked to post a feedback on the behavior of their counterpart as soon as the transaction is completed. The introduction of such a technical tool provides a twofold positive effect: on the one hand, each potential buyer or seller can profit from the preceding activity performed by other users in order to determine the credibility of the offer and of the seller (E. Katsh, J. Rifkin & A. Gaitenby, 'E-Commerce, E-Disputes, and E-Dispute Resolution: In the Shadow of eBay Law', 15 *Ohio St. J. on Disp. Resol.* 705 (1999–2000)); on the other hand, whenever a transaction is positively concluded, the reputation of the website itself increases owing to the fact that the participants indirectly attribute part of the successful outcome to the electronic platform itself, thus encouraging both the participation of more users and the correctness of their behavior in the performance of contracts.

The FSC complaint system provides that: 'Any individual or organization may submit a formal complaint against the FSC Certification Scheme' (certification scheme is thereby defined broadly and also includes the accreditation or the policy and standards program, etc.) see: http://www.fsc.org/fileadmin/web-data/public/document_center/international_FSC_policies/procedures/FSC-PRO-01–009_V2–0_Processing_Formal_Complaints.pdf

[106] Given the differences between judicial systems this is certainly a generalization for the purpose of contrasting with non-judicial enforcement mechanisms.

within TPR, the lower the cooperative attitudes in enforcement practices.[107] However, through recent changes, new forms of judicial mediation and conciliation have reshaped the features of judicial enforcement, moderating the adversarial aspects while increasing cooperation. Several forms of cooperative enforcement have in fact been adopted in the domain of judicial enforcement.[108]

Non-judicial enforcement by private bodies, on the contrary, has endorsed, since the outset, a more cooperative approach, often characterized by different stages, aiming for an agreed upon solution.[109] In TPR, the litigants often share common interests in the regulatory process (protection of consumer safety along the supply chain, protection of the environment, labor standards), which increases the incentives to cooperate to appropriately resolve the dispute. This can explain why judicial enforcement is used more in disputes between members (regulator and/or regulated) and third parties, but rather rarely between members, where, given the long-term relationship between disputants, dispute resolution should not have disruptive effects over organization or the regulatory process.[110] In TPR the juxtaposition between adversarial (judicial) and cooperative (non-judicial) is, however, less significant than that emerging in traditional international business litigation between judicial enforcement and arbitration.

7.3 Access to Justice

Access to private enforcement mechanisms, especially by third parties, is more limited than access to judicial enforcement where public policy and

[107] Cooperative enforcement tends to occur in homogeneous business communities typical of conventional private regimes like *lex mercatoria*, not in multi-stakeholder regulatory regimes like the ones considered in this chapter.

[108] In the context of TPR, litigants can be regulatees who share an interest in the regulatory process. Even in judicial enforcement the litigation has to be reconciled with the necessity to cooperate in the common regulatory enterprise. Remedies can also trigger forms of cooperative enforcement when, for example, the outcome is a judgment ordering implementation of programs that ensure a higher level of compliance by the regulated, and thereby stronger effectiveness of the regulatory principles.

[109] Conventionally the two main models are associated with the ideal types of mediation and arbitration. This characterization, developed in the domestic realm, does not find perfect equivalence matching in the transnational world. See W. Mattli, 'Private Justice in a Global Economy: From Litigation to Arbitration', 55 *International Organizations*, 919 (2001); A. Casella, 'On Market Integration and the Development of Institutions: The Case of International Commercial Arbitration', 40 *Eur. Econ. Rev.* 155 (1996).

[110] Empirical research is needed to test and qualify this hypothesis.

constitutional principles require open accessibility.[111] Private enforcement often deploys membership in identifying those who have access to the dispute settlement mechanism and those to whom access is denied. Increasingly, exceptions arise, where private regimes have allowed for third-party access to non-members.[112]

Standing rules are generally more restrictive in private regimes than those applicable in national courts. In private regimes, organized through an associational model, standing is often granted exclusively or primarily to members. Such rules might undermine the legitimacy of the regulatory process since parties would neither have access to the proceeding nor the capacity to seek remedies for the violations. More significant differences concern the nature of the proceedings, that is, the degree of adversarial structure and the impartiality of the enforcer.[113]

---

[111] See J. Braithwaite, *Regulatory Capitalism: How it Works, Ideas for Making it Work Better*, Edward Elgar, 2008, pp. 174ff., proposing the introduction of organizational rules opening access to justice by private organizations.

[112] In the field of advertising, access has been widely granted. Not only do consumers, both individuals and organizations, have access, but public bodies can even bring a claim before the private enforcement body. While such bodies undertake monitoring exercises of their own accord, these claims constitute the main avenue for the regulator to discover code violations. This practice even feeds into the rule-making process: complaints filed with the enforcement body are used as a proxy by the regulator to determine where new codes need to be adopted or existing ones need to be amended.

[113] ISO only grants the right of appeal of decisions to national bodies (http://www.iso.org/iso/about/how_iso_develops_standards.htm), see ISO/IEC Directives and ISO supplement (http://www.iso.org/iso/standards_development/processes_and_procedures/iso_iec_directives_and_iso_supplement.htm); the FSC on the other hand allows for complaints of stakeholders, certifiers and other concerned parties (see: http://www.fsc.org/706.html). ICANN provides in its bylaws for 'a process by which any person or entity materially affected by an action of ICANN may request review or reconsideration of that action by the Board' (Section 2 reconsideration) (http://www.icann.org/en/general/bylaws.htm#IV). The MSC also provides that a third party which can establish that the 'failure of certification body to follow procedures prevented or substantially impaired the objecting party's participation in the fishery assessment process' may submit a notice of objection (Technical Advisory Board Directive TAB D-023 v3, Sec. 4.4.1.(c), available at: http://www.msc.org/documents/scheme-documents/directives/TAB_D_023_Objections_Procedure.pdf).

In the case of advertising, the enforcement procedures followed before the SRO juries differ widely. In the UK, the procedure assumes an inquisitorial nature in which the British SRO (the Advertising Standards Authority) acts very much like a public prosecutor in investigating and trying the advertising complaint. In France and the Netherlands, by contrast, the proceedings are more adversarial in nature and allow the complainant to submit his views during the SRO proceedings. In

In judicial enforcement, there is generally wider scope to file complaints but less opportunity for direct participation in litigation. The right to access to justice constitutes a fundamental component of national legal systems' defining criteria for participation in judicial proceedings. Stakeholder accessibility to enforcement mechanisms has become ever more important in private non-judicial disputes resolution for the relevance of due process which limits the exercise of freedom of contract.

In non-judicial private enforcement, standing is generally narrower but the effects of enforcement have a wider scope. Often, for example, individual consumers or consumer organizations can bring a complaint but will not technically participate in the proceedings.[114] They are 'used' as monitoring agents but the private enforcer conducts the investigation and proceedings.[115] This occurs when the model, adopted by the private enforcer, is inquisitorial rather than adversarial.

7.4 The Nature and Scope of Remedies

This section concerns the objectives of sanctioning in TPR and the choice and scope of remedies and the principles driving enforcers' decisions. In particular, differences relate to the combination of compensation and deterrence, both the role of organizational sanctions and the relevance of repeated violations.

First, in relation to principles, it should be noted that while the right to an effective remedy has been recognized within judicial enforcement, both domestically and internationally, the effectiveness principle has not received the same recognition in private non-judicial enforcement.[116] This general principle provides the judge with a significant discretionary power, especially if no adequate remedies are available. The recognition of the effectiveness principle in non-judicial enforcement would permit a wider discretion,

---

addition, the EASA has tried to make sure that all of its SRO members have a jury, taking its decisions independently of the industry that funds its operations. With the exception of the German Deutscher Werberat, all SRO members have a jury that is partly composed of non-industry members. See P. Verbruggen, in this volume, Chapter 11.

[114] See below at note 136.

[115] References to NGOs as private prosecutors are generally made less often in the context of judicial enforcement than in non-judicial enforcement. See J. Braithwaite (above, note 111), pp. 73ff.

[116] For example, the right to an effective remedy has been recognized at the European level by ECHR Article 6. Given the application of Article 6 to private enforcers, albeit within limits defined by the Court, effectiveness should also be required in non-judicial private enforcement.

providing greater adaptability, especially when procedural rules are relatively narrow. Clearly, this recognition should not translate into arbitrary, discretionary power of the enforcer. Effectiveness and due process must be carefully balanced to define the sanctioning power of private enforcers.

Similarly, the principle of proportionality, related both to procedural and sanctioning aspects, has been recognized within judicial enforcement but is applied unevenly across transnational private regimes and types of enforcers.

Secondly, different remedies are available in judicial and private enforcement since they are aimed at protecting divergent complementary interests.

In judicial enforcement, remedies focus primarily on redress for the violation. They are not concerned with regulatory incapacity, but rather with the motivation that induced the infringer to breach the rule. Compensatory remedies are predominant, though injunctive relief plays some role.[117] Little relevance is attached to organizational sanctions and to the repeat nature of the infringement. The focus is primarily on individual behavior, not on the impact of the violation on the overall regime or its collective or 'community' dimension.[118] The credibility of the regulator when punishing the regulatee is not of paramount concern. Judicial remedies rarely capture the effects of the violation on the regime and rewards are similarly often missing.

In private non-judicial enforcement, sanctions have a double scope: deterring wrongful behavior and inducing cooperation among the members, regulator and regulated entities to increase regulatory capacity. The violation is understood to simultaneously harm both individual and collective interests. In many instances sanctioning aims at restoring the effectiveness of the regulatory process and at preserving the objectives of the

---

[117] In the advertising field injunctive relief was, for example, requested by advertisers whose ads have been considered to violate the British Advertising Standards Authority Act. However, courts hardly granted relief, see *R.* v *Advertising Standards Authority Ltd ex parte Direct Line Financial Services* [1997] EWHC 770 (Admin); and *R.* v *Advertising Standards Authority ex parte Debt Free Direct* [2007] EWHC 1337 (Admin). In the financial markets area the Belgian Trade Practices and Consumer Protection and Information Act, for example, explicitly provides for injunctions in order to stop a supplier or provider from continuing with forbidden practices.

[118] Clearly judges are well aware of the interests harmed by the violation. It is often the law that does not provide adequate tools to protect collective interests, focusing rather on the individual. This question has been recently addressed in the debate concerning the expansion of aggregate litigation and its 'exceptionalism' in civil justice. See S. Issacharoff & G. Miller, 'Will Aggregate Litigation Come to Europe?', 62 *Vanderbilt L. Rev.* (2009) 179.

regime. There is a stronger link to responsiveness and the collective nature of the regulatory regime than in judicial enforcement.

Among pecuniary remedies, compensatory damages are very rare, while private fines are used to deter wrongful behavior and reward effective monitoring.[119] The amount of the pecuniary sanction is generally not correlated to the victim's harm, but rather to the 'seriousness' of the violation. In sum, compliance rather than compensation is the primary goal, even when pecuniary remedies are adopted.

Consequently in TPRs' enforcement by private bodies, when a breach of the contract between regulators and regulated or a violation of the code of conduct occurs, significant weight is attributed to the *repeat nature of the violations*. When the member of the organization is a repeat infringer, several TPRs correlate the sanction and its severity to the seriousness of the breach; repeat violations naturally trigger stronger sanctions.[120]

In private non-judicial enforcement, sanctions are often combined with rewards, which is rather rare in judicial enforcement. A typical example concerns access to other regulatory regimes conditional upon compliance in the field of certification. Compliant regulated entities are allowed to take part in other regulatory regimes and/or are recognized with higher reputational status.[121] Often, only regulated entities compliant with codes of

---

[119] In the case of advertising, sector-specific agreements between sectoral organizations and the SROs might render the SRO competent to levy private fines. In the field of sports, TAS/CAS and the lower enforcers have the power to levy fines. In the field of e-commerce, some electronic trade platforms (Craigslist) have the power to fine traders who commit violations.

[120] See in e-commerce the eBay case where the seller rating requirements define a minimum performance standard, and where, after three negative complaints from a buyer's counterparties, eBay can provide for the following consequences ' ... your search placement will be lowered and there may be limits to your selling activity until your ratings improve. You may also be restricted from selling items on eBay if your performance falls significantly below the minimum requirements. If your account doesn't meet the standards, you: Need to resolve all issues on the account before buying or selling with other accounts; Can't register for a new account; Can't use an existing eBay account to avoid buying and selling limits or other policy consequences' (http://pages.ebay.com/help/policies/seller-non-performance.html).

In food safety GLOBALGAP provides an interesting example where the sanctions range from warnings, to product suspension, and, finally, to contract cancellation. Each of the steps requires a different intervention of the regulator and increasing limitations to the member.

[121] The use of rewards occurs in many sectors, ranging from electronic trading platforms to food safety and environmental regulation: for example in the online behavioral advertising framework, compliance is rewarded with a seal which can subsequently be removed in the case of a failure to comply. See European self-regulation for online behavioral advertising, IAB, 2011. 'Through an innovation in

conduct or soft law principles are allowed to access a market. This is the case for private companies engaged in military activities.[122]

7.5 The Discretion of the Enforcer and its Relationship with the Litigants

Differences between the two families of enforcement also concern the discretion of the enforcer in selecting remedies not defined by the law or by private regulatory instruments like the code, charter, or bylaw.

In public adjudication, the enforcer enjoys some level of discretion but it is often constrained by the menu of legal remedies available and more generally, by the due process principle.[123] Remedies are often defined in mandatory provisions and the scope for private autonomy is limited.[124] The power of selecting remedies differs between interim and final measures. In the domain of the former the judge enjoys more discretion than in that of the latter. Those regimes that still distinguish between equity and law provide additional leeway to the judge while finding the adequate and effective remedy.

In enforcement by private bodies, the power of the enforcer is constrained within the remedies stated by the contract or by the charter and the bylaw. As the litigation concerning review of arbitral awards shows often there might be no coincidence between the choices made by contracting parties and the applicable laws indicated in the arbitration clause giving the arbitrator some degree of interpretive discretion. Here, parties enjoy wider powers to define remedies than in judicial enforcement where they are 'bound' by the law. However, constitutional constraints, grounded on international or domestic charters, similarly apply, albeit with limited effects on private non-judicial enforcement.[125] Whether the private enforcer

---

self-regulation, the OBA framework introduces a new procedure to measure compliance with the commitments and establishes a system of pan-European enforcement for signatory companies. Compliant companies will receive a periodically renewable B2B seal. Should a company fall behind and not remedy a significant breach of its obligations within a limited timeframe, the seal would be removed'. See the OBA framework, available at http://www.iabeurope.eu/media/51925/iab%20 europe%20oba%20framework_merged%20ii.pdf

[122] See, generally F. Francioni & N. Ronzitti (eds) *War by Contract: Human Rights, Humanitarian Law, and Private Contractors*, Oxford University Press, 2011; L.A. Dickinson, *Outsourcing War and Peace: Preserving Public Values in a World of Privatized Foreign Affairs*, Yale University Press, 2011.

[123] See A. Zuckerman, *Zuckerman on Civil Procedure: Principles of Practice*, 2nd edn, Sweet & Maxwell, 2006, Chapter 22.

[124] However contracting over procedural terms is growing; see Davis & Hershkoff, note 60 above.

[125] See above at p. 14.

enjoys more freedom than the judge in the choice of the appropriate remedies requires further investigation.[126] Furthermore the legal form of the enforcer has an impact on its discretion. For example, the adoption of a non-profit form does in principle imply compliance with the business judgment rule, which might be incompatible with the principles of fair trial in a regulatory environment. In particular it might reduce the impartiality and transparency and overall accountability of private enforcement. However, some decisions by private enforcers suggest that the pursuit of regulatory objectives could limit the scope of the business judgment rule and enhance accountability via due process.[127]

In judicial enforcement, both the enforcer's discretion and the parties' freedom to seek new remedies are narrow. The opposite is true in private non-judicial enforcement where both domestic and constitutional due process limitations apply.[128]

---

[126] For example GLOBALGAP, when listing sanctions for the certification bodies (see General Regulations, Integrated Farm Assurance, Part II, 2), groups the performance of certifiers into categories from #1 (very bad performance) to #5 (high performance). If the certification is within a lower category, particular sanctions prescribed within the regulations will be issued by the Integrity and Surveillance Committee (General Regulations, Integrated Farm Assurance, Part II, Annex II).

eBay provides: 'Without limiting other remedies, we may limit, suspend or terminate our service and user accounts, prohibit access to our sites and their content, services and tools, delay or remove hosted content, and take technical and legal steps to keep users off the sites if we think that they are creating problems or possible legal liabilities, infringing the intellectual property rights of third parties, or acting inconsistently with the letter or spirit of our policies (for example, and without limitation, policies related to shill bidding, conducting off-eBay transactions, feedback manipulation, circumventing temporary or permanent suspensions or users who we believe are harassing our employees or other users). Additionally, we may, in appropriate circumstances and at our discretion, suspend or terminate accounts of users who may be repeat infringers of intellectual property rights of third parties. We also reserve the right to cancel unconfirmed accounts or accounts that have been inactive for a long time, or to modify or discontinue eBay sites, services or tools' (http://pages.ebay.com/help/policies/user-agreement.html).

[127] *International Centre for Dispute Resolution, ICM Registry, LLC* v *Internet Corporation for Assigned Names and Numbers*, Declaration of the Independent Review Panel, ICDR Case No. 50 117 T 00224 08, February 19, 2010, pp. 61ff. The Panel limited the applicability of the Business Judgment Rule on a decision made by the ICANN Board, stating that: ' … ICANN is no ordinary non-profit California corporation. The Government of the United States vested regulatory authority of vast dimension and pervasive global reach in ICANN'.

[128] Paradigmatic is the example of arbitration, where the scope for identifying ad hoc remedies is higher.

A second related difference concerns the relationship between the enforcer and litigants: while in private non-judicial enforcement, the relationship is repeated, as it would be in the administrative enforcement by public regulators, in judicial enforcement the relationship is random unless the parties specify a particular forum, identifying a single competent court.

7.6 Compliance with Sanctions

One of the most important differences between the two modes of enforcement is related to the means used to ensure compliance with the sanctions. In order to increase incentives for compliance, the codes of conduct or the association bylaws often provide clauses defining compliance as a legal obligation to which members of the regulatory regime subscribe. In the case of non-compliance, a claim for breach of contract can be brought by the private enforcer or by some of the members before the competent domestic court. In addition, parties may insert a contractual term that binds them to comply with the judgment issued by the private enforcer.[129]

While judicial enforcement employs strong means to deter non-compliance with sanctions, private systems are relatively weak and they rely on judicial intervention as the last legal resort. Enforceability of the awards, as arbitration shows, may become a problem.[130] If the sanctioned party does not comply – for instance, in the case of a misleading advertisement, the correction does not take place, or in food safety, the changes to the

---

129 See Article 26 ICC Code on Advertising and Marketing Communication Practice 2006: 'All parties are encouraged to include in their contracts and other agreements pertaining to advertising and other marketing communication, a statement committing the signatories to adhere to the applicable self-regulatory rules and to respect decisions and rulings made by the appropriate self-regulatory body'. The code is available at www.iccwbo.org.

130 Within arbitration, enforcement of awards is more problematic in ad hoc arbitration than in institutional arbitration. It is generally acknowledged that institutional arbitration increases the prospective enforceability of arbitral awards by domestic courts, as institutional procedures involve a number of procedural safeguards which ensure that the conduct of the proceedings is in accordance with the parties' will expressed in their agreement. Although arbitral awards rendered both in ad hoc or institutional proceedings shall be enforced in the same manner and according to the same criteria, it is widely acknowledged that both the parties and national courts have more trust in institutional awards. As regards institutional arbitration, there is also a reputational factor which may have a psychological impact on the enforceability of institutional arbitral awards. See L. Mistelis, *International Arbitration: Corporate Attitudes and Practices 2008*, available at: http://www.pwc.co.uk/pdf/PwC_International_Arbitration_2008.pdf; A. Clarke, 'International Arbitration: Current Corporate Concerns', 20 (2) *ICC Int'l Court of Arbitration Bulletin* (2009).

production process in compliance with the standards to which the regulated entity has subscribed are not effectuated – the private enforcer has no effective legal power to ensure compliance. It can resort primarily to organizational sanctions: shaming, suspension or termination of membership.[131] The effectiveness of these sanctions is proportional to the infringer's benefits in retaining membership in the regime. When incentives are low, enforceability of sanctions by private enforcement is primarily ensured by domestic courts because organizational sanctions do not represent a credible threat. This is a clear case of enforcement complementarity: organizational sanctions are primarily administered by private enforcers but their compliance needs to be assured by (the threat of) domestic courts.

7.7 Due Process

The level of procedural guarantees concerning, in particular, the impartiality of the enforcer and transparency of the proceedings remains much higher in judicial than in private enforcement, due primarily to constitutional principles prescribing due process.[132] Domestic courts are bound to comply with due process requirements and in particular with transparency and impartiality. More recently, the right to an effective remedy has been deemed enforceable before national and international courts.[133]

Private enforcers' activity is regulated by contractual or by organizational arrangements where freedom of contract of the litigants within the regime is warranted a much stronger role. Parties' freedom of contract is

---

[131] In the case of advertising, a powerful mechanism at the disposal of the separate enforcement bodies to enforce compliance with their decisions is the request to the affiliated media to stop the publication or use of the advertising that violated the code. Since the bulk of advertising made today relies on the media to reach its audience, the request to the media can enforce compliance with the decisions in the majority of cases. See J.J. Boddewyn, 'Advertising Self-regulation: True Purpose and Limits', 18(2) *Journal of Advertising*, 19 (1989).

[132] See R. Caponi, *General Report, XIV International Congress of Civil Procedure, Procedural Justice in a Globalized World*, Heidelberg, 2011.

[133] See e.g. Article 47 of the Charter of Fundamental Rights of the European Union, which states: 'Right to an effective remedy and to a fair trial. Everyone whose rights and freedoms guaranteed by the law of the Union are violated has the right to an effective remedy before a tribunal in compliance with the conditions laid down in this Article ...'. Taking the *Bosman* (C-415/93) ruling into consideration this would also apply to such cases of private regulation.

nevertheless limited by the principles of procedural fairness.[134] International charters and domestic constitutions also impose principles of due process on private justice.

Due process also affects the governance of the private enforcer, who is often part of the same organization in which the rule-maker sits. Insufficient functional separation still exists, thereby undermining the impartiality of the enforcer. Recently, however, as a result of pressure from external, and to some extent even internal, actors, many transnational regimes have opted for an external and independent enforcement mechanism. These transformations have taken place in two different ways: by creating a new body with a different composition and independent resources or by externalizing enforcement to existing bodies, either private or public.

Recent developments show greater openness of private enforcement towards non-members and third parties. The wider degree of participation in the rule-making process by way of recognizing rights to participate and to be heard is partly mirrored in the enforcement proceedings.[135]

Private enforcers have to comply with somewhat different procedural rules from those of judicial enforcement. Some of them have been recently reformed to include higher transparency and openness of the proceedings. Others still feature enforcement as an internal matter of the 'organization', rendering it inaccessible to the public. Lack of publicity impacts the

---

[134] As mentioned above, freedom of contract plays a different role according to the class of the dispute. Symmetrically, the limitations imposed by procedural fairness operate differently. See above text and note, p. 103ff. For procedural fairness in arbitration, see G.A. Bermann, 'Mandatory Rules of Law in International Arbitration', 18 *American Review of International Arbitration* (2007) 1; and id., 'Mandatory Rules in International Commercial Arbitration', in: F. Ferrari & S. Kroll, *Conflict of Laws in International Arbitration*, Sellier, 2010, p, 325, in relation to the Arbitration Fairness Act and the new UNCITRAL Principles.

[135] In the case of advertising, the participation of third parties (e.g. consumers, NGOs, public authorities) has moved from involvement in enforcement procedures (as members of the separate bodies enforcing codes of conduct) to the involvement of third parties in the adoption of codes via consultation processes. See, for a discussion, J.J. Boddewyn, *Advertising Self-regulation and Outside Participation: A Multinational Comparison*, Quorum Books, 1988, and for the new practice in Europe: EASA Best Practice Recommendations, 'Code Drafting and Consultation' 2008, available at: http://www.easa-alliance.org/page.aspx/162. See also the FSC Dispute Settlement regime which provides that: 'Any individual or organization may submit a formal complaint against the FSC Certification Scheme' ('certification scheme' is thereby defined broadly and also includes the accreditation or the policy and standards program, etc.) (http://www.fsc.org/fileadmin/web-data/public/document_center/international_FSC_policies/procedures/FSC-PRO-01–009_V2–0_Processing_Formal_Complaints.pdf).

effectiveness of the enforcement process and undermines social and economic control, thereby decreasing accountability.

7.8 Effects of the Judgment

Different concerns relate to the judgment's precedential character and the reach of its binding nature. Very seldom do private regimes regulate the precedential value of judgments issued by their enforcers. In many private regimes, the effects of the judgment related to the individual dispute are binding on all members.[136] This rule demonstrates the strong community dimension of private enforcement and the resonant correlation with the rule-making process, since rules defined within the adjudicatory process become part of the common rules regulating members' activity. On the contrary, in judicial enforcement, the judgment generally affects only the litigants, and specific rules are required to further extend its effect. Unlike judicial enforcement, where the decentralized model reduces the regulatory function, judgments issued by private enforcers have a powerful regulatory function.

8. WHY DO DIFFERENCES SUGGEST COMPLEMENTARITY BETWEEN JUDICIAL AND PRIVATE ENFORCEMENT OF TPR?

The two systems, judicial and non-judicial private enforcement, should be understood as complementary rather than alternative. They generally operate on parallel tracks, but for mandatory arbitration or equivalent clauses that prevent parties from using the judicial system to solve disputes, except in cases of public policy violations.[137] In that case, private non-judicial enforcement becomes the almost exclusive avenue for dispute resolution. The notion of parallel tracks does not imply absence of coordination

---

[136] For example in the field of advertising some codes explicitly state the rule. See the Spanish Code of Advertising Practice: Scope of Application and General Rules, Article 7 Enforceability of the decisions, 'The Jury's decisions are binding for the interested parties and for the remainder of the members' (http://www.autocontrol.es/pdfs/cod_pub _ingles.pdf).

Similar provisions exist in the British Code of Advertising, Sales Promotion and Direct Marketing 2008 (Article 60.21; available at: http://bcap.org.uk/The-Codes/CAP-Code.aspx) and the Italian Code of Marketing Communication (Article 41; available at: http://www.iap.it/en/code.htm).

[137] See below at p. 127.

through different devices, including hierarchy.[138] Coordination may be regulated by domestic laws or by the private regulator and by the contracts signed by regulatees to implement the regimes. However, the definition of complementarity by private autonomy is limited. For example, many legal systems do not allow private parties to define the scope of judicial review of their agreements, even when they would like to expand the review in order to increase regulatory accountability.

As we shall see, both temporal and spatial coordination constitutes the key concern in implementing complementarity effectively.

In relation to the two mechanisms, the differences with domestic enforcement are clear. While the regulatory function of judicial enforcement is generally stronger than that of private justice at the domestic level, the opposite might be true in relation to individual regulatory regimes at the transnational level.[139]

These differences render complementarity attractive but costly. The relationship between private non-judicial and judicial enforcement presents specific characteristics, depending on the sector. It is useful to distinguish between a structural and functional perspective of institutional complementarity between enforcement mechanisms.

9. STRUCTURAL COMPLEMENTARITY MAY OPERATE IN RELATION TO PLACE AND TIME

As we have seen, in theory, both judicial and private non-judicial enforcement may have a centralized or a decentralized structure, or a combination of the two.

---

[138] There is some review power by domestic courts of the judgments issued by the private enforcers to scrutinize their compliance with general contract, or organizational rules. This review power defines also some, albeit limited, hierarchical features of the relationship between the two.

[139] Private dispute resolution mechanisms are characterized by secrecy and confidentiality, rarely produce effects beyond the litigants, and their 'precedential' value is limited. Similar features exist also at the transnational level, where the dialogue between enforcement and rule-making is much closer, especially for disputes arising between the regulator and the regulated entities and among the latter.

Judicial enforcement of TPR generally forms a multilevel structure across territorial domains,[140] with domestic enforcement being complemented by supranational courts operating at regional or global level.

Private enforcement is primarily organized through functional rather than territorial boundaries. It operates either through centralized mechanisms or through a decentralized set of enforcers, as in the case of advertising and certain areas of CSR, organized within multilevel systems.

Spatially, four different combinations of the two enforcement systems can be identified in relation to the multilevel enforcement architecture of transnational private regulation:

1. Purely decentralized (plurality of domestic courts and private enforcers).
2. Mixed (Domestic courts and a centralized private enforcer).
3. Mixed (International court and a plurality of local private enforcers).
4. Purely centralized (one international court and one private international enforcer).

The first and last scenarios are rare (1) or non-existent (4). The main concentration occurs between the two intermediate scenarios, giving rise to different coordination problems, since two rather different concepts of jurisdictions operate: one territorial and the other functional.

9.1 Simultaneous and Sequential Enforcement: Judicial and Non-judicial

A second structural dimension of complementarity is the timeframe. From this perspective, it is useful to distinguish between simultaneous and sequential enforcement.[141] Both represent complementarity but each presents specific features.

Simultaneous enforcement occurs when the same or different claims are simultaneously brought before one or more domestic courts and a private enforcement body.

---

[140] On multilevel judicial governance see E.U. Petersmann, 'Justice as Conflict Resolution: Proliferation, Fragmentation and Decentralization of Dispute Settlement in International Trade', 2 *U. Penn. J. Int'l Econ. L.* 273 (2006); H. Buxbaum, 'Territory, Territoriality and the Resolution of Jurisdictional Conflict', 57 *Am. J. Comp. L.* 631ff. (2009).

[141] This distinction is commonly employed while describing the relationship between administrative (public) and judicial (private) enforcement.

Sequential enforcement takes place when, either by virtue of choice or legal constraints, infringements must be scrutinized firstly by one type of enforcement mechanism, and, only subsequently, by the other.

Sequentiality can be required by law or by private arrangement, when parties undertake the obligation to bring the claim first before the private enforcer and only thereafter before the competent domestic court.[142] Sequential enforcement takes place when the private enforcer's judgment does not constitute *res judicata* as is the case in arbitration, but it allows the subsequent enforcer a high degree of freedom to reconsider the dispute. Different links might exist: the most natural is the appeal before a court, but in theory, a separate and unconnected claim can be brought before a court without reference to the decision made by the private enforcer. At national level, independent private enforcement regimes often require that litigants wait until the judgment has been issued;[143] the opposite occurs when litigants are asked to mediate or arbitrate before they avail themselves of judicial proceedings.[144] This is rarely the case at the transnational level because claims may be brought before several domestic courts simultaneously and the outcomes may differ. An additional advantage of sequentiality is the possibility of reducing inconsistency among judgments. As we have seen, inconsistency among domestic courts is one of the main problems for transnational regimes, and can be tackled in different ways.[145] Some regimes, in response to inconsistency, include a clause defining a

---

[142] In the case of advertising, in Europe administrative authorities may require prior recourse to private enforcers. See Article 11(1) of EC Directive 2005/29 on unfair commercial practices and Article 5(2) of Directive 2006/114 on misleading and comparative advertising.

[143] In the case of advertising, procedural rules often require the private enforcer to suspend its proceedings until the domestic courts have decided the case.

[144] See the case in the Italian user agreement, where it is provided that 'Mediazione e Arbitrato. Tutte le controversie derivanti dal presente Accordo, ove il valore complessivo della controversia sia inferiore a EUR 10.000 (diecimila euro), potranno essere devolute al tentativo di conciliazione previsto dal Servizio di Mediazione e Conciliazione Online della Camera Arbitrale di Milano. Nel caso di mancata conciliazione, la controversia sarà risolta da un arbitro unico, in conformità al Regolamento Arbitrale della Camera Arbitrale di Milano. L'arbitrato avrà luogo presso la sede della Camera Arbitrale di Milano'.

[145] Some have claimed, mainly in relation to international public law, that international rule of law requires consistency even among courts which are not part of the same legal system. See J. Waldron, 'Partly Laws Common to All Mankind: Foreign Law in American Courts', Storrs Lectures delivered at Yale Law School, p. 25, available at http://www.iilj.org/

single applicable law and a single *lex fori* in order to avoid this problem.[146] In this context, all the matters concerning violations of the regulatory regime are brought before a single domestic court, which must apply one state's law. The monopoly of a single court can provide more certainty and stability but decreases regulatory innovation.

When parties can choose between simultaneous or sequential enforcement, the choice is based on several factors that we can briefly examine in order to clarify the notion of complementarity between the enforcement systems.

Sequentiality may occur as a result of strategic considerations of the litigants. A first consideration concerns the evidentiary role of the private judgment in court. If courts allow the private judgment as evidence in their proceedings, parties might have incentives to bring the claim before the private enforcer first and then use the results in the court proceedings.[147]

A second factor affecting the choice between simultaneous or sequential enforcement relates to the nature of available remedies and their influence on the choices between different enforcement mechanisms. When remedies are complementary, claimants may choose to bring simultaneous claims before different enforcers. When they are alternative, they will probably choose sequentiality in order to maximize the chances for access to the most favorable remedy.

The identity of the litigants, whether they are third parties, NGOs or other firms, and their strategic incentives to litigate, may also influence the choice of enforcement mechanism and the sequence, if both will be activated.

A third and, perhaps, more important dimension of complementarity, related to sequentiality, concerns the role of courts in enforcing private

---

[146] See e.g. ICANN, where any dispute outside the foreseen arbitration venue should be brought before a court located in Los Angeles, California (see: http://www.icann.org/en/registrars/ra-agreement-21may09-en.htm); eBay provides in its user agreements that conflicts shall be exclusively resolved by state or federal courts located in Santa Clara County, California (http://pages.ebay.com/help/policies/user-agreement.html?rt=nc).

[147] See in the case of ICANN, where the possibility to initiate legal proceedings before a court is not only allowed but it is also included in the UDRP procedure, either before the end of the dispute resolution proceeding, stopping the latter; or when the decision has already been taken, stopping the enforcement of the decision. In this sense, the court proceedings could be interpreted as a 'safety net' for the protection of the interests that were not taken into account within the dispute resolution systems (e.g. damages).

sanctions or scrutinizing the liability of private enforcers. Private non-judicial enforcement often operates, therefore, 'under the shadow' of judicial enforcement. Often, the private regimes lack the legal means to enforce the sanctions if the wrongdoer refuses to comply. Since most of these regimes are contractual or organizational, there is a legal duty on the wrongdoer to comply, and the private enforcer or the victim can bring a legal claim before a court to enforce the imposed private penalty. Non-compliance amounts to a breach of contract or a breach of the duty of loyalty in organizational models. As noted earlier, many of the private regulators seek immunity from liability through contractual disclaimers. Domestic courts are frequently asked to verify whether contractual immunity can be enforced according to domestic contract and tort law. Accordingly, domestic private law regimes complement internal regulation concerning immunity from liability or limitations concerning remedies and other rules of (civil) procedure.

A fourth related aspect of sequentiality concerns the domestic courts' review of awards issued by private enforcers. Courts are asked in the field of arbitration, and to a very limited extent but increasingly and more broadly in other types of non-judicial enforcement, to review judgments in relation to sanctions to verify whether they comply with public policy.[148]

10. THE INSTITUTIONAL DESIGN OF TRANSNATIONAL ENFORCEMENT: REFRAMING COMPLEMENTARITY

The four structural dimensions of complementarity just described suggest that coordination between the two enforcement mechanisms encompasses

---

[148] In the field of sport, reviews of TAS/CAS awards by the Swiss Federal Tribunal are allowed if there is a violation of public policy that can translate into violations of general principles like sanctity of contracts, abuse of right, violation of non-discrimination, violation of good faith. The Swiss Federal Tribunal contends that a TAS ruling will be annulled if not only the reasoning but also the result is contrary to public policy. See Federal Tribunal, Decision of November 24th 2010, BGE 132 III 389 SC.2 2 pp. 392ff; Federal Tribunal, Decision of January 5th 2007, 4P 240/2006, Federal Tribunal, Decision of September 28th 2010, 4A 144/2010.

In the field of internet governance, it is well settled under federal law that a federal court may overrule a UDRP panel decision, see *Storey* v *Cello Holdings, L.L.C.*, 347 F.3d 370 (2d Cir. 2003); *Sallen* v *Corinthians Licenciamontos LTDA*, 273 F.3d 14 (1st Cir. 2001). Moreover, review of UDRP decisions in a federal court is *de novo*, as in cases *Barcelona.com, Inc.* v *Excelentisimo Ayuntamiento de Barcelona*, 330 F.3d 617 (4th Cir. 2003); *Dluhos* v *Strasberg*, 321 F.3d 365 (3d Cir. 2003).

very complex variables, especially in decentralized systems, where both judicial and private enforcement may spawn several proceedings concerning the same violations.

From a functional perspective, complementarity permits mixing between enforcement proceedings operating with different goals. The private enforcement mechanisms are often primarily directed at protecting the collective interests of the regulatory regime by ensuring the compliance of regulated entities and providing protection from third parties' interference. They reflect an ongoing relational process between regulators and regulated and feed back into the rule-making process. There is an increasing, albeit still limited, role of beneficiaries and third parties where the system is made accessible to consumer and human rights organizations by granting them standing or, at least, scope to lodge a complaint. Limited attention is paid to the violation of fundamental rights, although in some areas, like CSR and advertising, the protection of human rights is increasingly becoming the focus of private enforcement mechanisms. However, judicial enforcement remains the milestone for the protection of fundamental rights in private regulation. This is true both to ensure compliance with commitments made in codes of conduct by MNCs and to ensure that private regulation violating general principles of non-discrimination, freedom of association, and labor standards are set aside. The important role of judicial enforcement does not imply that full and satisfactory protection is currently achieved through international and domestic courts.[149]

Complementarity emerges in relation to sanctions. Judicial enforcement is mainly focused on the compensation of violations, and only to a limited extent on deterrence. The predominance of compensatory goals renders the relationship between enforcement output and rule-making less significant. Only when domestic courts use injunctive power, for example in the area of product and food safety or advertising, as well as in some environmental sub-sectors, does the correlation with rule-making become more prominent, because the remedy affects the regulatory instruments, and, indirectly, the relationship between ends and means.[150] Non-judicial enforcement instead focuses primarily on deterrence and on improving the regulatory relationship between regulator and regulatees. The link with rule-making is much stricter; the primary goal is to ensure effectiveness of the regulatory

[149] On the limits of judicial enforcement see C. Estlund, in this volume, Chapter 8.

[150] For example, if a court issues an injunction to correct an advertisement, reducing its deceptiveness, this affects the activity of the regulated entity and, indirectly, that of the private regulator, more effectively than a compensatory remedy.

process. Organizational rather than individual sanctions are the main instruments. The combined operation of both enforcement mechanisms against the same violation facilitates the integration of the different protection of different interests relevant in the disputes. Generally, however, remedies deployed are only partially tailored to meet regulatory needs as they were developed for different purposes. Transnational private autonomy can operate to reshape them, but only within the limits afforded by national constitutions and international principles.

Complementarity pertains also to the combination of procedural and substantive requirements. Domestic courts, in particular in the US, have been particularly sensitive to procedural requirements and due process principles in private non-judicial enforcement. However, many procedural guarantees, recognized before domestic courts, are often still ignored or rejected by private enforcers.

Clearly, functional complementarity of enforcement mechanisms presents advantages that should be more carefully scrutinized when domestic courts are asked to consider the enforceability of mandatory arbitration or similar functional equivalents, thereby preventing parties from accessing courts.

11. CONCLUSIONS

In this chapter, the importance of enforcement for transnational private regulation has been highlighted. Different enforcement mechanisms are in place, mainly operating as complementary devices to pursue different goals or similar goals through different means. We have illustrated the complementarity of both instruments and objectives. Complementarity is partly a consequence of constitutional principles at domestic level and partly a choice in the design of enforcement by law or by private actors. It is a necessary consequence because there are limits on private parties' scope to exclude judicial enforcement and to opt for purely private mechanisms. Judicial enforcement by national courts preserves values and interests of sovereign states confronted with increasing transfer of regulatory powers to private actors, often outside their borders. Complementarity also occurs because private enforcement regimes must resort to judicial enforcement when wrongdoers do not comply with the private judgments.

A multiplicity of enforcement mechanisms poses both coordination problems within enforcement policy, and requires more complex governance responses to preserve the 'dialogue' with transnational private law makers. The notion of judicial comity and the German concept of *Verbund* represent different perspectives on judicial coordination. It is likely, however, that coordination between courts and private enforcers requires more innovation given that it applies to enforcement systems already internally fragmented.

The dialogue between enforcers and rule-makers is of strategic importance for the development of TPR. This dialogue occurs both with domestic courts and private enforcers, subject to the potential divergences or conflicts described earlier. Within the sphere of private non-judicial enforcement, the analysis has evidenced a trend towards higher independence of private non-judicial enforcement from standard setters, which enhances legitimacy but which may also reduce the effectiveness of the regulatory process. Independence is part of procedural due process and must be pursued, but it comes with costs that must be factored into the institutional design. The alternative between first and third-party enforcers illustrates some of these complex trade-offs. A clear trade-off between legitimacy and effectiveness of transnational private regulation is posed by independence and decentralization of enforcement. Independent enforcers may not fully internalize systemic considerations concerning regimes as internal adjudicatory bodies would. As independence and decentralization increase, coordination costs increase, while the levels of effectiveness decline. However, effectiveness can also be undermined by complementarity if coordination costs rise too high. TPR is enforced by complementary mechanisms, which combine judicial and private enforcement at the domestic and international level, giving rise to several possible combinations between space (decentralized versus centralized) and time (simultaneous versus sequential).

The ability of private regulators to define coordination mechanisms, through contract and by choosing applicable substantive law and the *lex fori*, establishes significant coordination power among the enforcement mechanisms.[151] However, these choices are often made in order to minimize liability or to limit third-party litigation rather than as a result of considerations of efficacy. Often, the choice of decentralized or even fragmented enforcement impedes consistency and legal certainty, but is motivated by strategic behavior towards other actors.

---

[151] See above text and note, p. 127ff.

3. National courts and transnational private regulation

Eyal Benvenisti and George W. Downs

I. INTRODUCTION

In recent years, the growing reliance on private actors in the domestic sphere[1] to perform functions and deliver services traditionally provided by governmental actors has migrated to the international sphere. Transnational private regulation (TPR) bodies composed of either private actors or a hybrid of public and private actors have increasingly either replaced direct governmental regulation or have begun regulating areas that have never been subject to governmental oversight. Such private initiatives result from full or partial delegation of authority by governments to private actors, or from new private initiatives that are approved, tolerated, or left unnoticed by overburdened governments. These TPR bodies either regulate their own behavior by deciding, for example, which food safety measures they will adopt for their own purchases of agricultural products,[2] or

[1] On privatization in the domestic sphere and its public law implications see e.g. Gillian E. Metzger (2003), 'Privatization as delegation', 103 *Colum. L. Rev.* 1367, Jody Freeman (2000), 'The private role in public governance', 75 *NYU L. Rev.* 543, Harm Schepel (2005), *The Constitution of Private Governance: Product Standards in the Regulation of Integrating Markets*, Hart Publishing; Martha Minow (2002), *Partners, Not Rivals: Privatization and the Public Good*, Beacon Press.

[2] Jan Wouters, Axel Marx and Nicolas Hachez (2008), 'Private standards, global governance and transatlantic cooperation – the case of food safety governance', 3, Leuven Centre for Global Governance Studies; Fabrizio Cafaggi (2010), 'Private regulation, supply chain and contractual networks: the case of food safety', 1, European University Institute, EUI Working Paper RSCAS; Fabrizio Cafaggi, 'Product safety, private standard-setting and information network', in F. Cafaggi and H. Muir Watt (eds) (2009), *The Regulatory Function of European Private Law*, Edward Elgar, pp. 215.

regulate others' activities, by accumulating, processing or disseminating information for the consumption of third parties.[3]

The sources of power and authority of private actors vary. At times, the large market share that these private regulators possess is itself sufficient to generate the compliance of those who transact with them. At other times, as in the case of professional associations, they are backed by statutory delegation of authority from the state to control entry to the profession, and regulate the conduct of the professionals. With or without delegation of public authority from the state, such privately set policies often shape the choices of third parties as much, or sometimes even more, than official state functionaries. As in the case of the domestic sphere, opinion remains divided about the potential consequences of TPR. While some extol the virtues of what they view as impartial, expertise-driven standard-setting,[4] others express concerns about the efficacy and legitimacy of governance by bodies that are subject to little oversight and can potentially advance narrow private interests through the creation of standards tailored to their own needs rather than those of the affected publics.

Not surprisingly, *transnational* private regulation poses even more dramatic challenges than *domestic* private regulation.[5] Globalization and the increased international regulatory coordination that it has fostered accelerated the long-standing shift in the political balance of power in most democratic states from the legislative to the executive branch and, in addition, have advantaged those private actors with mobile economic resources.[6] As a consequence, key venues of regulatory policy making have tended to migrate – with governmental approval or by default – from the

3 Fabrizio Cafaggi (2010), 'Private regulation, supply chain and contractual networks: the case of food safety', 25, European University Institute, EUI Working Paper RSCAS.

4 See Freeman, *supra* note 1, at 666 ('Public/private arrangements can be more accountable because of the presence of powerful independent professionals within private organizations. The background threat of regulation by an agency can provide the necessary motivation for effective and credible self-regulation. The two principal partners in a regulatory enterprise (the agency and the regulated firm, or the agency and the private contractor) might rely on independent third parties to set standards, monitor compliance, and supplement enforcement.').

5 Benedict Kingsbury (2009), 'Weighing global regulatory rules and decisions in national courts', *Acta Juridica* 90; David Kennedy (2005), 'Challenging expert rule: the politics of global governance', 27 *Sydney L. Rev.* 5.

6 On the impact of globalization on national executives, especially of powerful states, see Eyal Benvenisti and George W. Downs (2007), 'The empire's new clothes: political economy and the fragmentation of international law', 60 *Stan. L. Rev.* 595; on the benefits for small interest groups from globalization see Eyal Benvenisti (1999), 'Exit and voice in the age of globalization', 98 *Mich. L. Rev.* 167.

national to the global arena and from the public to the private sphere. Such privately-ordered, informal arrangements facilitated coordination without entailing long-term commitments, rigid rules that might constrain state executives, and avoidance of public scrutiny.[7] In this sense, TPR which is emblematic of both trends is doubly removed from the public sphere and from the ideal of deliberative democracy. More disturbingly, by increasing the information asymmetries among the various (domestic and global) stakeholders, and by evading or rendering obsolete traditional constitutional checks and balances and other oversight mechanisms, TPR threatens to exacerbate the already existing regulatory oversight deficit that globalization is widely believed to have created in many democratic states.

TPR has potential geopolitical implications as well with respect to further diminishing the bargaining power of developing countries. For example, TPR in the food safety context concentrates power in the hands of Northern large retailers[8] and creates an imbalance between them and producers who are mainly in the South.[9] Developed countries refuse to regard these TPRs as barriers to trade while Southern countries express concerns about them as the North's disingenuous way to overcome WTO obligations.[10] Such suspicions are not allayed by the fact that the modest amount of positive evidence that the developed state defenders of TPRs have marshaled in defense of their democratizing effects often collapses under close scrutiny. For example, as Vogel has observed '[a]dvocates of civil regulations claim that, by providing nonbusiness constituencies with new political and market mechanisms to affect business decisions, these regulations can help address the democratic deficit in global governance. But virtually all these nonbusiness constituencies are located in developed countries.'[11]

---

[7] Benvenisti and Downs, *supra* note 6, at 617–18; Eyal Benvenisti, '"Coalitions of the willing" and the evolution of informal international law', in C. Calliess et al. (eds) (2007), *'Coalitions of the Willing' – Avantgarde or Threat?*, available at: http://ssrn.com/abstract=875590

[8] Fabrizio Cafaggi, 'Private regulation, supply chain and contractual networks', *supra* note 2, at 3; Wouters et al., *supra* note 2, at 12.

[9] Cafaggi, 'Private regulation, supply chain and contractual networks', *supra* note 2. Also G. Chia-Hui Lee (2006), 'Private food standards and their impacts on developing countries', European Commission – DG Trade Unit G2 Paper, available at: http://trade.ec.europa.eu/doclib/docs/2006/november/tradoc_127969.pdf

[10] On this debate Wouters et al., *supra* note 2, at 18–22.

[11] David Vogel (2008), 'Private global business regulation', 11 *Annu. Rev. Polit. Sci.* 261, 276, available at http://www.annualreviews.org/journal/polisci

While the move to TPRs characteristically improves the leverage of Northern capital owners over more diffuse (Northern and especially Southern) constituencies, a few affected stakeholders have found ways to push back and revise the consequences of the delocalization of markets. Perhaps the most effective example of such resistance involves a global union association, the International Transport Workers' Federation (ITF), whose most successful campaign to date has focused on eliminating the adverse consequences for seafarers from the reflagging of ships under flags of convenience.[12] The ITF, based in London, draws its strength from the solidarity that exists between dock workers and seafarers. While ship owners can hire and fire seafarers at will, doing so exposes them to retaliatory boycott threats by dock worker unions. The ITF has managed to successfully leverage this threat to create improved employment conditions and wages in the shipping industry. It has set up a Fair Practices Committee (FPC) to reduce 'flags of convenience' abuses and to oversee ITF minimum collective agreements for seafarers designed to 'ensure decent salaries and conditions for FOC seafarers, thus helping to prevent unfair wage-based competition'.[13] While the International Finance Corporation (IFC) protected the interests of unions from both developed and established, labor-supplying developing countries, it effectively cut out new competitors to this market such as seafarers from China and Indonesia.[14] Vogel's warning is applicable also for transnational labor unionism which manages to exclude important voices, such as the Chinese and Indonesian seafarers.

In what follows we discuss the prospect that national courts (NCs) will take it upon themselves to directly or indirectly review such TPRs and thereby address some of the challenges that the TPRs potentially raise with respect to economic efficiency, democracy and equality. Below we briefly

---

[12] International Transport Workers' Federation (http://www.itfglobal.org/about-us/moreabout.cfm): 'The ITF defines a ship that flies a Flag of Convenience, or FOC as one that has no "genuine link" between the real shipowner and the flag the vessel flies. An FOC ship is one that flies the flag of a country other than the country of ownership. The beneficial ownership and control of the vessel belong to a different country than that of the flag of the vessel'. On this campaign see Nathan Lillie (2004), 'Global collective bargaining on flag of convenience shipping', *British Journal of Industrial Relations* 42(1), 47–67.

[13] http://www.itfglobal.org/itf-americas/fpc.cfm

[14] The ITF's so-called 'Athens Policy' requires that vessels engaged in international ferry service provide employment standards equivalent to one or the other of the countries they service. This policy was invoked when the Finnish ferry *Viking Line* wished to reflag under the Estonian flag in order more effectively compete with Estonian-based ferries in the Baltic ferry trade, an incident that will be discussed further below. Lillie, *supra* note 12, at 58.

flesh out some of the concerns that TPRs raise as a prelude to assessing the prospects for effective NC oversight. Similarly to inter-governmental standard setting exercises through inter-governmental institutions or informally, NCs' involvement can be at least partially instrumental in promoting accountability and representativeness of TPR processes. In order to accomplish this, NCs can resort to tools that they have developed over the years in response to privatized regulation at the domestic level. These are doctrines that seek to provide either direct or indirect judicial review of the policies adopted by private regulators or review of the act of delegating governmental authority to private actors. Part II surveys the available doctrines that NCs could use and the procedural norms that shape private law litigation as opposed to public law litigation. Part III assesses the constraints that NCs face when confronted with such tasks. Part IV concludes with an assessment of the potential and limits of NC regulation of TPRs.

II. NC TOOLS FOR REGULATING TPRs

Despite the fact that private regulation takes part below the radar screen of public law and does not necessarily depend on prior authorization or subsequent approval by public authorities, national courts have developed legal doctrines that successfully identify and alleviate at least some of the adverse effects of domestic private regulation. These doctrines can often be used to regulate TPRs. This Part examines the tools that NCs have used in this context. Section (a) will focus on doctrines of substantive law. Section (b) will examine procedural norms and examine their impact on NCs' review of private regulation. The aim in this Part is not to discuss these doctrines exhaustively, but to outline their potential effect on containing the discretion of TPRs.

(a) Substantive Law

(i) Public law doctrines

Formally or informally, many TPRs exercise public authority, either because they act under explicit or implicit state authorization or because their exercise of 'public functions', however vaguely defined, impacts individual rights and interests that are protected by domestic constitutions, domestic administrative law norms, or by supranational bills of rights. As we have already noted, NCs in several countries have developed a number of doctrines in the domestic context that subject such domestic actors to public law obligations, including administrative law requirements (as if they were administrative agencies) or constitutional law obligations. These doctrines typically have different titles and different scopes of application (e.g. the US 'State Action' doctrine),[15] but they all share the effort to treat private bodies that exercise public functions as if they were administrative agencies subject to at least some public law constraints and hence to judicial review.

Such review may or may not involve the private actor directly. The executive and even legislator might be subjected to judicial review by virtue of their decision either to delegate authority to the private body, or by virtue of their failure to effectively oversee its activities. The Supreme Court of Canada, for example, reasoned that '[j]ust as governments are not permitted to escape *Charter* scrutiny by entering into commercial contracts or other 'private' arrangements, they should not be allowed to evade their constitutional responsibilities by delegating the implementation of their policies and programs to private entities'.[16] Courts in several other countries have applied similar principles of administrative law to private entities that perform public functions.[17] These are tools developed in the domestic context by many NCs in response to executive branch attempts to pass, disguised as private actors, below the radar of administrative or constitutional courts. There is no doctrinal reason that would prevent NCs from responding in a similar fashion to the use of TPRs for similar objectives, and, for example, subject the TPR body responsible for organizing the Olympic Games to the obligation to maintain gender equality in the games.

---

[15] Stephen Gardbaum (2006), 'Where the (state) action is', *International Journal of Constitutional Law* 4(4), 2; Andras Sajo and Renata Uitz (eds) (2005), *The Constitution in Private Relations: Expanding Constitutionalism*, Eleven International Publishing; Freeman, *supra* note 1; Harold J. Krent (1990), 'Fragmenting the unitary executive: congressional delegations of administrative authority outside the federal government', *NW. U. L. Rev* 85(1), 62, at 65–6 (noting that Congress has delegated administrative authority also to private individuals and private groups to implement and execute legislative plans); F. Cafaggi (2006), 'Rethinking private regulation in the European regulatory space', European University Institute, EUI Working Paper, 13, 1, pp. 7, 16.

[16] *Eldridge* v *British Columbia (Attorney General)* [1997] 2 S.C.R. 624, para. 42.

[17] In the UK the leading judgment is *R* v *Panel for Takeovers and Mergers, ex parte Datafin plc* [1987] QB 815 (decisions of a private body – the City's self-regulating mechanism for dealing with mergers and acquisitions – exercising public functions may be amenable to judicial review). See also *YL* v *Birmingham City Council and others* [2007] UKHL 27, paras 20, 30 (a majority of 3 to 2 held that a private care home providing care and accommodation for elderly people under contract with a local authority was not exercising 'functions of a public nature' within s. 6(3)(b) of the Human Rights Act 1998); Colin D. Campbell (2009), 'The nature of power as public in English judicial review', *Cambridge Law Journal* 68(1), 90–117.

The failure of the Canadian and the US courts to decide against the organizers of these Games[18] should be attributed not to the lack of legal tools but to the collective action problem that NCs face, a problem to be dealt with below.

(ii) Doctrines of private law

TPRs may be bound by statutes that regulate market activities, most prominently competition law, corporate law and the law of associations that offer different rationales and opportunities for NC review of TPR activities that affect third parties.[19] Beyond such specific statutory obligations, TPR bodies could be subjected to the general obligations imposed on private actors. In both contract law and tort law there are open-ended standards such as good faith (in contract) or reasonableness (in tort) that can be employed by NCs to review private regulations. In both areas of law, the reliance of one party to a contract or the defendant in torts on a relevant TPR standard could be regarded as complying (or not) with their contractual or tort law obligations.[20] This provides courts with an opportunity to address the relevant TPR and assess its proper impact on the parties' obligations.

In many legal systems, courts interpret private law obligations on the basis of underlying public law principles. In some jurisdictions, Germany for example, courts readily acknowledge the indirect effect of constitutional rights on private law. The German doctrine of '*Drittwirkung*' is based on the judicially-supported understanding that in a coherent legal system, the constitution must be regarded as having not only vertical effects on the

---

[18] *Sagen* v *Vancouver Organizing Committee for the 2010 Olympics and Paralympic Winter Games 2010* (Supreme Court of British Columbia, 2009 BCSC 942) (rejecting a suit alleging gender discrimination). In *Martin* v *International Olympic Committee* 740 F2d 670 (1984) the Ninth Cir. rejected the suit on procedural grounds but added: 'we find persuasive the argument that a court should be wary of applying a state statute to alter the content of the Olympic Games. The Olympic Games are organized and conducted under the terms of an international agreement – the Olympic Charter. We are extremely hesitant to undertake the application of one state's statute to alter an event that is staged with competitors from the entire world under the terms of that agreement'. The dissenting judge lamented the missed opportunity to use 'America's commitment to human rights ... to tip the scales of justice in favor of equality'.

[19] See e.g. *Broadcom Corp* v *Qualcomm Inc.* 501 F.3d 297 (3rd Cir., 2007) (private standard setting governed by competition law); *Coalition for ICANN Transparency, INC.* v *VeriSign* 611 F.3d 495 (9 Cir., 2010) (accepting the framing of standards set by ICANN as potentially infringing anti-competition law). See in general Freeman, *supra* note 1, Cafaggi, *supra* note 15, at 31–3.

[20] See Kingsbury *supra* note 5, at 97–8; Cafaggi, *supra* note 15, at 25–6.

relations between government and governed but also horizontal effects among the governed. As a consequence, the constitution sets forth not only 'subjective' rights against the state but it also creates an objective order of values that permeates the whole legal system.[21] Such a doctrine is not explicitly recognized in the US. However, as the case of *New York Times* v *Sullivan*[22] demonstrates, civil rights inform the interpretation of the responsibilities of individuals *inter se*, due to the immediate effect that imposing civil liability has on the exercise of civil rights like free speech.[23] The European Court of Justice (ECJ) explained the indirect applicability of Community law obligations not on the basis of a certain theory but on the functional need to ensure the effectiveness of community law:

> the abolition, as between Member States, of obstacles to freedom of movement for persons and freedom to provide services would be compromised if the abolition of State barriers could be neutralised by obstacles resulting from the exercise, by associations or organisations not governed by public law, of their legal autonomy.[24]

The 2007 case of *International Transport Workers' Federation and Finnish Seamen's Union* v *Viking Line*[25] offers an example of indirect judicial review of a TPR. The ECJ invoked the principle of indirect effect of community law as the basis for examining and potentially superseding the policy of the ITF, which is a TPR that sought to set standards for the reflagging of ships under flags of convenience,[26] and subjected the TPR to a proportionality analysis that includes examination of whether the initiated action is aimed at pursuing legitimate interests, and is 'suitable for ensuring the achievement of the objective pursued and does not go beyond what is necessary to attain that objective'.[27]

---

21 See e.g. Andrew Clapham (2006), *Human Rights Obligations of Non-State Actors*, Oxford University Press, 521.

22 *New York Times Co.* v *Sullivan* 376 U.S. 254 (1964).

23 Gardbaum, *supra* note 15, at 6; Cafaggi, *supra* note 15, at 43.

24 Case C–36/74 *B.N.O. Walrave and L.J.N. Koch* v *Association Union Cycliste Internationale, Koninklijke Nederlandsche Wielren Unie and Federación Española Ciclismo* [1974] ECR 1405, para. 18. For the EU see Joanna Krzeminska-Vamvaka (2009), 'Horizontal effect of fundamental rights and freedoms – much ado about nothing? German, Polish and EU theories compared after *Viking Line*', Jean Monnet Working Paper 11/09, available at: http://centers.law.nyu.edu/jeanmonnet/papers/09/091101.pdf

25 Case C-438/05 *International Transport Workers' Federation and Finnish Seamen's Union* v *Viking Line ABP and OU Viking Line Eesti*: http://eur-lex.europa.eu/LexUriServ/LexUriServ.do?uri=CELEX:62005J0438:EN:HTML

26 Ibid., at para. 73.

27 Ibid., at para. 84.

(b) Procedural Norms

Historically, an NC review of private regulations has usually taken place in private law litigation. As we saw above, courts possess several legal doctrines that enable them to import public law principles to private law disputes and thereby bridge the normative gap between public and private law litigation. However, the procedural dimension of the litigation adds complexity: while private litigation offers some benefits to potential claimants, it also imposes some restrictions on them.[28]

Private law litigation is relatively less open to public participation than public law litigation which frequently offers more possibilities for members of the general public, either to initiate litigation or to take part in it. The requirements of standing for initiating public law adjudication are also lower than in private action: in common law systems one has to demonstrate a personal stake (not necessarily unique) in the outcome of the litigation rather than that a right had been infringed by the defendant. Some jurisdictions are ready to open their doors to *actio popularis* petitions that raise public concerns. Those systems that require a showing of a right that was infringed as the basis for public law litigation are ready to interpret that right widely and read into it the reciprocal state obligation to protect that right against encroachment by private parties. Public law litigation is also relatively more open for input from members of the public as respondents or amici.[29] As a result, public law litigation is likely to generate better information for the judges to process and decide upon. Courts that do not satisfy themselves that the information they have is comprehensive and full tend to intervene less in regulatory decisions.[30]

An additional burden of private law litigation is the relatively high litigation costs when seeking to challenge the private regulators. The costs of private litigation are often significantly higher than public petitions, and private defendants may react to suits by bringing counterclaims for lost revenues as a result of the litigation or injunctions that were issued by the court. Attorney fees often constitute a significant obstacle for individuals

---

[28] On private *ex post* enforcement see Samuel Issacharoff and Ian J. Samuel (2009), 'The institutional dimension of consumer protection', Public Law & Legal Theory Research Paper Series Working Paper No.09–18, 5. Electronic copy available at: http://papers.ssrn.com/sol3/papers.cfm?abstract_id=1369744

[29] Hannah L. Buxbaum (2010), 'National jurisdiction and global business networks', *Indiana Journal of Global Legal Studies* 17(1), 165–82, at 173–4.

[30] Ibid., at 178; Robert Wai (2005), 'Transnational private law and private ordering in a contested global society', *Harvard International Law Journal* 46(2), 475–6, at 482.

who consider challenging a TPR in court. Attention in this context should be given to the growing availability of class action suits.[31]

At the same time, however, private law litigation can overcome barriers that exist in public law. First, private litigation that involves a foreign private regulator does not raise concerns about foreign sovereign immunity, foreign act of state or other doctrines designed to prevent domestic courts from encroaching on foreign sovereigns. The 'effects doctrine' has been recognized by NCs to empower them to adjudicate foreign private activity that produced adverse economic consequences within their jurisdiction and to impose on that foreign practice domestic antitrust or other regulatory norms.[32] Also, sophisticated discovery tools developed in private law litigation more than in public law could be used to obtain crucial information that could assist in reviewing TPR.

Just like in the case of the evolution of public law doctrines, it is safe to assume that courts will react to the need to restrain executive branch attempts to evade the review of administrative or constitutional courts. The private identity of the reviewed bodies could even enable courts to overcome barriers that exist in public law litigation.

III. TRANSNATIONAL REGULATION MEETS TRANSNATIONAL NC COOPERATION

The question remains as to just how useful the tools developed by NCs to review private regulation will be for regulating transnational regulation. The fact that private regulation is now set by foreign private actors poses a challenge to many NCs. If one NC refused to give effect to a certain TPR, the TPR could then ignore the judgment (for example, because of the insignificant market share of the forum state) and even punish domestic actors for their court's activism. To the extent that TPRs reflect the private

---

31 Samuel Issacharoff and Geoffrey P. Miller (2009), 'Will aggregate litigation come to Europe?' 62 *Vanderbilt L. Rev*. 179.

32 See e.g. the decision to assert jurisdiction over KPMG, a UK-based accounting group: *Rocker Management, L.L.C.* v *Lernout & Hauspie Speech Products N.V.* 2005 WL 3658006, *7 (D.N.J. 2005). The court concluded that general jurisdiction could be sustained over KPMG UK: 'There can be no doubt that KPMG offices are integral parts of a single global enterprise that conducts business in the United States. That KPMG UK deliberately markets and promotes itself as part of an integrated global network severely undercuts its present attempt to divest itself of a relationship with that network in order to defeat the exercise of personal jurisdiction'. See Buxbaum, *supra* note 29, at 181–2. Similarly *Ernst & Young Bermuda: Cromer Finance Ltd.* v *Berger*, 137 F. Supp. 2d 452, 462 (S.D.N.Y. 2001).

interests of major commercial actors, NCs may be deterred from exercising review over the TPRs out of the concern that such actors will retaliate by moving their business elsewhere. For example, if credit rating agencies were to be penalized by one court for negligent rating[33] they might simply choose to stop rating local issuers or even relocate to a more amenable jurisdiction, or facing a demand to respect athletes' rights[34] could prompt the Olympic Games committee to choose another country as the venue of the Olympic Games. Past judicial practice indicates that NCs are quite sensitive to such adverse economic pressures.[35] NCs will tend not to volunteer their services simply to promote global economic interests or the global rule of law: they are national courts and they perceive themselves as the guardians of their respective domestic legal systems. NCs are unlikely to intervene in TPR review if there are no adverse domestic consequences that call for remedial action by the courts.[36] In other words, NCs must cope with the fact that regulating TPRs is a collective action problem.

But this collective action problem need not necessarily lead to failure to react to TPRs. Because we can expect that TPRs could cause adverse economic effects in several jurisdictions rather than in few, and thus pose a challenge to several courts simultaneously, we can anticipate that NCs will respond by exploring ways to collectively review those TPRs. National

---

[33] See e.g. *Abu Dhabi Commercial Bank* v *Morgan Stanley and Co. et al.* 08 Civ. 7508 (SAS), one of the class action suits filed by investors against credit rating agencies in the Southern District of New York.

[34] See *supra* note 18.

[35] See the refusal of the US courts to litigate the consequence of the Bhopal disaster *In Re Union Carbide Corp. Gas Plant Disaster at Bhopal, India in December, 1984* 634 F. Supp. 842 (S.D.N.Y. 1986), *aff'd*, 809 F.2d 195 (2d Cir. 1987) (on this case see Upendra Baxi (ed.) (1986), *Inconvenient Forum and Convenient Catastrophe: The Bhopal Case*, N. M. Tripathi Pvt Ltd; Jamie Cassels (1993), *The Uncertain Promise of Law: Lessons from Bhopal*, University of Toronto Press). A similar case was the unwillingness of US courts to adjudicate class action suits against Texaco by Ecuadorian and Peruvian citizens alleging that Texaco had severely polluted rainforests and rivers in Ecuador and Peru as a result of its oil exploitation activities in Ecuador (*Aquinda* v *Texaco, Inc.* 945 F. Supp. 625 (S.D.N.Y. 1996), *vacated*, 157 F.3d 152 (2d Cir. 1998); *Sequihua* v *Texaco, Inc.* 847 F. Supp. 61 (S.D. Tex. 1994). In the same vein is the refusal to litigate the consequences of the bankruptcy of the International Tin Council in UK courts (*J.H. Rayner Ltd.* v *Dep't of Trade & Indus.* [1989] 3 W.L.R. 969, 81 I.L.R. 670 (H.L.)). For more examples see Eyal Benvenisti (1993), *Judicial Misgivings Regarding the Application of International Norms: An Analysis of Attitudes of National Courts*, 4 *Eur. J. Int'l L.* 159 (1993).

[36] See *Morrison* v *National Australia Bank* 130 S. Ct. 2869 (2010); *F. Hoffmann-La Roche Ltd.* v *Empagran* S.A. 542 155 (2004); Buxbaum *supra* note 29, at 173.

courts have, since the end of the Cold War, developed practices of coordination and cooperation to collectively confront global challenges to their authority. Especially since 2000, we are witnessing an increasing willingness by NCs to cooperate across political borders. NCs have probably realized that globalization made judicial cooperation both necessary and possible. It was necessary to seek a common judicial front that would limit the possibilities of foreign actors to shop for lower standards of environmental protection or labor rights, or of migrant workers to benefit from a particularly lenient application of the refugee convention. It was perhaps even more necessary to counter the growing practice of executives setting up global policies without regard to domestic constitutional guarantees. It was also necessary to resist lawmaking by the newly established or recently invigorated international tribunals. Fortunately, the technological innovations in the area of communications that sustained globalization also facilitated the evolution of cooperation among NCs. As a result, in recent years NCs have evidenced an increased willingness to venture into the international arena, to take issue with the positions of their governments regarding the interpretation of treaties, and to otherwise constrain what had previously been governments' free hand in international bargaining.

This emerging practice of NC cooperation should eventually become self-enforcing as TPRs continue to develop. As it becomes routine, NC cooperation can be expanded to other transnational phenomena which are believed to generate serious negative externalities that affect a significant proportion of states. While regulating TPRs poses a host of challenges, it does not raise special political or economic concerns that are beyond the courts' reach. After all, if NCs have managed to make the UN Security Council modify its procedures for delisting suspected supporters of terrorism there is no reason that they would not be able to insist that private athletic associations improve the due process rights of athletes accused of using illegal drugs.

IV. THE PROMISE AND LIMITS OF NC REVIEWS OF TPRs

In recent years a growing number of NCs have signaled a willingness to cooperate with their peers. They have conveyed information about their commitment to cooperate by their reasoning and decisions and the tendency to rely on the same or similar legal sources. Using web-based forums,[37] e-mail lists, conferences and informal interaction NCs have set collective policies and informally monitored each other's compliance. The same practice can be repeated in the TPR context where NCs are in a position to serve as their nations' last national line of defense against skewed or unfair TPRs in circumstances where the political channels are dominated by powerful lobbies.

There are several opportunities for direct or indirect judicial review of TPR standards or practices.[38] Judicial endorsement of TPRs will be required, for example, for accepting a certain TPR standard as the 'state of the art' practice in tort litigation, for endorsing a certain decision-making procedure as compatible with due process requirements, for supporting an administrative agency's decision to comply with a TPR-based standard, or for recognizing private arbitration or alternative dispute resolution mechanisms that justify judicial deference to them under the doctrine of *forum non conveniens* as bar to litigation[39] or for recognizing its award as enforceable.[40]

An important factor that has facilitated NCs' cooperation across jurisdictions is their ability to resort to similar norms (based on similarly worded bills of rights) or on the very same norm (in the case of multilateral treaties) to communicate with each other and signal their commitment to coordinated outcomes. Thus, for example, NC cooperation in reviewing executive policies has been facilitated by the use of comparative constitutional law and international law.[41] Unfortunately in the context of TPR review there is more diversity in the legal doctrines available in the different jurisdictions, and reliance on general concepts such as human rights and due process may be too open-ended to serve as a focal point. In the future, NCs will therefore have to streamline their respective private and public law doctrines if they are to succeed in promoting coordination.

To the extent that NCs flex their muscles and exercise effective review, TPRs will need to take into account the potential NC reactions to their policies rather than simply rely on the acquiescence (or collaboration) of national regulators. Over time, this should prompt TPRs to peremptorily

---

37 See e.g. the website of the IARLJ – International Association of Refugee Law Judges, available at: http://www.iarlj.org/general/index.php

38 For examples see Kingsbury (2009) *supra* note 5, at 97–9.

39 *In re Assicurazioni Generali S.p.A. Holocaust Ins. Litigation* 228 F.Supp. 2d 348 (S.D.N.Y. 2002).

40 *Barcelona.com* v *Excelentisimo Ayuntamiento* 330 F.3d 617 (4th Cir. 2003).

41 Eyal Benvenisti (2008), 'Reclaiming democracy: the strategic uses of foreign and international law by national courts', *American Journal of International Law*, 102(2), 241–74, at 243.

adopt reforms in response to anticipated criticism by courts and to shield themselves from future judicial intervention in their policies. Some evidence of such preemptive initiatives can be found in global sport regulation. The intervention of some courts that expressed an interest in protecting the due process rights of athletes has led a number of global sport TPRs to adopt standards that protect athletes' due process rights.[42] The threat of NC intervention was probably also instrumental in motivating these TPRs to accept an expansive role for the Court of Arbitration for Sport which ensures that decisions affecting athletes comply with international principles of human rights.

We are, of course, still in the early stages of NC intervention in this area and it is not clear what the future will bring. However, it can be expected that increasing reliance on TPRs will be countered by growing NC willingness to review the standards for compatibility with their domestic laws and concerns. To the extent that NCs have reason to believe that TPRs are effectively acting as proxies for national executives, we can expect a similar dynamic to take place. For example, if national political branches delegate authority to special TPRs to regulate environmental standards, there is no reason for NCs to treat the standards developed by the TPRs differently than those issued by the political branches themselves.

The promise of NC review of TPRs and its resulting impact also depends on the distribution of factors that shape the inclination of NCs to review TPRs. These factors will include the types of regulatory activities to be addressed and their impact on the economic, social, political and cultural condition of the forum state. There is some evidence that suggests that courts in India, for example, protect upper-middle-class interests such as a clean environment, but pay less attention to the interests of the poor farmers in the countryside or of the dwellers in informal settlements.[43] Where judicial scrutiny of TPRs will burden certain economic actors to the extent that they might boycott the forum state, we can expect significant internal pressure on the NC to avoid such review. TPRs that address the social and environmental impact of commercial activities in ways that

---

42 Alec Van Vaerenbergh (2005), 'Regulatory features and administrative law dimensions of the Olympic movement's anti-doping regime', IILJ Working Paper 2005/11, at pp. 17–19.

43 Upendra Baxi (2003), 'A known but an indifferent judge: situating Ronald Dworkin in contemporary Indian jurisprudence', 4 *Int'l J. Cons. L.* 557, 568; Usha Ramanathan (2006), 'Illegality and the urban poor', 41 *Economic and Political Weekly* 3193, available at: http://www.ielrc.org/content/a0606.pdf (suggesting that Indian courts give precedence to urban developers over slum dwellers and interpret narrowly laws that protect the poor).

benefit Northern interests over Southern ones will probably be treated differently in Northern courts than in Southern ones (if the latter ever get to adjudicate them). The more judicial intervention is likely to create adverse economic, social or environmental ramifications in the forum, the more NC intervention would require coordination with similarly situated NCs so that NCs make sure their forum does not suffer the adverse consequences of their activist court.

The parochial biases of NCs and their lack of experience in engaging in coordination with each other could also be mitigated by the assistance of regional and international tribunals when the latter have opportunities to respond to NC judgments. For example, the ECJ has an important role in imposing community obligations on private parties across the EU.[44] In theory, international tribunals could also step in to ameliorate North/South imbalances and thereby limit NC discretion. The WTO Appellate Body, for example, can be in a position to review the legality of national implementation of TPRs that effectively create barriers to trade.[45]

V. CONCLUSION

In contrast to NC intervention in standard setting by intergovernmental organizations, indirect NC regulation of TPRs seems less likely to offer systematic responses to the challenges that they pose, at least in the short run. Private law doctrines vary among national legal systems to a greater degree than public law doctrines, and there is paucity of relevant international treaties that NCs could use if and when they seek to coordinate their policies with other NCs. Over time, however, this situation is likely to change as NC experience accumulates with NC cooperation in general and with addressing TPR-related cases in particular, and there is broader public awareness of the challenges that they pose. An increase in the number of TPR cases is likely to lead NCs to begin citing each other, and eventually to reducing the barriers to inter-court coordination by streamlining their respective doctrines on the direct or indirect applicability of public law obligations in private law.

Two other important distinctions between public and private litigation lie in the fact that the latter is less open to public participation and far more costly. NCs are likely to be or feel less informed and therefore unable to intervene. Here too we may anticipate changes introduced through developing similar class action requirements that would encourage private

---

44 Cafaggi *supra* note 15, at 21–2.
45 Ibid., at 22–3.

initiatives to sue on TPR issues. Even more than streamlining the doctrines on substantive legal obligations of TPRs, it will be important to consider reforms to comparative civil procedure law, especially the possibility of lowering the threshold of bringing class action suits.

At least initially, the more active NCs are likely to be those of Northern countries and to be informed by predominantly Northern stakeholders. This means that they are unlikely to receive complete information about the distributional stakes involved in connection with TPRs that have differential North/South effects and those that regulate the social and environmental impacts of commercial activities. As a result, the review processes driven by these NCs is likely to lead TPRs to become more egalitarian and democratic from the perspective of previously disregarded Northern constituencies, but only rarely from those in the South. It is also not clear whether Southern NCs, if they ever choose to review TPRs, will protect the interests of average citizens or elites.

4. Non-judicial enforcement of transnational private regulation

Colin Scott

1. INTRODUCTION

Transnational private regulation (TPR) is a phenomenon of growing significance across a wide range of policy domains, including the environment, food standards, labour rights and financial markets. Thinking about regulatory regimes generally, they are now conventionally described as comprising three distinct elements – some norms, rules or goals around which the regime is organized; feedback or monitoring mechanisms to detect deviations from the norms; and mechanisms for modifying behaviour which deviates (Hood et al. 2001). The making of both national and transnational private norms has received a significant amount of attention in the literature (e.g. Hallström 2004; Schepel 2005), but monitoring and enforcement have been relatively neglected. In this chapter I ask to what extent the enforcement of TPR regimes is similar to or different from national public regimes of regulation, and what effect do differences in enforcement have on the reach of regimes. Reach is perhaps narrower in one way because it is dependent on contracts in many instances (in contrast with generally applicable public law instruments), but more extensive in other ways because less restricted by jurisdictional boundaries. Weaknesses associated with the voluntary character of much TPR are likely to be more apparent than real in circumstances where participation in TPR, whether through adopting widely accepted technical standards or norms of Corporate Social Responsibility, or participating in associational codes, is a de facto condition of market participation. Given the ubiquity and significance of TPR in many sectors it is striking that the world of enforcement of private regulation is carried out in relative privacy and that this lack of transparency is liable to affect the credibility and legitimacy of regimes.

Some of the weaknesses, both of reach and legitimacy, associated with TPR regimes may be addressed in hybrid regimes involving public enforcement of transnational norms which are set privately, and the private transnational enforcement of public norms. Research on global business regulation suggests that there is frequently a significant gap between the generation of regulatory norms and their enforcement within global and transnational regimes. Expectations that globalized norms might and should be accompanied by global enforcement are both implausible and unnecessary. Self-regulatory and private mechanisms of enforcement are significant both for the implementation of inter-governmental and governmental norms and for privately generated norms (Braithwaite and Drahos 2000: 10).

Whilst it is possible to draw analytical distinctions between public and private norms and enforcement I suggest that it may be more fruitful simply to think of multiple actors within regulatory regimes with a range of capacities and motivations (Hancher and Moran 1989). I am aware also that considerations of relationships between public and private activity are liable to play differently in different legal systems. In this chapter I start with a brief analysis of the nature of regulatory enforcement and its application to TPR regimes, and then go on to consider the varied nature of hybrid enforcement regimes.

2. ENFORCEMENT OR COMPLIANCE?

There are a number of schools of thought on the nature of regulatory enforcement. For some, enforcement is about the formal processes through which agencies address infractions of regulatory rules which they discover through a variety of mechanisms, including complaints, market surveillance and inspections. For others, the puzzle of behavioural modification within regulatory regimes is about understanding how and why regulatees comply with regulatory rules, and the relationship of such compliance, broadly conceived, with a more limited set of enforcement practices (Parker 2000b). In their classic work on *Responsive Regulation* Ayres and Braithwaite offer the enforcement pyramid model (Figure 4.1) which seeks to link the two approaches, suggesting that the capacity for low-level and non-coercive steering of behaviour is linked to the capacity to escalate up a sanctions pyramid, through warnings and civil penalties to more stringent sanctions such as criminal penalties and licence revocation (Ayres and Braithwaite 1992).

The enforcement pyramid model is derived from Braithwaite's earlier empirical research on regulatory enforcement (e.g. Grabosky and

Source: Adapted from Ayres and Braithwaite (1992).

Figure 4.1 Example of an enforcement pyramid

Braithwaite 1986). The strategy for deploying the enforcement pyramid is derived in part from a game theoretic approach which is capable of addressing the variety or orientations towards compliance exhibited by regulated firms. The analysis draws on the well-known classification of regulatees in respect of compliance which basically combines assessments of motivation and capacity. Those who have both the motivation and the capacity to comply are fundamentally compliant, those with capacity but lacking motivation (unless it is made the most financially attractive path) are the 'amoral calculators', and the incompetents simply lack capacity and motivation is irrelevant (Kagan and Scholz 1984; but see also Baldwin and Black 2008). This analysis is conventionally deployed to understand the varied responses of businesses to regulatory requirements.

For firms which fundamentally seek to be compliant, education and advice, at the base of the pyramid, are liable to be sufficient to steer behaviour back to compliance. Infractions are treated as accidental and are corrected once pointed out. For the 'amoral calculators', the firms which seek to take the path towards maximizing profit, the pyramidal approach suggests that enforcement activity should start at the base of the pyramid but with the credible capacity to escalate up the pyramid where compliance is not forthcoming. Once the enforcement approach is clear, enforcers should be 'contingently forgiving' and return to the base of the pyramid in the expectation that firms will understand that the financial and reputational losses associated with criminal prosecution or licence revocation are more costly than complying (Ayres and Braithwaite 1992). Such an approach is dependent on enforcers having available sufficiently stringent sanctions, and the capacity to use them, such that compliance at the base of the pyramid is the most profitable course of action for the firms (Gunningham and Grabosky 1998: 402). In many jurisdictions formal enforcement is time consuming and costly, and may involve uncertainty, for example over the stringency of penalties to be handed down by a court (or even over whether there is judicial agreement that an infraction has occurred). Where, for whatever reason, effective escalation up the enforcement pyramid is not possible, the capacity for 'speaking softly' is limited because there is no big stick to back it up (Ayres and Braithwaite 1992). A third class of regulatees is the incompetents with whom neither education and advice nor the threat of stringent enforcement is likely to yield compliance because the firms concerned lack the capacity to implement regulatory norms within their businesses. Unless such firms can be encouraged to develop implementation capacity, the favoured enforcement approach is to seek their incapacitation through licence revocation or other equivalent measures, such as compulsory administration or disqualification of directors.

The pyramidal approach to regulatory enforcement raises the important questions of why some firms are fundamentally more compliant than others and what are the internal orientations and processes of firms which lead them not only towards compliance but also beyond compliance with regulatory requirements, in the sense that they may adopt and implement standards which exceed legal minima so as achieve better environmental or employee welfare outcomes (Gunningham and Sinclair 2002). For some firms the commitment to go beyond compliance is represented in internally developed codes of corporate social responsibility (Parker 2007), for others it is found in the membership of self-regulatory or other private regulatory regimes. Critically the motivations lying behind such initiatives are frequently not strongly connected to anxieties about formal enforcement, but rather are more concerned with addressing market processes affecting financial and/or reputational positioning of firms or the participation of firms within their wider community (Taylor 2005).

Set within this context, the question of how behaviour is modified within regulatory regimes, whether private or public, is as much concerned with compliance as with enforcement. Accordingly a strict contrast drawn in the literature between authoritative centralized enforcement of public regulatory rules, on the one hand and non-authoritative private rules with limited capacity for enforcement on the other (Jacobsson and Andersson 2006: 258–259) appears to be wide of the mark. Enforcement of public and private rules is far from systematic, and in each case is contingent on a range of factors.

3. PRIVATE NON-JUDICIAL ENFORCEMENT OF TPR

There is widespread recognition that transnational private regulation, to be considered regulation at all, must involve effective enforcement (Meidinger 2003: 252). But what constitutes effective enforcement? Much of the empirical research on regulatory enforcement generally suggests that the informal techniques of education, advice and warnings are central in many cases, but backed by the capacity for occasional application of more stringent measures, including civil and criminal penalties, and in some cases, licence revocation and analogous incapacitating measures such as the disqualification of directors or the issuing of prohibitions. The legal basis for such formal enforcement within public regimes is typically the grant of statutory powers to enforcement officials, variously in government departments, local government authorities or regulatory agencies, with a degree of operational independence.

The available mechanisms for formally enforcing and promoting compliance with transnational private regulation are closely linked to their legal basis. One way to analyse the mechanisms of enforcement is to distinguish them by reference to who enforces (Figure 4.2). The redeployment of the capacity/motivation analysis assists in the identification of actual and potential enforcers. Many private regulatory regimes stem from the limited capacity of governments and seek to address the problem that those with the capacity may lack the motivation. Arguably the greatest capacity for enforcement lies with the targets of regulation, and so the issue is one of understanding and keying into their motivations. Beyond the targets of regulation, capacity is typically widely diffused and dependent on context. The point is illustrated by the role of third-party gatekeepers in transnational private enforcement of some public regimes, as diverse as the role of airlines in enforcing immigration rules on passengers (and sometimes in ways that would not be open to governments themselves) (Gilboy 1997), and the role of banks in enforcing US prohibitions on internet gaming in a context where prosecution authorities cannot reach the owners of gaming servers located in other countries (Scott 2005). Elaborating on the potential for NGO strategies for making global and transnational rules stick, Braithwaite and Drahos argue that the targeting of those with gatekeeping capacity, not only by governments and not only in respect of public rules, provides a generalized means to promote enforcement. Many of those organizations with gatekeeping capacity are categorized as 'soft targets' for enforcement as they do not benefit from regulatory infractions (Braithwaite and Drahos 2000: 618). Requiring 'regulated actors to pay for gatekeepers to audit their compliance' and effectively monitoring the integrity and performance of such private monitors provides a central mechanism for overseeing both public and private rules, they suggest (Braithwaite and Drahos 2000: 69). There are concerns that such private audit processes may mask the variability of substantive obligations in private codes, and that they are insufficiently transparent to provide robust reassurance to consumers and other stakeholders (Haines 2005: 133–134).

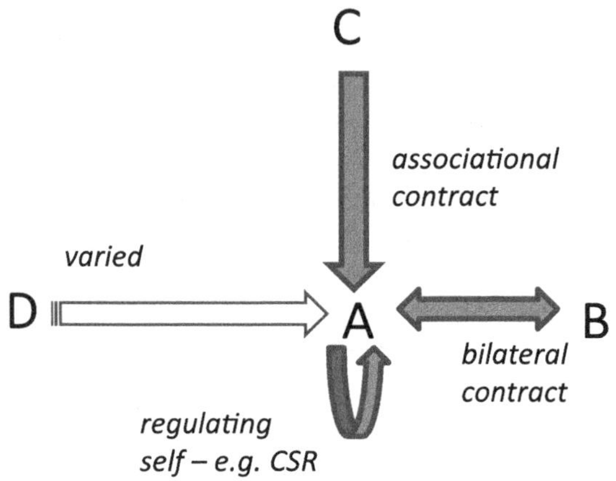

A – Organization subject to private regulation
B – Contracting party – e.g. buyer
C – Association of which A is a member
D – Third parties – e.g. consumers, auditors, certification bodies, investors

Figure 4.2 Modes of transnational private regulatory enforcement

In the case of corporate social responsibility and other self-imposed norms, a multinational enterprise has to devise ways both to detect deviation from the norms and to correct such deviations. In this corporate context the implementation of private norms is likely to be complementary to, or in competition with, efforts to comply with publicly set norms (Parker 2000a). In some instances the capacity for formal sanctions may reside with a trade association or other self-regulatory body, but in other cases the enforcement capacity may lie elsewhere, with buyers, certification bodies, consumers or investors (Haufler 2003). For example, the capacity to apply social sanctions such as gossip (which punish through reputational damage with adverse market consequences (Bernstein 2001)) and related market sanctions such as ending contracts or declining to enter them, is liable to be diffused. Where regulatory norms are incorporated into contracts the capacity to apply formal sanctions through enforcing contract terms is also diffused, not only amongst the contracting parties, but sometimes also amongst third parties contracted by either party to certify compliance. Investors and insurance companies may also enforce private (and public) regulatory norms as part of their regular commercial practices (Furger 1997; Richardson 2002).

Where a firm sets down its own codes then enforcement potential is aligned to the ordinary employment relationships within the firm. The capacity of multinational enterprises for the promulgation and enforcement of norms within their own company structure is of great potential significance, though challenging to implement within diffuse organisations (Engwall 2006: 170–171). It is suggested that firms generally follow a set of internal norms rather than strict legal rights in dealing with employees (Rock and Wachter 1996). Large firms also have substantial capacity to set and enforce rules for others through bilateral contracts (discussed below).

Regimes of self-regulation are typically based on collective contracts between member organizations. The rules, the available sanctions and the processes for detection and enforcement are each liable to be set down in the collective contract between the members. In her work on self-organizing regulation of common pool resources, Elinor Ostrom has suggested that the availability of monitoring and graduated sanctions is a key principle of successful regime design (Ostrom 1990: 94–101). How well self-regulatory arrangements for monitoring and enforcing are specified and implemented is likely to be shaped by the interests of the members in establishing and participating in the regime. Penalties may range from warnings to financial penalties and ultimately expulsion from the group. The credibility of such sanctions, and the capacity to create an enforcement pyramid will be based on the importance of membership to the members. In some sectors participation in an effective self-regulatory regime, or a particular regime, is a *sine qua non* for market participation. There may be some competition for membership and so regimes may need to compete on their credibility in the marketplace (Ogus 1995). Where regimes are successful and important for market participation members are likely to comply with enforcers well before expulsion is invoked as a sanction. In other instances self-regulatory regimes may only work where they are gentle with their members, with the regime being more dependent on the members than the members on the regime. In such instances rigorous enforcement is unlikely.

There is a good deal of contingency around the capacity for enforcement within self-regulatory and private regulatory regimes. However, in some instances they are bolstered externally through a variety of forms of bilateral contractual arrangements. Indeed, it has been suggested that the supply chain constitutes the primary institutional setting and the 'ultimate source of authority' for giving effect to mechanisms of 'non-state market driven governance' (Cashore et al. 2004: 23, 25). Some purchasers of products specify in their contracts not only the product specification but also the private regulatory standards with which a supplier must comply. The specification of private standards extends beyond self-regulatory regimes to include other forms of private standards regimes, such as those administered by the International Organization for Standardization (ISO) and various general and more specific standards bodies operating at international, European and national level. Contractual specification of private standards is likely to be accompanied by sanctions within the contract for failure to follow the applicable standards and may also include mechanisms of accreditation, certification or inspection by the purchaser or, increasingly, by a third-party organization.

How are such contractual regimes enforced? The first point to make is that enforcement is likely to take place in private. A certain amount of research has been undertaken on the resolution of contractual disputes and has found a surprisingly (to lawyers) large amount of dispute resolution involves the parties in reaching workable solutions without reference to the contractual provisions or to their lawyers (Macaulay 1963; Beale and Dugdale 1975). Remedies are likely to involve the rejection of products that do not meet or do not sufficiently meet required specifications, financial arrangements including return of or suspension of payments made under the contract, and, in many instances, measures to bring conduct back into compliance and provide some assurance that it is and will remain in compliance.

Many supply chains are organized around 'relational contracts' in which we might expect social and economic rather than strictly legal solutions to predominate. We might also expect, even within social settings, an implicit form of enforcement pyramid to emerge, as adverse remarks and disapproval provide initial steps for addressing problems in a context where there may be potential for formal enforcement of contractual penalties. Lisa Bernstein's research on the global regulatory system which links national diamond trading cartels, the World Federation of Diamond Bourses, for example, finds there is a high degree of informality in concluding and enforcing executory agreements, but potential for escalation to pre-arbitration and arbitration processes for resolving disputes. A member of one of the cartels who does not speedily abide by an arbitration decision is liable to have the arbitration decision and their photograph published in prominent places in the rooms of each of the national cartels (not just the one in which the trader was a member). Suspension and expulsion are also possible remedies for members who do not honour commitments (Bernstein 1992: 128).

Even where agreed remedies for breach of contractual terms are invoked, this is largely a matter for the parties, unless they find themselves unable to resolve the dispute. Resort to arbitration and litigation may itself be regarded as a form of escalation, since it involves costs to the parties, some uncertainty of outcomes, and, in the case of litigation, the risk of adverse publicity. An alternative form of escalation within relational contracts is for one of the parties to exit the arrangement. The potential for exit depends on the economic positioning of the parties. Retailers with strong brands have found themselves able to exert a good deal of power over suppliers, including the ending of contractual relationships. This phenomenon of retailer power has become increasingly significant in the groceries industry, with large supermarket chains dominating supply in an increasing number of OECD countries, and with increasing requirements being placed on suppliers to comply with private standards such as those developed by GlobalGap (Havinga 2006). Small and medium suppliers are sometimes highly dependent on one or a small number of retailers for the sale of their products and for them options are much more limited.

In instances where disappointed buyers have weak capacity to enforce contractual norms individually, some aggregated mechanisms to discipline sellers have emerged. Amongst the best known are the mechanisms for rating sellers on EBay. Buyers are invited to, and many do, rate sellers' performance. Sellers with poor ratings are liable either to find it difficult to sell or, other things being equal, will have to sell at a lower cost than higher ranked sellers (Scott 2004; Calliess 2008). In this case the standards are, in effect, market norms on such matters as speed of delivery, consumer expectations of the product, and so on. Monitoring is carried out by diffuse buyers, and behaviour modification derives from the anticipated damage to the ability of sellers to sell in the market place should ratings be adverse. This interesting example of enhancing consumer information in order to facilitate regulation by the market, however imperfect, is likely to shape new mechanisms of transnational private regulation in years to come.

Collective action by consumers is also a feature of the enforcement of other regimes. The market for ethical and sustainable products has grown significantly on the back of consumers exhibiting 'preferences for processes' (Kysar 2004), prioritizing assurances that producers have been paid a fair price, child labour has not been employed, or only sustainable sources have been used for production. The emergence of certification linked to labelling (C & L programmes) has been of particular significance (McNichol 2006). C & L programmes offer a market mechanism to demonstrate compliance to consumers (Meidinger 2008). The marketing potential associated with participation in regimes such as Fairtrade and the Forest Stewardship Council (FSC) would be completely undermined if consumers could not be confident that the norms associated with these regimes were enforced. Transparency of such regimes is becoming increasingly important to their credibility (Meidinger 2008). In the case of the FSC, enforcement has a double dimension since the initial NGO campaigns of boycotts and public information were concerned with persuading major retailers to sign up to private regulatory principles to which they did not previously subscribe (Meidinger 2003). The widespread adoption of FSC standards in the UK was subsequently brokered by a UK government agency (McNichol 2006: 362–363).

The potential for private enforcement of regulatory norms is not restricted to situations where contracts are present. In their research on environmental compliance that goes beyond legal requirements, Gunningham, Kagan and Thornton have suggested that the existence of an implicit social licence with local residents, community groups and NGOs enables these groups 'to act as effective watchdogs and de facto regulators, shaming and otherwise pressurising companies into beyond-compliance environmental performance' (Gunningham et al. 2003: 152). Whilst this analysis originates with the local community relationships surrounding extractive industries, it is possible to conceive of social licences operating transnationally around such issues as labour rights.

4. HYBRID NON-JUDICIAL ENFORCEMENT OF TPR

Thus far I have focused on public enforcement of public regulatory regimes and then on private enforcement of private regimes. I turn now to mixed models, including public enforcement of TPR regimes and private enforcement of public regimes. The full set of instances of public enforcement of TPR regimes would, of course, include judicial enforcement. There is a lively debate as to the extent to which the courts should seek to discover and give effect to private norms (Bernstein 1996), but that need not concern us here. Such debates are more concerned with the bilateral resolution of disputes than with some more broadly conceived idea of regulation. Furthermore, just as the overwhelming majority of public enforcement of public regulation occurs without reference to courts, towards the base of the enforcement pyramid the same is likely to be true of public enforcement of TPR regimes. In this respect public enforcement of private regimes is not analogous to private enforcement of public regimes, the latter emphasizing litigation as the chief mechanism of enforcement in such areas as environmental regulation and competition law (Boyer and Meidinger 1985).

An initial question is why would public authorities become involved in enforcing TPR norms? Within some TPR regimes regulatory capacity is incomplete, in the sense that there may be no mechanisms for monitoring and/or enforcement. Alternatively mechanisms that exist may be weak. In other instances norms from TPR regimes may be optional, as with technical standards and codes of corporate social responsibility (CSR), but national or supranational legislators may want to incorporate them into public regulatory regimes to reduce public costs and exploit private expertise in setting such norms. In the case of CSR, implementation by firms may offer mitigation in regulatory enforcement actions, or may be a condition for setting a regulatory action or for issuing a licence (Parker 2007: 218–220). In a third case private regulators, seeking to promote compliance with their rules may find that their organizational capacity and expertise, by themselves, are insufficient to promote compliance and the authority of others, notably state actors, should be invoked to give more robust effect to the regime (Jacobsson and Andersson 2006: 259). Rees has described how the self-regulatory regime over the US nuclear power industry is, in some cases, dependent on the capacity to invoke state enforcement of safety rules and he refers to this as the 'gorilla in the closet' (Rees 1997). In this instance public enforcement constitutes a form of escalation towards the apex of what turns out to be a hybrid enforcement pyramid. Intriguingly, the ultimate sanction within some private regimes, to expel a member, may be too drastic (and also counter-productive if it leaves the expellee unregulated or liable to use their knowledge to disrupt the regime (Bernstein 1992: 129)), such that invoking a less drastic public enforcement action provides a significant escalation short of the ultimate sanction (Figure 4.3). These are the kind of considerations which have placed many TPR regimes within a set of hybrid arrangements under which enforcement (and prior to that incentives to join a non-state regime) may be pursued by public regulators. More generally it has been observed that states have become increasingly important in some sectors as 'mediators, arbiters and legitimacy providers' (McNichol 2006: 371), and that whereas regimes have previously been characterized as state, business or civil society, there is a degree of convergence of regimes on a centre ground characterized by the participation of each of these groupings (Abbott and Snidal 2009).

A broader recognition of hybrid enforcement capacity amongst businesses, civil society and governments caused Gunningham and Grabosky to re-cast the pyramid in three dimensions with each of these societal groups identified on one face (Grabosky 1997; Gunningham and Grabosky 1998: 397–404). The enforcement capacity represented shows the capacity of each kind of actor to escalate sanctions, with considerable potential both for overlap and for hybrid approaches. Thus, for example, some low-level, but well publicized publicly enforced sanction such as securing an undertaking of compliance against a business, might be amplified by civil

Source: Adapted from Ayres and Braithwaite (1992).

Figure 4.3 A hybrid enforcement pyramid

society organizations such as the media or NGOs giving publicity to the sanction, and businesses re-evaluating the riskiness of current or future contracting with the firm involved. As noted above there is no monopoly over coercion held by the state.

EU regimes for consumer protection provide a number of examples of different forms of relationship with TPR regimes. It is quite common for national regulatory regimes to refer to technical standards set by the ISO and other standardization bodies. The International Organisation of Securities Commissions (IOSCO), an international body of national public regulators, has indicated its approval for standards put forward by the International Accounting Standards Board (IASB), a private body, thus effectively incorporating IASB rule-making into supranational and national regulatory practice. It has been suggested that not only does the IASB gain authority for its rules through this action, but that the IOSCO derives authority from the technical expertise of the private body (Jacobsson and Andersson 2006: 261).

Within the EU regime on product safety a hierarchy of legislative and private standards is created. Compliance with the general product safety requirement may be demonstrated first by compliance with an EU legislative standard, second by compliance with a national legislative standard, third by compliance with a European private standard, emanating from, for example, CEN or CENELEC, the general and electrical standards bodies, respectively, and fourth by compliance with a national standard, originating with national standards bodies such as AFNOR, DIN or the BSI (Directive 2001/95/EC, Article 3 (Scott 2010)). Such standards are, for some products, mandatory under national legislation. Where they are not, compliance with the standards provides a means of demonstrating compliance and reducing the discretion involved in monitoring and enforcing for consumer protection agencies. Enforcement measures for unsafe consumer products include voluntary and mandatory recall (arrayed pyramidally, one assumes), application of fines, and, in some cases imprisonment, and destruction of products. My understanding is that the destruction sanction is not applied in pyramidal fashion. An importer or producer may be given an option to destroy an unsafe product themselves, but where a non-compliant product presents a serious risk, destruction by the firm involved, or by the enforcement agency is applied as a sanction without recourse to lower-level sanctions.

EU consumer protection legislation also provides a mechanism for public enforcement of self-regulatory codes where private enforcement is absent or inadequate. Under the terms of the Unfair Commercial Practices Directive, prohibited conduct includes holding oneself out to be a member of a self-regulatory regime where either the firm is not a member, or, even if a member, does not routinely comply with the requirements of the regime (Directive 2005/29/EC Article 6(2)(b)). The latter circumstance may, in practice, be difficult to identify with precision since a degree of non-compliance and punishment by the regime is anticipated by the EU regime. Perhaps routine refusal to accept the judgments of the enforcers of the self-regulatory regime would be an appropriate indicator. National legislatures have set down the mechanisms for enforcement for such misleading practices. Under Irish legislation there is an a elaborate architecture for enforcement by the National Consumer Agency which includes the informal mechanism of education, advising and warning, with a range of formal low-level steps including seeking undertakings and issuing prohibition notices prior to the more punitive steps of applying administrative penalties and seeking fines and/or imprisonment in criminal litigation. For each measure the agency is entitled to publish details of the infractions and the sanctions, thus creating an additional, socially-based sanction of naming and shaming wrong-doers (Consumer Protection Act 2007). Adverse publicity and reputational damage is thought to concentrate minds in firms with valuable brand images to protect to a greater extent than relatively small fines.

Instances of transnational private enforcement of public rules are perhaps less visible than public enforcement of private rules. The compliance functions of multinational enterprises involve understanding and implementing public regulatory requirements, including national variations, across the enterprise (Kagan 2000). The examples of gatekeeping by banks in respect of online gaming and of airlines in respect of immigration, noted above, also exemplify transnational private enforcement of public rules.

One last variation on the theme is private enforcement of private regimes, transnationally, over public actors. One set of examples which spring to mind are the development of performance league tables by trade associations and media organizations over public bodies such as competition and telecommunications regulators and universities. Such league tables implicitly set standards through the selection of the indicators which are measured, involve the producer of the league table in collecting data, and then steer behaviour of the targeted organizations by reference to publication of performance comparative to others in the league table. The hypothesis with performance indicators generally is that organizations which are regulated in this way focus adjustments to their behaviour on the aspects of performance that are measured and published (Miller 2001). The publication of credit ratings in respect of sovereign debt also exemplifies the application of private regime over public sector bodies, in this case governments (Scott 2002).

5. CONCLUSIONS

The enforcement of TPR regimes occurs very largely in a secret world, frequently as dependent on markets and networks as they are on hierarchy for effectiveness. Weaknesses which are shaped by such contingencies are, to some extent, compensated for by the potential for public enforcement, or indeed the displacement of private with public regimes. The hidden nature of such enforcement should not surprise us too much, since in many jurisdictions low-level regulatory enforcement is also fairly opaque. Accordingly there are common questions which may be asked of regulatory enforcement generally as to its legitimacy.

Legitimacy, the sense that some set of governance arrangements are more or less acceptable (and thus followed), is liable to be a product both of procedural and substantive considerations, inputs- and outputs-based legitimacy (Scharpf 1998). Legal scholarship has tended to emphasize the procedural basis for legitimacy which includes considerations of compliance with rule of law values such as equality of treatment, transparency and non-retrospectivity and extends to such matters as the giving of reasons and meeting of legitimate expectations. Other approaches have placed greater emphasis on outcomes displacing a more traditional legal emphasis on input or process criteria for legitimacy with substantive evaluations. Law and society scholarship on regulation, for example, has chiefly concerned itself with the effectiveness of implementing regulatory norms – for example aiming to maximize compliance (Parker 2000b).

Within the literature which applies principles of law and economics to the emergence and operation of social norms, the chief criterion of evaluation is economic efficiency, although other possible values which might underpin substantive legitimacy are recognized, including equity and corrective justice (Katz 1996: 1745). The issue of legitimacy of private regimes is significant, in part, because it may guide decisions as to when deference to such regimes by governments should be shown (Katz 1996: 1752). However, we should recognize that in many instances private regimes, particularly at the transnational level, have come about, in part, because of the limited capacity of government to provide appropriate, or any, regimes. This may be for political reasons – a reluctance to impose public roles which might scare off foreign direct investment for example – or because of a lack of reach of national governments over targeted activities as they occur wholly outside the jurisdiction. Within regulatory scholarship, advocacy of broad principles-based regulation, which tends to create spaces for various forms of private regulation to fill in detailed requirements, is seen to be a superior form of outputs-based regulation than the kind of detailed public rules which invite creative compliance (McBarnet and Whelan 1991; Parker 2000b: 547).

Few instances of enforcement of TPR regimes are ever likely to be litigated, although there may be potential for 'appeal' to arbitrators or courts over enforcement action which gives rise to contractual disputes. The linkage between TPR regimes and public enforcement does give some potential for public oversight of TPR regimes, chiefly at national level. Most obviously national regulators may blow the whistle on regimes which they consider to be fraudulent in the claims they make about benefits to consumers from products produced within such regimes.

To a large extent the effectiveness and legitimacy of TPR regimes and their enforcement is likely to be a product of market and social processes in combination with private law and public oversight or engagement. The more trustworthy and effective regimes are liable to emerge where there is a range of commercial, NGO and perhaps also governmental actors involved. It has been noted that TPR regimes are increasingly taking on this kind of tripartite form as each type of participant brings to the regime something lacking in the others (Abbott and Snidal 2009).

REFERENCES

Abbott, K. and D. Snidal (2009). 'The Governance Triangle: Regulatory Standards Institutions and the Shadow of the State'. In W. Mattli and N. Woods (eds), *The Politics of Global Regulation*. Princeton, Princeton University Press.

Ayres, I. and J. Braithwaite (1992). *Responsive Regulation: Transcending the Deregulation Debate*. Oxford, Oxford University Press.

Baldwin, R. and J. Black (2008). 'Really Responsive Regulation'. *Modern Law Review* **71**: 59–94.

Beale, H. and T. Dugdale (1975). 'Contracts Between Businessmen'. *British Journal of Law and Society* **2**: 45–60.

Bernstein, L. (1992). 'Opting Out of the Legal System: Extralegal Contractual Relations in the Diamond Industry'. *Journal of Legal Studies* **21**: 115–157.

Bernstein, L. (1996). 'Merchant Law in a Merchant Court: Rethinking the Code's Search for Immanent Business Norms'. *University of Pennsylvania Law Review* **144**: 1765–1821.

Bernstein, L. (2001). 'Private Commercial Law in the Cotton Industry: Creating Cooperation Through Rules, Norms, and Institutions'. *Michigan Law Review* **99**: 1724–1790.

Boyer, B. and E. Meidinger (1985). 'Privatising Regulatory Enforcement: A Preliminary Assessment of Citizen Suits Under Federal Environmental Laws'. *Buffalo Law Review* **34**: 835–964.

Braithwaite, J. and P. Drahos (2000). *Global Business Regulation*. Cambridge, Cambridge University Press.

Calliess, G.-P. (2008). 'Transnational Consumer Law: Co-Regulation of B2C E-Commerce'. In O. Dilling, M. Herberg and G. Winter (eds), *Responsible Business: Self-Governance and Law in Transnational Economic Transactions*. Oxford, Hart.

Cashore, B., G. Auld and D. Newsom (2004). *Governing Through Markets: Forest Certification and the Emergence of Non-State Authority*. New Haven, CT, Yale University Press.

Engwall, L. (2006). 'Global Enterprises in Fields of Governance'. In M.-L. Djelic and K.S. Andersson (eds), *Transnational Governance: Institutional Dynamics of Regulation*. Cambridge, Cambridge University Press.

Furger, F. (1997). 'Accountability and Systems of Self-Governance: The Case of the Maritime Industry'. *Law and Policy* **19**: 445–476.

Gilboy, J. (1997). 'Implications of "Third Party" Involvement in Enforcement: The INS, Illegal Travellers, and International Airlines'. *Law and Society Review* **31**: 505–530.

Grabosky, P. (1997). 'Discussion Paper: Inside the Pyramid: Towards a Conceptual Framework for the Analysis of Regulatory Systems'. *International Journal of the Sociology of Law* **25**: 195–201.

Grabosky, P. and J. Braithwaite (1986). *Of Manners Gentle: Enforcement Strategies of Australian Business Regulatory Agencies*. Melbourne, Oxford University Press.

Gunningham, N. and P. Grabosky (1998). *Smart Regulation: Designing Environmental Policy*. Oxford, Oxford University Press.

Gunningham, N. and D. Sinclair (2002). *Leaders and Laggards: Next-Generation Environmental Regulation*. Sheffield, Greenleaf Publishing.

Gunningham, N., R. Kagan and D. Thornton (2003). *Shades of Green: Business, Regulation and Environment*. Stanford, Stanford University Press.
Haines, F. (2005). *Globalization and Regulatory Character*. Aldershot, Ashgate.
Hallström, K.T. (2004). *Organizing International Standardization: ISO and IASC in Quest of Authority*. Cheltenham UK and Northampton, MA, USA, Edward Elgar.
Hancher, L. and M. Moran (eds) (1989). *Capitalism, Culture and Regulation*. Oxford, Oxford University Press.
Haufler, V. (2003). 'New Forms of Governance: Certifications Regimes as Social Regulations of the Global Market'. In E. Meidinger, C. Elliott and G. Oesten Regmagen-Oberwinter (eds), *Social and Political Dimensions of Forest Certification*. Available at: http://www.forstbuch.de/
Havinga, T. (2006). 'Private Regulation of Food Safety by Supermarkets'. *Law & Policy* **28**: 515–533.
Hood, C., H. Rothstein and R. Baldwin (2001). *The Government of Risk*. Oxford, Oxford University Press.
Jacobsson, B. and K.S. Andersson (2006). 'Dynamics of Soft Regulations'. In M.-L. Djelic and K.S. Andersson (eds), *Transnational Governance: Institutional Dynamics of Regulation*. Cambridge, Cambridge University Press.
Kagan, R.A. (2000). 'Introduction: Comparing National Styles of Regulation in Japan and the United States'. *Law and Policy* **22**: 225–244.
Kagan, R. and J. Scholz (1984). 'The "Criminology of the Corporation" and Regulatory Enforcement Strategies'. In K. Hawkins and J. Thomas (eds), *Enforcing Regulation*. Boston, Kluwer-Nijhoff.
Katz, A. (1996). 'Taking Private Ordering Seriously'. *University of Pennsylvania Law Review* **144**: 1745–1763.
Kysar, D.A. (2004). 'Preferences for Processes'. *Harvard Law Review* **118**: 525–642.
Macaulay, S. (1963). 'Non-Contractual Relations in Business: A Preliminary Study'. *American Sociological Review* **28**: 55–83.
McBarnet, D. and C. Whelan (1991). 'The Elusive Spirit of the Law: Formalism and the Struggle for Legal Control'. *Modern Law Review* **54**: 848–873.
McNichol, J. (2006). 'Transnational NGO Certification Programs as New Regulatory Forms: Lessons from the Forestry Sector'. In M.-L. Djelic and K.S. Andersson (eds), *Transnational Governance: Institutional Dynamics of Regulation*. Cambridge, Cambridge University Press.
Meidinger, E. (2003). 'Forest Certification as a Global Civil Society Regulatory Institution'. In E. Meidinger, C. Elliott and G. Oesten Regmagen-Oberwinter (eds), *Social and Political Dimensions of Forest Certification*. Available at: http://www.forstbuch.de/
Meidinger, E. (2008). 'Multi-Interest Self-Governance Through Global Product Certification Programmes'. In O. Dilling, M. Herberg and G. Winter (eds), *Responsible Business: Self-Governance and Law in Transnational Economic Transactions*. Oxford, Hart.
Miller, P. (2001). 'Governing by Numbers: Why Calculative Practices Matter'. *Social Research* **68**: 379–396.
Ogus, A. (1995). 'Re-Thinking Self-Regulation'. *Oxford Journal of Legal Studies* **15**: 97–108.
Ostrom, E. (1990). *Governing the Commons: The Evolution of Institutions for Collective Action*. Cambridge, Cambridge University Press.

Parker, C. (2000a). 'The Ethics of Advising on Regulatory Compliance: Autonomy or Interdependence?' *Journal of Business Ethics* **28**(4): 339–351.
Parker, C. (2000b). 'Reinventing Regulation Within the Corporation – Compliance-oriented Regulatory Innovation'. *Administration & Society* **32**(5): 529–565.
Parker, C. (2007). 'Meta-Regulation: Legal Accountability for Corporate Social Responsibility'. In D. McBarnet, A. Voiculescu and T. Campbell (eds) *The New Corporate Accountability: Corporate Social Responsibility and the Law*. Oxford, Oxford University Press.
Rees, J. (1997). 'The Development of Communitarian Regulation in the Chemical Industry'. *Law and Policy* **19**: 477–528.
Richardson, B. (2002). *Environmental Regulation Through Financial Organisation: Comparative Perspectives on the Industrialised Nations.* The Hague, Kluwer Law International.
Rock, E.B. and M.L. Wachter (1996). 'The Enforceability of Norms and the Employment Relationship'. *University of Pennsylvania Law Review* **144**: 1913–1952.
Scharpf, F.W. (1998). *Interdependence and Democratic Legitimation*. Cologne, Max Planck Institute for the Study of Societies.
Schepel, H. (2005). *The Constitution of Private Governance: Product Standards in the Regulation of Integrating Markets.* Oxford, Hart Publishing.
Scott, C. (2002). 'Private Regulation of the Public Sector: A Neglected Facet of Contemporary Governance'. *Journal of Law and Society* **29**: 56–76.
Scott, C. (2004). 'Regulatory Innovation and the Online Consumer'. *Law & Policy* **26**: 453–482.
Scott, C. (2005). 'Between the Old and the New: Innovation in the Regulation of Internet Gambling'. In J. Black, M. Lodge and M. Thatcher (eds), *Regulatory Innovation*. Cheltenham, UK and Northampton, MA, USA, Edward Elgar.
Scott, C. (2010). 'Enforcing Consumer Protection Laws'. In G. Howells, I. Ramsay, T. Wilhelmson and D. Kraft (eds), *Handbook of Research on International Consumer Law*. Cheltenham, UK and Northampton, MA, USA, Edward Elgar.
Taylor, P.L. (2005). 'In the Market But Not of It: Fair Trade Coffee and Forest Stewardship Council Certification as Market-Based Social Change'. *World Development* **33**: 129–147.

PART II

Judicial enforcement of transnational public regulation

5. Judicial models of international law enforcement[1]

Francesco Francioni

1. A MODERN APPROACH TO AN OLD PROBLEM

For more than a century the issue of international law enforcement by domestic courts has been monopolised by the debate over monism and dualism as theoretical models for conceptualising the relationship between international law and domestic law. Triepel[2] and Anzilotti,[3] the champions of legal positivism at the end of the 19th century and in the first half of the 20th century, postulated a separation of the two legal orders and the necessity of a formal incorporation of international law in municipal law as a condition for domestic courts to enforce the former. This construction was the result of a normative perspective in which domestic legal orders are original, independent and self-sufficient, and therefore 'separate' from international law. This conception was reinforced by judicial practice and especially by some decisions of international courts.[4] At the opposite end, proponents of monism followed in the footsteps of natural law, which by definition presupposes a *universal* idea of the law and a coherent and homogeneous legal order with no place for relativism. In its modern version, monism has found its most accomplished form in the pure theory of law of Hans Kelsen where the universe of law responds to the formal

[1] This chapter elaborates and updates ideas already expressed by the author in his article 'International Law as a Common Language for National Courts', 36 *Texas Int. L. J.*, 2001, pp. 587ff.

[2] H. Triepel, *Voelkerrecht und landesrecht*, 1899.

[3] D. Anzilotti, *Corso di diritto internazionale,* 1928.

[4] See in particular the judgment of the Permanent Court of International Justice in the case of *German Interests in Upper Silesia*, where it is explicitly stated that 'Au regard du droit international et de la Cour qui en est l'organe, les lois nationales sont des simples faits, manifestations de l'activité des Etats au meme titre que les decisions judiciares et les mesures administratives' (CPJI, S.A. n. 7, 19).

logic of a hierarchical architecture of the legal order based on a *grundnorm* on which the validity of all other norms is based.[5]

Although the contrast between dualists and monists could be easily liquidated today as an outdated academic dispute of time past,[6] contemporary practice shows that it continues to re-emerge in different forms and with new implications. It has happened in the context of the fashionable rediscovery of the theory of pluralism of legal orders,[7] in relation to the increasing insistence on the non-derogable character of national law on fundamental rights, and, in its more extreme forms, in the variety of theories that tend to challenge or deny the democratic legitimacy of international law in the name of the sanctity of national constitutions and of popular consent. Many manifestations of judicial practice confirm this trend. One needs only to think of the much commented *Kadi* judgment of the European Court of Justice,[8] which has held that an EU measure implementing a Security Council sanction with direct effect for the targeted individual could not trump the fundamental principles of due process of EU law. Along the same lines we can find the ruling of the United States Supreme Court in the notorious *Medellin* case,[9] which has brought the separation of international law and national law to the extreme consequence of holding the courts of Texas free to apply its own criminal law in contrast with a judgment of the International Court of Justice that mandated the reopening and reconsideration of criminal proceedings in a death penalty case involving the breach of the right to consular assistance of the sentenced individual. Even in the much more closely knit system of interactions between international law and national law as in the European Convention on Human Rights, the eternal debate between dualism and monism re-emerges with respect to the persistent difficulties of enforcing

---

5 H. Kelsen, *Allgemeine Staatslehere*, Leipzig, 1925 and *Principles of International Law*, New York, 1952.

6 In this sense, see Soerensen, who states: '… le sentiment general aujourd' hui, est que ce débat théorique est epuisé … les historiens futurs de la doctrine du droit international le considérerons peut-être comme une des characteristiques de la première moitié du vingtième siecle', *Recueil des Cours*, 1960 (III), p. 109.

7 I use the word 'rediscovery' because the contemporary debate over plurality and interaction of legal orders owes much to the original work of Santi Romano and his 'institutional' theory of the legal order and of the consequent pluralità of legal orders, corresponding to the plurality of the social groups that organise themselves in legal and institutional structures independent one from another. See Romano, *L'Ordinamento giuridico*, 1918.

8 For a comment, Francioni, 'Kadi and the Vicissitudes of Access to Justice' in *Challenging the EU Counter-Terrorism Measures Through Courts,* Cremona, Francioni, Poli (eds), EUI Working Paper, Academy of European Law, 2009/10.

9 *Medellin* v *Texas*, decision of 25 March 2008, 552 US 491 (2008).

the judgments of the Strasbourg Court in the domestic systems of the State Parties.[10] Recently, we have even observed open calls by influential sectors of the national judiciary to put an end to the perceived quasi constitutional role of the Strasbourg Court in stepping over State Parties' margin of appreciation and its overlooking the diversity of national cultural and legal traditions that shape the interpretation of human rights in different countries.[11]

So, far from being dead, the issue of dualism and monism continues to condition the way in which courts and other national enforcement bodies treat and implement international law. The reasons for this persistence are clear also in the context of the topic of this book. On the one hand globalisation produces a quantitative expansion of the international and transnational regulation of many areas of economic and social life that in the past were subject to the exclusive jurisdiction of the state, with a corresponding increase in the number and range of international claims that private actors bring before domestic courts. On the other hand international law is undergoing a qualitative transformation in the sense of moving away from its original matrix of a purely inter-governmental legal order to that of a composite system of norms, addressing, besides states, also individuals, private actors, and the international community as a whole. If we take into account this structural transformation, the real question today is not whether and how to re-open the old abstract debate over the theoretical model in which to frame the normative relationship between international law and domestic law, but rather to ask what role national courts and enforcement agencies can play when they are confronted with claims and disputes that involve the application of international norms. So posed, the question presupposes that one way or another international law – both customary and treaty law – is recognised as binding on the state as a political social structure, and not as a pure system of norms.[12] It entails that international law is considered to be functioning in harmony with domestic law, and that, therefore, the latter does not exist in total separation from, and systemic conflict with, the

---

[10] For an updated overview of these difficulties, see A. Caligiuri, 'The Application of the ECHR in the Domestic Systems', Symposium on the Future of the ECHR System, XX *Italian Ybk Int. L.* (forthcoming).

[11] The position of the UK has been especially critical in this respect. See Lord Hoffman, 'Human Rights and the House of Lords', *Modern Law Review*, 1999, pp. 159ff., and the speech, 'The Universality of Human Rights', Judicial Studies Board, London, 19 March 2009.

[12] On this point see the penetrating reflections of R. Quadri, *Diritto Internazionale pubblico*, Napoli, 1968, p. 5.

former. This is a fact in the contemporary world. Modern constitutions recognise and sometimes give superior status to international law,[13] and court made rules, as in the United Kingdom and the United States, establish that 'international law is part of the law of the land'.[14]

But even if this reality has attenuated the dogmatic counter-position of dualists and monists, adjudication of cases involving international law remains fraught with difficult questions. National judges face the challenge of interpretation of legal concepts that may have different meanings in different legal orders, such as human dignity, public morals, state of necessity, national security, just to give a few examples. The identification of the proper addresses of relevant obligations may pose problems, since normally national judges apply the law to individuals and private entities, whereas international law is mainly concerned with relations between states. More important, national courts will always face the problem of how to solve unavoidable conflicts between norms of the two legal orders and of how to reconcile fundamental principles of separation of powers between the executive and the judiciary with the international rule of law and the independence of judges.

This chapter will address these issues from a policy oriented perspective of how national courts can best participate in the process of enforcement of international law and thus serve the function of international justice, together with, and in addition to, international courts and traditional diplomatic means.

2. ENFORCING CUSTOMARY INTERNATIONAL LAW

As pointed out above, there is no dispute today that customary international law is recognised in domestic law and must be applied by domestic courts. By definition, however, customary law is in a constant flux and its transformation reflects the changing social necessities and aims of the international society. This is clearly evidenced by the dynamic evolution of many sectors of international law like sovereign immunities, international

[13] See, A. Cassese, 'Modern Constitutions and International Law', *Recueil des Cours*, 1985, pp. 331–368.

[14] For the United Kingdom, see e.g. *Triquet* v *Bath*, 3 Burr. 1478 (K.B. 1764); *R.* v *Keyn*, 2 Ex. D.63 (1876); *West Rand Central Gold Mining Co.* v *R.*, 2 K.B. 391 (1905); *Mortensen* v *Peters*, 8 F. (j) 93(1906) (Scotland). For the United States, see e.g. *The Paquete Habana*, 175 U.S. 677 (1900); *Edye* v *Robertson*, 112 U.S. 580 (1884); *Sei Fujii* v *California*, 38 Cal. 2d 718 (1952).

criminal law, the law of the sea, and of the body of human rights law, to mention just a few examples. When customs undergo such transformation, national courts need to keep intact the lifelines that connect national jurisdiction with the evolving structure of international law. In practical terms, national courts need to explore and discover the world of state practice, international jurisprudence and comparative case law to try to capture the essence of *opinio iuris* and consolidation of practice that are the decisive elements in the formation of customary rules of international law. Today, this task is facilitated by the widely available means of information and communication technology, which permit facilitated access to international legal material and decisions of foreign courts. Unfortunately, all too often national courts show the tendency to ascertain the existence and content of a norm of customary international law on the basis of precedents found in national law and national judicial practice. This, of course, may lead to the consolidation of misconceived ideas of customary law and to unilateral interpretation of the law inconsistently with the character of international customs, as the manifestation of the collective will of the international society and not of the unilateral assessment of a single state. Sometimes this 're-nationalisation' of customary international law is not the result of a free choice of judges but is imposed on courts by legislative act. This happens, for instance, in cases where conditions and limits on sovereign immunities are set by national legislation in a way that does not reflect generally accepted practice, or with regard to the prohibition of torture and cruel and inhuman treatment or punishment. This is an international crime defined under customary international law and restated in specific treaties, such as the 1984 Torture Convention[15] and the UN Covenant on Civil and Political Rights.[16] Yet, in some countries a tendency has emerged to leave the definition of torture to the exclusive determination of national law,[17] which may lead to the practical elusion of the international law obligation to prevent and suppress torture and to the manipulation of its definition, as has happened in the case of official authorisation of severe forms of interrogation in the fight against terror.

By reaching out to foreign judgments, by making use of the method of comparative evaluation of the case law of different jurisdictions, and by

---

[15] Convention against Torture and Other Cruel, Inhuman or Degrading Treatment or Punishment, Dec. 10, 1984, 1465 UNTS 85.

[16] International Covenant on Civil and Political Rights, Dec. 16, 1966, 999 UNTS 171.

[17] The United States has attached a specific understanding to the Torture Convention to the effect of accepting only the definition of torture that is in accordance with the United States Supreme Court.

discovering the world of international practice, national courts do not only contribute to the development of a correct model of judicial enforcement of international law, they may also contribute to the evolution and consolidation of international law. In the important and topical area of sovereign immunity it is the jurisprudence of national courts that has produced the transformation from the old regime of absolute immunity to the current regime of restrictive immunity, which is much more responsive to the contemporary need to ensure the individual right of access to justice. It is unavoidable that during the process of transformation national courts may take different attitudes with regard to the applicable rule of international law. It took half a century for the courts of common law countries to reconcile themselves with the new norm of customary international law excluding state immunity for commercial activities.[18] At the time of writing national courts are again the focus of international attention and even of a litigation adjudicated before the International Court of Justice[19] over the question of whether the rule of sovereign immunity should be set aside when the recourse concerns a victim of alleged breaches of human rights so grave as to constitute violations of *jus cogens.* Some national courts, notably the Italian Court of Cassation[20] and the Greek Supreme Court,[21] have construed international law so as to set aside the immunity of the respondent state in order to give priority to the right of the victim to have access to justice. Other courts have interpreted international law in a more traditional fashion and have maintained immunity notwithstanding the alleged violation of a norm of *jus cogens*.[22] These divergent interpretations

---

[18] In *Trendtex* v *Central Bank of Nigeria* (16 ILM 471, 1977), the House of Lords contributed to the universalisation of the rule of restrictive immunity by recognising that, although such doctrine was not at the relevant time (1977) recognised by all states, yet it was 'consonant with justice'.

[19] See ICJ Jurisdictional Immunities of the State (Germany v Italy: Greece Intervening), 3 February 2012, in which the Court upheld immunity.

[20] See in particular *Ferrini* v *Repubblica Federale di Germania, Corte di Cassazione (Sezioni Unite Civili)*, 11 March 2004, No 5044. For an extensive comment in English, see M. Iovane, 'The Ferrini Judgment of the Italian Supreme Court: Opening up Domestic Courts to Claims of Reparation for Victims of Serious Violations of Fundamental Rights', XIV *Italian Ybk Int. L.*, 2004, pp. 165ff.

[21] *Prefecture of Voiotia* v *Federal Republic of Germany*, case No 11/2000, 4 May 200, discussed in M. Gavouneli and I. Bantekas, *AJIL*, 2001, pp. 198ff.

[22] See in particular the judgment of the House of Lords in *Jones* v *Saudi Arabia*, 14 June 2006, and the decision of the European Court of Human Rights, Grand Chamber, in *Al Adsani* v *United Kingdom,* Application 35763/97, 21 November 2001 (http:// www,echr.coe.int/eng/judgments.htm) where, however, a substantial minority of judges (Rozakis, Caflisch, Costa, Cabral Barreto, Vajic) dissented and argued

of international law are part of the physiological evolution of international law. What is important is the continuing interaction between national courts, and between them and international practice, including the case law of the international courts and tribunals, which has already been called upon to pronounce on this issue.

3. ENFORCING TREATY LAW

More than in relation to customary law, which is akin to common law in the Anglo-American legal systems, the legacy of dualism still displays its effects in the field of treaty law. This is so because treaties, as much as statutory legislation in domestic law, are the product of a specific act of will of the law maker, rather than the result of a progressive formation of a collective conscience and of a corresponding sense of obligation of a given behaviour, as in the case of custom. This explains the instinctive sense of distrust that national judges may have towards norms of 'external' origin which sometimes may even be of uncertain consistency with domestic law. To this, one has to add that even the most important treaties, such as the UN Charter, contain norms of indeterminate character which are hardly conducive to their enforceability by domestic courts, as the already cited *Medellin* case[23] amply demonstrates. However, when the applicable provision of a treaty is complete, sufficiently precise, well defined in its normative content, and properly incorporated in domestic law, there is no reason for a national court to decline its implementation simply on the basis of the argument that the treaty has established obligations only between states. This is especially true when the applicable international norm concerns primarily the interest of individuals, as in the case of human rights, with respect to aliens' rights or the rights of immigrants and refugees. In these cases the traditional doctrine of non self-executing treaties should not be used to hinder the invocation of international law by private actors who are the addressees of the applicable norm or the ultimate beneficiaries of it. A considerable evolution has taken place towards this end in the field of human rights.[24] But the doctrine of non self-executing treaties re-emerges

---

that in case of torture the victim should have access to remedial process notwithstanding sovereign immunity.

[23] See *supra* note 9.

[24] For a comparative analysis of the domestic law jurisprudence in the enforcement of human rights, see Conforti and Francioni (eds), *Enforcing International Human Rights in Domestic Courts*, The Hague, Boston, London, 1997.

occasionally in certain states[25] and is systematically maintained in the area of international trade law under the case law of national courts, and the jurisprudence of the European Court of Justice.[26]

Enforcement of treaties by domestic courts requires the preliminary operation of interpretation of the relevant treaty provisions. This operation presupposes a good knowledge of international law and of the techniques of treaty interpretation that today are codified in the 1969 Vienna Convention on the law of Treaties. These techniques are especially important in relation to the passing of time and the consequent evolution that certain terms and concepts used in the treaty may undergo from the time of the adoption of the treaty to the time of its enforcement. Although the Vienna Convention sanctions the objective method of interpretation, that is a method which is '... in accordance with the ordinary meaning to be given to the terms of the treaty in their context and in light of its object and purpose' (Article 31 para. 1, Vienna Convention), it is important that the treaty is interpreted taking into account the political, social and legal context in which it is to be enforced. This is a good practice that finds confirmation in the case law of the GATT-WTO, especially in the well-known *Shrimp–Turtle* case,[27] in which the Appellate Body read the expression 'exhaustible natural resources' of GATT Article XX (g) not in the original 1947 sense of mineral resources, but in the contemporary context of a rapid exhaustion also of the living resources of the sea. This type of 'evolutive' interpretation is consistent with Article 31 (3) (c) of the Vienna Convention on the Law of Treaties which provides that in ascertaining the meaning of a treaty norm there shall be taken into account '... any relevant rule of international law applicable in the relation between the parties'.

Contextualising treaty interpretation can permit not only giving a compelling contemporary meaning to an old term such as 'exhaustible natural resources' , but also 'internationalising' national concepts such as 'human dignity', 'public morality', 'equity', 'necessity', or 'denial of justice', whose

---

[25] See for instance the position of the United States, which at the time of the ratification of the International Covenant on Civil and Political Rights has attached reservations and declarations to the effect of holding human rights provisions non self-executing in the domestic law of the United States. See D. Stewart, 'US Ratification of the Covenant on Civil and Political Rights: The Significance of the Reservations, Understandings and Declarations', 14 *Human Rights L.J.*, 1993, p. 77.

[26] See Case C-149/96 *Portuguese Republic* v *Council (Textiles)*, Decision of 23 November 1999, 1999 ECR I.8395.

[27] *United States – Import Prohibition of Certain Shrimp and Shrimp Products*, Report of the Appellate Body, WT/DS58/AB/R

shared understanding in comparative and international jurisprudence may facilitate the gradual development of a common language for national courts.[28]

Besides matters of interpretation and enforcement, the role of national courts is critical also in relation to matters of treaty termination and invalidity. The resolution of a dispute may depend on the applicability of a treaty whose validity or efficacy is challenged on grounds of constitutional rules, *jus cogens*, war, fundamental change of circumstances or of breach by another party. A good judicial model in these circumstances is to allow courts to reach an independent decision on the concrete case at hand without prejudging the executive decision to resolve the matter at the level of international relations through the formal denunciation of the treaty, its suspension or re-negotiation.[29] This solution permits the reconciliation of the need to prevent the enforcement in domestic law of a treaty that is vitiated or terminated under rules of international law with respect to the separation of powers between the executive and the judiciary.

4. NATIONAL COURTS AND THE EXECUTIVE

A more difficult question arises when courts are called upon to decide on matters of international law that involve sensitive issues of foreign policy or when enforcement of international law may even run counter to specific decisions of the executive. Should courts in such cases follow a model of judicial deference to the executive or a model of total independence in the enforcement of the relevant rules of international law? In his seminal work for the Institut de Droit international on 'The Activities of National Judges and the International Relations of their State',[30] Professor Conforti advocated a robust model of judicial independence in the interpretation and enforcement of international law by national judges. Even if one has to concede that not all questions of international law may be left entirely in the hands of national judges, especially when national security and fundamental foreign policy goals are involved, Professor Conforti's model is the correct one to the extent that it makes a general presumption that courts

---

[28] See Francioni, 'International Law as a Common Language for National Courts', 36 *Texas Int. Law J.*, 2001, pp. 587ff.

[29] See B. Conforti and A. Labella, 'Invalidity and Termination of Treaties: The Role of National Courts', 1 *EJIL*, 1990, p. 44.

[30] See *Annuaire de l'Institut de Droit International*, Vol. 65-I, 1993, pp. 327, 331, 337.

have the power to interpret and enforce customary international law and treaties when they are the applicable law to the case. This is a principle that the International Court of Justice has also accepted in the 1980 *Case Concerning United States Diplomatic and Consular Staff in Tehran*.[31] Faced with the Iranian objection to admissibility, on the ground that the taking of the hostages was only an 'incident' in a complex political context not amenable to resolution by adjudication, the Court held that, notwithstanding the political questions surrounding the controversial US–Iran relations, the dispute presented clear issues of law, related to the application of customs and treaty norms on diplomatic relations, immunities and individual rights, so as to render the case justiciable.

The general presumption of justiciability may suffer an exception in situations where the existence of an international 'fact' depends on a political decision of the government. This is the case in the recognition of a state or of the insurgents in a foreign state, has happened with the insurrection in Libya, which led to the control of a substantial part of the territory by the popular movement opposed to Qaddafi and to its recognition by a number of countries even before the outcome of the internal conflict was clear. In these cases national courts should defer to the executive on the point of whether a 'social fact' – that is, the existence of a legal entity for the purpose of the application of international law – has to be judicially recognised or not. But even in such situations, there is a limit beyond which the existence of the relevant international 'fact' also depends on the application of a well established set of norms. Take for instance the question of the continuity or extinction of a state as a consequence of its breaking apart. In the case of the dissolution of the former Republic of Yugoslavia and of the Soviet Union, the question was debated in the United Nations, and, in the case of Yugoslavia, it was the object of the ICJ's rulings with respect to the status of Serbia as a member of the United Nations and the addressee of some international obligations arising under treaties concluded by the predecessor state.[32] Thus, in these situations even 'international facts' are intertwined with legal questions which are suitable for judicial determination on the basis of applicable rules of international law.

Besides being unfounded in point of logic, the doctrine of absolute judicial deference to the executive in all matters touching upon international relations can run afoul of basic considerations of justice. A case in

---

[31] ICJ Reports 1980, pp. 3ff.

[32] For a discussion of the Yugoslav situation at the United Nations, see Y. Blum, 'UN Membership of the "New" Yugoslavia : Continuity or Break?', 86 *AJIL*, 1992, p. 830.

point is offered by the legislation in force in Italy until 1992 which stated that legal action for the execution of judgments against foreign states and their property was subject to authorisation by the Minister of Justice pursuant to a statute adopted in 1926.[33] At the time the statute had been adopted, such authorisation was consonant with the then prevailing regime of absolute immunity. But with the gradual erosion of absolute immunity and the emergence of the doctrine of immunity only for acts *iure imperii* and not for acts of a commercial nature, the maintenance in force of the ministerial authorisation amounted to leaving to the executive the power to frustrate the operation of the new rule of customary international law. This was bad enough, inasmuch as it precluded courts from fulfilling their constitutional mandate, under Article 10 para. 1 of the Italian Constitution, to guarantee the implementation of customary international law. To make things worse, for many years, the executive discretion was used by the Minister of Justice in a way so as to systematically deny authorisation for the execution over foreign states' property even when such property related to commercial activities rather than to some public function. This way, reasons of political convenience took precedence over the requirement of effective access to justice and of correct implementation of the rules of international law. This situation was remedied by a decision of the Italian Constitutional Court of 15 July 1992 which declared the 1926 statute unconstitutional because of its contrast with Article 10 para. 1 of the Constitution[34] mandating the enforcement of general norms of international law in the domestic legal system.

5. NATIONAL COURTS AND THE INTENTIONAL BREACH OF INTERNATIONAL LAW

A more radical conflict between the judiciary and the executive arises when national courts are faced with acts of the government that are expressly intended to breach international law. Some authors have argued that the power of the executive to breach international law is implied in the power to contribute to the making of international law.[35] This is true, of course. The

---

[33] Law 15/7/1926 n. 1263, reprinted in *Rivista di diritto internazionale*, 1926, p. 407.

[34] Corte Costituzionale, 15 July 1992 n. 329, in *Rivista di diritto internazionale*, 1992, p. 356.

[35] See e.g. J. Charney, 'May the President Violate Customary International Law?: The Power of the Executive Branch of the United States Government to Violate Customary International Law', 80 *AJIL*, 1986, pp. 913–920.

making of customary international law includes the power to change existing norms by way of a new practice that, at least at its initial stage, constitutes a breach of existing law. Many rules of customary international law have emerged as a consequence of practices that at their inception were at variance with existing norms of international law. So, the establishment of the continental shelf in the 1950s and of the Exclusive Economic Zone in the 1970s were at variance with the principle of the freedom of the high seas;[36] human rights law has become established 'in violation' of the old principle of domestic jurisdiction, and the more recent principle of the 'responsibility to protect' tends to modify the principle of non intervention in the domestic affairs of a foreign state and the fundamental norm on the prohibition of the use of force. But does this mean that any governmental act in breach of international law should be beyond the reach of judicial review by national courts, simply because of its professed or presumed intention to change international law for the better? The answer, of course, is no. First, because the dynamic transformation of customary international law does not depend of the single act of will of a state and its government; it involves a collective process of the international society as a whole. This process is gradual, not instantaneous, and it involves all the branches of government, the judiciary included. So, even a bona fide assertion by the executive of the need to act contrary to existing norms of international law for the virtuous purpose of reforming the law will have to meet the test of the generalised support of such reform by a critical mass of the international community and of its *opinio iuris.* The independent role of domestic courts in interpreting and enforcing international law remains a necessary component in the process of transformation of customary international law and in the final consolidation of the *opinio iuris* that may sanction the emergence of a new rule. Given the importance of *opinio iuris* in the consolidation of new rules of customary international law, one can easily understand that this element can find its source and evidence in reasoned decisions given by courts, especially when they are familiar with international practice and with the judgments of foreign courts. Their independence and the institutional obligation to explain the legal foundation of any given judgment is a better guarantee of *opinio iuris* than the self-judging statement of the executive branch.

Therefore, leaving courts open to the review of executive breaches of customary international law, even when they are justified by the professed

---

[36] F. Durante, 'Norme generali e regole convenzionali per la delimitazione della piattaforma continentale', *Rivista di diritto internazionale*, 1970, pp. 5ff; J. Charney, 'The Exclusive Economic Zone and Public International Law', 15 *Ocean Devt & Int. L.*, 1985, pp. 233ff.

need to change the law, has a double advantage. First, it provides a remedy against possible executive abuses. Second, it preserves the important role of domestic courts as agents in the process of creation and transformation of international law. By allowing courts to second-guess the wisdom of a governmental decision to breach customary international law, we can contribute to moderate unilateral and self-serving assertions of the need to make new law by the executive and thus to safeguard the integrity of the process through which customary international law is created and transformed.

6. THE EXTERNAL DIMENSION OF JUDICIAL ENFORCEMENT OF INTERNATIONAL NORMS

The increasing interdependence of national societies, the transnational movement of persons, goods and services, as well as the possibility of instantaneous communication permitted by information technology has placed an ever greater demand on national courts to deal with situations that are not localised in the forum state but rather originate or display their principal effects in a foreign country. An individual may face prosecution in his/her country of residence for sexual offences committed abroad against foreign children in the course of one of many instances of sex tourism. A foreign official may be arrested and prosecuted in country A for the alleged commission of war crimes or crimes against humanity in country B. Victims of human rights abuses suffered as a consequence of corporate conduct in country A may sue the parent company in its home state, country B. A foreign ship may be stopped in a port, and its officers may be arrested, in connection with a serious incident of marine pollution that occurred on the high seas or in the exclusive economic zone of a third state. What is the role of national courts in these cases? Should they restrictively apply rules of national jurisdiction, invoke the doctrine of *forum non conveniens*, and thus decline to adjudicate the case for lack of sufficient connection with the forum? Or should they rather strive for the application of relevant rules of international law to expand as far as possible the opportunity for its enforcement, even when such enforcement will affect situations abroad? It is not difficult to understand that in the normative perspective adopted in this chapter the latter alternative provides the appropriate judicial model. This is for several reasons. First, international law has recognised the existence of global public goods and of corresponding obligations established in the public interest and binding every state towards the international community as a whole rather than reciprocally one state to another.[37] Second, a constantly expanding web of treaty law in the areas of human rights, international criminal law, protection of the environment, anti-corruption, safeguarding of cultural heritage, just to mention a few examples, has given concrete content to the idea of *erga omnes* obligations, thanks to the introduction of third-party remedies which necessarily involve the enforcement role of domestic courts. Third, domestic legislation and national judicial practice in the most advanced legal systems support the exercise of jurisdiction and the application of international law to foreign situations when important public interests are involved. This is evident in the field of human rights, where a growing jurisprudence indicates that they do not necessarily stop at the forum state boundaries, but, given certain circumstances, must be secured also in relation to situations occurring abroad;[38] in the field of criminal law with its expanding list of crimes that require international cooperation in their suppression and prosecution; and even with regard to the prevention of 'potential' breaches abroad, which has led to judicial restraints on the

---

[37] Since the famous dictum of the International Court of Justice in the *Barcelona Traction Case* (ICJ Reports 1970, pp. 3ff.) such public goods have been exemplified with respect of human rights, the maintenance of peace, self-determination of peoples, and the safeguarding of the natural environment against massive pollution, and have been legally formalised in terms of *erga omnes* obligations. The 2001 Articles of the International Law Commission on the Responsibility of States for Internationally Wrongful Acts have recognised this type of obligation at Article 48 (1) (b) which foresees the possibility for any state other than the injured state to invoke the responsibility of another state if '... the obligation breached is owed to the international community as a whole'. See Report of the ILC, Official Records of the General Assembly, Fifty-sixth session, Supp. N. 10 (A/56/10) ch. IV.E.1, November 2001.

[38] The extraterritorial application of human rights obligations under Article 1 of the European Convention on Human Rights has been the object of a dense jurisprudence of the Strasbourg Court which has recognised the possibility of extraterritorial application of the Convention on the basis of: (1) the overall control of a geographical area by the respondent state (*Loizidou*, judgment of December 18, 1996, *Ilascu*, judgment of the Grand Chamber of July 8, 2004); (2) the effective control over the individuals involved (*Issa*, judgment of November 16, 2004); and (3) the residual power of a legitimate government deprived of effective control over a part of its territory to influence the respect of convention rights (*Ilascu*, cit. In this case the Court held Moldova bound by convention obligations even though it had lost to Russia the effective control over the separatist region of Transnistria, because there was evidence that Moldova could still exercise some influence over the enjoyment of the convention rights by the applicants). For a trans-judicial application of the above criteria in the Inter-American human rights system, see the recent report of the Inter-American Commission concerning the operation of Colombian military forces in the territory of Ecuador: IACHR Report No 112/10, 21 October 2010, at: http://www.cidh.oas.org/casos/10.eng.htm

power of expulsion or extradition of aliens who may be subject to human rights abuses in another country.[39]

7. CONCLUSION

The expansion of international law in areas that in the past were restricted to the domestic jurisdiction of states, the rise of transnational private regulation in many areas of economic and social life, and the increasing role of non state actors, such as business corporations and non-governmental organisations, in the promotion and enforcement of international standards, require that national courts adjust to this reality by functionally redefining their role as active participants in the enforcement of international law. This chapter has argued that this task may be successfully performed by meeting three distinct challenges. The first is the removal or minimisation of the obstacles that traditionally have hindered the effective implementation of international law in the domestic sphere (judicial deference to the executive, unnecessary use of the doctrine of non self-executing treaties, incorrect interpretation of the rules on immunity, etc.). The second is the infusion into domestic law of international law concepts which permit national courts to keep in touch with the evolutive dynamics of international law, and, by the same token, to contribute by the technical expertise of judges to the progressive development of international law as a true legal order and not a simple system of power politics. The third is the widening of the sphere of justice beyond the traditional boundaries of the nation state, by way of judicial application of international law also to private actors and public officials who operate abroad in parts of the world where weak governance, conflict situations or the absence of the rule of law make local enforcement agencies unable or unwilling to implement international law.

---

[39] After the *Soering* (Judgment of July 7 1989, 11 EHRR 439, Series A. No 161, Application No 14038/88) case in which the Strasbourg Court held the United Kingdom bound to enforce Article 3 of the Convention in order to prevent the 'probable' breach of the applicant's human rights as a consequence of his extradition to the United States where he could be placed on death row, the Court has applied the same principle in cases of expulsion of aliens who could face 'probable' torture or inhuman treatment in the nationals' country.

6. Multilevel judicial protection of 'rule of law' in transnational regulation requires 'struggles for justice'

Ernst-Ulrich Petersmann

> The law is not mere theory, but living force. And hence it is that Justice which, in one hand holds the scales in which she weights the rights, carries in the other the sword with which she executes it. The sword without the scales is brute force; the scales without the sword is the impotence of law.[1]

I. INTRODUCTION

Globalization has decreased the scope of national regulatory powers and dramatically increased intergovernmental regulation and transnational private regulation (TPR) without adequate democratic, parliamentary and judicial 'checks and balances'. Not only the effectiveness and enforceability of both TPR and public international regulation, but also their democratic legitimacy depend on judicial protection of constitutional rights of citizens and Rule of Law (RoL), with due respect for the legitimate diversity of national constitutional guarantees of human rights and democratic self-governance. In addition to dispute prevention, dispute settlement and judicial clarification of the contested meaning of legal rules and principles, national and international courts also engage in 'judicial governance' by adjusting 'incomplete agreements' and under-theorized legal systems to the changing needs of citizens and governance. The effectiveness of transnational RoL and multilevel judicial remedies depends on their active use by citizens and on 'comity' and cooperation among courts at national, transnational (e.g. in cases of arbitration), regional and worldwide levels, based on judicial justification of multilevel protection of RoL by overlapping 'principles of justice', such as respect for common constitutional principles, 'judicial balancing' of conflicting human rights, and due process

[1] J. von Jhering, *The Struggle for Law* (translated by J. Jay Lalor, 1876), 1–2.

of law. Multilevel judicial review can both limit and enforce TPR. The universal recognition of human rights requires 'courts of justice' to review also the 'rules of recognition' governing private and public regulation by construing international economic, environmental and human rights law no longer only as 'international law among states', but also as 'integration law' among peoples and individuals entitled to judicial protection of human rights, private and democratic self-governance, and transnational RoL. In view of the ground covered in Chapter 5 of this volume on 'Judicial Models of International Law Enforcement', this chapter refrains from describing the different methods of dispute settlement and enforcement in international economic law (IEL) and their increasing 'judicialization' and 'decentralization', notably in European economic law and international commercial, investment and intellectual property law.[2]

II. THE ENFORCEMENT OF TPR DEPENDS ON JUDICIAL REMEDIES

If transnational private and public regulation – as described in the various contributions to this book – is not voluntarily complied with 'in the shadow of the law', its enforcement ultimately depends on judicial protection of RoL. In addition to their dispute settlement and enforcement functions, private and 'mixed' arbitration, national and international courts also engage in 'judicial governance' by means of clarifying, adjusting and progressively developing incomplete rules and under-theorized legal systems in response to new challenges. This is particularly true in the field of IEL in view of its often imperfect regulation of economic relations, competing private law, 'conflicts law', 'global administrative law', international law and constitutional conceptions, and ever more obvious 'regulatory failures'.[3] Clarification of whether, and to what extent, TPR is legally enforceable is ultimately a judicial task. In constitutional democracies and citizen-driven transnational relations, 'judicial dialogues' among 'courts of justice' and litigants are an ever more important part of 'deliberative

---

[2] For an overview see E.U. Petersmann, 'Justice as Conflict Resolution: Proliferation, Fragmentation and Decentralization of Dispute Settlement in International Trade Law', *University of Pennsylvania Journal of International Economic Law* 27 (2006), 273–366.

[3] For a critical discussion of the diverse conceptions of IEL see E.U. Petersmann, 'The Future of International Economic Law: A Research Agenda', in: C. Joerges and E.U. Petersmann (eds), *Constitutionalism, Multilevel Trade Governance and International Economic Law* (Oxford: Hart Publishing, 2nd edition, 2011), Chapter 18 (also published in EUI Working Paper Law Department 2010).

democracy', clarifying 'public reason' necessary for protecting the legitimacy, enforceability and consistency of law with 'principles of justice'. Examples include the multilevel judicial dialogue among national and European courts (such as the European Court of Justice (ECJ), the EFTA Court and the European Court of Human Rights) over how to 'balance' and delimit market freedoms, human rights and labor rights, or the current controversies about the legal scope of the 'no bail-out clause' in Article 125 of the Treaty on the Functioning of the European Union (TFEU) and the resultant legal limitations on the European Central Bank to purchase government bonds from insolvent EU member states and their national banks. Just as private and public regulation interact, so do private and public enforcement, for instance of privately agreed restraints of competition and their legal and judicial limitations by competition laws, unfair trade regulation and human rights. This is particularly true for the recognition and enforcement of commercial arbitration awards on the basis of international agreements like the New York Convention of 1958.

III. THE EFFECTIVENESS OF TRANSNATIONAL JUDICIAL REMEDIES DEPENDS ON MULTILEVEL JUDICIAL COOPERATION

All 193 UN member states have undertaken legal obligations to respect, protect and promote human rights and interpret international treaties 'in conformity with principles of justice' and human rights, as explicitly recalled in Article 1 of the UN Charter and in the Preamble to the Vienna Convention on the Law of Treaties. The frequent neglect of human rights in worldwide economic regulation – for instance, in the Bretton Woods agreements and in GATT/WTO practices – and the failures of governance to protect 'global public goods', entail increasing challenges by civil society to the legitimacy of IEL.[4] The 'constitutional functions' of 'courts of justice' to 'administer justice' and protect constitutional rights justify judicial protection of 'constitutional justice' also in TPR.[5] In transnational

---

[4] Cf. E.U. Petersmann, 'Administration of Justice in the WTO: Did the WTO Appellate Body Commit "Grave Injustice"?', *The Law and Practice of International Courts and Tribunals* 8 (2009), 329–373.

[5] Cf. E.U. Petersmann, '"Constitutional Justice" Requires Judicial Cooperation and "Comity" in the Protection of "Rule of Law"', in: F. Fontanelli, G. Martinico and P. Carozza (eds), *Shaping Rule of Law Through Dialogue* (the Netherlands: Europa Law Publishing, 2009), 1–19; *idem*, 'Constitutional Theories of International Economic Adjudication and Investor-State Arbitration', in: P.M. Dupuy,

relations, the enforcement of arbitral awards and other judicial dispute settlement rulings often depends on cooperation among national, transnational and international courts across jurisdictions, as illustrated by judicial review of investor–state arbitration inside the EU by national courts and related preliminary rulings by the ECJ.[6] The constitutional functions of courts to protect constitutional rights and RoL require judicial cooperation (comity) not only in the sense of deference towards national jurisdictions, but also in the cosmopolitan sense of regard to legitimate concerns of foreign jurisdictions, transnational governance procedures and the need for judicial protection of transnational 'principles of justice', with due regard to the values of conflict (e.g. in the sense of reasonable disagreement), complementarity (e.g. in multilevel protection of RoL) and comity in relationships among private and public, national and transnational regulatory orders.

IV. MULTILEVEL JUDICIAL REVIEW CAN LIMIT AND ENFORCE TPRs: EXAMPLES FROM IEL

In view of the extensive description of TPR in the other contributions to this book, this section is confined to a few illustrations of the 'limiting' and 'enforcement functions' of multilevel judicial review of TPR in IEL.

1. Intergovernmental GATT/WTO Dispute Settlement Procedures Challenging TPR

Several GATT/WTO dispute settlement procedures have challenged government support for private 'voluntary export restraints' and other restrictive business practices concerning trade in goods and services.[7] Even though GATT/WTO law prescribes access to justice at national levels (e.g. Article X GATT) and international levels (e.g. in the WTO Dispute Settlement Understanding), and domestic courts often apply the 'consistent interpretation principle' requiring interpretation of domestic laws in conformity with international legal obligations of the country concerned, GATT/

F. Francioni and E.U. Petersmann (eds), *Human Rights in International Investment Law and Arbitration* (Oxford: Oxford University Press, 2009), 137–194.

[6] Cf. H. Wehland, 'Intra-EU Investment Agreements and Arbitration: Is European Community Law an Obstacle?', *ICLQ* 2009, 297–320.

[7] Examples include *Japan – Trade in Semi-Conductors* (BISD 35S/116), *Japan – Measures affecting Consumer Photographic Film and Paper* (WT/DS44/R adopted in 1998) and *Mexico – Telecoms* (WT/DS204/R adopted in 2004).

WTO law does *not* guarantee domestic judicial enforcement of GATT/WTO rules. Most WTO dispute settlement rulings are complied with by legislative or administrative measures rather than by national court injunctions (e.g. by the Brazilian Supreme Court in 2009 regarding the WTO Appellate Body findings concerning Brazilian restrictions of retreaded tires).

2. Intergovernmental GATT/WTO Dispute Settlement Procedures Enforcing TPR

GATT/WTO dispute settlement proceedings may be invoked in order to enforce privately agreed product standards and production standards that are legally recognized by WTO rules (e.g. in the TBT and SPS Agreements) or WTO decisions (e.g. on the Kimberley Protocol restricting trade in conflict diamonds). Such GATT/WTO legal and judicial remedies can protect the effectiveness of TPR at international levels but are, so far, rarely used for TPR.

3. Private Arbitration Administered in the WTO of Disputes among Private 'Pre-shipment Inspection Entities' and Exporters

Such an exceptional dispute settlement procedure has been established on the basis of Article 4 of the WTO Agreement on Pre-Shipment Inspection in cooperation with the International Chamber of Commerce in Paris. Although rarely invoked so far, it can contribute to enforcing public and private trade rules in transnational relations among private parties.

4. ECJ and National Dispute Settlement Procedures Challenging TPR

Examples include judicial enforcement of common market rules and competition rules against restrictive business practices and other private market access restrictions (e.g. by actions of trade unions in the *Viking* and *Laval* disputes among European companies invoking the market freedoms of EU law, and trade unions resorting to strikes so as to dissuade the companies concerned from using their EU market freedoms).[8] Such judicial proceedings clarify and enforce public law limits imposed by EU law on TPR.

---

[8] Cf. Case 341/05, *Laval un Partneri* [2007] ECR-I 11767; Case C-438/05, *Viking Line*, ECR 2007 I-10779. On the need for judicial 'proportionality balancing' of competing economic, social and human rights see E.U. Petersmann, *International Economic Law in the 21st Century* (Oxford: Hart Publishing, 2012), Chapter VII.

5. ECJ and National Dispute Settlement Procedures Enforcing TPR

Examples include judicial enforcement of privately agreed collective agreements among management and labor (Article 155 TFEU) or among private energy suppliers aimed at ensuring 'security of energy supply in the Union' (Article 194 TFEU), or judicial application of privately agreed product standards (e.g. agreed upon in the European Committee for Standardization).

6. National Courts and ICSID Annulment Proceedings Challenging TPR

Depending on the applicable procedures, private investment contracts and transnational investor–state arbitration awards – as privately agreed forms of TPR – may be challenged in national courts (e.g. on the basis of Article V of the 1958 New York Convention), possibly after a preliminary ruling of the ECJ. Investor–state arbitration based on the procedures of the International Center for the Settlement of Investment Disputes (ICSID) provides for transnational ICSID annulment procedures without additional review by national courts. Such national and transnational review enforces limitations of TPR under public law or under privately agreed investment contracts between foreign investors and host states (acting *jure gestionis*).

7. National Courts and Arbitral Tribunals Enforcing TPR

Commercial and transnational arbitral awards are legally binding and enforceable in domestic courts subject to a few circumscribed procedures for challenging arbitral awards.[9]

V. COURTS OF JUSTICE SHOULD PROMOTE TRANSNATIONAL RULE OF LAW BASED ON COSMOPOLITAN CONCEPTIONS AND DECENTRALIZED ENFORCEMENT OF IEL

The move to transnational and global regulation has shifted vast regulatory powers to the executive branches of powerful states as well as to transnational companies without adequate institutional safeguards for holding international regulation and certain transnational business practices legally

---

9 Cf. A. Redfern and M. Hunter, *Law and Practice of International Commercial Arbitration* (London: Sweet & Maxwell, 1999), Chapter 9.

and democratically accountable. In most worldwide economic organizations, international economic regulation continues to be designed in close cooperation among governments and business without effective control by national parliaments and courts. The financial crisis which began in 2008, like the oil pollution in the Gulf of Mexico, illustrate that inadequate public supervision of transnational financial regulation and of environmental business practices can lead to the destruction of billions of dollars in private savings and huge environmental damage to the detriment of citizens. This Section argues that 'struggles for rights' by adversely affected citizens and their judicial protection by courts are essential 'constitutional checks and balances' against welfare-reducing, intergovernmental and transnational business regulation.

1. Multilevel Judicial Cooperation Depends on the Prevailing Conceptions of Law

The functional interrelationships between private and public, national and international economic regulation are perceived differently by international private law, 'conflicts law', 'global administrative law', public international law and 'multilevel constitutional conceptions' of IEL.[10] While national courts in the EU, the ECJ and the European Court of Human Rights (ECtHR) cooperate in the context of shared conceptions of 'multilevel constitutional regulation', national courts in the European Economic Area (EEA) cooperate with the European Free Trade Area (EFTA) Court on the basis of more deferential interpretations of EEA law, without supranational principles of legal primacy, direct effect and direct applicability of the common market guarantees of the EEA Agreement inside EFTA countries.[11] Cooperation among national and international courts in regional free trade areas (like the North American Free Trade Agreement (NAFTA)) and common markets outside Europe (like Mercosur) is much less developed compared with Europe.[12] The diverse conceptual and regulatory approaches in multilevel economic regulation (e.g. in regional free

---

[10] Cf. Petersmann *supra* note 3 and Section VI below.

[11] Cf. E.U. Petersmann, 'Human Rights, International Economic Law and "Constitutional Justice"', *European Journal of International Law* 19 (2008), 769–798; C. Baudenbacher, *The EFTA Court in Action* (Stuttgart: German Law Publishers, 2010), at 35ff.

[12] Cf. N. Lavranos (ed.), 'Multilevel Judicial Governance between Global and Regional Economic Integration Systems', EUI Working Paper MWP 2009/41; J.A. Huerta-Goldman, 'Trade Remedies Disputes – Reciprocal Relationships between WTO and NAFTA Tribunals', in: Fontanelli, Martinico and Carozza (*supra* note 5), 299–318.

trade areas like NAFTA and common markets like Mercosur) are inevitable consequences of the legitimate reality of 'constitutional pluralism'.[13] Yet, the refusal by many domestic courts and the ECJ to implement legally binding WTO dispute settlement rulings also illustrates the numerous deficits in transnational RoL: citizens often cannot rely on compliance by governments with their self-imposed treaty obligations under international law and lack effective judicial remedies against governments that violate IEL for the benefit of powerful interest groups and exclude their judicial accountability for abuses of regulatory powers. As collective supply of many international public goods (like an efficient world trading system and prevention of climate change) depends on voluntary cooperation by citizens and transnational RoL (e.g. for decentralized carbon-emission trading systems and complementary border adjustment taxes), democratic and judicial struggles challenging government violations of internationally agreed economic, social and environmental regulation are likely to be major challenges in the 21st century.

Most governments and most textbooks continue to perceive IEL as 'public international law regulating the international economy'.[14] An alternative conception of IEL as multilevel economic regulation underlies many international trade and investment agreements. It focuses on the 'functional unity' of private and public, national and international regulation of the economy,[15] on the advantages of mutually coherent, decentralized forms of market regulation (e.g. by means of multilevel competition rules) and dispute settlement (e.g. as provided for in Chapters 11 and 19 of NAFTA), and on individual economic and social rights and judicial remedies as provided for in regional economic integration law, and, more one-sidedly, in bilateral investment treaties and intellectual property rights conventions.

---

[13] On the diverse conceptions and practices of 'constitutional pluralism' see e.g. M. Avbelj and J. Komarek (eds), 'Four Visions of Constitutional Pluralism', EUI Law Working Paper No. 21 (2008). My use of the terms 'constitution', 'constitutionalism' and 'constitutionalization' is explained in Petersmann (*supra* note 8), Chapter II, as well as in: E.U. Petersmann, 'Constitutional Justice and the Perennial Task of "Constitutionalizing" Law and Society through "Participatory Justice"', EUI Working Paper Law 2010/03.

[14] See e.g. A.H. Qureshi and A. Ziegler, *International Economic Law* (London: Sweet & Maxwell, 2nd edition, 2007), at ix: 'This book focuses on that branch of Public International Law which is concerned with international economic relations between States.'

[15] The concept of 'functional unity' tends to be construed in diverse ways by different authors depending on their legal, political and economic methodologies; cf. E.U. Petersmann, 'International Economic Theory and International Economic Law', in: R.S.J. Macdonald and D.M. Johnston (eds), *The Structure and Process of International Law* (Leiden: Nijhoff Publishers, 1983), at 239ff.

This 'multilevel economic law perspective', like the 'multilevel constitutional conceptions' of economic law applied in the jurisprudence of the ECJ and the ECtHR, emphasizes potential synergies of 'public–private partnerships'. For instance, private regulation can supplement and complement incomplete, intergovernmental regulation and offers decentralized enforcement mechanisms empowering citizens as self-interested guardians of the rule of law. Public–private co-regulation may also increase the legitimacy, effectiveness and scope of economic and environmental regulation (e.g. of the reduction of carbon-emissions and private trade in carbon permits). But it also risks facilitating 'protectionist collusion' and restrictive business practices to the detriment of consumer welfare. In contrast to the universally agreed 'rules of recognition' of public international law, as codified in Article 38 of the Statute of the International Court of Justice, multilevel economic regulation at public and private levels lacks a single unifying rule of recognition in view of its broad coverage of private and public, national and international sub-systems of IEL. It understands and analyzes IEL as interdependent 'social practices' which regulate economic activities and transactions, including the 'private ordering' of the international division of labor among billions of producers, investors, traders and consumers in UN member states. The functional interrelationships between public regulation (e.g. by means of competition law, banking law, investment law, labor law, environmental law) and private legal practices (such as TPR) are rightly perceived as core problems of economic regulation, as illustrated by the 'near-death experience' of the 2008 financial crisis which has discredited the 'market fundamentalism' advocated by many economists (i.e. the notion that unfettered markets, all by themselves, can ensure economic prosperity and growth) in the same way as the fall of the Berlin Wall discredited communism.[16]

2. Human Rights Require Reviewing the 'Rules of Recognition' of IEL

In a globalizing world where citizens rightly insist on the human rights obligations of all UN member states and on more effective protection of 'global public goods', IEL and TPR (like the transnational 'law merchant' governing international sales of goods and trade in financial products) cannot remain effective and legitimate over time unless they are justifiable by 'overlapping principles of justice', like respect for human rights, rule of law and corresponding 'corporate social responsibilities'. Especially in

---

[16] J.E. Stiglitz, *Freefall: America, Free Markets and the Sinking of the World Economy* (New York: W.W. Norton, 2009).

those areas of international relations where production, investments, trade, environmental pollution and consumption of scarce resources are driven by supply and demand of private actors, the legitimacy and effectiveness of IEL depend on empowering citizens as legal subjects to be protected by constitutional and legislative rights (e.g. labor rights) and political, administrative and judicial remedies against the ubiquitous 'market failures' and 'governance failures'.[17] The more national and international 'primary rules of conduct' evolve dynamically in response to 'globalization' and 'global regulation' by governments and powerful private actors, the more urgent becomes the need for interpreting the 'secondary rules' for changing the law and adjudicating disputes in conformity with 'principles of justice' and human rights, as explicitly required by the customary rules of international treaty interpretation and actually practiced by European courts in their multilevel protection of human rights and constitutional rights in European economic law. Courts of justice are constitutionally required to identify and interpret valid rules in conformity with the *opinio juris* not only of governments but also of citizens as 'democratic principals'.[18] The universal recognition of 'inalienable' human rights requires interpreting the traditional 'rules of recognition' of international law no longer only from the point of view of the rulers but with due regard also to the *opinio juris sive necessitatis* of civil society, democratic parliaments and independent 'courts of justice'. In the public clarification of such claims through 'deliberative democracy' and 'judicial dialogues', human rights require respecting 'reasonable disagreement' among individuals and democratic societies.

---

17 On the need for a 'cosmopolitan conception' of IEL see Petersmann, *supra* note 8.

18 On law as a union of 'primary rules' of conduct and 'secondary rules' of change, adjudication and recognition, see H.L.A. Hart, *The Concept of Law* (Oxford: Oxford University Press, 2nd edition, 1994), Chapter V. Hart's emphasis on law as social practices depending on agreed sources of law and rules of recognition justifies that international treaty rules focusing on recognition by 'the international community of states as a whole' (e.g. Article 53 VCLT concerning determination of *jus cogens*), must today be interpreted in conformity with the obligations of all UN member states to respect, protect and promote 'inalienable' human rights deriving from respect for human dignity. Like the 'constitutional distinction' between constitutional, legislative, executive and judicial rules and institutions at national and international levels of governance, the distinction between primary and secondary rules is of crucial importance for understanding the systemic character and dynamic evolution of IEL as an integrated, legal system of private and public, national and international legal sub-systems which can protect 'justice' and human rights across borders only in a multilevel constitutional framework protecting overall coherence, legitimacy and 'public reason'.

3. Justice Requires Judicial Protection of Cosmopolitan Rights

The human rights obligations of all UN member states entail that human rights – as 'the foundation of freedom, justice and peace in the world' (Preamble of the Universal Declaration of Human Rights (UDHR)) – constitutional democracies and courts of justice are the constitutional foundations of the legitimacy also of IEL. 'Equal freedoms' as 'first principle of justice' (in terms of Kantian legal philosophy) and welfare economics justify the liberalization and regulation of mutually beneficial international division of labor among free citizens, including TPR. Protection of human rights by rule of law across frontiers, and limitation of international 'market failures' as well as of 'governance failures', require constitutional restraints of abuses of public and private power, including TPR. The UN principles of 'sovereign equality of states' and of 'self-determination of peoples', and the 'subsidiary function' of UN human rights law vis-à-vis protection of human rights in constitutional democracies, justify national and regional diversity of human rights conceptions. IEL must respect reasonable disagreement about interpreting human rights, including the intergovernmental practice of separating economic regulation (e.g. in the WTO) from human rights protection on the basis of 'exception clauses' recognizing sovereign rights to protect human rights (e.g. on the basis of Article XX GATT if construed in conformity with the human rights obligations of all WTO members).

Human rights require treating citizens as subjects and 'democratic principals' of international regulation of mutually beneficial economic co-operation among citizens. Just as economic competition derives its constitutional legitimacy from protecting 'equal freedoms' (as 'first principle of justice') and general consumer welfare, so does international economic regulation derive its constitutional legitimacy from protecting equal rights of citizens (normative individualism) and constitutionally agreed 'public goods'. Unnecessary poverty, violation of human rights, treatment of citizens as mere objects and environmental pollution in so many states undermine the legitimacy of authoritarian 'Westphalian paradigms of IEL'. Also TPR will not remain effective unless the rules are recognized by citizens and parliaments as fair and enforceable in domestic courts of justice. IEL should be conceived not only as 'international law among states', but also as 'law of peoples' and 'cosmopolitan law' with individual rights to RoL, including judicial protection of precise and unconditional international guarantees of freedom, non-discrimination and social justice. Multilevel economic regulation requires multilevel constitutional protection of equal rights, democratic governance and judicial protection of RoL, as recognized by the 47 member countries of the European Convention on Human Rights and Fundamental Freedoms (ECHR).

4. TPR as Part of IEL

From the constitutional perspective of equal freedoms as 'first principle of justice' (in terms of Kantian and Rawlsian legal philosophy), TPR and other fields of IEL can be conceptualized as a 'science of liberty' (F.C. von Savigny). Judicial protection of equal liberties, like judicial enforcement of competition rules and of RoL protecting the market processes resulting from the exercise of individual freedoms, are of constitutional importance for the capacity of constitutional democracies to protect national and international 'public goods'.[19] Multilevel regulation of economic markets, including multilevel judicial protection of constitutional rights and RoL, are indispensable also for TPR, as illustrated by the financial crisis of 2008 caused by 'regulatory failures' regarding legal accountability of bankers and other financial market actors. As in European economic integration, multilevel judicial governance and citizen-driven, decentralized enforcement of common market law, competition law, environmental regulation and TPR can operate as a 'guardian of the constitutional unity of IEL', including of 'principles of justice' justifying, limiting and complementing TPR and its judicial enforcement.[20] The 'constitutional failures' of the 'Westphalian system of international law' suggest that – without TPR and its multilevel judicial review and enforcement – most international public goods, like an efficient world trading system, transnational RoL and

---

[19] On the defining characteristics of 'public goods' (like their non-excludable and non-rivalrous use benefiting all citizens), the 'collective action problems' impeding the supply of international 'public goods' (like the 'jurisdictional gap', the 'participation gap', 'incentive gap' and 'prisoner dilemmas'), and the increasing democratic insistence on devolving decision-making powers to the lowest possible level ('subsidiarity') in order to promote 'stakeholder participation' in the decentralized implementation and enforcement of multilevel regulation, see I. Kaul, I. Grunberg and M.A. Stern (eds), *Global Public Goods: International Cooperation in the 21st Century* (New York: Oxford University Press, 1999).

[20] Cf. E.U. Petersmann, 'Multilevel Judicial Governance as Guardian of the Constitutional Unity of International Economic Law', in: *Loyola International and Comparative Law Review* 30 (2008/2009), 101–152. On the increasing acknowledgment also by US lawyers of 'enabling constitutionalization', 'constraining constitutionalization' and 'supplemental constitutionalization' by means of 'international constitutional norms' see J.L. Dunoff and J. P. Trachtman (eds), *Ruling the World? Constitutionalism, International Law and Global Governance* (Cambridge: Cambridge University Press, 2009), at 10ff.

prevention of climate change, cannot be effectively supplied by governments. Yet, in view of the 'market failures' regarding supply of public goods and social justice, the legal and institutional choices necessary for transforming IEL and TPR into more effective instruments for protecting private and public goods depend not only on economic and political efficiency arguments as explained by welfare economics, public choice theory and comparative institutional analyses;[21] they must also be based on, and justified by, international agreement on 'overlapping principles of justice' and their multilevel constitutional, legislative, administrative and judicial protection – also in the field of TPR – for the benefit of citizens.

VI. OBSTACLES TO OVERCOMING FRAGMENTED CONCEPTIONS OF 'RULE OF LAW' IN TRANSNATIONAL ECONOMIC COOPERATION

In Resolution 62/70 of 8 January 2008, the UN General Assembly continues to distinguish RoL at the international level and RoL at national levels in view of the differences between the primarily 'horizontal structures' of the 'international law among states' and the primarily 'vertical structures' of national legal systems constituting and limiting governance powers vis-à-vis citizens.[22] The preceding Sections have argued that human rights, the citizen-oriented functions of IEL and the need for transnational 'rule of law communities' in the global division of labor require overcoming the traditional dichotomy of rule of law at national and international levels in international economic and environmental cooperation. If the UN Charter and modern international law require all UN member states to respect, protect and promote human rights also in transnational cooperation among citizens, including rights 'to a social and international order in which the rights and freedoms set forth in this Declaration can be fully realized' (Article 28 UDHR 1948), then national and international governments and courts should cooperate in protecting 'international rule of law' for the benefit of citizens also in their transnational division of labor. Mutually consistent rule-making and multilevel, judicial protection of 'international rule of law' are likely to strengthen both national as well as

---

[21] Cf. N. Komesar, *Imperfect Alternatives: Choosing Institutions in Law, Economics and Public Policy* (Chicago: University of Chicago Press, 1994); *idem*, *Law's Limit: The Rule of Law and the Supply and Demand of Rights* (Cambridge: Cambridge University Press, 2001).

[22] Cf. A. Nollkaemper, 'The Internationalized Rule of Law', *Hague Journal on the Rule of Law* 1 (2009), 74–78.

international law following the 'plywood principle'. As illustrated by the *Kadi* judgment of the ECJ of September 2008, domestic courts may rightly insist that compliance with international law must remain consistent with human rights and common constitutional principles.[23] Vice versa, WTO dispute settlement rulings and investor–state arbitral awards may rightly insist that domestic governments and courts must protect transnational RoL in conformity with their international legal obligations. From the point of view of citizens, the ever more intense impact of national and international rules on transnational economic transactions require 'integrated conceptions of rule of law' in international economic cooperation among producers, investors, traders and consumers. Such common conceptions of RoL must be based on the common constitutional principles underlying national and international human rights law. 'Rule of law' – as a constitutional restraint on 'rule by men' and their often selfish 'rule by law' (e.g. in limiting the legal accountability of bank managers for the 'social costs' of their banking and compensation practices) – will help not only national governments to resist protectionist pressures for violating IEL; it will likewise help international organizations to overcome the 'collective action problems' in promoting legal security and justice across national borders as a constitutional precondition for effective supply of 'international public goods'.

It remains contested whether and how the 'fragmentation' and 'legal pluralism' of the hundreds of national and functionally limited international legal systems can be interpreted coherently on the basis of agreed 'principles of justice' (like human rights, democratic governance, RoL) and other 'conflict rules' (like peaceful settlement of disputes on the basis of 'due process of law', judicial comity and respect for 'reasonable disagreement'). Just as there have been only three court proceedings among EC member states in the ECJ since the 1950s that were settled by judgments of the ECJ, many intergovernmental WTO disputes could be avoided and 'decentralized' by enabling private complainants to settle their disputes (e.g. about alleged trade discrimination, illegal customs duties, trade-related intellectual property rights, restrictive business practices) in domestic courts – provided WTO Members (notably the EU and the USA) did not prevent domestic courts from applying WTO law.[24] Yet, proposals for

---

23 Joined Cases C-402/05P & C-415/05P, *Kadi & Al Barakat Foundation* v *Council and Commission*, ECR [2008] I-6351.

24 Cf. E.U. Petersmann, 'Preventing and Settling Transatlantic Economic Disputes: Legal and Policy Recommendations from a Citizen Perspective', in: E.U. Petersmann and M.A. Pollack, *Transatlantic Economic Disputes* (Oxford: Oxford University Press, 2003), 3–64, 577–594.

decentralizing and depoliticizing intergovernmental disputes over trade practices vis-à-vis private parties by means of strengthening the *domestic dimensions* of the WTO legal and dispute settlement system – and the underlying conception of empowering citizens and domestic courts to protect 'rule of international law' for the benefit of citizens – tend to be opposed by diplomats interested in limiting their legal and judicial accountability, for instance if they use 'hegemonic international law' for the benefit of powerful interest groups at home (e.g. cotton, textiles, agricultural and industrial producers dominating trade policy-making in GATT 1947) in exchange for political support. Authors perceiving international law as a 'law for states'[25] applaud the diplomatic focus on power-oriented approaches in promoting *national interests* (as defined by government elites and domestic interest groups),[26] for example in view of the fact that WTO law does not explicitly commit governments to promotion of consumer welfare and to individual rights and judicial remedies protecting citizens against non-compliance with WTO law.

1. Diverse Conceptions of the Interrelationships between Private and Public, National and International Rules

Due to their diverse conceptions of international economic rules, diplomats, economists, public international lawyers, private lawyers, and administrative and constitutional lawyers often 'theorize' the complex interrelationships between private and public, national and international rules and policies in diverse ways. For instance:

- *Public international lawyers* tend to focus on 'international law among states' and on inter-governmental bargaining, such as reciprocal commitments among governments for trade liberalization and inter-governmental dispute settlement proceedings in the WTO, without regard (e.g. in most textbooks on WTO law and IEL) to the customary law requirement of settling disputes 'in conformity with the principles of justice and international law', including human rights.

---

[25] Cf. J. Goldsmith and D. Levinson, 'Law for States: International Law, Constitutional Law, Public Law', *Harvard Law Review* 122 (2009), 1791–1868.

[26] For a criticism of such power-oriented conceptions of the WTO dispute settlement system see E.U. Petersmann, 'Why Rational Choice Theory Requires a Multilevel Constitutional Approach to International Economic Law – the Case for Reforming the WTO's Enforcement Mechanism', *Illinois Law Review* 1 (2008), 359–382.

- *Private lawyers* tend to focus on international transaction law and private commercial arbitration among private economic actors and on reducing conflicts among national legal systems, for example by allocating the jurisdiction to one single country for the settlement of commercial disputes, often without adequate regard to the constitutional limits of private party autonomy and to the public law dimensions of transnational dispute settlement proceedings (e.g. in case of investor–state arbitration requiring judicial 'balancing' of private and public interests).
- *Administrative lawyers* perceive many areas of IEL – such as the WTO agreements coordinating rules for customs administration, national government procurement procedures, national sanitary measures, technical standards or intellectual property regulation – as 'global administrative law', often without adequate regard to the systemic context of administrative law in constitutionally limited legal systems and the need for constitutional safeguards limiting administrative discretion also in IEL so as to protect citizens against abuse of administrative powers.[27]
- *Constitutional lawyers* increasingly acknowledge the constitutional dimensions of IEL, such as the need for preventing and settling the inevitable conflicts of interests and disputes among citizens and governments by means of a 'limiting constitution' as well as an 'empowering constitution' providing for constitutional protection (e.g. by means of EU law, EEA law and WTO law) of economic freedoms, market competition and third-party adjudication. But many constitutional lawyers focus one-sidedly on 'nation states' without adequate regard to the 'constitutional functions' of IEL for the collective supply of international public goods, for instance by limiting and compensating national 'governance failures' and protecting cosmopolitan rights in the global division of labor. The value premises of democratic constitutionalism – such as 'normative individualism', respect for the diversity of value preferences and for the ubiquity of conflicts among rational self-interests, which need to be reconciled on the basis of common 'public reason' (e.g. reasonable interests in constitutional principles of justice, in non-discriminatory

---

[27] G. Van Harten and M. Loughlin, 'Investment Treaty Arbitration as a Species of Global Administrative Law', *EJIL* 17 (2006), 121–150, admit that 'the defining features of global administrative law are rather fluid' (at 121f). As there is no centralized system of administration in international law, international regimes make use of diverse legal approaches limiting the administrative functions of states to different degrees.

conditions of market competition and other constitutional 'checks and balances') – differ fundamentally from power-oriented conceptions of 'international law among states'.

As discussed in Section V, the diverse conceptions of IEL can be reconciled and integrated most convincingly through multilevel 'constitutional interpretations', focusing – as in the diverse forms of economic integration law in Europe – on the common constitutional principles underlying national and international human rights law, democratic rule-making and multilevel judicial protection of human rights by 'courts of justice'. Constitutional democracies risk being undermined in a globally integrated world unless they promote 'constitutionalization' of intergovernmental power politics through international and judicial protection of RoL and 'cosmopolitan rights'. Intergovernmental 'public international law conceptions' – which perceive IEL as an integral part of 'international law among states' – run counter to the 'human rights imperative' of treating citizens as legal subjects and 'democratic masters' also of international law and diplomacy. Multilevel 'economic law perspectives' – which perceive IEL as a functional unity of private and public, national and international regulation of the economy – may lack constitutional legitimacy, for instance if they advocate economic utilitarianism or 'constitutional nationalism' without regard to reasonable citizen interests in the collective supply of global public goods.

2. Diverse Formal and Substantive Conceptions of International 'Rule of Law'

The diverse private and public, constitutional, administrative or 'foreign policy' conceptions of IEL are often related to diverse conceptions of 'rule of law'.

- A *formal understanding of rule of law* is often promoted by commercial lawyers, 'utilitarians' and free-market economists. For example, according to Nobel Prize-winning economist F.A. Hayek, rule of law 'means that government in all its actions is bound by rules fixed and announced beforehand – rules which make it possible to foresee with fair certainty how the authority will use its coercive powers in given circumstances, and to plan one's individual affair on the basis of this knowledge'.[28] Yet, *substantive conceptions of rule of law* have emphasized since antiquity that rule of law differs from 'rule by law' and

[28] F.A. Hayek, *The Road to Serfdom* (London: IEA, 1944), at 54.

'rule by men' in terms of additional legal safeguards such as judicial protection of principles of justice (e.g. legal equality, due process of law) and judicial enforcement of law vis-à-vis all private persons as well as public authorities.[29]

- *Human rights approaches to rule of law*, as reflected in the 1948 UDHR and its call for 'equal protection of the law' (Article 7) and of human rights 'by the rule of law' (Preamble UDHR), emphasize that the making, administration and implementation of law derive their 'input legitimacy' and 'output legitimacy' from respecting, protecting and fulfilling civil, political, economic, social and cultural human rights as 'the foundation of freedom, justice and peace in the world' (Preamble UDHR); 'everyone is entitled to a social and international order in which the rights and freedoms set forth in this Declaration can be fully realized' (Article 28); 'in the exercise of his rights and freedoms, everyone shall be subject only to such limitations as are determined by law solely for the purpose of securing due recognition and respect for the rights and freedoms of others and of meeting the just requirements of morality, public order and the general welfare in a democratic society' (Article 29).
- *Democratic approaches to rule of law* share the basic premise of human rights approaches that the only legitimate interest a government is entitled to pursue is that of its citizens and other subjects. Yet, democratic approaches often focus less on human rights and constitutional rights than on parliamentary, popular and 'communitarian discourses' (e.g. in terms of 'deliberative democracy'), majority voting and 'representative governance' in defining 'national interests' in

---

[29] In his later works such as *The Constitution of Liberty* (London: Routledge, 1960), F.A. Hayek emphasized the need for general legislation and judicial protection as defining elements of RoL: it is 'because the lawgiver does not know the particular cases to which his rules will apply, and it is because the judge who applies them has no choice in drawing the conclusions that follow from the existing body of rules and the particular facts of the case, that it can be said that laws and not men rule' (at 153). On 'rule of men' as domination, and 'rule of law' as non-domination, see P. Pettit, *Republicanism: A Theory of Freedom and Government* (Oxford: Oxford University Press, 1997). L. Fuller, *The Morality of Law* (New Haven: Yale University Press, 1969), identifies (in Chapter 2) eight moral requirements as being constitutive of 'rule of law' (i.e. generality, clarity, promulgation, stability, consistency of rules and social behavior, non-retroactivity and the non-contradictory nature of rules, which must also not require the impossible). J. Raz, *The Authority of Law* (Oxford: Clarendon Press, 1979), at 214ff., emphasizes the need for additional requirements (such as judicial independence, judicial review, fair hearings).

domestic legislative, administrative and foreign policy measures. Proponents of 'deliberative democracy' (like Habermas) tend to perceive the individual self-interest and the common 'public interest' as two mutually consistent sides of the same coin. Rights-based conceptions of liberal democracy often emphasize the 'constitutional functions' of courts of justice as ultimate guardians of constitutional rights vis-à-vis abuses by democratic majority decisions.

- *'Constitutional justice' approaches to rule of law* emphasize the constitutional function of supreme courts as 'exemplars of public reason'[30] and instruments of reasoned, social ordering[31] by means of independent, impartial interpretation, application, clarification and enforcement of legal principles, rules, rights and obligations in fair procedures protecting 'procedural' as well as 'substantive justice' (e.g. in the presentation of proof, reasoned arguments by all affected parties, and reasoned, equitable and peaceful settlement of disputes). Just as common law and civil law systems have evolved by means of judicial clarification and enforcement of principles and rules, so does international rule of law depend on judicial clarification of international rules in incomplete agreements as well as on judicial cooperation among courts in different jurisdictions so as to coordinate fragmented national and international legal regimes.[32] The Kantian

---

[30] According to J. Rawls, *Political Liberalism* (Cambridge: Harvard University Press, 1993), at 231ff., 'in a constitutional regime with judicial review, public reason is the reason of its supreme court'; it is of constitutional importance for the 'overlapping, constitutional consensus' necessary for a stable and just society among free, equal and rational citizens who tend to be deeply divided by conflicting moral, religious and philosophical doctrines. The content of the Rawlsian 'public reason' comprises substantive principles of justice (such as fundamental rights) as well as procedural principles of justice (such as due process of law, independence and impartiality of courts, and democratic governance).

[31] For common law conceptions of RoL and 'adjudication as a form of social ordering' see L.L. Fuller, 'The Forms and Limits of Adjudication', *Harvard Law Review* 92 (1978), 353–409.

[32] On the dependence of international RoL on multilevel judicial protection of 'constitutional justice' see E.U. Petersmann, 'Judging Judges: From "Principal-Agent Theory" to "Constitutional Justice" in Multilevel Judicial Governance of Economic Cooperation among Citizens', *JIEL* 11 (2008) 827–884; and R. Higgins, *Themes and Theories: Essays, Speeches and Writings in International Law* (Oxford: Oxford University Press, 2009), at 19–43. The term 'constitutionalism' is used here for denoting a political and legal method for constituting governance authorities and limiting their delegated powers for the protection of the constitutional rights of citizens and human rights.

constitutional ideal of protecting equal liberties by means of constitutional restraints on abuses of public and private power in all human interactions inside countries and among countries, as well as in transnational relations of citizens vis-à-vis foreign states, requires international and transnational rule of law no less than rule of law inside constitutional democracies.[33]

3. Competing Conceptions of 'Rule of Law' Inside European Integration Law

The above survey confirms that 'rule of law' remains a contested concept that is regulated and implemented in national and international legal systems in often diverse ways. Due to the worldwide adoption of national constitutions and international treaties, traditional conceptions of 'government by law and not by men' are increasingly limited by national constitutional restraints and international legal obligations. In England, for instance, the traditional claim to 'parliamentary sovereignty' and to legal primacy of later legislation (*lex superior* rule) has become increasingly limited by judicial compliance with European law, including the ECHR, as confirmed by the British Human Rights Act of 1998.[34] The judicial review – by ever more national and international courts – of the 'proportionality' of legislative and administrative restrictions of individual rights in terms of the 'rationality' (suitability), 'necessity' and 'proportionality *stricto sensu*' of the restrictions continues to enhance individual remedies, 'public reason' and the constitutional functions of courts of justice.[35] The Treaty on European Union (TEU) includes numerous commitments to 'the principles of liberty, democracy and respect for human rights and fundamental freedoms and of the rule of law' (Preamble TEU): 'The Union is founded on the values of respect for human dignity, freedom, democracy, equality, the rule of law and respect for human rights' (Article 2 TEU), including

---

[33] On the Kantian explanation of multilevel constitutionalism as a precondition for RoL see Petersmann (*supra* note 8), Chapter III. For a modern explanation of why foreign policy discretion and 'the government's own freedom of action is not an intrinsic value as it is for individual citizens' see J. Waldron, 'Are Sovereigns Entitled to the Benefit of the International Rule of Law?', New York University School of Law Working Paper No. 1/2009.

[34] Cf. F.G. Jacobs, *The Sovereignty of Law: The European Way* (Cambridge: Cambridge University Press, 2007).

[35] On this use of 'proportionality analysis' in ever more national and international jurisdictions see A. Stone Sweet and J. Mathews, 'Proportionality, Judicial Review and Global Constitutionalism', in G. Bongiovanni, G. Sartor and C. Valentini (eds), *The Reasonableness of Law* (Heidelberg: Springer Verlag, 2009), 173–214.

'strict observance and the development of international law' and 'the principles of the United Nations Charter' (Articles 3, 21 TEU). Inside the common market law, the ECJ has long since applied stricter standards of judicial review regarding *national* restrictions of common market freedoms compared with *EC* restrictions, especially if the EC law-makers exercised legal discretion or a margin of appreciation concerning complex economic facts. In the 'area of freedom, security and justice' as well as in the common foreign and security policy of the EU, the EU treaties limit the jurisdiction of the ECJ.[36] In the areas of WTO law and the UN Convention of the Law of the Sea, the ECJ has voluntarily limited its jurisdiction (e.g. by denying individuals and EU member states rights to enforce WTO or UNCLOS obligations against the EU institutions) in view of the intergovernmental dispute settlement procedures provided for in WTO law and in the Law of the Sea Convention.[37] Hence, even though EU law protects communitarian conceptions of formal and substantive rule of law among its 27 member states through constitutional restraints of a higher legal rank and multilevel judicial remedies, the scope of judicial review by European courts varies among different areas of European integration law. For instance, whether investor–state disputes inside the EU can be settled by investor–state arbitration on the basis of bilateral investment agreements remains controversial in view of the non-applicability of the preliminary rulings procedure of the ECJ.[38] The diverse, internal and external conceptions of RoL and 'double standards' of 'justiciability' in the EU illustrate that judicial protection of RoL remains culture- and context-dependent.[39] Yet, the reasons for judicial self-restraint vis-à-vis parliamentary rule-making inside constitutional democracies are less prevalent in intergovernmental economic regulation, which is not effectively controlled by most parliaments and national courts in most countries.

4. Nationalist vs Cosmopolitan Conceptions of IEL

The different private and public, national and international legal approaches to IEL interact and complement each other in many ways. For

---

[36] Cf. E.O Wennerström, *The Rule of Law and the European Union* (Uppsala: Iustus Förlag, 2007); A. Hinarejos, *Judicial Control in the EU: Reforming Jurisdiction in the Intergovernmental Pillars* (Oxford: Oxford University Press, 2009).

[37] Cf. M. Mendez, 'The Legal Effect of Community Agreements: Maximalist Treaty Enforcement and Judicial Avoidance Techniques', *EJIL* 21 (2010), 83–104.

[38] Cf. H. Wehland, (note 6).

[39] Cf. L. Pech, 'The Rule of Law as a Constitutional Principle of the EU', Jean Monnet Working Paper 04/2009 NYU School of Law.

example, the US veto power in the IMF, the World Bank and GATT 1947 entailed not only that many global governance decisions (e.g. on the termination of the gold–dollar convertibility in August 1971, GATT exceptions discriminating against cotton, textiles and agricultural exports from less-developed countries) were essentially taken by the United States. Conceptions of 'hegemonic international law' also explain the insistence by the US Congress (e.g. in US laws implementing the results of the eight GATT Rounds of multilateral trade negotiations) that worldwide economic treaties (like GATT and WTO law) are not enforceable in US courts against federal restrictions. Worldwide WTO guarantees and UN human rights guarantees protect equal freedoms and non-discrimination in international relations, yet without providing for directly applicable legal and judicial remedies empowering individuals against violations of international law.

'Global administrative law' approaches tend to be concerned more about administrative 'rule by law' and intergovernmental regulation of 'public interests' than about constitutional limitations of national and international governance powers so as to protect human rights and 'rule of law'. The constitutional approach to IEL emphasizes that the collective supply of global public goods – like international legal security and a mutually beneficial, efficient world economy promoting general consumer welfare – is confronted with the same constitutional problems as in national and regional market economies. My 1991 book on *Constitutional Functions and Constitutional Problems of International Economic Law*[40] argued that, from the perspective of reasonable citizens interested in constitutional protection of their individual rights across national frontiers:

- international legal guarantees of private freedoms, property rights, non-discrimination and RoL – as in WTO law, European integration law as well as in international human rights law – could be perceived as functionally limited extensions of the 'empowering constitution' necessary for citizen-driven competition and economic and legal self-government;
- similarly, international agreements (like the WTO Agreement) constituting international organizations providing for collective rule-making and compulsory jurisdiction for the peaceful settlement of international disputes could be conceived as functional parts of a multilevel 'limiting constitution', restraining adverse 'externalities' of

[40] E.U. Petersmann, *Constitutional Functions and Constitutional Problems of International Economic Law* (Fribourg: Fribourg University Press, 1991).

national 'governance failures' and other 'collective action problems' from impeding the collective supply of international public goods; and

- domestic courts of justice should interpret domestic laws in conformity with these 'constitutional functions' of IEL so as to protect equal freedoms of domestic citizens and non-discriminatory conditions of competition in economic cooperation across frontiers.

5. Diverse Conceptions of 'Governance Failures' and 'Constitutional Failures'

Power-oriented and 'global administrative law' approaches to IEL often reject citizen-oriented interpretations of international rules and compulsory jurisdiction of international courts on the ground that the reality of international power politics justifies foreign policy discretion and 'cost–benefit analyses' regarding whether, and how, international obligations should be complied with by governments. Citizen-oriented and constitutional perspectives of IEL argue, by contrast, that prioritizing government discretion over legal and judicial protection of equal liberties and other citizen rights in international trade and financial relations reinforces 'constitutional failures' in IEL. For example:

- *Market failures* (like abuses of market power reducing consumer welfare, environmental pollution, social injustice) are not effectively regulated and controlled in many areas of IEL, as illustrated by the lack of WTO competition rules prohibiting international restrictive business practices (like export cartels), and by the obvious inadequacy of consumer protection in international financial regulation.
- *Governance failures* (like certain forms of trade protectionism, underregulation of international banking services) are not effectively restrained in many areas of IEL. The WTO system, for instance, continues to treat citizens as mere objects of authoritarian governments without offering producers, investors, traders and consumers effective legal and judicial remedies to protect consumer welfare and RoL against welfare-reducing abuses of discretionary trade policy powers.
- Discretionary '*member-driven governance*' in international organizations for the collective supply of global public goods continues to focus one-sidedly on power politics and rent-seeking interest groups rather than on collective long-term interests of citizens (e.g. in international RoL, a clean environment). Trade governance in the WTO is not democratically controlled by most parliaments and citizens and –

as illustrated by more than 40 years of trade protectionism in many economic sectors (like cotton, textiles and agriculture) discriminating against less-developed countries – tends to respond one-sidedly to 'rent-seeking' pressures from domestic interest groups.

- Due to the perceived lack of legitimacy of WTO governance dominated by political self-interests of governments in limiting their legal and judicial accountability vis-à-vis domestic citizens for discriminatory trade protectionism, WTO dispute settlement rulings are widely ignored by domestic courts.

VII. RECONCILING STATE- AND CITIZEN-CENTERED INTERPRETATIONS OF IEL REQUIRES STRONGER JUDICIAL PROTECTION OF CONSTITUTIONAL RIGHTS

The 'human rights approach' to IEL proposed by the UN High Commissioner for Human Rights raises the question of why the WTO commitments for promoting 'sustainable development' (WTO Preamble) and 'providing security and predictability to the multilateral trading system' (Article 3 DSU) should not be interpreted as requiring recognition of citizens as legal subjects of WTO rights and obligations.[41] For example, rather than interpreting the exclusive and compulsory jurisdiction of WTO dispute settlement bodies (Article 23 DSU) as preventing domestic courts from holding their own governments judicially accountable for violations of WTO law (as suggested by some EU and US trade lawyers),[42] the human right of access to justice and the WTO guarantees of individual access to courts offer (con)textual arguments that Article 23 DSU establishes an exclusive jurisdiction only for intergovernmental disputes; the multilevel 'dispute settlement system of the WTO' should provide 'security and predictability to the multilateral trading system' (Article 3 DSU) also for citizens engaged in, and benefiting from international trade whenever citizens request domestic courts to interpret trade rules in conformity with the WTO obligations ratified by domestic parliaments. Just as European courts have justified citizen-oriented interpretations of the intergovernmental EC Treaty rules as constituting fundamental rights of EU citizens

---

41 Cf. E.U. Petersmann, 'The "Human Rights Approach" Advocated by the UN High Commissioner for Human Rights and by the ILO: Is it Relevant for WTO Law and Policy?', *JIEL* (2004), 605–628.

42 Cf. R. Bhala and K. Kennedy, *World Trade Law* (Newark: Lexis Publishing, 1998), at 43.

as legal subjects of European integration law, so do the human rights obligations of all WTO members offer arguments against one-sided, intergovernmental definitions of 'state interests' without regard to general citizen interests in being recognized as legal subjects of IEL. The rational self-interest of EU institutions in limiting their legal and judicial accountability for violations of WTO law to the remedies conceded in the WTO dispute settlement system should not prevent European courts from protecting the legitimate rights of EU citizens and EU member states to judicial protection of RoL inside the EU, including respect for the international WTO obligations ratified by all parliaments inside the EU.[43] The more citizens, their democratic representatives and judges insist on 'rule of international law' as constitutional restraints on abuses of foreign policy powers, as well as on a 'moral duty of justice ... to help ensure that all persons have access to institutions that protect their basic rights',[44] the better are the chances for a rules-based trading system preventing and settling international economic disputes peacefully through domestic courts rather than only through intergovernmental dispute settlement proceedings and medieval 'trade wars'.

---

43 The ECJ case law denying 'direct applicability' of all GATT/WTO rules no longer repeats its earlier, incorrect claims that GATT/WTO rules are not precise and unconditional enough for their judicial application (cf. the case law mentioned by Mendez *supra* note 37). The current judicial reasoning of the ECJ wrongly claims that Article 22 DSU – which provides for the possibility of mutually agreed compensation as a means for avoiding lawful retaliation by other WTO members – excludes judicial application of WTO rules by the ECJ; but such compensation does not change the illegality of the measures concerned under WTO law. The ECJ's politically motivated refusal to protect EU compliance with WTO rules undermines RoL inside the EU and is unjustified vis-à-vis EU citizens and EU member states which have neither access to WTO dispute settlement proceedings nor other judicial remedies in order to restore RoL in the EU.

44 See A. Buchanan, *Justice, Legitimacy and Self-Determination: Moral Foundations for International Law* (Oxford: Oxford University Press, 2004), at 27, 86. The author bases his book on such a 'natural duty of justice' and rejects the realist perception of international relations as anarchic struggles for power and military dominance (the Hobbesian war of all against all). Chapters 4 and 5 discuss the controversial questions of how to define 'principles of justice' and legitimate tolerance in international law and international relations among liberal and non-liberal states, and to what extent principles of justice in constitutional democracies can and should be extended to international economic regulation. The main conclusion is that existing international human rights law already prescribes far more comprehensive protection of human rights than the minimalist protection suggested by John Rawls in his proposals for *The Law of Peoples* (Cambridge: Harvard University Press, 1999).

The prevailing disregard – in state-centered WTO negotiations and WTO legal practices – for the human rights obligations of all WTO members reflects not only the limited jurisdiction of WTO bodies and the lack of expertise of trade diplomats regarding human rights. There is also concern by trade diplomats and economists that too many human rights advocates appear to be more interested in redistributing other people's welfare than in creating the legal conditions for empowering the poor to increase their own economic resources (e.g. through more effective legal protection of open markets, non-discriminatory conditions of competition and international RoL).[45] Economists and trade politicians fear a divisive 'politicization' of reciprocal trade liberalization and trade regulation by 'human rights fundamentalists' who all too often ignore the necessary economic foundation of constitutional democracies in consumer-driven trade, competition and a mutually welfare-increasing division of labor. Yet, protection of human rights requires constitutional construction not only of citizen-driven democracies, but also of consumer-driven 'social market economies' that protect the economic as well as non-economic dimensions of human liberty and of non-discriminatory competition in conformity with the 'indivisibility' of the human rights of citizens. The unnecessary poverty of more than 1 billion people living on US$ 1 per day or less, and the continuing failure of UN member states to protect RoL and global public goods effectively in so many UN member states, as well as in transnational relations, demonstrate that these human rights dimensions and constitutional tasks of IEL continue to be widely and unduly neglected.

---

[45] Cf. E.U. Petersmann, 'Taking Human Dignity, Poverty and Empowerment of Individuals More Seriously: Rejoinder to Alston', *EJIL* 13 (2002) 845–851.

PART III

Transnational private regimes: contrasting judicial and non-judicial enforcement across sectors

7. Privatizing the adjudication of international commercial disputes: the relevance of organizational form

Kevin E. Davis[1]

1. INTRODUCTION

Should profit-maximizing private firms be responsible for governing commercial transactions? In recent years several commentators have argued that profit-oriented private actors ('for-profits') ought to play a greater role in governing commercial transactions (Hadfield 2001, 2009).[2] This presents a profound challenge to the conventional idea that law is a quintessentially public good that ought to be provided by public actors, and adds an important dimension to debates over who should govern the commercial transactions that sustain our economic life.

Advocates of privatization emphasize the superior – relative to public actors – incentives and resources of for-profits operating in competitive markets. This chapter tests that claim by examining a setting in which the advantages of for-profits should be most pronounced, namely, the market for adjudication of international commercial disputes. Remarkably, for-profits do not dominate. The actors who adjudicate international commercial disputes include for-profits, not-for-profits, international organizations, publicly-sponsored courts, and hybrid organizations. The organizational diversity is striking.

[1] I am grateful to Gary Bell, Franco Ferrari, Clayton Gillette and participants in the Workshop on Enforcement of Private Transnational Regulation for helpful comments and conversations, as well as to Maxwell Kardon for research assistance. All errors are my own. Financial support from the Filomen D'Agostino and Max E. Greenberg Research Fund at NYU School of Law is gratefully acknowledged.

[2] For earlier treatments of this topic see Landes and Posner (1979), and other contributions to the same volume, as well as Benson (1989). For a more recent and general treatment of private lawmaking see Snyder (2003).

Understanding that organizational diversity and its ramifications requires a new theoretical framework. To begin with, it requires a framework that goes beyond a simple public/private dichotomy and recognizes a range of organizational forms. It also requires acknowledgement of the fact that the 'market' for adjudication of international commercial disputes bears little resemblance to the kinds of perfectly competitive, undistorted externality-free markets whose virtues privatization advocates invoke.

The theoretical framework developed below takes these factors into account and shows that under certain conditions the incentives of and resources available to for-profits may be inferior to those of actors that adopt other organizational forms. At the same time, it shows that there is no reason to presume that the organization best suited to adjudicate any given dispute will be a publicly-sponsored court. Taking organizational form into account offers the possibility of new answers to questions about who should govern international commerce.

Section 2 of this chapter lays out the case for relying on for-profits to help resolve international commercial disputes. Section 3 describes current practices and shows that for-profits actually play a limited role in adjudicating international commercial disputes. Section 4 examines the theoretical connections between organizational form on the one hand, and on the other hand, incentives of and resources available to organizations that provide international commercial dispute resolution services. This analysis both explains and justifies current practices. It also casts doubt on the merits of proposals to expand the role of for-profits in the adjudication of international commercial disputes. Section 5 concludes.

2. THE CASE FOR FOR-PROFITS

What is a For-profit Organization?

Economic actors can take a variety of organizational forms but the three main categories are: for-profit, not-for-profit, and public. For present purposes the for-profit category will be defined to include actors with private residual claimants, encompassing familiar organizational forms such as sole-proprietorships, corporations and partnerships. The not-for-profit category contains actors without residual claimants that are not controlled by the state. The public category consists of actors controlled by the state. These categories are neither comprehensive nor mutually exclusive. In other words, hybrids, such as publicly-controlled for-profits, and alternatives such as international organizations or private actors with limited residual claims, are possible.

The Case for For-profit Production of Commercial Law

In recent years the strongest proponent of having for-profits play a greater role in governing commercial transactions has been Professor Gillian Hadfield (Hadfield 2001, 2009; Hadfield and Talley 2006). Her central argument seems to be that when it comes to the production of commercial law, for-profits operating under reasonably competitive conditions are likely to be more efficient and innovative than public actors.[3] This argument rests in turn upon important assumptions about determinants of the relative competence of private and public actors, including both the *incentives* that public and private actors have to provide rules that are valued by parties to commercial transactions, and the *resources* they can draw upon to create those rules.

There are several reasons to believe that for-profits differ systematically from other actors in terms of their incentives to provide commercial law efficiently. For instance, in an article co-authored with Eric Talley, Hadfield claims that although for-profits' incentives to provide differentiated 'products' to 'consumers' of corporate law may not be socially optimal, in competitive settings their offerings will be closer to being optimal than those of legislatures (Hadfield and Talley 2006; Snyder 2003). In making this argument Hadfield and Talley rely heavily on the rather cynical assumption that the individuals who control public actors are motivated primarily by the prospect of receiving personal benefits. Starting from this premise, they reason that the incentives of public actors are compromised because their members receive limited personal benefits from maximizing public revenues. Consequently, elected officials will have only attenuated incentives to maximize public revenues from attracting the business of incorporating firms. Reasoning by analogy implies that elected officials will have similarly attenuated incentives to provide rules to govern the enforcement of commercial transactions.

Even public actors motivated by public interests may have limited incentives to produce optimal rules. This is particularly true when it comes to the rules that govern international commercial transactions. The gains from

---

[3] In this context efficiency means that goods are produced at the lowest possible cost, given the producer's existing knowledge (productive efficiency), that the prices of those goods are set at levels that approach the costs of production, and that goods are allocated to those who value them most highly (allocative efficiency). This chapter follows Hadfield in assuming that the primary objective of the rules that govern contractual relations between legal entities such as corporations is to maximize efficiency, although I will pay more attention than she does to externalities associated with the production of commercial law.

commercial transactions are usually divided between the parties to the transaction. Thus, if a public actor invests in improving the rules that govern international commercial transactions a portion of the benefits will typically redound to foreign actors. As a result, public actors whose objective is to maximize the benefits that flow to local actors, or who simply attach more weight to the interests of local actors than foreign actors, will not have incentives to invest in improving the regime to the point that maximizes global gains from trade. So, for example, when developing procedural rules of general application, local lawmakers may fail to take sufficient account of the benefits of harmonization with the law of other jurisdictions since some of the benefits will accrue to foreign firms.

On the other hand it seems unreasonable to presume that for-profits always have superior incentives to provide commercial rules. Such rules are a form of intellectual property. For-profits' incentives to invest in creating and disseminating intellectual property depend on the extent to which their ideas can be appropriated without compensation, which in turn depends on factors such as their ability to assert copyright and the feasibility of placing physical or electronic restrictions on distribution (Hadfield 2001, pp. 44, 45; Hadfield 2009, pp. 249–250; Hadfield and Talley 2006). There is no particular reason to believe that those incentives are, on balance, socially optimal.[4] More generally, it is well understood that a variety of 'market failures' can undermine for-profits' incentives to make socially optimal decisions. For-profit producers have limited incentives to minimize (maximize) negative (positive) externalities created by their activities, abide by unenforceable commitments, or refrain from exploiting market power or superior information (Hadfield and Talley 2006, p. 439).

For-profits and public actors can also differ in terms of the *resources* they can draw upon to create and implement rules. Public actors may have limited fiscal resources because ideological or legal factors constrain their ability to impose taxes or user fees or to set aside public resources for the benefit of commercial actors. But it is not clear that public actors generally face greater fiscal constraints than private organizations. In any event, advocates of privatization tend to stress the importance of access to another kind of resource, namely, information. Hadfield and others emphasize the fact that private actors, collectively, may have more expertise than public actors because they can draw upon a broader range of information (Benson 1989, p. 650; Bernstein 1992; Dixit 2004). In particular,

[4] Here it is particularly important to distinguish the incentives of organizations, of any kind, from those of their agents. Agents' incentives to innovate may be influenced by additional factors such as, on the one hand, the desire for fame or career advancement, or, on the other hand, leisure. See, Gillette (1999).

communities of merchants can draw upon their experience to formulate laws that best fit their needs. This argument is less than compelling though because it is unclear why for-profits are likely to be any better than public actors at tapping the information possessed by merchants. In principle, the state should be just as capable as a private firm of hiring individuals with commercial experience and allowing its agents to solicit information from merchants.

The proponents of privatization of commercial law must also confront the fact there is one resource to which public actors typically have better access than private actors: coercive force. While states do not necessarily have a monopoly on the use of force within their territory, states usually try to discourage private actors from using force for the purposes of enforcing commercial obligations, and well-ordered states tend to be quite successful in enforcing those restraints. This means that private actors engaged in enforcing commercial obligations will either have to find alternatives to coercive enforcement – of which there are several – or solicit the assistance of at least one public actor.[5]

Application to International Commercial Adjudication

For the foregoing reasons, purely theoretical arguments that for-profits are better placed than public actors to govern commercial transactions efficiently are inconclusive. So what does the evidence say?

We can begin by examining a context in which the argument in favor of relying on for-profits seems strongest, namely, adjudication of international commercial disputes. Why focus on adjudication? After all, adjudication is only one of three main stages in the governance of international commerce – the others being making rules, and, when necessary, enforcing the rulings of an adjudicator. The answer is that, as we have seen, the risk of unauthorized copying may undermine for-profits' incentives to make socially optimal rules. At the same time, lack of direct access to coercive force may limit for-profits' enforcement capabilities. However, neither of these problems should affect for-profits' competence to engage in adjudication.

---

[5] As far as alternatives are concerned, Benson (1989) argues that the history of the law merchant suggests that commercial boycotts can serve as substitutes for coercive enforcement. Bernstein (1992) makes similar claims about more recent enforcement of obligations among Jewish diamond dealers. For general discussions of alternatives to third-party enforcement as methods of inducing firms to perform their obligations, see Klein and Leffler (1981), Telser (1980), Williamson (1983), and Charny (1990).

One could argue that public actors still have an advantage in undertaking adjudication because rule-making, adjudication and enforcement are often bundled together by providers of 'dispute resolution' services, and public actors are in the best position to provide at least two elements of the bundle. But, as noted above, public actors' incentives to invest in governance of *international* commercial disputes are attenuated by the fact that a portion of the benefits will flow to foreign actors. In addition, a public actor's superior access to coercive force within a particular territory may be less significant in the international context where enforcement is likely to entail coordination of the use of force across multiple jurisdictions. So far inter-jurisdictional efforts to coordinate enforcement of judgments rendered by publicly-sponsored courts have been relatively unsuccessful, at least when compared to efforts to coordinate enforcement of the awards of private arbitrators (Dammann and Hansmann 2008).

3. FORMS OF ADJUDICATION IN INTERNATIONAL COMMERCE

Does current practice bear out the claim that for-profits have an advantage in adjudicating international commercial disputes? The main approaches to adjudicating such disputes are as follows:

- Internal processes
- Commercial arbitration
- Investor–state arbitration
- Courts.

As we shall see, each of these forms of adjudication is associated with particular organizational forms, personnel and procedural rules, some of which straddle the public/private divide. No single organizational form appears to play a dominant role.

Internal Bodies

When disputes arise in commercial transactions the parties to such agreements often try to resolve them internally, that is to say, without referring them to a third party. This process is often conceptualized as a form of 'bargaining in the shadow of the law', meaning that it involves negotiation by interested parties rather than adjudication by an independent actor. However, when the parties to the agreement are large organizations, as is typically the case in international commercial transactions, internal dispute resolution mechanisms can look more like adjudication than negotiation.

Large organizations can often find personnel who are relatively independent of the personnel responsible for negotiating or performing a contract to adjudicate any disputes that arise. In fact, Gilson, Sabel and Scott claim that governance mechanisms that involve such 'contract referees' are common in contracts that contemplate deeply collaborative relationships (Gilson et al. 2009). So, for example, some contracts specify that disputes concerning parties' obligations are to be referred initially to an inter-firm group that is directly responsible for overseeing the collaboration, then to senior Vice Presidents for each firm, and then, if necessary, up the respective firms' hierarchy to the two CEOs. These party-affiliated referees are still far from impartial. But Gilson et al. claim that the knowledge they bring to the dispute resolution process offsets, at least to some extent, their partiality.

Institutional Arbitration

It is often useful to have disputes resolved by a true third party. In many international commercial transactions the parties specify that the third party will be a private arbitrator.

There are two basic kinds of international commercial arbitration: institutional and ad hoc. Institutional arbitration involves the adjudication of a dispute by an arbitrator under the auspices of an organization known as the arbitration institution. The services provided by the arbitration institution often include: default procedural rules; lists of potential arbitrators (as well as, if necessary, names of specific arbitrators); guidelines for arbitrators' fees; custody of documents and funds; registration and archiving of filings and correspondence; physical facilities for hearings; and mechanisms for resolving disputes over procedural rules. In return the arbitration institution is typically paid a fee which generally includes both a fixed and a variable component. The variable component may depend on the amount at issue in the dispute or the time spent by the arbitration institution in administering the case.[6]

---

6 The LCIA's fees comprise a registration fee of £1500 as well as 5% of the fees charged by the tribunal (which can depend upon the complexity of the proceedings), fees for time spent on the matter by members of the LCIA Secretariat and Court, and expenses (see http://www.lcia.org/Dispute_Resolution_Services/LCIA_Arbitration_Costs.aspx). By contrast under the ICC rules administrative expenses and arbitrators' fees are based on the sum in dispute (ICC 2010, Art. 4.).

Well-known international commercial arbitration institutions include the American Arbitration Association's International Centre for Dispute Resolution (ICDR), the China International Economic and Trade Arbitration Commission (CIETAC), the Hong Kong International Arbitration Centre (HKIA), the International Chamber of Commerce's International Court of Arbitration (ICC), Judicial Arbitration and Mediation Service (JAMS), the London Court of International Arbitration (LCIA), and the Singapore International Arbitration Centre (SIAC). The World Intellectual Property Organization (WIPO) also provides an arbitration facility designed primarily for disputes concerning intellectual property.

Interestingly, all but two of these institutions are organized as not-for-profit entities. One of the exceptions is JAMS, which is a for-profit based in the United States.[7] The other exception is WIPO, which is an international organization. There is, however, variation among the not-for-profit institutions. The LCIA was originally administered by the City of London Corporation and the London Chamber of Commerce.[8] Meanwhile CIETAC,[9] HKIA,[10] and SIAC (*Straits Times* 1991; Yong Tong 2000) were all initially sponsored, at least to some extent, by their respective governments.

Commercial actors who choose institutional arbitration do not always look for wholly independent institutions; in some cases they look to arbitral institutions with which they have fairly strong economic ties. The classic examples are actors who choose arbitrations run by international trade associations. Trade associations concern themselves primarily with disseminating market information, lobbying various regulators, and producing standard form contracts for the benefit of their members. But a few of them also provide arbitration services. The most notable examples are the Federation of Oils, Seeds and Fats Associations (oilseeds, oils and fats, and groundnuts)[11] and the Grain and Feed Trade Association (grain and feed).[12] These trade associations are also organized as non-profit entities.

---

[7] JAMS Arbitration, Mediation and ADR Services, see http://www.jamsadr.com/aboutus_overview/ (accessed July 22, 2010).

[8] The London Court of International Arbitration, see http://www.lcia.org/LCIA/Our_History.aspx (accessed July 22, 2010).

[9] CIETAC was established in 1956 under the China Council for the Promotion of International Trade (CCPIT) which was then a government agency, but CIETAC is now said to be financially independent of the Chinese government (Inoue 2006, pp. 171, 175–176).

[10] Hong Kong International Arbitration Centre, see http://www.hkiac.org/index.php/en/hkiac/about-us

[11] Fed. of Oils, Seeds & Fats Ass'ns, http://www.fosfa.org

[12] Grain & Feed Trade Ass'n, http://www.gafta.com.

Credit card processing companies also provide arbitration institutions that are not wholly independent of the disputants (Morriss and Korosec 2005). These arbitrations are designed to resolve disputes that arise between issuers of credit cards and the banks of merchants who accept credit cards (these banks are called 'acquirers'). Many of these disputes are initiated by customers who claim that their credit card statement reflects unauthorized or incorrect charges, or charges for defective merchandise.[13] The process serves to determine which financial institution should bear responsibility for a charge. The responsible institution will often pass the charge on to a cardholder or merchant, as the case may be. Consequently, the outcome of the dispute resolution process is of interest to merchants and cardholders, even though they are not strictly speaking parties to the proceedings. The credit card processors are far from independent third parties to these disputes since they have contractual relationships with the disputants and participate in the series of transactions that give rise to the disputes.

The two major credit card processing companies, Visa and MasterCard, began life as cooperatives owned by their member banks (Visa Inc. 2007; MasterCard Worldwide 2010a). In the United States both are now publicly-traded for-profits. MasterCard changed its ownership and governance structure in a process that concluded in 2006 (MasterCard Incorporated 2006); Visa followed in 2007 (Visa Inc. 2007). The dispute resolution procedures described above pre-date the change in ownership structure (compare Morriss and Korosec (2005) with Visa (2009) and MasterCard Worldwide (2010b)). In Europe, Visa continues to be organized as a member-owned firm (Visa Europe 2009).

Ad Hoc Arbitration

Much international commercial arbitration is not administered by any arbitration institution, but instead is governed by ad hoc arrangements formulated by the parties to the transaction. In these cases the arbitrators are private individuals selected in accordance with the mechanism selected

---

[13] In these proceedings arbitration is only the final stage in a highly structured process that requires issuers and acquirers to classify their reasons for asserting and rejecting charges using numerical classification schemes, to collect and provide particular kinds of evidence, and to transmit information in prescribed electronic formats in a prescribed sequence and within prescribed time limits. If a party (typically the issuer) decides to initiate arbitration, limited opportunities to submit additional evidence are provided. Rights of appeal are also limited. For a general description of these procedures see Morriss and Korosec (2005).

by the parties. These arbitrators are typically either agents of for-profit law firms or sole proprietors. The procedural rules are also specified by the parties, who often draw on previous agreements as well as rules formulated by either an arbitration institution or an international organization such as the United Nations Commission on International Trade Law (UNCITRAL).

Investment Arbitration

International commercial disputes in which one of the parties is a state can be resolved through institutional or ad hoc commercial arbitration, but they can also be resolved using mechanisms specially designed for disputes between states and foreign investors. The most important mechanism of this sort is the International Centre for Settlement of Investment Disputes (ICSID). Many modern investment treaties require disputes involving a state party on the one hand and, on the other hand, investors who are nationals of the other state party, to be submitted to some form of international arbitration, and ICSID arbitration is commonly listed as one of the options (Born 2009, p. 107).

ICSID is an international organization created by a multilateral treaty that entered into force in 1966 (*Convention on the Settlement of Investment Disputes between States and Nationals of Other States*). It was designed to provide a mechanism for resolving disputes between member states and investors who qualify as nationals of other member states (with the consent of the disputing parties). Since 1978, ICSID's facilities have also been available for the resolution of other kinds of disputes. Like other arbitration institutions, ICSID provides procedural rules (ICSID actually has two separate sets), a panel of arbitrators, physical facilities for hearings, and various administrative services. These services can be unbundled, in the sense that ICSID will provide administrative services in connection with ad hoc proceedings that are not governed by its procedural rules. The World Bank covers the costs of the ICSID Secretariat but the costs of proceedings are borne by parties to the dispute.

Judicial Proceedings

International commercial disputes can also be resolved in proceedings administered by national courts. Courts are the quintessential examples of publicly-sponsored organizations, but it is worth keeping in mind that private actors play a significant role in some judicial proceedings. For instance, in some jurisdictions tribunals that preside over commercial cases – at least in the first instance – include lay people selected for their business acumen; sometimes the panel is composed entirely of lay judges (Kessler 2010, pp. 679, 681; Vermeule 2007, pp. 1569, 1573). In other cases publicly-employed judges rely on private-sector experts or are at least willing to entertain arguments from representatives of the business community.

4. A NEW THEORETICAL MODEL

The dispute resolution mechanisms listed above have all been in existence for many years and are well known. Moreover, choice-of-forum and arbitration clauses are regularly enforced. As a result, commercial parties interested in specifying how their disputes will be resolved have many options to choose from.

The variety of organizational forms represented among those options is striking. Parties to international commercial transactions do not face a binary choice between for-profits on the one hand and wholly public national courts on the other hand. To be sure there are examples of for-profit providers, including arbitration institutions such as JAMS, Visa and MasterCard, as well as the individuals who serve as arbitrators in ad hoc arbitrations; but the providers of dispute resolution mechanisms also include not-for-profit trade associations (the Grain and Feed Trade Association; GFTA), other not-for-profit organizations enjoying various levels of state support (ICC, LCIA, SIAC), member-owned firms (Visa and MasterCard in Europe), international organizations (WIPO and ICSID), and national courts staffed or advised, in whole or in part, by private individuals or organizations.

This evidence suggests that a satisfactory theory of the relationship between organizational form and ability to resolve commercial disputes has to account for the possibility of dispute resolution being provided simultaneously by a variety of organizations, including hybrids. It is clearly unrealistic to assume that for-profits and national courts are the only two options.

A theory of this sort is sketched below. The building blocks are the same as Professor Hadfield's: the efficiency with which any given kind of organization provides dispute resolution services depends on the extent to which it has appropriate incentives or resources.[14] However, at each step the

[14] Here I follow Hadfield in focusing on the efficiency implications of alternative ways of adjudicating disputes. A more expansive analysis would pay greater attention to factors such as whether the dispute resolution provider in question is democratically accountable and respects values such as individual autonomy and

theory takes into account the possibility that a non-profit or international organization, or some sort of hybrid organization, will be more appealing than either a for-profit entity or a national court.[15]

Incentives to Behave Opportunistically

Commercial parties often select providers of dispute resolution mechanisms at the outset of their relationship and long before any dispute has arisen. In making their choices parties will tend to favor providers who can be counted on to perform commitments to provide dispute resolution services, that is to say, commitments that may be long term and inherently difficult for third parties, or even the commercial parties themselves, to enforce. This in turn implies that commercial parties will favor providers who do not face incentives either to shirk their responsibilities or to take risks that jeopardize their ability to fulfill those responsibilities.

As Henry Hansmann has shown, for-profits are not ideally suited to be dependable trading partners (Hansmann 1980, pp. 868–872; Hansmann 1996, pp. 24–34). The reason is simple: for-profits deciding whether to invest resources in ensuring that they perform their obligations can be expected to respond primarily to financial incentives. If obligations are so difficult to enforce that there is no financial penalty for poor performance, then there is no reason to expect a for-profit to try to deliver anything better. By contrast, not-for-profits and public actors lack similar financial incentives to shirk their obligations, and so may be more dependable.

This general point suggests that for-profit providers of dispute resolution mechanisms will, all other things being equal, be less dependable than not-for-profits or public bodies. Consider for example, an arbitral institution deciding whether to make costly investments in screening the arbitrators it appoints to chair proceedings for conflicts of interest. Assume that disputing parties would benefit from having their institution provide a list of pre-screened arbitrators, even if only as a starting point in the process of deciding who will ultimately adjudicate their dispute. Finally, imagine a situation in which no one is in a position to impose a financial penalty on the institution for failing to invest in screening. In these circumstances, parties choosing between institutions can expect any for-profit institution they select to respond to the incentive to shirk its 'responsibilities' and refrain from screening. In addition, a for-profit institution is likely to

equality. These issues have been discussed extensively in the literature on private rule-making (e.g. Scott 2008, pp. 254–268; Snyder 2003, pp. 425–437; Levit 2008).

[15] The material which follows draws on Davis (2006).

respond to financial incentives that require positive action – such as announcing surprise fee increases after parties have selected them – that can be equally pernicious. Finally, in deciding whether to make risky investments that have the potential to threaten its survival – consider for example a risky expansion into a new overseas market – a for-profit institution has no incentive to consider the interests of commercial parties whose plans for dispute resolution will be disrupted if the institution fails. Knowing all this, commercial parties ought to systematically favor not-for-profit or public arbitration institutions over for-profits.

There are, of course, ways in which for-profit institutions can compensate for the limitations inherent in their organizational form. One way is to provide a warranty, that is to say, some sort of legally enforceable commitment (Choi 2003, p. 1238; Rutledge 2004). For a provider of dispute resolution services this would mean signing contracts with commercial parties who intend to use its services. Those contracts would contain legally binding commitments to meet certain performance standards. Moreover, sanctions for breach of those standards would have to be sufficient either to deter breach or provide satisfactory compensation. Ideally, the contracts would be formed at the time the parties selected their provider so as to guard against the risk of opportunistic behavior between the time of selection and the time a dispute arises. Interestingly though, parties typically contract with the arbitration institutions they have selected only after a dispute has arisen and those contracts generally disclaim liability for all but deliberate wrongdoing (see e.g. ICC 2010, Article 34; JAMS 2005, Article 1.6; LCIA 1998, Article 31.1; Singapore International Arbitration Centre 2010).[16] This may reflect the difficulty of verifying compliance with the kinds of commitments that would be valuable to consumers of dispute resolution services.

A second way in which a for-profit provider might enhance its credibility is by exposing itself to the prospect of substantial loss in the event that it defaults on its obligations. In other words, it can post a bond (Charny 1990; Klein and Leffler 1981; Telser 1980; Williamson 1983). The most straightforward way to do this is to invest in establishing a reputation for providing high-quality services that will be destroyed in the event of a scandal. So, for example, an arbitration institution could invest so much in advertising the integrity of the arbitrators it appoints as chairs that it would suffer prohibitive losses if it failed to invest in proper screening and one of its chairs proved to be corrupt. Similarly, individual arbitrators might be

---

16 For an overview of the law concerning the legal liability of arbitrators see Cafaggi (Chapter 2, this volume).

motivated to avoid conflicts of interest by the fear of tarnishing their reputation in the legal community and losing future business.

Unlike a warranty, a reputational bond need not involve casting commitments in legal form, nor does it require the invocation of costly legal proceedings in the event of default. On the other hand, a reputational bond does not serve to compensate disappointed stakeholders in the event of default – in our example, the arbitration institution's loss would not be the clients' gain. Reputational mechanisms also do not necessarily have the most reliable enforcement mechanisms – the media may be inconsistent in its taste for and ability to uncover scandals, and social networks may be incomplete. Moreover, some firms' public relations advisers may be better than others at blunting the impact of scandal.

Both warranties and reputational bonds only work if defaults are observable by the affected party. It helps if they are also verifiable by third parties. This is because neither mechanism works unless defaults can be detected by parties in a position either to enforce the warranty or damage the dispute resolution provider's reputation. This in turn suggests that both warranties and bonds are likely to be particularly effective if combined with some sort of credible commitment to transparency. So, for example, an arbitration institution could make a commitment to regular reporting of its performance and submit to audits of its reports by independent third parties. In practice though, the fact that commercial parties typically have an interest in keeping their disputes confidential counteracts any such incentives to provide transparency.

It is only fair to note that even if for-profit firms face inherent limits on their dependability that cannot be fully overcome by warranties or reputational bonds, not-for-profits, international organizations or hybrid organizations may not be perfectly dependable either. It would be convenient to assume that for-profits always strive to maximize financial returns while the other types of organizations are faithfully committed to promoting the interests of disputants. But that assumption is unlikely to be universally valid. For example, if dispute resolution is only one of many activities pursued by a not-for-profit or international organization it may wish to use the profits from dispute resolution to subsidize other activities. Not-for-profits or international organizations in this situation can be predicted to behave in exactly the same way as for-profits. Similarly, if a not-for-profit depends for its survival on revenue from disputants and faces significant competition (from either for-profits or other non-profits) then it may be just as responsive to financial incentives as any for-profit. Generally speaking, the assumption that not-for-profits are immune to financial incentives generated by disputants is only plausible for organizations that can count on financing from other sources, such as donors, or members, or the profits associated with the exercise of market power.

It is also important to consider the possibility that the behavior of any given organization will reflect the interests of the individuals who staff it rather than organizational objectives. There is reason to believe that these sorts of 'agency costs' will be particularly significant in organizations which have no residual financial claimants. Residual financial claimants such as the shareholders in a for-profit corporation have a strong incentive to hold agents of the organization accountable. In their absence, agents of the organization, including the agents who deliver dispute resolution services, may have a great deal of latitude to pursue their own interests.[17] Those interests can be quite varied. For example, some agents may be inclined to shirk their responsibilities simply in order to enjoy more leisure time. Alternatively, some agents, particularly senior managers, may wish to maximize profits because they benefit indirectly in the form of higher salaries and greater job security. On the other hand, staff motivated by professional pride might have interests that are fairly well aligned with broader organizational objectives, such as promoting the interests of disputants.

Incentives to Mitigate Externalities

So far we have discussed reasons why for-profits motivated exclusively by financial interests will tend to ignore the effects of their decisions on disputants who hope to benefit from their services. Similar reasoning shows that for-profits that fit this description will tend to ignore ways in which their resolutions of disputes affect the broader public (Davis and Hershkoff 2011).

There are several ways in which the adjudication of an international commercial dispute can affect the broader public (Cutler 2003; Wai 2002). To begin with, the outcome of the dispute may have important distributional effects. This is most likely to occur in high-stakes cases where the decision transfers substantial amounts of wealth from individuals located in one country to individuals located in another. The most important examples of such cases are investor–state arbitrations in which damages ranging into the hundreds of millions of dollars have been awarded against relatively poor states (see e.g. *CMS* v *Argentina* and *Lauder* v *Czech Republic*).

[17] This is not to deny that for-profit firms can be affected by agency costs.

Adjudication can also have normative effects (Fiss 1984, pp. 1085–1087; Landes and Posner 1979, pp. 238–240). To the extent that reasons for decisions are made public they can shape other parties' views on how laws of general application or widely used contractual language will or should be interpreted. This is true even when the decisions do not technically qualify as binding precedent. By condemning or condoning particular conduct – whether it happens to be failure to mitigate damages or bribery of a public official – each decision has the potential to influence the norms that govern subsequent international commercial dealings. Moreover, even if a particular decision does not shift anyone's beliefs about the prevailing norms, it may influence the level of certainty surrounding those beliefs. These normative effects are particularly significant in investor–state dispute resolution where the norms being established concern the appropriateness of government policies that affect entire societies (Kingsbury and Schill 2009).

Adjudication can also affect the world beyond the parties to the dispute by influencing the production of information. To begin with, adjudication inevitably generates information about the facts of the transaction giving rise to the dispute. When those facts involve misconduct such as bribery or sale of defective products, third parties may find the information very valuable. Information about the dispute resolution process itself may also be of value to third parties. For example, information about successful procedural innovations may be of considerable value to other providers of dispute resolution services. In fact, even information about snags encountered in a particular proceeding may be useful as a spur to subsequent procedural innovation.

Finally, the provision of dispute resolution services by a particular actor to a particular set of clients has the potential to affect, either for better or worse, the accountability of other providers to other actors. For example, a new arbitral institution might attract clients who would otherwise do a great deal to hold publicly-sponsored courts accountable for poor performance. The consequent reduction in accountability of the courts could easily have a negative effect on less vocal litigants who lack access to the arbitral forum. Alternatively, the new arbitral institution could have the positive effect of stimulating healthy competition for litigants (Dammann and Hansmann 2008; Gillette 1996).

Providers of dispute resolution services make many decisions that affect the welfare of third parties along these dimensions. Individual adjudicators naturally bear primary responsibility for the impact of decisions on third parties. But on the margins the processes that govern the vetting and selection of adjudicators seem likely to influence the pattern of outcomes.

So, for instance, the approach that an arbitration institution takes toward selection of arbitrators seems likely to determine whether arbitrators in their pool typically approach their task primarily as a technical problem, a problem of giving effect to the will of the parties, or as a problem of balancing the will of the parties against rights and duties owed to the general public. Meanwhile, the procedural rules that providers of dispute resolution services adopt will determine the evidence that is gathered in connection with each dispute, how vigorously factual claims are contested, the extent to which third parties are permitted to make arguments and the overall level of transparency concerning the proceedings. Finally, the members of any given dispute resolution organization can devote greater or fewer resources to constructive criticism of other providers of dispute resolution services.

Theory predicts that for-profit organizations will only take the interests of third parties into account in their decision-making to the extent that they derive some financial benefit from doing so. To the extent that providers of dispute resolution services are paid by potential disputants – some for-profits are likely to have other sources of revenue, especially arbitrators that are sole proprietorships – and those disputants are themselves devoted to profit-maximization, it is difficult to see why for-profit providers would design their processes to permit third parties' interests to affect the outcome.[18] Why would profit-maximizing commercial actors choose a dispute resolution mechanism that permits its processes to be delayed by interventions from NGOs? Why would they submit themselves to the uncertainty of publicly-oriented rules like the doctrine of public policy? Why would they lobby for continued investment in the publicly-sponsored courts? Thus, the demand for publicly-oriented dispute resolution from firms that focus exclusively on maximizing financial returns seems likely to be small. If there is any such demand it is likely to come from commercial actors who wish to cultivate a reputation for social responsibility, or governments who feel bound to uphold public interests even when they engage in commercial dealings. This suggests that for-profits might find niche markets for publicly-oriented approaches to resolving disputes between states and foreign investors, as well as disputes among large firms committed to social responsibility.

---

[18] The discussion here assumes that providers of dispute resolution services are not subject to legal liability for failing to protect the interests of third parties. For a proposal that involves the imposition of such liability, see Guzman (2000).

It is unclear to what extent providers of dispute resolution services capture financial benefits from producing information about their activities. The disputants typically will not pay for the production of such information.[19] However, as we have already seen, a commitment to transparency can be useful as a way of reassuring potential clients about the value of a dispute resolution mechanism.

Broad dissemination of information about a particular mechanism's procedural rules can also be a useful way of attracting new clients in settings where network externalities are significant. Network externalities arise where the value derived from use of a product is an increasing function of the number of users. This can occur with dispute resolution mechanisms: the cost of using a particular mechanism may decline as the number of attorneys familiar with its practices increases, both because of the effects of competition among attorneys and because inexperienced attorneys may delay proceedings. A rational for-profit provider might respond to this phenomenon by subsidizing the dissemination of information about its procedural rules.

It is also difficult to generalize about the extent to which not-for-profits or international organizations that provide dispute resolution services will take public interests into account. As we have already seen, this will depend in part on the extent to which those organizations are immunized from financial pressures to cater exclusively to the interests of disputants. A great deal also seems to turn on the mandate of the organization, which in turn seems likely to be a function of its membership.[20] For instance, a trade association whose members are drawn exclusively from the for-profit members of a particular industry has little incentive to design a dispute resolution mechanism that takes broader interests into account. As for international organizations, in principle they represent the interests of member states but in practice they represent the interests of member states' *governments*. Those governments may have good reasons to disregard broader interests in social responsibility or transparency, or to neglect the task of monitoring staff of the organization. Another point to keep in mind is that the members of a not-for-profit or international organization

---

[19] Landes and Posner (1979, pp. 238–239) suggest that for-profit judges might publish their opinions on the law as a way of advertising their competence and impartiality. They go on to note, however, that the absence of written opinions in commercial arbitration suggests that other forms of advertising are more effective.

[20] See Wai (2002, pp. 258–264) for a general discussion of how the interests and values of private actors influence international commercial law. Gillette and Scott (2005) examine how participants' interests influence specific kinds of rule-making processes in international commercial law.

may have conflicting views on how to protect the public interest. It is not difficult to imagine disagreements between publicly and privately held firms, or between more and less democratic countries, on issues such as whether arbitral proceedings ought to be open to the public.

Access to Volunteers

For-profits may also differ from not-for-profits in the sense that they enjoy different levels of access to the resources required to provide dispute resolution services. One such resource is volunteer labor.[21]

Having the option of tapping volunteers to assist in the design or operation of a dispute resolution mechanism may be quite advantageous. One reason is that it may be difficult for users of a dispute resolution mechanism to assess its quality. Consequently, for-profit providers have an incentive to shirk on any commitments to provide high quality services. Devices such as warranties and bonds (reputational or otherwise) can mitigate this problem. To the extent that these fail, however, it will be helpful if internal factors such as altruism, professional pride or the desire to exercise and improve skills motivate agents to exert themselves. This will frequently be true of volunteers. So, for example, it may be useful for an arbitration institution to create a volunteer advisory board whose members provide information on how to improve the overall quality of its services.[22] On the other hand, there is no guarantee that volunteers' internal motivations will align their interests with those of either disputing parties or the public.

Volunteers may also be helpful in generating innovations in procedural rules. It is difficult for any single person, or even small group of people, to foresee all of the cases in which a given set of procedural rules might be applied. For this reason it may be ideal to have such rules reviewed by a large group of individuals, even if each member of the group only devotes a relatively small amount of time to the task. The reason is that if the group is sufficiently diverse each member will bring different experiences to the table and will identify and focus on different circumstances in which the rules

---

21 The term volunteer is used broadly here to refer to any individual or organization which provides goods or services on terms that are more favorable than fair market value.

22 See e.g. SIAC's Council of Advisors, which is described as 'a number of respected arbitration practitioners and counsel who will act on a voluntary basis to offer their expertise and assistance to the SIAC Board' (http://www.siac.org.sg/cms/index.php?option=com_content&view=article&id=50&Itemid=70).

might be applied.[23] In addition, allowing readers to play a role in selecting the problems upon which they focus may be a useful way to harness the private information that they possess about their own capabilities. Providing monetary compensation to members of such a large group might be prohibitively costly, because of both the transaction costs of processing payments and the difficulty of assigning a price to each contribution. If, however, the members of the group provide their services on a voluntary basis then this sort of collective enterprise becomes a viable mode of production. In fact it may be superior to production by a smaller group whose members provide their services in exchange for monetary compensation.[24]

For-profits may have less access to volunteers than other kinds of organizations. Leaving aside altruism,[25] many people volunteer in order to socialize or to exercise and hone their professional skills or to obtain status in the eyes of their peers. There is no obvious reason why these sorts of benefits cannot be obtained by volunteering on behalf of a for-profit enterprise. However, for some people the direct personal benefits they could receive from volunteering on behalf of a for-profit organization might be outweighed by an aversion to gratuitously conferring benefits on the owners of a for-profit organization.[26] This aversion might lead even people who are not exactly altruistic to prefer to volunteer for not-for-profits. It is unclear, however, how prevalent this attitude is. In fields such as software development and the publication of academic journals, people frequently volunteer to benefit for-profit organizations (Benkler 2002, pp. 440–441). For-profit firms also are frequently able to induce their customers to provide volunteer labor in forms that range from responses to customer satisfaction surveys to voluntary transfers of significant technological innovations.[27]

---

23 Cf. 'Given enough eyeballs, all bugs are shallow', Raymond (2000).

24 This is the logic that has been offered to explain the success of open source software projects and other instances of what Yochai Benkler (2002) calls peer production.

25 I am dubious whether many actors in this sector are motivated primarily by altruism in the sense of being interested in benefiting, for example, 'the members of the grain and feed industry', or 'inhabitants of countries seeking foreign investment'. To the extent there are such altruists, they are even more likely than other actors to be dissuaded from volunteering for a for-profit by the concerns set out below.

26 The existence of such an aversion seems particularly plausible when the for-profit organization is a competitor. So, for instance, law firms might donate their services to a trade association but not to another private law firm.

27 For discussion of more extreme examples, see Harhoff et al. (2003).

Access to Tax-exempt Capital

In many countries, including the United States, for-profits enjoy less favorable tax treatment than not-for-profits. Under US law not-for-profits are exempt from certain state and local taxes, most notably franchise and property taxes.[28] These exemptions clearly give not-for-profits a competitive advantage over for-profits by lowering their relative costs of production. Many not-for-profits are also exempt from federal income tax, which tends to reduce their cost of capital.[29] To see this, consider the following example. Suppose that an organization needs to raise $10 000 to finance the creation of an arbitration institution. Assume that the normal after-tax rate of return on an investment in a venture such as this would be 10 percent and that the tax rate is 30 percent. If the organization is a for-profit, it will have to provide an investor with an after-tax return of $1000, meaning that it will have to earn roughly $1428.57 in before-tax income. Suppose, however, that the organization is a tax-exempt not-for-profit. In this case it might try to finance the business by charging its members dues in return for an implicit promise to provide dispute resolution services at below-market prices in the future. In a sense, therefore, the members can be characterized as 'investors'. Assume that, like other investors, they demand a return of 10 percent on their investment. Notice that the not-for-profit will only have to earn $1000 in before-tax income to generate this return. This means that the not-for-profit will be able to charge a lower price for its services than a for-profit while still generating an acceptable return for its investors. Alternatively, it can charge the same price and generate a relatively high return for its investors, thus encouraging them to invest.[30]

---

[28] The details vary from state to state (Hill and Kirschten 1994, para. 14.04).

[29] I.R.C. § 501(c) (2000) (listing exempt organizations). § 501(c)(6) refers to '[b]usiness leagues, chambers of commerce, real-estate boards, boards of trade, or professional football leagues (whether or not administering a pension fund for football players), not organized for profit and no part of the net earnings of which inures to the benefit of any private shareholder or individual'. Income from exempt not-for-profits' unrelated business activities – that is to say, activity unrelated to the purposes that form the basis of the not-for-profit's exemption – is subject to a federal tax called the unrelated business income tax ('UBIT'). However, for many not-for-profits, providing dispute resolution services seems unlikely to qualify as an unrelated business activity (I.R.C. § 511(a) 2000; Hansmann 1989).

[30] The consequences would be similar if not-for-profits were not exempt from income taxation but typically were able to avoid generating taxable income by offsetting income from business activities with expenses incurred in providing benefits to members. However, Internal Revenue Code (I.R.C.) § 277 limits the

Access to Public Subsidies

Subsidies from public bodies constitute a significant source of funding for some providers of dispute resolution services (see e.g. ICSID). It would be unwise for a public body to provide such a subsidy without taking steps to control the use of funds. In principle it would be possible to assert such control over a for-profit by, for example, using a contract that contains appropriate performance standards. In practice though it might be difficult to attain the requisite level of control without relying on a more direct form of oversight, such as a seat on the board of directors of the organization. This suggests that organizations designed to attract public subsidies ought to be controlled, at least to some extent, by public actors. This hypothesis would explain the existence of both wholly public and hybrid (public–private) organizations.

Access to Information

In resolving commercial disputes it is often helpful to have prior familiarity with the underlying transaction. Access to specialized information does not seem to be systematically related to organizational form. For example, in some contexts the individuals with greatest access to relevant information can be found within the disputing parties themselves. On other occasions a trade association will have the best access to expert decision-makers since its *raison d'être* is to maintain relationships with a broad range of industry professionals. In still other cases, an intermediary like Visa or MasterCard will have the requisite expertise. As these examples suggest, the situation is further complicated by the fact that there is typically a trade-off between expertise and impartiality: individuals or organizations that are familiar with a transaction may also be connected to the parties in a way that creates bias in favor of one party or another.

5. CONCLUSION

Commercial law represents the infrastructure of international commerce. As with other forms of infrastructure, the case for provision by for-profit actors is complex. Conventional economic theory suggests that under certain conditions for-profits offer advantages in terms of efficiency and

scope for this practice. That provision prevents certain non-tax-exempt organizations from treating expenditures on member benefits as deductions from income generated from business activities.

innovativeness. However, other theoretical considerations point in different directions. For one thing, for-profits do not have obvious incentives to be dependable providers of high-quality services, particularly for parties to long-term contracts. They also lack incentives to take public interests into account when determining the outcomes of disputes. Moreover, there are circumstances in which for-profits will be at a disadvantage compared to other institutions in terms of access to labor, capital or information.

These theoretical observations are consistent with evidence that actors involved in adjudication of international commercial disputes take a variety of organizational forms. On the other hand, both the theoretical and the empirical analyses set out above are too preliminary to show precisely when any given organizational form is optimal, from the perspective of either the parties to commercial transactions or society as a whole. Therefore, the lesson seems to be that a great deal remains to be learned about how international commerce is actually governed, but taking organizational form into account adds an important dimension to the inquiry.

REFERENCES

Benkler, Yochai (2002), 'Coase's Penguin, or, Linux and The Nature of the Firm', *Yale Law Journal* **112** (3), 369–446.

Benson, Bruce L. (1989), 'The Spontaneous Evolution of Commercial Law', *Southern Economic Journal* **55** (3), 644–661.

Bernstein, Lisa (1992), 'Opting Out of the Legal System: Extralegal Contractual Relations in the Diamond Industry', *Journal of Legal Studies* **21** (1), 115–157.

Born, Gary B. (2009), *International Commercial Arbitration* (3rd edition), The Hague: Kluwer Law International.

Charny, David E. (1990), 'Nonlegal Sanctions in Commercial Relationships', *Harvard Law Review* **104** (2), 373–467.

Choi, Stephen J. (2003), 'The Problem with Arbitration Agreements', *Vanderbilt Journal of Transnational Law* **36** (4), 1233–1240.

Cutler, A. Claire (2003), *Private Power and Global Authority: Transnational Merchant Law in the Global Political Economy*, New York: Cambridge University Press.

Dammann, J. and H. Hansmann (2008), 'Globalizing Commercial Litigation', *Cornell Law Review* **94** (1), 1–71.

Davis, Kevin E. (2006), 'The Role of Non-profits in the Production of Boilerplate', *Michigan Law Review* **104** (5), 1075–1103.

Davis, K.E. and H. Hershkoff (2011), 'Contracting for Procedure', *William & Mary Law Review* **53**, 507–565.

Dixit, Avinash (2004), *Lawlessness in Governance and Economics*, Princeton: Princeton University Press.

Fiss, Owen (1984), 'Against Settlement', *Yale Law Journal* **93** (6), 1073–1090.

Gillette, Clayton P. (1996), 'Opting Out of Public Provision', *Denver University Law Review* **73** (4), 1185–1219.

Gillette, Clayton P. (1999), 'Harmony and Stasis in Trade Usages for International Sales', *Virginia Journal of International Law* **39** (3), 707–741.

Gillette, C.P. and R.E. Scott (2005), 'The Political Economy of International Sales Law', *International Review of Law and Economics* **25** (3), 446–486.

Gilson, R.J., C.F. Sabel and Robert E. Scott (2009), 'Contracting for Innovation: Vertical Disintegration and Interfirm Collaboration', *Columbia Law Review* **109** (3), 431–502.

Guzman, Andrew T. (2000), 'Arbitrator Liability: Reconciling Arbitration and Mandatory Rules', *Duke Law Journal* **49** (5), 1279–1334.

Hadfield, Gillian K. (2001), 'Privatizing Commercial Law', *Regulation* **24** (1), 40–45.

Hadfield, Gillian (2009), 'The Public and the Private in the Provision of Law for Global Transactions', in Volkmar Gessner (ed.), *Contractual Certainty in International Trade: Empirical Studies and Theoretical Debates on Institutional Support for Global Economic Exchanges*, Oxford: Hart Publishing, pp. 239–256.

Hadfield, G. and E. Talley (2006), 'On Public versus Private Provision of Corporate Law', *Journal of Law, Economics, & Organization* **22** (2), 414–441.

Hansmann, Henry (1980), 'The Role of Nonprofit Enterprise', *Yale Law Journal* **89** (5), 835–901.

Hansmann, Henry B. (1989), 'Unfair Competition and the Unrelated Business Income Tax', *Virginia Law Review* **75** (3), 605–635.

Hansmann, Henry (1996), *Ownership of Enterprise*, Cambridge, MA: The Belknap Press of Harvard University Press.

Harhoff, D., J. Henkel and E. von Hippel (2003), 'Profiting from Voluntary Information Spillovers: How Users Benefit by Freely Revealing their Innovations', *Research Policy* **32** (10), 1753–1769.

Hill, F.R. and B.L. Kirschten (1994), *Federal and State Taxation of Exempt Organizations*, Boston: Warren Gorham & Lamont.

Inoue, Taroh (2006), 'Introduction to International Commercial Arbitration in China', *Hong Kong Law Journal* **36** (1), 171–196.

International Chamber of Commerce (ICC) (2010), *ICC Rules of Arbitration*, available online at: http://www.iccwbo.org/court/arbitration/id4093/index.html

JAMS (2005), *JAMS International Arbitration Rules*, available online at: http://www.jamsadr.com

Kessler, Amalia D. (2010), 'Marginalization and Myth: The Corporatist Roots of France's Forgotten Elective Judiciary', *American Journal of Comparative Law* **58** (3), 679–720.

Kingsbury, B. and S. Schill (2009), 'Investor–State Arbitration as Governance: Fair and Equitable Treatment, Proportionality and the Emerging Global Administrative Law', in Albert Jan van den Berg (ed.), *50 Years of the New York Convention, ICAA Congress Series no 14*, The Hague: Kluwer Law International, pp. 5–68.

Klein, B. and K.B. Leffler (1981), 'The Role of Market Forces in Assuring Contractual Performance', *Journal of Political Economy* **89** (4), 615–641.

Landes, W. and R. Posner (1979), 'Adjudication as a Private Good', *Journal of Legal Studies* **8** (2), 235–284.

LCIA (1998), *LCIA Arbitration Rules*, available online at: http://www.lcia.org/Dispute_Resolution_Services/LCIA_Arbitration_Rules.aspx (accessed August 20, 2010).

Levit, Janet Koven (2008), 'Bottom-Up Lawmaking: The Private Origins of Transnational Law', *Indiana Journal of Global Legal Studies* **15** (1), 49–73.

MasterCard Incorporated (2006), *Prospectus*, 24 May.

MasterCard Worldwide (2010a), 'The MasterCard Story', available online at: http://www.mastercard.com/us/company/en/ourcompany/the_mastercard_story.html (accessed July 22, 2010).

MasterCard Worldwide (2010b), *Chargeback Guide*, 16 April, available online at: http://www.mastercard.com/us/merchant/pdf/TB_CB_Manual.pdf

Morriss, A.P. and J.A. Korosec (2005), 'Private Dispute Resolution in the Card Context: Structure, Reputation, and Incentives', Case Legal Studies Research Paper No. 05–12, Case Research Paper Series in Legal Studies, Jonathan H. Adler and Erik M. Jensen (eds), Case Western Reserve University School of Law.

Raymond, Eric Steven (2000), *The Cathedral and the Bazaar*, Version 3.0, http://www.catb.org/~esr/writings/cathedral-bazaar/cathedral-bazaar (follow 'Release Early, Release Often' hyperlink) (accessed September 30, 2010).

Rutledge, Peter B. (2004), 'Toward a Contractual Approach for Arbitral Immunity', *Georgia Law Review* **39** (1), 151–214.

Scott, Colin (2008), 'Regulating Private Legislation', in Fabrizio Cafaggi and Horatia Muir-Watt (eds), *Making European Private Law*, Cheltenham, UK and Northampton, MA, USA: Edward Elgar, pp. 254–268.

Singapore International Arbitration Centre (2010), *Arbitration Rules of the Singapore International Arbitration Centre* (4th edition, 1 July), available online at: http://www.siac.org.sg/cms/images/stories/documents/news/2010/SIAC_Rules_2010.pdf.

Snyder, David V. (2003), 'Private Lawmaking', *Ohio State Law Journal* **64** (2), 371–449.

Straits Times (1991), 'International Arbitration Centre Set Up in S'pore', 6 July.

Telser, Lester G. (1980), 'A Theory of Self-Enforcing Agreements', *Journal of Business* **53** (1), 27–44.

Vermeule, Adrian (2007), 'Should We Have Lay Justices?', *Stanford Law Review* **59** (6), 1569–1611.

Visa (2009), *Visa International Operating Regulations – Dispute Resolution Rules*, 2 November.

Visa Europe (2009), *Annual Report*.

Visa Inc. (2007), Registration Statement, Form S-4 under the Securities Act of 1933, filed with the Securities Exchange Commission on 22 June.

Wai, Robert S. (2002), 'Transnational Liftoff and Juridical Touchdown: The Regulatory Function of Private International Law in an Era of Globalization', *Columbia Journal of Transnational Law* **40** (2), 209–274.

Williamson, Oliver E. (1983), 'Credible Commitments: Using Hostages to Support Exchange', *American Economic Review* **73** (4), 519–540.

Yong Tong, Ang (2000), 'SIAC: Arbitration in the New Millenium', *Singapore Law Gazette*, January, available online at: http://www.lawgazette.com.sg/2000–1/Jan00–23.htm (accessed August 5, 2010).

Treaty

Convention on the Settlement of Investment Disputes Between States and Nationals of Other States, produced at Washington DC, 18 March 1965. Found at 575 U.N.T.S. 159 (No. 8359) (1966), available at: http://icsid.worldbank.org/ICSID/

FrontServlet?requestType=CasesRH&actionVal=ShowHome&pageName=Documents_Home (accessed July 23, 2010).

Cases

CMS v *Argentina*, Award, May 12, 2005, 44 ILM (2005) 1205 (annulled in part by decision dated 25 September 2007).
Lauder v *Czech Republic*, Award, September 3, 2001, 9 ICSID Reports 66.

Legislation

I.R.C. §§ 277, 511(a), 501(c) (2000).

8. Enforcement of private transnational labor regulation: a new frontier in the anti-sweatshop movement?

Cynthia Estlund

1. INTRODUCTION

Anti-sweatshop activists, now veterans in the corporate social responsibility (CSR) movement, have been working for decades to improve wages and working conditions in the factories of the developing world, where most of the world's clothing, toys, and electronics are now produced. While public law, domestic and international, plays an important role in those efforts, its focus is on developing mechanisms of private, voluntary regulation by the large branded multinational corporations (MNCs or 'lead firms') at the top of the supply chains that link poor workers in the developing world to affluent consumers in the developed world.[1]

Critics of those efforts abound. Some see a misguided assault on the salutary flow of desperately needed capital to impoverished people and communities.[2] Others, including many trade unionists, view CSR as meaningless at best and harmful at worst in its tendency to divert energy and attention from the more useful projects of strengthening public enforcement of labor standards and supporting independent trade unions.[3] In the

[1] MNCs' own employees' labor conditions may become a source of controversy. But our focus here is the more complicated business of regulating labor conditions in factories that are not operated by the MNCs, but that contract with them to supply goods or components.

[2] See, e.g., Nicholas D. Kristof, In Praise of the Maligned Sweatshop, *N. Y. Times* (6/6/2006); Nicholas D. Kristof & Sheryl WuDunn, Two Cheers for Sweatshops, *N. Y. Times Magazine* (9/24/2000); Paul Krugman, In Praise of Cheap Labor, available at: http://web.mit.edu/krugman/www/smokey.html; Allen R. Meyerson, In Principle, A Case for More 'Sweatshops', *N. Y. Times* (6/22/2002).

[3] See, e.g., Harry W. Arthurs, Private Ordering and Workers' Rights in the Global Economy: Corporate Codes of Conduct as a Regime of Labour Market

meantime, many within the CSR community struggle daily to push corporations along the path from promise to performance, and from the bare commitment to promote decent labor standards among suppliers to increasingly ambitious mechanisms for realizing those standards. Environmental and human rights activists are traveling that same path, and are confronting similar issues in promoting effective private transnational social regulation.

The topic at hand is 'enforcement'. Enforcement has many dimensions, even in the context of this one particular kind of private transnational regulation.[4] Much of the history of the anti-sweatshop movement has been about one kind of enforcement: pressing firms to improve enforcement of labor codes of conduct against their suppliers by instituting better monitoring procedures, training, and other procedures to improve supplier compliance. On the horizon is another more challenging set of enforcement issues: the ability of workers or their advocates to enforce code provisions against suppliers or lead firms. Legal enforcement of CSR commitments by or on behalf of the workers they are intended to benefit might be the next frontier in CSR.

To get the measure of the challenge facing demands for enforcement, it will be helpful to look back at the history of the struggle to induce lead firms to enact and enforce private, voluntary codes of conduct against suppliers. Through that history runs a recurring dilemma that follows from the voluntariness that is a defining feature of *private* transnational social regulation. Regulated entities must be induced to submit to private regulation. Stakeholders' efforts to ratchet up the strength and efficacy of regulatory regimes are thus in tension with their efforts to induce voluntary submission to those regimes. That tension is bound to constrain efforts to secure enforceable commitments in this as in other arenas of private transnational social regulation.

Regulation, in Joanne Conaghan et al. (eds), *Labour Law in an Era of Globalisation*, pp. 471, 485–87 (Oxford University Press, 2002); Adelle Blackett, Global Governance, Legal Pluralism and the Decentered State: A Labor Law Critique of Codes of Corporate Conduct, 8 *Ind. J. Global Legal Stud.* 401, 406–18 (2001); Kimberly D. Krawiec, Cosmetic Compliance and the Failure of. Negotiated Governance, 81 *Wash. U. L.Q.* 487, 510–54 (2003). For a fascinating ongoing online debate about these issues, hosted by Timberland, Inc., see http://www.earthkeeper.com/Forum/default.aspx?g=posts&t=8

[4] See Fabrizio Cafaggi, Chapter 2, this volume.

2. CSR AND PRIVATE TRANSNATIONAL LABOR REGULATION: THE ROAD SO FAR[5]

Milton Friedman famously said: 'There is one and only one social responsibility of business – to use its resources and engage in activities designed to increase its profits so long as it stays within the rules of the game'.[6] But in the last few decades, the proponents of CSR have managed to change the rules of the game, particularly with regard to corporate responsibility for labor conditions in suppliers' factories.

2.1 Corporate Social Responsibility: The Inside and Outside Games

Friedman represents one side in a long-running debate over whether corporate officers (may or should or do) pursue the interests of shareholders only, or of other 'stakeholders' as well. Most US corporate law scholars hold that corporate fiduciaries are not *permitted* to pursue social goals unless they are consistent with long-term profit maximization.[7] Others doubt that fiduciaries are *motivated* to do so. Either or both of these beliefs have led proponents to emphasize, with considerable success, 'the business case for social responsibility'.[8] Big corporations vocally proclaim their commitment to go 'beyond compliance' in protecting workers' rights, human rights, community development, and environmental sustainability. In particular, firms have been induced to accept some responsibility for the conditions of workers to whom the firm is not legally liable in places where

---

[5] This section is adapted from Cynthia Estlund, *Regoverning the Workplace: From Self-Regulation to Co-Regulation*, Ch. 4, pp. 97–103 (Yale University Press, 2010).

[6] Milton Friedman, *Capitalism and Freedom*, p. 133 (University of Chicago Press, 1962).

[7] See Frank H. Easterbrook and Daniel R. Fischel, *The Economic Structure of Corporate Law*, pp. 36–9 (Harvard University Press, 1991); Stephen Bainbridge, In Defense of the Shareholder Wealth Maximization Norm: A Reply to Professor Green, 50 *Wash. & Lee L. Rev*. 1423, 1427–8 (1993); John Macey, An Economic Analysis of the Various Rationales for Making Shareholders the Exclusive Beneficiaries of Corporate Fiduciary Duties, 21 *Stetson L. Rev.* 23, 24–5 (1991). Others contend for a less constrained view of corporate social responsibility. See Margaret M. Blair & Lynn Stout, A Team Production Theory of Corporate Law, 85 *Va. L. Rev.* 247, 254 (1999); Einer Elhauge, Sacrificing Corporate Profits in the Public Interest, 80 *N.Y.U. L. Rev*. 733, 737 (2005); Antonio Vives, Corporate Social Responsibility: The Role of Law and Markets and the Case of Developing Countries, 83 *Chi.-Kent L. Rev*. 199, 216–21 (2008).

[8] See David Vogel, *The Market for Virtue: The Potential and Limits of Corporate Social Responsibility*, pp. 16–45 (Brookings Institution Press, 2005).

there is a dearth of effective legal authority.[9] It would be naïve simply to take these proclamations at face value; but it would be foolish to ignore them.

CSR proponents pursue their objectives through both an 'outside game' and an 'inside game'. The 'outside game' seeks to galvanize public and consumer sentiment against (or in favor of) the corporation's reputation, brand, and products on the basis of conditions or practices within the corporation's operations or supply chain.[10] Revelations about inhumane working conditions, persecution of labor activists, destructive toxic emissions, or clear-cutting of ancient forests may arouse public outrage, bruise the corporate brand, or trigger a boycott; while exemplary programs may earn a 'Sweat-Free' or 'Fair Trade' label, and the favor of advertisers and customers. The inside game involves shareholders – including large public pension funds and socially responsible investment (SRI) mutual funds – pressing firms to adopt socially responsible positions and programs.[11] Another 'inside game' kicks in once a firm staffs its CSR programs. In-house CSR personnel seek credibility and expertise by joining a larger professional CSR community; within the firm, they become an internal constituency for taking CSR commitments more seriously. The outside and inside strategies are intertwined; the threat of bad publicity (or the promise of good) from outside advocates motivates corporate directors and managers to accede to some CSR demands of shareholders or staff.

Firms that initially offer verbal commitments of social responsibility, perhaps aiming to deflect outside pressures, often find themselves propelled by advocates' skillful deployment of inside and outside tactics down a path toward serious investments in regulatory procedures – especially monitoring and reporting procedures – to back up those commitments.[12] The evolution of the anti-sweatshop movement provides a case in point.

---

[9] See Vogel, *supra* note 8, at pp. 96–109.

[10] See ibid. at pp. 77–82; Michael E. Porter and Mark R. Kramer, Strategy and Society: The Link Between Competitive Advantage and Corporate Social Responsibility, 84 *Harv. Bus. Rev.* 78, 80 (2006); Romen Shamir, Mind the Gap: The Commodification of Corporate Social Responsibility, 28 *Symbolic Interaction* 229, 231 (2005).

[11] See Vogel, *supra* note 8, at pp. 63–4. Both SRI investment assets and SRI proxy resolutions have grown significantly in recent years (ibid.).

[12] See Peter Utting, Corporate Responsibility and the Movement of Business, 15 *Development in Practice* 375, at 383–6 (2005).

2.2 Private Transnational Labor Codes and their Enforcement against Suppliers

The global anti-sweatshop movement has mounted a decades-long effort to make corporate codes of conduct meaningful instruments for improving labor standards, and for filling a regulatory gap that multinational corporations – especially in toy, garment, and footwear manufacturing – were taking advantage of in the developing world.[13] The goal of the movement is to activate corporate regulatory resources that, in the aggregate, swamp those of the relevant government bodies.

Big global garment brands like Gap and Nike were particularly sensitive to consumer responses to shocking exposés of the child labor, forced labor, subsistence wages, and grueling hours that went into producing their expensive sneakers and jeans. Advocates argued that the brands profited from the relentless cost-based competition that their contracting practices encouraged, and that the brands had the economic and organizational capacity to monitor and influence suppliers' labor practices. Brands like Nike claimed to be 'just the buyer'; but advocates managed to tighten the perceived link through images of third-world workers sewing on big-brand logos. The anti-sweatshop activists pursued both an outside and an inside strategy. Exposés, publicity campaigns, and boycotts sought to make Gap, Nike, Wal-Mart and others 'socially liable' for the conditions of their suppliers' workers.[14] That set the stage for sympathetic shareholders and investors to pressure corporate fiduciaries to cultivate a 'sweat-free' reputation. The result was a profusion of corporate supplier codes requiring suppliers to comply with basic labor standards.

The early schemes were a mixed bag. Code provisions were vague, and most ignored workers' freedom of association, a 'core' international labor right. There was little effort to inform workers of code provisions or to elicit

---

[13] See Kimberly Ann Elliott & Richard B. Freeman, *Can Labor Standards Improve Under Globalization?*, pp. 49–72 (Institute for International Economics, 2003); Mark Barenberg, Toward a Democratic Model of Transnational Labour Monitoring?, in Brian Bercusson & Cynthia Estlund (eds), *Regulating Labour in the Wake of Globalisation: New Challenges, New Institutions*, p. 37 (Hart, 2008); Mark Barenberg, Law and Labor in the New Global Economy: Through the Lens of United States Federalism, 33 *Colum. J. Transnat'l L.* 445, 447–8 (1995).

[14] See, e.g., Archon Fung, Dara O'Rourke & Charles Sabel, *Can We Put an End to Sweatshops?* (Beacon Press, 2001); Michael P. Vandenbergh, *The New Wal-Mart Effect: The Role of Private Contracting in Global Governance*, 54 *UCLA L. Rev.* 913 (2007).

their concerns, or to ensure suppliers' compliance.[15] The ubiquitous Wal-Mart offers a textbook illustration of the weaknesses of early supplier codes and a first cut at the problem of legal enforcement. From 1992, Wal-Mart in its 'Standards for Suppliers'[16] required suppliers to comply with certain local and international labor standards (though not freedom of association) and to allow monitoring by Wal-Mart.[17] But monitoring was not independent, inspections were rarely unannounced, and results were not made public. In 2005, labor advocates filed a class action lawsuit on behalf of workers in China, Bangladesh, Indonesia, Swaziland, and Nicaragua alleging that Wal-Mart failed to enforce its code, and thus 'reign[s] over a sweatshop gulag that condemns workers around the world to provide forced and uncompensated labor'.[18] Wal-Mart's legal response was revealing, and successful: it argued that the Standards for Suppliers created no legal duty on Wal-Mart's part to inspect supplier factories, and no legal duty at all toward suppliers' workers, but at most a contractual right for Wal-Mart to monitor factories.[19]

But Wal-Mart's response outside court was equally revealing. In 2005 Wal-Mart revised its Standards for Suppliers, recognizing workers' freedom of association (although most Wal-Mart suppliers are in China, where workers have no right to choose their own union), and improving the quality of monitoring. According to Wal-Mart:

> We have one of the most active Ethical Standards programs in the retail industry. In 2005, we audited more factories than any other company in the world, performing more than 13,600 audits of 7,200 factories. We increased the number of unannounced audits by 100 percent. When violations are found, our first priority is to work with our suppliers to ensure their factories achieve compliance. We are confident that this collaborative approach is the best way to help

---

15 On corporate codes in practice, see Jill Esbenshade, *Monitoring Sweatshops: Workers, Consumers, and the Global Apparel Industry* (Temple University Press, 2004); Barenberg, Toward a Democratic Model, *supra* note 13; Blackett, *supra* note 3, at 416–17 (2001); Dara O'Rourke, Outsourcing Regulation: Analyzing Nongovernmental Systems of Labor Standards and Monitoring, 31 *Pol'y Stud. J.* 1, 20–25 (2003); Dara O'Rourke, Monitoring the Monitors: A Critique of Corporate Third-Party Labour Monitoring, in Rhys Jenkins, Ruth Pearson & Gill Seyfang, *Corporate Responsibility and Labour Rights: Codes of Conduct in the Global Economy*, pp. 196–207 (Earthscan, 2002).

16 See http://www.laborrights.org/sites/default/files/publications-and-resources/Supplier-Standards-2005.pdf

17 Ibid.

18 See http://www.iradvocates.org/walmartcase.html

19 See *Doe* v *Wal-Mart Stores, Inc.*, 572 F.3d 677 (9th Cir. 2009).

our suppliers understand the business benefits of operating factories meeting labor, environmental, and health and safety standards.[20]

Wal-Mart's actions suggest how far activists have succeeded in extending the ethos of corporate responsibility to lead firms' supply chains. Putting aside for now questions of efficacy, this is a remarkable accomplishment given the lack of hard law behind that profession of responsibility. Many major US and European corporations – especially those that market directly to consumers – have felt compelled to extend their regulatory commitments, and to develop their latent monitoring capabilities, to reach far flung factories for which they bear no legal responsibility and which themselves often face little legal pressure to comply with domestic labor standards, given weak local regulatory institutions.

In an effort to improve upon corporate labor codes, several multi-stakeholder initiatives, often with trade union participation, have arisen.[21] For example, the US-based Social Accountability International (SAI) trains and certifies factory monitors and companies in accordance with SAI's model code, SA8000, which draws from core ILO conventions as well as domestic law.[22] Multi-stakeholder initiatives like SAI, the Ethical Trading Initiative (ETI), and the Fair Labor Association (FLA) generally include provisions on 'freedom of association' that are often omitted in corporate codes, and set standards for independent monitoring. In addition, most encourage the creation of grievance procedures by which workers can bring complaints within the factory. Some (FLA, for example) include 'third party complaint procedures' by which stakeholders can complain of violations and trigger a review by the organization.

These multi-stakeholder initiatives seek to focus diffuse reputational forces in order to recruit corporate adherents, deliver reputational rewards to them, and pressure them to improve standards. They represent the current state of the art in enforcement of private transnational labor regulation against lead firms. Yet these organizations' efforts to improve corporate accountability are in chronic conflict with their effort to gain

---

20 See Wal-Mart Stores, Inc., 2005 Report on Ethical Sourcing, available at: http://walmartstores.com/Sustainability/7951.aspx

21 For an excellent overview of the major multi-stakeholder initiatives as of 2006, see Dara O'Rourke, Multi-stakeholder Regulation: Privatizing or Socializing Global Labor Standards?, 34 *World Development* 899 (2006).

22 Social Accountability International, see About Us: http://www.sa-intl.org/index.cfm?fuseaction=Page.viewPage&pageId=472

voluntary corporate adherents.[23] This tension constrains efforts to improve enforcement of these voluntary private regulatory undertakings, and may be the Achilles heel of private transnational social regulation. The major multi-stakeholder organizations attempt to deal with the tension in part by maintaining tiers of participation with varying levels of commitment; a firm may be able to sign onto a multi-stakeholder initiative by proclaiming an aspiration to improve performance and agreeing to report on progress toward meeting prescribed standards. That is not nothing, for even this can create soft pressure toward improving labor standards; but it is far from legal enforceability.

Practices have improved as worker advocates, including multi-stakeholder organizations, have pressed to ensure that monitors are independent of employers, have complete information about factory locations, make unannounced visits, and conduct confidential interviews with workers, as well as ensuring that workers are made aware of code provisions and protected against retaliation.[24] Central to those efforts is the education and involvement of workers, widely recognized as the best if not the only effective monitors of labor standards.[25] For example, the Fair Wear Foundation, a factory monitoring group that works in China, recently issued a set of 'best practices' calling for extensive education of workers in labor rights, both international and domestic, and in 'committee building and representation skills'. The aim should be to '[equip] workers with the skills to organise meetings, negotiate with management and represent the views of others. Part of the training process is that workers are chosen by means of fair election'.[26]

---

[23] The Workers Rights Consortium (WRC) is an exception. It has no corporate adherents, and it does not certify factories. Rather, it investigates complaints by workers or unions. O'Rourke describes its model as a 'fire alarm' model, and concurs with advocates' and scholars' praise of the democratic nature, transparency, and thoroughness of WRC's investigations. But the WRC model is too labor intensive to be capable of large-scale replication, and appears to work best in collaboration with more traditional monitoring organizations like the FLA. See O'Rourke, Multi-stakeholder Regulation, *supra* note 21, at 905–906.

[24] Esbenshade, *supra* note 15, at 60–119. Wal-Mart's post-2005 program, for example, appears designed to meet some of these demands.

[25] See, e.g., Barenberg, Toward a Democratic Model, *supra* note 13, at 63; Blackett, *supra* note 3, at 436; Elliott & Freeman, *supra* note 13, at 69–72; Linda Shaw & Angela Hale, The Emperor's New Clothes: What Codes Mean for Workers in the Garment Industry, in Jenkins et al., *supra* note 15, at 104–105.

[26] See Fair Wear Foundation, Best Practices in Factory Training in China: Contributing to More Worker Participation in the Improvement of Working Conditions (Sept. 2009), available at: http://fairwear.org/images/2010-01/fwf_-_factory_training_paper_-_september_2009.pdf.

Still unclear, however, is whether monitoring works for workers. Good empirical research on efficacy is difficult and scarce – though it is now at the top of the CSR agenda.[27] A recent independent study commissioned by Nike, which maintains one of the most ambitious and transparent factory monitoring programs among global brands,[28] concluded:

> [N]otwithstanding the significant efforts and investments by Nike and its staff to improve working conditions among its suppliers, monitoring alone appears to produce only limited results. Instead, our research indicates that when monitoring efforts are combined with other interventions focused on tackling some of the root causes of poor working conditions – by improving the ability of suppliers to better schedule their work and improve their quality and efficiency – working conditions appear to significantly improve.[29]

In particular, frequent and intense interaction between suppliers and Nike *production* staff was associated with significant improvements.

Recurring revelations of labor rights violations by factories that are subject to supposedly state-of-the-art monitoring raise doubts about efficacy. Such revelations may become more rather than less frequent as firms accede to demands for greater transparency in their monitoring programs. Part of the problem with factory monitoring programs is that suppliers have become increasingly adept at the monitoring 'game', using duplicate books, scripts for workers, and consultants who 'guarantee' a factory's passing muster.[30] According to ETI:

---

[27] For example, in addition to Nike, see *infra*, ETI has commissioned independent assessments of its impact on workers. See: http://www.ethicaltrade.org/resources/key-eti-resources/eti-impact-assessment-part-1-main-findings. Scholars are also actively engaged in assessing the efficacy of CSR programs. See, e.g., Robert A. Kagan et al., Explaining Corporate Environmental Performance: How Does Regulation Matter?, 37 *Law & Soc'y Rev.* 51 (2003).

[28] On Nike.com one finds Nike's supplier code, a description of factory monitoring protocols, a list of all active factories producing Nike goods, and recent monitoring reports (http://www.nikebiz.com/responsibility/workers_and_factories.html). Nike is nearly alone in having voluntarily disclosed the identity and location of their factories – crucial information for those seeking to ensure accountability, but closely guarded as a 'trade secret' by most lead firms. See David Doorey, Transnational Domestic Labour Regulation: Using Domestic Disclosure Regulation to Influence Foreign Labour Practices (unpublished dissertation, York University, 2009).

[29] Richard M. Locke et al., Does Monitoring Improve Labor Standards? Lessons from Nike, 61 *Indus. & Lab. Rel. Rev*. 3 (2007).

[30] See Secrets, Lies, and Sweatshops, *Business Week*, Nov. 27, 2006, available at: http://www.businessweek.com/magazine/content/06_48/b4011001.htm

> [A]udit fraud is now so common that a whole new industry has developed to facilitate it. For example, factory managers in China can now buy software packages that allow them to keep multiple sets of records, or get trained on how to falsify their records. The reality is that suppliers are developing an ever more sophisticated and wide range of practices, all with the single aim of hiding the truth and presenting an alternative reality to suppliers.[31]

The problem of evasion points to the larger flaw in the prevailing code enforcement model: its failure to address the economics of supply chains. As one leading critic explains: 'At present, brands publicly embrace [CSR], and then push their suppliers to accept prices so low that labor rights violations and sub-poverty wages are virtually guaranteed'.[32]

Transforming supply chain practices has thus become a major priority in the anti-sweatshop movement.[33] Advocates are pressing firms to shift away from an 'open' to a more 'closed' supply chain, with stronger ties to fewer contractors, and away from a 'policing' model to a more remedial approach to violations.[34] Some leading firms, as well as multi-stakeholder organizations, are picking up the refrain. Nike has announced that its 'Generation III' approach to improving labor standards is 'responsible competitiveness', and will focus on 'a sustainable sourcing strategy', '[i]ncreasing contract factory ownership of corporate responsibility, and [b]uilding industry coalitions'.[35] Wal-Mart similarly claims to be moving 'away from intermittent transactions with many suppliers toward longer-term arrangements with a

[31] Ethical Trade Initiative, Auditing Working Conditions: http://www.ethicaltrade.org/in-action/issues/auditing-working-conditions. See also Secrets, Lies, and Sweatshops, *Business Week*, Nov. 27, 2006.

[32] So wrote Scott Nova, of the Workers Rights Consortium, in a post on Timberland's Earthkeepers (CSR) website, http://www.earthkeeper.com/Forum/default.aspx?g=posts&t=8

[33] See, e.g., the Ethical Trading Institute's Purchasing Practices Project, http://wiego.org/sites/wiego.org/files/resources/files/ETI-Global-Trade-PP_step_by_step_guide.pdf

[34] See Blackett, *supra* note 3, at 418; Esbenshade, *supra* note 15. The Worker Rights Consortium (WRC), which recruits universities to pressure the brands that supply their 'logo' products, has been at the forefront of these efforts. The WRC's 'Designated Supplier Program' (DSP) would require brands to close the set of supplier factories, and to build closer relationships with suppliers based on a contract price that covers the cost of decent wages and conditions. See http://www.workersrights.org/dsp.asp. However, the DSP has not yet gotten enough universities to sign on to trigger the program's implementation.

[35] Workers in Contracting Factories, (http://info.nike.com/responsibility/documents/3_Nike_CRR_Workers_C.pdf), at17.

smaller group of manufacturers', as well as tightening standards and expanding monitoring.[36]

Underlying this move is an effort to link social and operational concerns in a strong version of the 'business case for social responsibility': It is not just that activists can *make* social irresponsibility costly to the firm's reputation, but that social irresponsibility *is* costly, in that abusive labor and environmental practices go hand in hand with poor quality, product safety, and productivity. Wal-Mart's then CEO Lee Scott echoed the argument in 2008:

> I firmly believe that a company that cheats on overtime and on the age of its labor, that dumps its scraps and its chemicals in our rivers, that does not pay its taxes or honor its contracts, will ultimately cheat on the quality of its products. And cheating on the quality of products is the same as cheating on customers.[37]

This approach to CSR could potentially align interests and constituencies that have been in conflict with each other, and promote the kind of operational engagement between lead firms and suppliers that appears to have a positive impact on labor conditions.[38] It is too early to know how widespread these changes are, much less their impact on workers.

The jury is still out on how much CSR programs actually improve labor standards at the bottom of global production chains. There is still too little research that rigorously evaluates them, and much skepticism about their meaningfulness.[39] But a preference by many worker allies for stronger public enforcement is increasingly tempered by a realization that production is too mobile and too global for traditional public regulatory methods to do the whole job. Moreover, CSR has followed an encouraging trajectory so far, from corporate acceptance of responsibility and adoption of supplier codes to escalating demands to follow through on fine-sounding promises. Advocates have steadily raised the bar for what counts as adequate follow-through, as each round of improvements teaches new lessons about what it takes for supplier codes to work.

---

[36] Stephanie Rosenbloom, Wal-Mart to Toughen Standards, *N. Y. Times*, Oct. 22, 2008, B1.

[37] Ibid.

[38] See Locke et al., *supra* note 29.

[39] See *supra* note 3.

3. THE ENFORCEMENT PROBLEM IN PRIVATE TRANSNATIONAL LABOR REGULATION

That brings us to what might be the next major step up the CSR ladder in the labor rights arena: enforcement by workers and their advocates against suppliers and especially lead firms, with the backing of recognizably legal processes and sanctions. Let us first pin down what is meant by 'enforcement' here: At a minimum, enforcement entails some process of identifying violations (of a labor code) that can, failing correction, lead to sanctions against the violator. Of course, the nature of the enforcement process and of potential sanctions matters a great deal – not least to the willingness of firms to undertake enforceable obligations. There is a world of difference between tort litigation that could culminate in a jury award of punitive damages, and a private third-party investigation leading to recommendations, mediation, and eventually termination of membership in a multi-stakeholder organization. That difference is only partly captured by the distinction between 'judicial' and 'non-judicial' enforcement. But for present purposes, both count as forms of 'enforcement'. (I leave for the jurisprudes the question whether the weakest and least coercive forms of private non-judicial enforcement count as 'legal enforcement'.)

Giving workers and their advocates the ability to enforce code provisions against suppliers and lead firms would help to counter the strong economic incentives that cause suppliers to cheat and cause lead firms to look the other way. Obviously, MNRs face a conflict of interest between their CSR commitments and the profitability of cost-squeezing contracting practices. Even NGOs engaged in monitoring face a potential conflict if they are chosen and paid (as most are) by the firms that are hoping for a clean report. Giving legal recourse to the workers whose rights and labor standards are at stake can potentially help keep these programs honest.

Yet these same conflicts will plague efforts to demand enforceability, for those demands are in tension with the desire to secure 'buy-in' to these programs. Given the voluntary nature of CSR commitments, demands for enforceability raise the cost of commitments and may discourage firms from participating.[40] To be sure, that might also have been said about

[40] This concern should not constrain the shape of rights, remedies, and procedures under public law, whose authority does not depend on the consent of the regulated entities. There is, however, the analogous problem of 'regulatory competition', and the ability and propensity of transnational firms to avoid jurisdictions with stronger labor standards and other regulations. On the problem of 'regulatory

earlier demands for independent monitoring, public disclosure of monitoring reports, or other elements that have now become 'best practices' for supplier code schemes. Reputation-conscious firms have signed on to CSR provisions that they would have rejected out of hand a decade ago. Still, the reputational pressures that have helped raise the bar for what counts as a reputable CSR system might be insufficient to secure legal enforceability.

The issue of enforceability strikes a very sensitive nerve for lead firms. Even proposals for third-party, non-binding mediation of code disputes have met strong resistance.[41] For the same reasons, multi-stakeholder groups are reluctant to demand forms of accountability that are too far ahead of the curve, and that may deter firms from signing on to their particular program (as opposed to another less demanding program). Some, as noted above, have incorporated 'third-party complaint procedures' that may result in reports and recommended remedial measures against signatory lead firms; but this is a very rudimentary form of enforceability. The dilemma of ensuring accountability in a private regime of voluntary CSR commitments means that advocates may have to lower their sights or lengthen their time horizons as they seek to induce lead firms to take this next step toward corporate responsibility.

One other basic dilemma is worth flagging at the outset. Some observers worry that private CSR schemes tend to 'crowd out' or inhibit the development of local public regulatory capacity. These schemes arose partly in response to a regulatory deficit in developing countries; economic development, spurred partly by global outsourcing, should help promote public regulatory capacity. Yet, the latter may lag if local factories are more concerned about the demands of private transnational firms and their monitors than about local public regulatory agencies, or if the latter come to rely on private regulation of local labor standards. Whatever the validity of these concerns, they might be either exacerbated or mitigated by the introduction of enforcement procedures, depending on the form they take. Let us keep that problem in our peripheral vision as we proceed.

3.1 Enforcement by Whom and Against Whom?

The most critical enforcement gap is the inability of workers or their advocates to enforce code provisions that are supposed to protect them. Before turning to the issue of enforcement by or on behalf of workers

---

competition', see Daniel C. Esty & Geradin Damien (eds), *Regulatory Competition and Economic Integration: Comparative Perspectives* (Oxford University Press, 2001).

[41] Personal communications from Arnold Zack, 3/4/10.

against the lead firm, let us briefly take up four other interesting pairs of potential disputants: lead firms versus suppliers; suppliers versus lead firms; workers versus suppliers; and consumers versus lead firms. Merely to enumerate these pairings illustrates the complexity of the issue of enforcement.

Lead firms versus suppliers

As suggested by the Wal-Mart litigation, a corporate supplier code is most readily understood as an agreement between the lead firm and its suppliers, establishing conditions on the supplier relationship, and giving the lead firm the power to monitor compliance. This agreement runs parallel to (or may be incorporated into) other contracts – discrete orders for given quantities of goods. But, subject to the fulfillment of those contracts, the contractual relationship between the lead firm and the supplier is generally terminable at will. (The insecurity of supply contracts and the resulting pressure to squeeze labor costs create their own problems; more on this shortly.)

The lead firm has no need for legal enforcement of its code of conduct against suppliers, for the contract is 'self-enforcing'.[42] Just as an employer in a typical US at-will employment relationship can 'enforce' its work rules by discharging an employee or threatening to do so, so the lead firm can enforce code provisions against suppliers by terminating the contract or threatening to do so. To be sure, a lead firm may hesitate to terminate the contract of a low-cost, dependable supplier that has failed to pay overtime; it may choose remediation or warnings, or even look the other way. But that is little different from an employer that hesitates to fire a wayward but productive employee (say, a sexual harasser). The point is that the lead firm has the economic power to enforce its contractual conditions for suppliers, and that this is a familiar way to enforce some contracts. Lead firms lack not the power to enforce labor standards, but only – perhaps – the *motivation* to enforce them against low-cost suppliers.[43] Similarly, employers always had the power to make and enforce rules against sexual harassment; what they lacked was the motivation to do so. That changed with the rise of sexual harassment litigation by aggrieved employees against employers. By that same logic, lead firms might be better motivated to enforce

42 Cafaggi, Chapter 2, this volume.

43 In contractually securing the *power* to regulate suppliers' labor practices, lead firms do not necessarily thereby acquire a legally-enforceable *duty*, or make an enforceable promise, to regulate.

labor provisions against suppliers if the lead firms themselves faced some kind of liability to the workers affected by those provisions.

One problem, of course, is that lead firms benefit economically from some of the practices that their codes prohibit. Suppliers who engage in cost-saving labor violations may be like managers who exact off-the-clock work or fail to pay overtime – as many Wal-Mart store managers have been found to do in the US. Wal-Mart clearly had the power not only to formally prohibit that conduct (which they did) but to prevent it; but Wal-Mart's interest in enforcing its rules was in conflict with its interest in the higher store profits these cost-cutting practices garnered. Decades of wage-and-hour litigation against Wal-Mart appear to have persuaded the firm to take more serious steps to enforce its formal policies in this area.[44] That suggests, once again, the role in the supply chain context of lead firm liability to aggrieved workers, to which we will turn shortly.

The other problem is that an adversarial 'policing' model of enforcement against suppliers may be fundamentally flawed, as suggested above. Many participants in the CSR monitoring world believe that a more remedial and reciprocal approach to performance problems – one that emphasizes transparency and continuous improvement – may do more to improve labor standards. On that view, our conception of what counts as effective enforcement of private transnational labor standards may have to change.

Suppliers versus lead firms

The notion of suppliers enforcing code provisions against lead firms may be puzzling until one recalls the economics of supply chains. Lead firms demand decent labor standards while instigating and profiting from suppliers' 'race to the bottom' in labor costs. Stakeholders are pressing firms to adopt new supply chain strategies in which supplier relationships are fewer, more stable, and more bilateral than under existing codes, with lead firms promising both an adequate contract price and operational support and engagement with suppliers. If that happened, one could imagine a process by which terminated suppliers could bring a complaint against the lead firm that it had violated commitments to suppliers. I simply flag this possibility; it is not our main concern here.

Workers versus suppliers

Enforcement of code provisions by workers or their advocates against the supplier factory itself requires a low-cost, accessible, and efficient process, in or near the workplace, for resolving frequent and mostly small-stakes

[44] See Estlund, *supra* note 5, at 6.

disputes – in short, 'some kind of hearing' before a neutral third party with the power to award basic make-whole relief. This would resemble the grievance-arbitrations systems that are ubiquitous under collective bargaining agreements in the US (though, crucially, without the power of a union behind it). A grievance system, including some form of worker representation, can help bring workers into the process of monitoring code compliance, which is one of the major goals of CSR labor rights advocates, and can also help both lead firms and stakeholder groups keep tabs on compliance. By making it more likely that code violations would come to light, a grievance system might indirectly spur lead firms to pursue their own enforcement (against suppliers) more assiduously.

The obvious virtues of employee grievance procedures have not escaped the stakeholder community. The major multi-stakeholder organizations and the best corporate codes require or encourage suppliers to maintain grievance procedures of some kind, though often with few details or assurances of fairness or accessibility to workers. This is clearly an area where improvement is possible. The principle of 'enforceability' through individual complaint procedures at the supplier level is among recognized 'best practices', and a vast pool of experience with internal grievance procedures, union and non-union, in the developed world gives much grist for the CSR mill.

Consumers versus lead firms

The primary targets of MNCs' professions of social responsibility are Western consumers, some of whom will pay more for 'sweat-free' goods. That has led to legal claims by consumers against MNCs for allegedly misleading public professions of CSR. In the one reported decision of this nature in the US, Kasky sued Nike under California law on the ground that Nike's false representations about its factory monitoring program constituted unfair competition and false advertising. Nike argued that its statements on these social and political matters were shielded from liability by the First Amendment of the US Constitution. The California Supreme Court disagreed, holding that Nike's statements aimed at consumers constituted 'commercial speech' that was subject to liability if false or misleading.[45] The courts did not pass on the underlying consumer protection

---

45 *Kasky* v *Nike, Inc.*, 45 P.3d 243 (Cal. 2002), cert. dismissed as improvidently granted, 539 U.S. 654 (2003). The US Supreme Court, after agreeing to hear the case, changed its mind on procedural grounds, leaving the California decision standing. Several (liberal) justices dissented, expressing concern that suits like Kasky's cast an intolerable shadow of liability over protected public discourse (539 U.S. at 663–5).

theory of *Kasky* v *Nike*, but it was certainly plausible. Nike eventually settled the suit by paying $1.5 million to the Fair Labor Association for improving factory monitoring programs.

The consumer protection claim provides a potential avenue of 'enforcement' against lead firms – indeed, of judicial enforcement – that strikes at the commercial heart of the CSR movement.[46] In doing so, it unfortunately reinforces the charge that CSR is about quelling the moral qualms of affluent Western consumers, not about improving workers' lives. Moreover, the remedies would run not to workers but to consumers, and might reflect only the price premium paid for 'sweat-free' goods (assuming such a premium could be proven). Still, suits by misled consumers constitute one indirect but potentially effective and underutilized way of enforcing CSR commitments on behalf of workers.

3.2 Enforcement Against Lead Firms under Existing Codes of Conduct

That brings us to the central question whether and how CSR labor commitments are or could be enforceable by or on behalf of workers against the lead firms. I will not pause long to explain why it is necessary to allow advocates – NGOs, local or otherwise – to act on behalf of workers, given the burdens of poverty, illiteracy, and fear that may inhibit workers from complaining on their own behalf. Still, tricky questions arise over what organizations can legitimately represent workers. A century of international law stands behind the proposition that workers should be free to choose their own representatives – that is, unions – through free and democratic processes; and more must be done to ensure workers' freedom to form unions. But where workers do not have the practical ability (or, in China, even the legal right) to choose their own representatives, some allowance must be made for other organizations to represent them in

[46] In the EU, such claims appear to be contemplated by the Unfair Commercial Practices Directive (UCPD), Directive 2005/29/EC of the European Parliament and of the Council of 11 May 2005. The UCPD allows for actions based on non-compliance with codes of conduct by firms that have publicly claimed adherence to such codes. The primary target may be codes of conduct relating to the quality of the product or service or the terms on which it is sold, but the Directive appears to reach codes of conduct relating to processes of production (e.g. labor and environmental codes) that are aimed at consumers. On the UCPD as a form of public–private transnational regulation, see Fabrizio Cafaggi, Private Regulation in European Private Law, *Towards a European Civil Code* (Wolters Kluwer, 4th edn, 2010).

enforcement processes. Many advocates are pressing for greater involvement of local NGOs, which might play that role.[47] (Others worry that this would exacerbate the tendency of CSR schemes to displace efforts to promote workers' freedom to form and bargain through unions.)

Let us consider the possibility of lead firm liability for serious or recurring violations of a sort that indicate defects in the firm's supply chain management and monitoring regime.[48] I will first take up potential theories of judicial enforcement under existing corporate codes, and then turn briefly to potential avenues of non-judicial enforcement under multi-stakeholder initiatives.

Corporate codes

One might imagine, first, that existing codes of conduct constitute express contracts that are judicially enforceable as they stand. That was the theory of the international labor advocates in the Wal-Mart litigation. It failed not because Wal-Mart's code of conduct was particularly narrow, or because judges construed it too narrowly, but because existing corporate codes of conduct simply do not contemplate worker enforcement. Perhaps needless to say, these codes were drafted by lawyers, presumably with an eye to avoiding this sort of lawsuit.

One contractual theory of enforcement asserts that workers are third-party beneficiaries of the code of conduct. Surely the codes purport to benefit workers. But a third-party beneficiary's rights derive from the rights of the promisee,[49] and under existing corporate codes the lead firm promises nothing to anyone. Lead firms arguably do make 'promises' on behalf of workers, if not in their codes of conduct, then in their corporate CSR publicity and reports. But those 'promises' are not enforceable as bilateral contracts, nor are they specific enough to be enforceable as binding unilateral contracts. If a court were to find otherwise, the supplier codes would likely be redrafted to avoid such liability in the future – unless firms can be persuaded to voluntarily assume enforceable contractual duties to workers.

Workers' advocates have also pursued tort and tort-like theories to enforce lead firms' CSR commitments on behalf of workers. The difficulty is mainly in finding a duty on the part of lead firms toward the workers of

---

47 See, e.g., O'Rourke, *supra* note 21.

48 One could also imagine direct liability for supplier violations along the lines of 'joint employer' liability under the US Fair Labor Standards Act (which depends on the degree of oversight the lead firm exercises). But it is not plausible that firms would voluntarily assume that sort of accountability.

49 See, e.g., Samuel Williston, *Treatise on the Law of Contracts* §37:8 (4th edn, 2010).

their suppliers. Plaintiffs in the Wal-Mart litigation pursued several tort claims on behalf of suppliers' employees, but all were rejected on the ground that Wal-Mart had no common law duty toward those employees.

Under emerging international human rights norms, promoted especially by the Special Representative of the United Nations' Secretary-General, John Ruggie, transnational corporations would have a 'duty to respect' workers' human rights (including freedom of association, freedom from forced labor, and several other labor rights), and would violate that duty if they were 'complicit' in violations committed directly by others. The meaning of 'complicity' in the context of labor violations by suppliers has not been fully elaborated, but it is clearly meant to reach some of the conduct at issue here.[50] By its own terms, that would extend the reach of public international law, and is beyond the scope of this chapter. But the notion of complicity could also seep into and expand the reach of private tort law for some labor violations.

The existing corporate codes were not intended to give rise to judicially enforceable duties on the part of lead firms to the workers of supplier firms, and are unlikely to do so. Nor would it clearly speed the progress of the CSR movement if firms learned that adopting a code of conduct for their overseas suppliers could *inadvertently* expose them to costly litigation and substantial liabilities. Legal enforceability of private labor standards by workers against lead firms is unlikely to come about either accidentally or without a fight. It will have to be granted by firms voluntarily, advisedly, and presumably after a long campaign like that which produced better monitoring protocols or greater transparency.

Multi-stakeholder initiatives

The major multi-stakeholder initiatives maintain labor standards and monitoring protocols, and certify the compliance of brands, factories, or monitors with those standards. None promises (or threatens) judicial enforceability; as things stand, that would defeat their efforts to recruit corporate participants. But they do create a structure through which non-judicial modes of enforcement can operate. For example, the FLA's third-party complaint procedure allows workers or worker advocates, among others, to trigger an investigation, first by the FLA-affiliated firm

---

[50] See John Ruggie, *Protect, Respect and Remedy: A Framework for Business and Human Rights*, *Report of the Special Representative of the Secretary-General on the Issue of Human Rights and Transnational Corporations and other Business Enterprises*, A/HRC/8/5, 7 April 2008.

and then by an independent third party, and potential remediation.[51] The FLA reports publicly on complaints that are not resolved by the company during the 45-day period.[52]

This complaint process is clearly a step beyond what is available under ordinary corporate codes of conduct. The process is somewhat formalized, though still wholly private and non-judicial; it culminates in recommendations and mediation; and the only sanctions appear to consist of adverse publicity, along with whatever pressure emanates from a firm's voluntary commitments and affiliation with the FLA. Is this 'enforcement' within our broad definition? If it is not, then perhaps our definition is too narrow.

4. FROM INFORMAL TO FORMAL ENFORCEMENT BY WORKERS AGAINST LEAD FIRMS

Workers' advocates have managed to make large, branded firms *socially liable*, and subject to reputational sanctions, for serious or recurring abuses by their suppliers, and have thus encouraged them to monitor suppliers' compliance with labor codes. Those soft mechanisms have proven surprisingly formidable, and have brought about substantive and procedural improvements in supply chain monitoring programs over several decades. Yet the field of private transnational labor regulation is arguably plagued by a large 'enforcement gap'. As long as submission to regulation is voluntary, that gap will persist until firms are persuaded to narrow it. What sort of enforcement clauses or mechanisms should worker rights advocates attempt to persuade firms to incorporate into their voluntary CSR commitments?

4.1 Judicial or Non-judicial Enforcement?

Among formal enforcement mechanisms, there is a basic divide between judicial and non-judicial processes. In the context of private transnational labor regulation, there are several reasons to focus on non-judicial mechanisms. Enforcement in the domestic courts of the developing nations where workers and factories are located makes little sense even if it were

[51] The FLA's 'complaint process is not intended to replace or undermine any existing internal grievance channels in the factory or through the affiliated company, or legal remedies available at the country level', but 'is meant to be a tool of last resort when other channels have failed to protect workers' rights'. http://fairlabor.org/fla/go.asp?u=/pub/mp&Page=ThirdPartyComplaints

[52] See http://fairlabor.org/fla/go.asp?u=/pub/mp&Page=ThirdPartyComplaints

acceptable to firms. Assuming the basic integrity of those judicial systems (a heroic assumption in many cases), their capacity is often limited. Adding private code-based labor claims to overburdened local court dockets would likely make those courts even less hospitable to workers' claims under domestic law (which, it is widely agreed, should be preserved and strengthened). As for litigation in the home jurisdiction of the lead firm, it is almost unthinkable at present that firms would voluntarily expose themselves to such litigation by the workers of supplier companies. At least that is true in the US, given the cost of litigation and the risk of large jury awards. I do not, of course, rule out the possibility of statutory reform allowing for judicial enforcement of private codes of conduct on behalf of workers in the supply chain; that kind of co-regulation may be conceivable in the EU. But I will focus here on the prospects for some non-judicial process based on voluntary agreements.

Arbitration is the conventional non-judicial mode of enforcement for disputes arising under private agreements of many kinds. To call arbitration a non-judicial enforcement process is to beg a crucial question: is arbitration meaningful or even conceivable without judicial enforcement (of the agreement to arbitrate and the resulting arbitration award)? That is among the issues to which we will shortly (and briefly) turn.

First, however, let us briefly flag another path not taken in this chapter: it would be possible to construct a freestanding non-governmental dispute resolution tribunal to which firms would agree to submit disputes under transnational codes of conduct. It is not obvious whether that strategy, perhaps spearheaded by the multi-stakeholder groups, is more or less feasible than getting firms to agree to arbitrate disputes under their own corporate codes, with resort to existing legal principles of arbitration. Still, I will focus on the latter set of issues – the legal principles that would or should govern individual firms' agreement to arbitrate disputes under a code of conduct – rather than the many interesting issues of institutional design that the former would entail.

4.2 Arbitral Enforcement of Labor Rights under Private Codes of Conduct: The Judicial Backdrop

In the world of arbitration, there is a useful distinction between the law *in* arbitration and the law *of* arbitration. The law *in* arbitration is the substantive law that arbitrators apply in the resolution of disputes. The law *of* arbitration is the law that governs the validity and enforcement of the arbitration agreement and of arbitral awards; and it is mostly applied by courts. We are primarily concerned here with the latter.

Where sophisticated parties, especially commercial actors, agree to arbitration, arbitration normally follows as a matter of course without judicial involvement. That may reflect social norms or voluntary commitments within a particular community. But arbitration generally takes place 'under the shadow of the law' – the law of arbitration that courts would apply in case of a dispute over arbitrability or the validity of an arbitration award.[53] In disputes between workers or their advocates and lead firms under codes of conduct, the law of arbitration is most likely to be at issue in three scenarios:

1. Judicial enforcement of the arbitration *agreement* may be sought if either
   (a) a lead firm refuses to arbitrate a claim by or on behalf of workers; or
   (b) a lead firm seeks to enforce an arbitration clause and to dismiss a lawsuit by or on behalf of workers over a putatively arbitrable dispute; or
2. Judicial enforcement of an arbitration *award* may be sought by or on behalf of workers if the lead firm refuses to comply with an award.

In any of these cases it is notable that the court, or forum, would be chosen in the first instance by the workers or their advocates.[54]

One might doubt that arbitration of disputes under private labor codes is viable absent judicial enforcement in the developing countries in which the disputes arise.[55] But in the case of arbitration agreements by and awards

---

[53] The norms and law favoring arbitration of some category of disputes – e.g. international commercial or athletic disputes – may become so well and widely established that we do not need to be overly concerned about where the arbitration takes place or where its enforceability is challenged. See Jan Paulsson, Arbitration in Three Dimensions (LSE Law, Society & Economy Working Papers, 2/2010), available at http://papers.ssrn.com/sol3/papers.cfm?abstract_id=1536093.

[54] If the forum is in the workers' (and the supplier's) home jurisdiction, the lead firm might try to claim *forum non conveniens* (though their links with the supplier firm and the obvious advantages for the workers would weigh against that claim). The lead firm's home jurisdiction would have some advantages for workers with international NGO backing, and would not be subject to challenge.

[55] This doubt resonates with a 'territorial' view of arbitration and of law, under which legal authority is exercised exclusively by states with sovereignty over a particular territory, and arbitral authority depends on the willingness of states and their legal systems to back up arbitration agreements and awards issued within their territorial jurisdiction. Under a more pluralistic view of legal authority, it might suffice that many or most states, under overlapping legal principles, would recognize and back up the arbitral process and award. See Paulsson, *supra* note 53.

against lead firms under their codes of conduct, it may suffice that the courts of the lead firm's home jurisdiction would recognize and enforce the agreement to arbitrate and the arbitral award. Even if the arbitration hearing itself took place where the factory and workers are located, enforcement could still be had in the lead firm's home jurisdiction. In the US, for example, arbitration agreements and awards of this nature would be generally enforceable in the federal or state courts (assuming a valid written arbitration agreement, on which more below) under either the Federal Arbitration Agreement (FAA)[56] or the Federal Convention Act (for enforcement of foreign arbitral awards),[57] depending on where the arbitration occurred or the award was issued.

The foregoing assumes an arbitration agreement or award that meets normal conditions of validity. That brings us to the next question: What sort of agreement would meet those conditions?

4.3 Arbitral Enforcement of Labor Rights under Private Codes of Conduct: What Would Be a Valid Agreement to Arbitrate?

Arbitration, under both the FAA and the UN Convention, is founded on an agreement to arbitrate, and specifically on a written agreement to arbitrate. Let us suppose that a lead firm were persuaded to assure workers that it would maintain decent, code-compliant conditions in supplier factories, and accept contractual liability for 'recurring' or 'egregious' violations, but only if all complaints were subject to binding arbitration. Let us suppose, too, that it is unrealistic to expect individual workers in overseas factories to agree in writing to arbitration. Is there an enforceable agreement to arbitrate such cases?

---

[56] 9 U.S.C. §1, et seq. US arbitration agreements and awards under a labor code of conduct would presumably constitute 'a contract evidencing a transaction involving commerce', 9 U.S.C. §2, covered by the FAA, and would probably not come within the exception for 'contracts of employment of seamen, railroad employees, or any other class of workers engaged in foreign or interstate commerce', 9 U.S.C. §1. The former phrase was broadly construed, and the latter narrowly construed, in *Circuit City, Inc.* v *Adams*, 532 U.S. 105 (2001).

[57] See 9 U.S.C. §§ 202–208 (2002) (the 'Convention Act'), implementing the United Nations Convention on the Recognition and Enforcement of Foreign Arbitral Awards, *opened for signature* June 10, 1958, 21 U.S.T. 2517, 330 U.N.T.S. 3. Foreign arbitration agreements or awards arising out of 'commercial' relationships are broadly enforceable under the Convention Act, and 'commercial' relationships include even more than the analogous scope provisions of the FAA. See *Bautista* v *Star Cruises*, 396 F.3d 1289 (11th Cir. 2005).

One possibility is that the firm could enter into an agreement with a designated worker representative that binds all parties, including individual workers, to arbitration of disputes under the agreement. Workers would then be actual third-party beneficiaries of the substantive agreement. But would they be bound by the agreement to arbitrate? Or would workers' substantive rights be litigable in court on the grounds that arbitration is strictly a matter of contractual consent, and that only signatories to a pre-dispute agreement to arbitrate are bound by the agreement? That is indeed the traditional rule; and if that rule prevailed, such that individual workers had judicial causes of action under an agreement giving them substantive rights, the deal is unlikely to be made. On the other hand, there has been movement in several jurisdictions in the direction of holding non-signatory beneficiaries subject to arbitration provisions.[58]

US labor law might suggest another way out of the dilemma (but with a catch). When an employer signs a collective bargaining agreement (CBA) with a union that represents its workers, the CBA confers contractual rights on the workers – job security, vacation pay, etc. – but those rights are enforceable exclusively by the union under the CBA's grievance-arbitration process. The union acts as a gatekeeper, screening out frivolous or trivial claims; even if the union refuses to arbitrate a meritorious contractual claim, employees cannot normally take their claims to court. However, the union's exclusive power to represent the workers, and the bar against employee lawsuits under the CBA, is qualified by the unions' 'duty of fair representation'; if and only if the union breaches that duty can the individual employee sue the employer directly under the CBA.

The point of this digression is this: it is perfectly conceivable in principle for a (quasi-)employer and an organization that represents workers to confer substantive rights on workers, and to submit disputes to exclusive and binding arbitration, where the workers are represented by the organization. But such agreements in the unionized workplace are legitimate because of an elaborate *sui generis* body of supporting legal principles and procedures; most importantly, the democratic process by which employees

---

[58] Karim Youssef, *Consent in Context: Fulfilling the Promise of International Arbitration* (Database updated December 2009) (Part II: Complex Jurisdiction or the Disintegration of the Arbitration Agreement, Ch. 5: Extension by Application of General Principles of Contract Law, IV: Third-Party Beneficiary, § 5:24: Compelled to arbitrate?). The UK Contracts Act of 1999 (Rights of Third Parties), §8(1), expressly provides that third-party beneficiaries of a contract are bound by an arbitration clause in the agreements. Some US courts have so held as well. *E.I. DuPont de Nemours and Co.* v *Rhone Poulenc Fiber and Resin Intermediates*, S.A.S., 269 F.3d 187, 200 (3d Cir. 2001); *American Bureau of Shipping* v *Tencara Shipyard* S.P.A., 170 F.3d 349 (2d Cir. 1999).

choose to be represented by a union, and the union's duty of fair representation. In short, a legal framework embodying principles of democracy, equal protection, and due process both supports and qualifies the system of labor arbitration under CBAs. That framework is missing in the case of labor codes of conduct.

Another route is suggested by the US law of employment arbitration, under which employers may require employees to agree to arbitrate future legal claims as a condition of employment. Indeed, employees may 'agree' to arbitration in some jurisdictions merely by continuing to work after getting notice of the arbitration provision.[59] The legitimacy of compelling arbitration of employees' *public law* claims under these circumstances is highly controversial, even in the US (though its legality appears settled absent new legislation). It is less problematic, however, to compel employees to arbitrate *contractual* claims, provided they are on notice of the arbitration provision of the contract (or code of conduct) under which they are making their claim. Assuming that employees' rights and remedies under public law are unaffected by an arbitration agreement in a code of conduct, then it seems fair to require employees to arbitrate contractual claims that were only granted on condition of arbitral enforcement. Both the substantive rights and the enforcement mechanisms created by the code are strictly supplementary to any rights the workers enjoy under public law, local or international, and were granted only on the condition that enforcement is exclusively through arbitration. If workers choose to invoke those additional rights, it seems fair to require them to use the arbitral process prescribed by the code for their enforcement. Workers would lose nothing that they otherwise had under background public law, and would potentially gain from having code of conduct rights that are subject to arbitration exclusively by a designated worker representative.[60]

So we might envision agreements between lead firms and designated worker representatives whose promises are enforceable not by workers, either directly or as intended third-party beneficiaries, but only by their designated representative through arbitration. One might question the

---

[59] *See Circuit City Stores* v *Adams*, 532 U.S. 105 (2001); *Gilmer* v *Interstate/Johnson Lane Corp.*, 500 U.S. 20 (1991). Similarly, consumers may 'agree' to mandatory arbitration merely by continuing to accept electrical or telephone service or to use a credit card after receiving notice of the arbitration provision in a monthly bill.

[60] The same cannot be said of the arbitration agreements that most US employees can be compelled to accept as a condition of employment, under which workers give up the right to litigate even inalienable statutory rights, as under antidiscrimination laws.

legitimacy of such an agreement absent any mechanism to ensure that the organization is a genuine representative of workers' interests. But under the logic of the *quid pro quo* (or 'better than nothing') argument, it may be enough to permit stakeholders and advocates to informally police the adequacy of the enforcement process or the representative entity, and to blow the whistle on sham procedures, much as just about every other aspect of CSR is currently policed and backed by reputational sanctions.

5. CONCLUSION

Enforcement of lead firms' labor CSR commitments, through binding arbitration or otherwise, is hardly on the horizon in private transnational labor regulation. But if we lower our sights from enforcement to dispute resolution and remediation, the landscape may look a bit more promising. The FLA's Third Party Complaint process is an example of an existing process of independent investigations, recommendations, and mediation that could potentially be improved with the addition of arbitration provisions. Accountability of lead firms for their CSR commitments, and compliance on the part of suppliers, would be enhanced by the introduction of a dispute resolution process with 'some kind of hearing' before a neutral third party whose ruling is judicially enforceable. And it is compliance, after all, rather than enforcement for its own sake, that is the ultimate objective.

9. Financial private regulation and enforcement

Geoffrey P. Miller

The topic of financial private regulation and enforcement concerns the activities of private firms in the financial sector which are involved in cross-border activities – Citigroup, Bank of America, HSBC, UBS, JPMorgan Chase, RBS, BNP Paribas, Barclays, Morgan Stanley, Goldman Sachs, Deutsche Bank, HBOS, Société Générale, Banco Santander, American Express, Nomura, and so on. For convenience of reference, I will refer to this type of organization as an 'internationally active financial services firm' (IAFSF). This chapter will categorize different types of private regulation and enforcement applicable to IAFSFs and then offer some tentative thoughts about the underlying forces that may determine the phenomena under observation, with special reference to the HiiL Concept Paper, 'The Added Value of Private Regulation in an Internationalised World? Towards a Model of the Legitimacy, Effectiveness, Enforcement and Quality of Private Regulation'. The principal subject of investigation will be the activities of IAFSFs under US law, but attention will be given to international standards and regulations as well.

I. TYPES OF PRIVATE REGULATION AND ENFORCEMENT

House Rules

All IAFSFs operate according to internal rules governing the day-to-day administration of the company.

Rules of organization define the roles of offices and allocate responsibility for operations. All large IAFSFs, like almost all large firms in any industry, take the form of complex corporate groups involving holding companies, subsidiaries, and subsidiaries of subsidiaries. These networks are partially the result of government regulation. The US Gramm-Leach-Bliley Act, for example, permits commercial banks to affiliate with securities firms and insurance companies, but only though the framework of a financial holding company. Similarly, commercial banks doing business abroad may be encouraged or compelled by host countries to operate their banking operations through separately chartered subsidiary banks rather than through branches. Often, however, the decision to structure an operation in an affiliate rather than a division is a matter of convenience or history rather than government mandate. In either case, the division of a firm into separate divisions or affiliates has important consequences for how the firm is managed: the organizational structure allocates and distributes power and authority in fundamental ways.

Companies or divisions within a corporate family also administer detailed standards and procedures for allocating power and responsibility. A securities firm may maintain separate trading divisions for fixed-income and equity securities – and within these categories, separate units specializing in different types of securities (bankers' acceptances, certificates of deposit, asset-backed securities, and so on). These internal structures also distribute, limit, and check the exercise of power and authority.

Rules of compensation and conditions of employment define stakeholder entitlements to share in the firm's fortunes. For IAFSFs, as for many service industry companies, the most important of such rules are those pertaining to senior managers. These rules may be established by a human resources department, or, for the most senior managers, by a compensation committee of the board of directors. Workplace rules also govern the compensation and working conditions of lower level workers such as clerical staff; these may also be set in part through a process of collective bargaining. Some employment rules are mandated by the government; workplace safety standards or pension policies are examples. Others are formulated within the sole discretion of the firm and its employees. In many of the latter cases the formal terms of the employment agreement capture only part of the relationship between the parties; the employment relationship is characterized by significant extra-contractual elements that bear more resemblance to gift exchange than to formal contractual conditions.[1]

House rules can sometimes be enforced by the government, either because they are mandated by law or because they take the form of legally binding contracts (as in the case of employment agreements). Much more often, however, house rules are principally enforced within the firm without

---

[1] See George A. Akerlof, Labor Contracts as Partial Gift Exchange, 97 *Quarterly Journal of Economics* 543–69 (1982).

government involvement. Enforcement can take the form of rewards or punishments on the job: a person may be sanctioned for not complying with the rules by being denied a promotion, not receiving an expected bonus, having his or her trading discretion restricted, or myriad other devices. Senior managers at IAFSFs usually serve under at-will employment contracts which entitle their supervisors to dismiss them with or without cause. Enforcement also occurs through informal mechanisms. Because reputation is an important asset in the financial services world, a person who is a conspicuous rule-breaker can suffer collateral career consequences even if they are not subjected to formal disciplinary action.

The category of house rules is the most 'private' of the strategies for regulation and enforcement discussed in this chapter. Both the formulation of rules and the enforcement of violations occur principally within the four walls of the firm.

Contracts

IAFSFs enter into many contracts with other firms. These contracts set norms and standards for behavior. Often they have a transnational dimension, either because the contract is with a foreign counterparty or because the subject matter of the contract is inherently international in dimension. Contracts for simple purchase or sale do not have a significant regulatory impact beyond the time of the closing. Other contracts, however, are more 'relational' in function.[2] They do carry long-term implications and accordingly can be seen as regulatory in scope.

Consider a line of credit issued by a bank in one country for the benefit of a foreign borrower. The credit agreement will usually specify the purposes for which the line is granted (which can be quite specific, or can be as general as 'to repay existing indebtedness'). They may require the borrower to submit regular financial statements; remain in compliance with legal rules; maintain minimum liquidity and operating income; satisfy specified financial ratios; not incur additional indebtedness; or not undergo a change in control. Credit agreements, in short, can operate as reasonably comprehensive regulatory systems, entered into by private contract and not compelled by any government action. All IAFSFs are party to many credit agreements, either as borrowers or as lenders.

---

2 See G. Baker, R. Gibbons and K.J. Murphy, Relational Contracts and the Theory of the Firm, 117 *Quarterly Journal of Economics* 39–84 (2002).

Private contracts are largely enforced by private action.[3] On the borrower side, enforcement takes the form of compliance with the terms of the lending agreement. Responsibility for performance is delegated bureaucratically to a defined individual or office. On the lender side, enforcement principally takes the form of monitoring.[4] Lenders designate personnel to review and track the performance of the borrower and to verify that the borrower remains in compliance with the terms of the loan agreement. Reputation is also important: a borrower who earns a bad name among lenders is likely to find it harder to obtain credit at a competitive price in the future.[5] The contracts themselves contain specific enforcement rules defining counterparty remedies in the event of specified future events. For suppliers of credit, these remedies may include the right to terminate further credit advances, to demand that the borrower post or increase collateral, or to declare an event of default and demand immediate repayment of the full loan amount. Some lending agreements give lenders specific management rights over the operations of distressed borrowers, including the right to veto large transactions, to prohibit the payment of dividends during the period of distress, or even to influence the selection or retention of senior management personnel. Because these remedies are explicitly spelt out in the loan agreements, there is usually no need for recourse to the courts for enforcement.

If these private mechanisms fail, the parties to the contract have other available means for enforcement short of relying on state action. Some contracts among sophisticated entities contain procedures for mediation of disputes that discourage recourse to legal processes. They may provide, for example, that in the event of disagreement over the terms of the contract, specified senior managers from both parties will meet to attempt a resolution. Recourse to legal remedies may also be discouraged by terms imposing a penalty on the first mover, such as venue rules that specify that the site for dispute resolution will be in the home city of the party who has not triggered the process. Contracts may also specify that disputes will be resolved by binding arbitration rather than litigation.[6]

---

[3] See generally B. Klein and K.B. Leffler, The Role of Market Forces in Assuring Contractual Performance, 89 *Journal of Political Economy* 615–641 (1981).

[4] See Douglas Diamond, Financial Intermediation and Delegated Monitoring, 51 *Review of Economic Studies* 393–414 (1984).

[5] See Douglas Diamond, Reputation Acquisition in Debt Markets, 97 *Journal of Political Economy* 828–62 (1989).

[6] Surprisingly, however, sophisticated commercial parties apparently agree to binding arbitration less frequently than might be supposed based on the supposed advantages of arbitration over litigation. See Theodore Eisenberg & Geoffrey

Ultimately, however, the courts provide a backstop: if the parties are unable to work out a disagreement or renegotiate terms after default, if the borrower enters formal bankruptcy proceedings, or if either party is unwilling to accept the terms of an arbitral award, the courts will step in and adjudicate rights and duties. Even then, however, the courts will often seek to maintain the fundamental terms of the relationship among the parties, so long as the arrangement has not broken down altogether.[7] Private parties, moreover, routinely include choice-of-law clauses and (less frequently) forum-selection clauses in their contracts, thus retaining a degree of control over the nature of the legal process by which contractual rights are tested and enforced.[8]

Internal Compliance

Now consider the setting where public authorities set the norms for behavior. Even here, private enforcement is the principal means by which public norms are enforced for IAFSFs.

The internal audit function, employed by IAFSFs as well as most other large companies, is a means by which the firm can monitor its own performance across a variety of dimensions, including ensuring that the firm is complying with applicable laws and regulations, probing to detect the presence of financial or other fraud, assessing the reliability of the firm's financial reporting systems, and generally checking on the overall efficiency of the firm's operations. Many firms maintain an internal auditing department headed by an official with a title such as 'chief of internal audit' or 'chief audit executive'. The head of the internal audit department typically reports directly to the chief executive officer and also to the audit committee of the board of directors. Audit committees and internal auditors are required for listing on the New York Stock Exchange.[9]

Complementing the role of the internal audit is the function of compliance management. Every major IAFSF maintains one or more compliance offices headed by an official with a name such as 'chief compliance officer',

---

Miller, The Flight from Arbitration: An Empirical Study of Ex Ante Arbitration Clauses in Publicly-Held Companies' Contracts, 56 *De Paul Law Review* 335 (2007).

[7] See S. Johnson, J. McMillan and C. Woodruff, Courts and Relational Contracts, 18 *Journal of Law, Economics and Organization* 221–77 (2002).

[8] See Theodore Eisenberg and Geoffrey Miller, The Flight to New York: An Empirical Study of Choice of Law and Choice of Forum Clauses in Publicly-Held Companies' Contracts, 30 *Cardozo Law Review* 1475 (2009); Theodore Eisenberg & Geoffrey Miller, Ex Ante Choices of Law and Forum: An Empirical Analysis of Corporate Merger Agreements, 59 *Vanderbilt Law Review* 1975 (2006).

[9] *New York Stock Exchange Listed Company Manual*, § 303A.

often reporting to a special compliance committee of the board of directors. These individuals and offices have become powerful over the past decade due to a combination of public and private factors. Within firms, managers realized that compliance costs and exposure could be reduced, and a favorable public appearance achieved, if responsibility for legal compliance, which had formerly been distributed across the firm along functional lines, were centralized in a single office. Accordingly, even without legal compulsion, many firms would have centralized their compliance function in a single unit. At the same time, public authorities increasingly mandated that IAFSFs maintain procedures and policies to manage the task of legal oversight and risk control.

Delaware Chancellor Allen's decision in the 1996 *Caremark* case provided much of the spur for this movement.[10] That opinion announced that a board of directors' duty of care involves, at a minimum, the duty to undertake minimal steps to ensure that a corporation has adequate reporting and information systems in place. The American Law Institute, an influential private organization devoted to promulgating best practices in various legal fields, added to the pressure with its Principles of Corporate Governance, which encouraged the establishment of a chief compliance and ethics officer with a 'major policymaking' function within the corporation.[11] In the same general vein, the Model Penal Code, another initiative of the American Law Institute, provides that a corporation may assert a defense against criminal liability if it can prove that the 'high managerial agent having supervisory responsibility over the subject matter of the offense employed due diligence to prevent its commission'.[12]

The Federal Sentencing Guidelines provide another important impetus to the development of formal compliance procedures by encouraging leniency in sentencing for corporations that maintain an 'effective compliance and ethics program'.[13] To qualify, such a program should 'exercise due diligence to prevent and detect criminal conduct' and 'promote an organizational culture that encourages ethical conduct and a commitment to compliance with the law'.[14] To ensure that the initiative is effective, the guidelines require that 'high-level' people in the organization should exercise overall responsibility for the program. The guidelines further require

---

[10] *In re Caremark International Inc. Derivative Litigation*, 698 A.2d 959 (Del. Ch. 1996).

[11] American Law Institute, Principles of Corporate Governance, § 1.27 cmt. c. (1994).

[12] Model Penal Code, § 2.07(5) (1985).

[13] Federal Sentencing Guideline, §8B2.1(a).

[14] Ibid.

qualifying firms to maintain and publicize effective whistle-blower programs under which employees may report or seek guidance about actual or potential criminal conduct.[15]

Section 404 of the Sarbanes-Oxley Act of 2002 added to the mix by requiring that management of listed firms annually produce an 'internal control report' which must 'state the responsibility of management for establishing and maintaining an adequate internal control structure and procedures for financial reporting' and 'contain an assessment, as of the end of the most recent fiscal year of the issuer, of the effectiveness of the internal control structure and procedures of the issuer for financial reporting'.[16] The management report must be evaluated and attested to by the external auditor.[17]

Many other rules and regulations encourage or require the creation of specialized compliance offices or functions.[18] Among the most pertinent to IAFSFs, the USA PATRIOT Act, the anti-terror law enacted in 2001, requires financial institutions to establish anti-money laundering programs that have, as essential elements, the development of internal policies, procedures, and controls, designation of a compliance officer, an ongoing employee training program, and an independent audit function.[19]

Management-based Regulation

Much of the regulation confronting IAFSFs does not take the traditional form of general pronouncements of an administrative agency applicable to all firms in the industry. Management-based regulation, which is individually tailored to particular firm operations, has assumed increasing importance in recent years.[20] The basic assumption of management-based

---

[15] Ibid., §8B2.1(b)(5)(c).

[16] 15 U.S.C. § 7262(a).

[17] 15 U.S.C. § 7262(b).

[18] See, e.g., Sarbanes-Oxley Act of 2002, 15 U.S.C. §§ 7262 (2006) (mandating internal controls to ensure the accuracy of financial reports and disclosures); 17 C.F.R. § 240.15c3–4(a) (2009) (requiring over-the-counter derivatives dealers to establish and maintain a 'system of internal risk management controls to assist it in managing the risks associated with its business activities, including market, credit, leverage, liquidity, legal, and operational risks'); § 31(b)(3) of the Investment Company Act (requiring the SEC to exercise its inspection authority with due regard for the benefits of internal compliance policies and procedures and the effective implementation and operation thereof).

[19] 31 U.S.C. § 5318(h)(1).

[20] See generally Cary Coglianese & David Lazer, Management-Based Regulation: Prescribing Private Management to Achieve Public Goals, 37 *Law & Society Review* 691 (2003).

regulation is that regulated firms have better information about their industry and their individual situations than do the regulators. Management-based regulation seeks to free-ride on these advantages by enlisting the regulated firm itself to participate in the formulation or application of rules pertinent to its operations. Firms are required to develop their internal processes and procedures and to share these with the regulators, whose review then focuses on whether the internal standards are rational, justifiable, and consonant with the regulatory purposes.

The Basel II Guidelines take the principle of management-based regulation to a new level. The Basel Committee on Banking Supervision was explicit on this point, recognizing that a 'significant innovation' of the revised framework is the 'greater use of assessments of risk provided by banks' internal systems as inputs to capital calculations'. Consistent with this philosophy, Basel II's IRB (internal ratings-based) approaches to credit risk rely explicitly on a bank's internal risk-management models to evaluate the credit risk for particular assets. The Foundation IRB approach allows banks to supply their own estimates of the probability of default for a client or group of clients. The Advanced IRB approach allows banks, in addition, to use their internal quantitative models to estimate exposure at default and loss given default.

Even more generous attitudes towards internal modeling are found in Basel II's approach to operational risk – the risk of the risk of loss resulting from inadequate or failed internal processes, people and systems, or from external events. The standardized approach to operational risk, which offers banks some potential to reduce capital charges if they qualify, is available if the institution's board of directors and senior management are involved in the oversight of the operational risk management framework and the firm has a sound and reliable operational risk management system. This approach calculates capital charges for operational risk by dividing the bank's activities along functional lines. The advanced management approach to operational risk is even more deferential. It permits banks to develop their own empirical models of operational risk, and provides 'significant flexibility' to such banks in the development of operational risk measurement and management systems.

These forms of management regulation go to the formulation of standards rather than to enforcement per se. Yet, because the standards to be formulated are specifically tailored to the facts and circumstances of each IAFSF, and because these firms are often allowed to use their own internal models in the development of rules pertaining to them, the functions of regulation and enforcement become blurred. In a real sense, the formulation of the rules pertinent to an institution is part of the enforcement process. Once the rules are in place, however, the enforcement function becomes similar to that utilized for any publicly formulated standards: internal compliance coupled with a backdrop of public enforcement processes.

Private Standard-setting Bodies

The activities of IAFSFs are importantly impacted by private standard-setting bodies. Among the most important of these in the United States is the Financial Accounting Standards Board (FASB). The FASB is an independent, private body consisting of five independent individuals who serve for five-year terms (renewable once). The FASB follows procedures for public comment and rule-making similar to those applicable to federal government agencies under the Administrative Procedure Act. Its Emerging Issues Task Force (EITF) tracks developing issues in the financial accounting world and promulgates consensus guidance which is usually accepted as authoritative by the FASB. The US Securities and Exchange Commission (SEC) has statutory authority to promulgate accounting standards for publicly traded firms, but it has consistently elected to defer to the FASB for the adoption of authoritative standards. While the FASB has very broad authority to set standards for financial accounting, it has essentially no enforcement authority. Violations of FASB auditing standards are enforced through the internal and external audit process and by means of public enforcement by the SEC and private litigation.

The Public Company Accounting Oversight Board (PCAOB), created by the Sarbanes-Oxley Act, has the powers to set auditing, independence, and quality control standards for the preparation of audit reports and to register public accounting firms performing an external audit function. Although legally and formally a private sector body, the PCAOB is closer to a government agency than is the FASB. Its powers are conferred by legislation. The SEC appoints PCAOB's members, approves its budget, oversees its operations, and has the power to censure or remove its members. Decisions by the PCAOB can be appealed to the SEC, which has the power to overturn its rules. (The public nature of PCAOB's activities has sparked an important constitutional challenge, *Free Enterprise Fund* v *Public Company Accounting Oversight Board*,[21] in which objectors to the board's activities claim that the authorizing statute unconstitutionally denies the President of the United States the constitutional authority to appoint federal officers.) The PCAOB exercises important regulatory functions: it can conduct investigations, require submission of documents and

---

21 No. 08–861, Supreme Court of the United States.

information, and administer sanctions against auditing firms subject to its jurisdiction.

The International Swaps and Derivatives Association (ISDA), a trade association of firms in the derivatives industry, is another important standard-setting body whose work impacts IAFSFs in important ways. Established in 1985, the ISDA is principally known for developing the ISDA Master Agreement, the authoritative contract used by industry participants. But the ISDA also engages in other activities that could be considered regulatory in nature. It claims as part of its mission statement the tasks of 'promoting practices conducive to the efficient conduct of the business', 'promoting the development of sound risk management practices', and 'fostering high standards of commercial conduct'. Because all IAFSFs participate in the derivatives market, some to a substantial extent, the ISDA is an important standard-setting body for the industry. However, the ISDA is not an enforcement agency; enforcement of contractual terms under the master agreement must take the form of the usual mechanisms of private pressure, arbitration or litigation.

Completing the quartet of important standard-setting bodies is the Financial Industry Regulatory Authority (FINRA). Like the other three just discussed, FINRA is officially a private organization, created in 2007 through the consolidation of NASD and the regulatory and enforcement functions of the New York Stock Exchange. FINRA's principal responsibility is to oversee the broker-dealer industry in the United States. In that capacity it has an important, although limited, regulatory authority over IAFSFs, most of which maintain a broker-dealer as part of their corporate structure. FINRA promulgates rules for the broker-dealer industry through a process resembling federal notice-and-comment rule-making. It also offers informal standard-setting by means such as interpretative letters, examination letters, and interpretations of financial and operational rules.

In addition to setting standards, FINRA exercises an enforcement function. It monitors markets to detect evidence of fraud, manipulation or insider trading, and conducts compliance examinations for firms subject to its jurisdiction. It is authorized by federal law to take disciplinary actions against its members, which can include fines, orders of restitution, censures, suspensions, or expulsion of firms or individuals from the industry. It also provides arbitration services to help resolve disputes between and among investors, securities firms and individual brokers. FINRA is substantially a private self-regulatory organization. Its board of governors is elected by the membership at an annual meeting, not appointed by the SEC or any other governmental agency. It ostensibly sets standards and conducts enforcement activities free of SEC oversight and supervision. Nevertheless, it is clear that the SEC exercises substantial influence over FINRA, extending even beyond its power to reject proposed rules for incompatibility with federal law.

Cartels

The past decades have witnessed the exposure and prosecution of numerous international cartels, ranging from the worldwide vitamins conspiracy to agreements to fix the prices of international air travel and air freight, aluminum, batteries, beta carotene, carbon electrical products, automotive glass, fine art auction services, DVD players, shipping – even the Three Tenors CD. Somewhat surprisingly, no major cartels have been discovered involving international financial services. Perhaps some of the reasons for this welcome absence are the ease of entry into the market, the lack of concentration, even with very large institutions playing pivotal roles, the relative transparency of pricing and other terms, and the heavily regulated nature of most segments of the industry. However, the fact that cartels have not been in evidence in international services does not mean that they do not or could not exist.

A cartel fits our definition of private regulation and enforcement. Even though the purposes of the cartel are contrary to the public interest, that fact – a public purpose – is not essential to the definition. Often, indeed, it is difficult to ascertain what the public interest requires in a given case: the difference between a cartel to fix prices in financial services and the requirement long in effect in the United States that banks could not pay interest on checking accounts is somewhat difficult to ascertain, aside from the fact that one is illegal and the other was legally required.

To be effective, cartels require coordination and agreement among industry participations to restrict production and to avoid undercutting of the agreed-on prices. These are, in effect, forms of regulation – no less so because they are typically formulated in secret and distributed in carefully disguised code. Cartels, moreover, require extensive policing if they are to be stable. Members must abide by the agreement despite ever-present temptations to enhance their profits by undercutting the cartel price; and must do what they can to discourage entry by persons not members of the club. Accordingly, we classify cartels as a form of private regulation and enforcement – albeit not one shown to have played a major role in the operation of IAFSFs.

Private Litigation

Private litigation is also a form of private enforcement. Private parties seek to obtain relief for themselves, but do so by establishing that the defendant has violated some applicable principle of law. When many plaintiffs are involved, as in the American-style class action, the relationship between private litigation and public enforcement is even clearer – so clear that one of the traditional justifications for class action litigation is that the representative plaintiff acts as a 'private attorney general' on behalf of a large group of similarly situated persons. We therefore should include private litigation in the general category of private mechanisms for regulating and enforcing rules pertaining to IAFSFs.

IAFSFs are subject to litigation in any country where they do business. As a practical matter, however, the risk they face from private lawsuits is relatively minor, except in the case of jurisdictions that recognize class actions or similar procedures. The principal such jurisdiction, of course, is the United States. Class actions are often brought against these companies for alleged false or misleading statements in financial disclosures. Claims are also framed as shareholders derivative litigation, alleging that the senior managers of an IAFSF violated a duty of care or loyalty to the company. IAFSFs can also be caught up in securities litigation brought against other companies with which the IAFSF has dealt. For example, a lawsuit for fraud arising out of a securities underwriting will nearly always join the underwriter on the ground that the underwriter signed the registration statement with knowledge of false or misleading statements of material fact. For a time it appeared that IAFSFs would face another, potentially unbounded liability as 'aiders' or 'abettors' of their customers' frauds. The Supreme Court has twice ruled that aider-and-abettor liability is unavailable under the federal securities laws.[22] But the liability cloud has not entirely cleared, since resourceful plaintiffs' attorneys are able to claim (sometimes with plausibility) that an IAFSF was an active participant in the alleged fraud, not just an aider and abettor.

---

[22] *Central Bank of Denver* v *First Interstate Bank of Denver*, 511 U.S. 164 (1994); *Stoneridge Investment Partners, LLC* v *Scientific-Atlanta, Inc. and Motorola, Inc.*, 552 U.S. 148 (2008).

II. ASSESSMENT

The discussion so far has identified a variety of different mechanisms for the private regulation and enforcement of norms pertinent to IAFSFs. What can we make of the information so compiled?

One point should be obvious, but bears emphasis because it is so commonly ignored. Scholars of regulation and enforcement have tended to focus, for understandable reasons, on public institutions and processes. They examine the activities of legislatures and administrative agencies, of investigators and police, of courts and hearing examiners. These, after all, are the sorts of regulation and enforcement that are most apparent, and also the ones that are most easily identified as part of a process for enforcing public norms. Yet a realistic examination of the behavior of IAFSFs – or of any major industry group – reveals that government regulation and enforcement is a small part of the overall processes by which rules of conduct are created, promulgated, and enforced. By far the greatest share of standard-setting and enforcement is conducted by private actors in one or more of the modalities described above. For this reason, among others, the study of private regulation and enforcement in the global economy is an eminently desirable avenue of research.

The foregoing discussion identified the following types of private regulation and/or enforcement for IAFSFs: (1) house rules; (2) contracts; (3) internal compliance and audit; (4) management-based regulation; (5) private standard-setting bodies; (6) cartels; and (7) private litigation. More modalities could be added to the list – for example, codes of corporate governance or codes of corporate ethics could be included. Even the items that have been discussed reveal a wide range of public involvement in the process of standard-setting and enforcement, ranging from minimal (in the cases of house rules, cartels and contracts), to moderate (internal compliance and audit, private standard-setting bodies, litigation), to substantial (management-based regulation). The government involvement, moreover, does not assume the same form for all of these modalities: sometimes the government plays a major role in the formulation of norms but not in their enforcement (e.g. litigation), other times the government stays out of norm-formation but plays a bigger role in enforcement (e.g. the FASB), and sometimes the government plays a role in both functions (management-based regulation). The pattern is complex, shaped in part by history, and not necessarily consistent from country to country. Nevertheless, some tentative judgments may be offered based on the evidence presented so far, with due caution for the fact that most although not all the data are from the United States.

The verdict on effectiveness is mixed. Certainly the system of overlapping public and private standard-setting for IAFSFs did nothing to prevent the financial meltdown of 2008. What is less clear is whether any other approach would have done better. Governments were no better than the private sector at foreseeing the grave risk to the world financial system posed by the enormous flood of cheap credit coursing through financial markets during the 2000s. Quite the opposite: governments, in the form of central banks operating monetary policy, were the chief culprits in setting loose the forces of disaster. The ebullient spirit that infuses a nation in the midst of an asset bubble affected government actors as well as private ones. On the other hand it appears clear that the system of overlapping regulation and fail-safe monitoring that appeared to be so carefully embedded in the mix of public and private regulation and enforcement, also failed in its mission. Risk management committees did not pick up on or adequately control the fat-tail potential inherent in financial markets. Corporate governance standards promulgated in the wake of the corporate scandals of the 1990s appear to have accomplished little. Very few people, and no one in a position of real authority, properly appreciated the fact that the financial world was teetering on the precipice of disaster during the credit boom of the 1990s.

The system of public–private regulation appears relatively successful at conferring legitimacy on the actions taken in the case of IAFSFs. There is an obvious value in vesting the rule-setting and enforcement powers in the group being regulated, in that the presence of self-regulation appears calculated to induce greater compliance and acceptance of the validity and reasonableness of the regulations being enforced. On the other hand, the enhanced legitimacy among regulated parties is offset, to an extent, by the reduced credibility they have as impartial champions of the public interest. The example of cartels proves all too clearly that the private sector cannot be relied on to regulate itself when the interests of private actors conflict substantially with the public interest. To deal with the suspicions of industry favoritism, self-regulatory organizations and private standard-setting bodies, such as FINRA or ISDA, make concerted and well-publicized efforts to conduct open rule-making procedures involving extensive input from all interested parties. The same dialectic occurs in the case of management-based regulation: the enlistment of company management into the regulatory and enforcement process both creates better-informed standards and induces potentially greater compliance by the regulated party; but allowing IAFSFs to supply their own models and assumptions could also be seen, by a critic, as an example of allowing the fox to guard the henhouse.

Difficult as it is to judge quality of regulation, it appears that the private involvement in regulation and enforcement may offer certain advantages as compared with 'top-down' government rules. Private regulation and enforcement may bring the expertise and a substantial knowledge base of the private sector into the regulatory mix, with good effect. On the other hand, what the private sector provides in expertise and knowledge, it may lack in overall perspective. The financial services industry cares about itself but not so much about the public interest; government regulators may score better on this front.

The presence of private sector actors in the process of enforcement also yields potential benefits and costs as regards IAFSFs. On the plus side, the private sector often is privy to valuable information pertinent to enforcement, including soft information such as gossip and rumor. No one knows more about what goes on at an IAFSF than people in other similar organizations. Private sector enforcement can take advantage of these and other bases of knowledge which are less accessible to the government. On the negative side, private sector enforcement may be hamstrung by the special interests of the industry being regulated or by the lack of strong sanctions for violations. Further research, ideally involving empirical tests and analyses, would be needed to assess the degree to which private sector involvement enhances or hinders effective enforcement of public norms.

The choice between the various regulatory options does not boil down to a single variable or criterion. Instead, multiple considerations appear to be determinative of the observed pattern, interacting in a complex and interrelated fashion. The major factors appear to include the following considerations, each of which apply on an 'other things equal' or *ceteris paribus* basis:

1. *Minimization of transactions costs.* The mix of private and public regulation seeks to minimize the transactions costs associated with the regulatory process.
2. *Access to information.* The regulatory and enforcement functions are vested in persons who can obtain relevant information rapidly and at reasonable cost.
3. *Expertise.* The mix of private and public regulation and enforcement takes advantage of specialized expertise in technical or rapidly evolving fields.
4. *Political power of the regulated industry.* The regulatory and enforcement functions reflect the political power and economic strength of the industry being regulated, as well as the power of potentially competing industries.
5. *Turf.* The mix of private and public regulation and enforcement

reflects competition of regulators for 'turf' – the power to set rules or conduct enforcement proceedings in a particular industry.

6. *Budget*. The mix of private and public regulation reflects the costs of the regulation and the financial constraints facing public regulatory bodies.
7. *History*. The structure of the regulatory and enforcement functions of private and public bodies is a function of history and path dependency. For this reason, we expect to see substantial differences in the pattern across national boundaries.

The study of private involvement in transnational regulation in a globalized world is still in its infancy. The foregoing discussion is intended as a preliminary effort towards developing a typology of private regulatory and enforcement activity pertinent to the business of internationally active financial services firms, identifying some of the determinants of the observed regulatory structure, and evaluating how the public–private mix of regulation and enforcement for IAFSFs measures up along the dimensions of effectiveness, quality, legitimacy and enforcement.

10. Transnational private regulation of the Internet: different models of enforcement

Federica Casarosa

1. INTERNET REGULATION: THREE LEVELS OF ANALYSIS

When we speak about 'the Internet' we all understand the overall concept, thinking of the global communication network that is accessed mainly through computers, and more recently through many other different devices, such as mobiles, games consoles, and the like. However, such common understanding does not always take into account all the different facets that characterize the large and complex concept of the Internet communication network.

To begin with, the Internet is a global network of interconnected packet-switched networks, based on a shared communication protocol (the so-called TCP/IP) that allows servers and computers to interact and communicate among themselves (Abbate, 1999; Leiner et al., 2003). The software application that is most commonly associated with the Internet platform is the World Wide Web, but these are not synonymous, as the latter is only one of the applications that the technical infrastructure of the Internet can host, which include, for instance email, file transfer protocol, and a variety of peer-to-peer file sharing programs. Thus, it is possible to affirm that the Internet includes different structural levels, comprising the technical infrastructure of hardware and software, the applications running on such technical infrastructure, and the content that is communicated or generated using those applications (Solum, 2008: 49).

This distinction is very important in the framework of this chapter because it clarifies that, in order to define Internet regulation, we should always define in advance the level that such regulation will apply to, namely:

- technical infrastructure;
- platform application;
- content sharing.

In each of the mentioned levels the possible choices for regulation can differ not only in terms of regulatory strategies, but also as a consequence of the actors involved in the definition of the rules and standards (Benkler, 2006), and of the role played by technology itself in the framing of possible activities within the network (Lessig, 2006).

1.1 Transnational Private Regulation on the Internet

Internet regulation in general terms – encompassing the three different levels previously mentioned – is at the center of an ongoing debate (Goldsmith and Wu, 2006; Deibert et al., 2008, 2010). If at the first implementation of the Internet infrastructure, pure self-regulation was the possible and most effective choice to regulate the government agencies, research centers and universities which were the unique users of the communication network, then the current developments in commercialization of Internet access and services, resulting in an exponential growth of Internet users and in multiple applications available through Internet connection, require a deeper deliberation over the type of regulatory strategy to be used.

In this sense Internet regulation is the answer to a clear necessity: on the one hand, online activities inevitably have an influence on individuals and other entities in the real world; on the other, any user of online services cannot escape his/her own legal system, regardless of anonymity claims (Weber, 2000; Stalla-Bourdillon, 2010). Moreover, the success of many of the most diffused Internet services is based on the availability of a stable and clear legal framework, whether national or international, private or public.

Private regulation of the Internet, and in particular self-regulation, is the option that has been strongly favored (and in some cases has also received incentives from states),[1] given the advantages it has with regard to public regulation in the online framework, namely the capacity to adapt to rapid technical progress and to the ubiquitous development of the new communication media. In addition to flexibility, it is claimed that self-regulation

[1] See that the US presidency supported a major self-regulatory initiative in particular with regard to privacy in electronic commerce (see Koops et al., 2006: 118), while on the other side of the Atlantic, the Council of Europe and the European Commission issued a series of reports and recommendations promoting Internet self-regulation (see Koops et al., 2006: 110).

offers the benefits of greater efficiency, increased incentives for compliance, and reduced costs (Price and Verhulst, 2005: 21; Koops et al., 2006: 109).

The models of private regulation of the Internet are able to take into account the transnational dimension of such a communication medium. Location of the users is irrelevant for the functionality of the infrastructure and for the running of the applications on the Internet; however, the rules and standards could conflict with the legal rules applicable to users on the basis of jurisdiction, raising cross-border disputes (Hörnle, 2009: 20).

In order to understand the models of transnational private regimes currently adopted to regulate the Internet (Hadfield, 2002; Schultz, 2007: 156), this chapter will provide two different examples, namely the case of the ICANN-led regime for the allocation of the Internet domain name system, and the case of online auction websites that provide the platform for commercial exchanges among registered users of such technological platforms. Within the above-mentioned classification of regulatory levels governing the Internet, the former would be clearly located on the first level, on Internet infrastructure, while the latter would be located on the third level, as a form of content regulation.

The following parts will then focus on the ICANN regulatory system (Section 2) and on the eBay system as example of online auction model (Section 3), describing in each case the structure of the private regime and its enforcement mechanisms. Then, a comparison between the choices taken in the two systems will be presented in order to understand the rationales that steer the use of different regulatory tools (Section 4). Concluding thoughts will follow (Section 5).

2. THE CASE OF ICANN

One of the essential resources that allow the operation of the Internet network is the Internet address system or 'domain name system' (DNS), which is a hierarchical system that assigns a human-readable identifier to any resource connected to the Internet. The logic of the communication system requires that each complete domain name must be unique and must be uniquely linked to the appropriate IP address (a 32-bit number string). In order to keep pace with the continuous growth of available resources on the Internet, coherence and hierarchical organization are imperative. The purpose of the domain name system is then to assure that every uniform resource locator (URL) and every email address is linked to a unique IP address which defines a specific resource on the Internet (Lenard and White, 2009: 5).

The domain name of a node is simply the list of names of the path from the node of the network to the DNS root. Conventionally, domain names are read from left to right, with the most specific on the left and the most general on the right. The hierarchical levels of the DNS, separated by a dot (.), continue until the name of the host computer is reached. For instance in the case of <example.co.uk>, the constituents of the last part of the domain name are defined as the Top-Level Domains (TLDs), while the left-hand-side parts are defined as Second-Level Domains and Third-Level Domains. In particular, TLDs can be distinguished into generic (the original seven created in 1994) and country code TLDs, which are related to geographical or national boundaries.[2] The hierarchy in the formal construction of the DNS is then reflected in the administration of such a system, which can be delegated to different entities (Lyndsay, 2007: 8).

Initially, responsibility for administering the Internet's name and addressing systems went to the engineers who had developed the Internet, with positive results until the mid-1990s (Botzem and Hoffman, 2008: 6). A few years later, as a response to the increasing number of disputes and to the reduced authority of the Internet Engineering Task Force in regulating the Domain Name system, the Internet Corporation for Assigned Names and Numbers (ICANN) was created under the aegis of the US government through the Commerce Department, in the form of a not-for-profit organization incorporated in California.

The 1998 Memorandum of Understanding (MoU) between the US government and ICANN laid down the division of responsibilities between them and a schedule for the foreseen (but not yet achieved) complete privatization of those responsibilities. The US government delegated the administration of the DNS, including the introduction of regulated competition in the domain name market and the allocation of Internet addresses to ICANN. However, the Department of Commerce asserted its authority to oversee the DNS management functions in order to ensure continuity and stability in the performance of technical management of the DNS in the transition to a private regime. The MoU adopted four guiding principles for DNS governance, namely:

- stability of the Internet;
- competition and consumer choice (in order to lower costs, promote innovation, encourage diversity and enhance user choice and satisfaction);

---

[2] The definition of the list of abbreviations is based on the ISO standard known as 'Code for the representation of names of countries' (ISO-3166).

- private sector bottom-up coordination (including all participating actors representing the interests of business and civil society); and
- representation (as management structures should reflect the functional and geographic diversity of the Internet and its users).[3]

The expiry date of the MoU was set one year after its entry into force; however, it was amended seven times and contextually extended its validity up to 2009, in order to achieve the final result of the transition to a private regime. As a matter of fact, the original program envisaged that business organizations and Internet users negotiate solutions to market problems on the basis of a self-regulatory process (Kesan and Gallo, 2008: 3). However, only the most recent amendments, in 2006, lowered the supervision activity of the Department of Commerce, giving more autonomy to ICANN to achieve its main responsibilities (Lyndsay, 2007: 60).

2.1 The (Regulatory) Functions of ICANN

ICANN has been at the center of a long debate over its functions, in particular whether it could be defined as a purely technical coordination body or as a policy-making body (Kesan and Gallo, 2008; Lenard and White, 2009). An intermediate position between the two was adopted by the structural reform process that was undertaken by the ICANN management:

> ICANN, today, inevitably has a global policy role ... ICANN provides a forum where policy development can occur through a process that strives to achieve reasonable consensus wherever it can, and move forward in instances where the consensus process is deadlocked. And that forum is necessary.
>
> In the view of the Evolution and Reform Commission, there is not any more a legitimate debate over whether ICANN has a role in policy development and implementation. It does. We also believe that role should be limited to those policy areas that are reasonably related to ICANN's technical mission.[4]

The overlap between technical coordination and policy making is clear also from the functions that ICANN is responsible for, in particular the control

---

[3] See the White Paper 'Statement of Policy, Management of Internet Names and Addresses', 63 Fed. Reg. 31741(1998), where these four principles were described in detail, available at: http://www.icann.org/en/general/white-paper-05jun98.htm

[4] Committee on ICANN Evolution and Reform, *ICANN: A Blueprint for Reform*, 2002, available at http://www.icann.org/en/committees/evol-reform/blueprint-20jun02.htm

over the DNS confers a de facto power on ICANN to decide over the criteria upon which consenting access to the Internet is granted: before any entity can appear on the Internet, it must register a domain name under the terms and conditions imposed by ICANN, more correctly by its accredited registrars.

ICANN has a number of functions:

- to decide on the number of generic TLDs (gTLDs), the potential categories of coverage that apply to each domain (e.g. what kinds of organizations can register for a website in a specific domain);
- to designate and contract with specific organizations to serve as the registries for specific gTLDs;
- to accredit and contract with the registrars with whom the registries deal;
- to negotiate with the country code managers for each country code TLD (ccTLD) to ensure that they carry out registry-like functions;[5]
- to maintain a system for settling disputes among website holders (e.g. as to who is entitled to specific character strings in their second-level domain name);
- to generally maintain the compatibility, capacity (in terms of IP addresses), and stability (in terms of the uniqueness of IP and DNS addresses) of the DNS; and
- through IANA[6] to coordinate the allocation of IP addresses and manage the DNS 'root', the master file of top-level domain names (TLDs).

Particular attention should be devoted to the registry and registrars agreements, given that these two roles are related to two different functions within the ICANN regulatory structure (see Figure 10.1).

The registry function involves the operation of the database for registering domain names for a gTLD, and is allocated to the 16 companies that are in charge of one gTLD (each)[7]; while registrar function involves the

---

[5] Unlike the gTLDs, over which ICANN has direct authority and control, the ccTLDs and their country code managers have a considerably looser relationship with ICANN.

[6] Note that also the Internet Assigned Numbers Authority (IANA) is managed by ICANN under contract to the Department of Commerce. The latter provides an ongoing oversight function, whereby it verifies additions and changes made in the root to ensure IANA complies with its policies.

[7] Currently, domain names under the following gTLDs are available, and the corresponding registries are under contract with ICANN: .aero, .asia, .biz, .cat, .com, .coop, .info, .jobs, .mobi, .museum, .name, .net, .org, .pro, .tel and .travel.

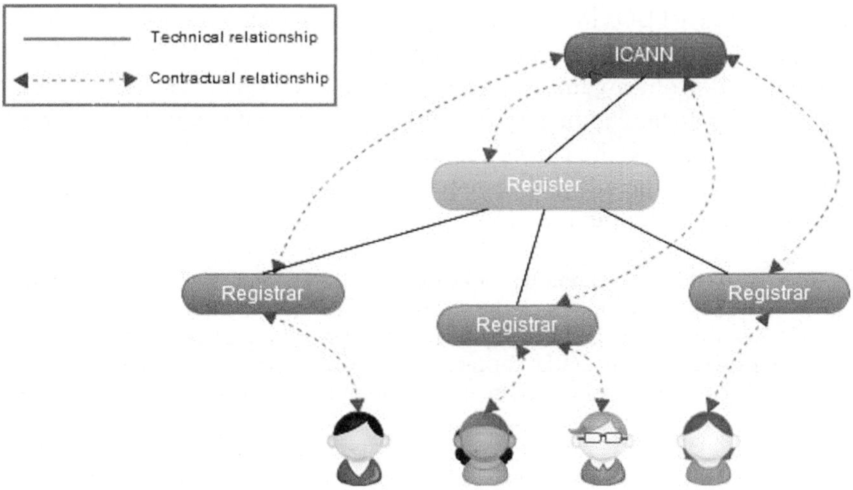

Figure 10.1 Existing relationships among ICANN, registers, registrants and users

registration of domain names for customers, and is allocated to the companies that fulfill the criteria for accreditation provided by ICANN.

Among the registries, a fundamental distinction exists, namely between sponsored and un-sponsored ones. Generally speaking, an un-sponsored gTLD registry operates under policies established by the global Internet community directly through the ICANN process. In particular, the main obligations of registries under the agreement with ICANN are the following:

- to comply with and implement all temporary specifications or policies established by ICANN that are necessary to maintain the stability or security of the Internet;
- to comply and implement all ICANN 'consensus policies' (the abovementioned bottom-up approach in developing the policies related to the DNS management);
- to comply with the process for consideration of proposed registry services, where ICANN could require a decision from a standing panel of experts over the possibility to implement any modification to registry services in case the latter could raise significant security, stability or competition issues.[8]

[8] See the agreements available at: http://www.icann.org/en/registries/agreements.htm.

A sponsored gTLD, instead, is a specialized gTLD that has a sponsor company representing a specific community that is served by the gTLD, such as non-profit organizations.[9] The sponsor company carries out delegated policy-formulation responsibilities and operates within an agreed charter that defines who can be a registrar and how the policy decisions will be made within the relevant community. In particular, with respect to the TLD the sponsor should:

(i) publish such standards, policies, procedures, and practices so they are available to members of the sponsored TLD community;
(ii) conduct its policy-development activities in a manner that reasonably provides opportunities for members of the sponsored TLD community to discuss and participate in the development of such standards, policies, procedures, or practices;
(iii) maintain the representativeness of its policy-development and implementation process by establishing procedures that facilitate participation by a broad cross-section of the sponsored TLD community; and
(iv) ensure, through published procedures, adequate opportunities for members of the sponsored TLD community to submit their views on and objections to the establishment or revision of standards, policies, procedures, and practices or the manner in which standards, policies, procedures, and practices are enforced.[10]

A different process characterized the ccTLDs, given that originally the delegation of responsibility was made informally on a 'first come first served basis'. Following the rapid growth of the Internet and its commercialization, such informal procedure was no more feasible and raised disputes among competing potential authorities (Lyndsay, 2007: 90). Thus, in 2006, ICANN provided a set of broad criteria, known as an accountability framework, to be the basis for formal agreements between ICANN and ccTLD managers (ccNSO, 2006). The accountability framework in practice can become a detailed agreement, or an exchange of letters depending on the specific conditions that characterize the ccTLD management in each country,[11] including clauses on obligations of the ccTLD managers and ICANN, dispute resolution systems and termination.

---

[9] See the cases of .coop, .museum, and .aero.

[10] The .coop sponsored TLD agreement, available at: http://www.icann.org/en/tlds/agreements/coop/coop-agmt-01jul07.htm

[11] See the different agreements available at: http://www.icann.org/en/cctlds/agreements.html

Looking at the case of registrars, instead, the so-called Registry Accreditation Agreement includes more detailed obligations for companies that want to become registrars.[12] In particular, the agreement requires registrars to enter into an electronic or paper registration agreement with domain name holders that includes the following provisions:

- the provision of accurate and reliable contact details of the domain name holder, where willful provision of inaccurate or unreliable information shall constitute a breach of contract and be a basis for cancellation of the registration;
- the information concerning the data treatment and the possibilities for rectification of personal data provided;
- the acceptance of a dispute resolution system, provided autonomously by the registrar or following the existing Uniform Domain Name Dispute Resolution Policy (UDRP).

This last point is very important as it shows the privatization of the regulatory regime with regard to the enforcement function (Hadfield, 2002: 263–4), either directly through the implementation of the UDRP on the relationships between domain name holders and registrars, or indirectly delegating such activity to the registrars, imposing on them the obligation to provide an alternative dispute resolution system. Moreover, given that the main beneficiaries of protection are third parties which have no direct relationship with ICANN nor the registrars nor the domain name holders, the UDRP has been described as a '*contractually-mandated private system for the benefit of non-contracting parties*' (Thornburg, 2002: 197).

2.2 The Dispute Resolution System of ICANN

As stated above, with the development of the Internet as a global exchange commercial platform, domain names not only retained an identification function, but acquired increased significance as business identifiers, which could be related with intellectual property rights. The so-called practice of 'cyber-squatting', in fact, is one of the negative effects of the hierarchical and unique nature of the domain name system, where third parties can

---

[12] See the model agreement available at: http://www.icann.org/en/registrars/ra-agreement-21may09-en.htm#5

preemptively register trademarks as domain names assigned on a first-come-first-served basis, offering them to the trademarks' owners at prices that are far beyond the cost of registration.[13]

In order to overcome this problem ICANN drafted the aforementioned Uniform Domain Name Dispute Resolution Policy (UDRP), providing a fast, convenient, and efficient dispute resolution procedure for the benefit of trademark holders whose marks have been unlawfully registered as domain names. At the moment of registering the selected domain name, any user must 'represent and warrant that ... the registration of the domain name will not infringe upon or otherwise violate the rights of any third party',[14] and contextually agrees to participate in arbitration-like proceedings where any third party would claim the existence of such rights.[15]

A complainant in a UDRP proceeding must establish three elements to succeed, as provided in art. 4 (a):

(i) The domain name is identical or confusingly similar to a trademark or service mark in which the complainant has rights;
(ii) The registrant does not have any rights or legitimate interests in the domain name; and
(iii) The registrant registered the domain name and is using it in 'bad faith'.

In particular, the definition of bad faith is to be interpreted on the basis of a non-exclusive list provided in art. 4 (b), which includes both the simpler example of cybersquatting, where the user has as primary purpose that of selling, renting, or otherwise transferring the domain name registration to the complainant who is the owner of the trademark or service mark, but also the case in which the user registered the domain name primarily for the purpose of disrupting the business of a competitor, or intentionally attempted to attract, for commercial gain, Internet users to his/her website, by creating a likelihood of confusion with the complainant's mark.

The only remedy the UDRP proceeding can award is a cancellation or transfer of the domain name to the complainant, and this can be directly

---

[13] See the definition provided in the Anticybersquatting Consumer Protection Act, codified as Lanham Act, § 43 (c), 15 USC § 1125 (c).

[14] ICANN (2010), Rules for Uniform Domain Name Dispute Resolution Policy at clause 2, available at: http://www.icann.org/en/dndr/udrp/uniform-rules.htm

[15] Note that five dispute resolution service providers have received ICANN approval, but only three are deciding cases under the UDRP: the Arbitration and Mediation Center of WIPO; the National Arbitration Forum (NAF); and the Asian Domain Name Dispute Resolution Centre (ADNDRC).

implemented by the registrar after the order of a panel. Nonetheless, the UDRP does not limit the possibility for the parties to initiate proceedings before a competent court after the panel's decision; however, the registrar will enforce the binding decisions if neither party commences litigation before the courts within the time limit defined in the policy.[16]

The main critics of the UDRP system are focused on the low level of fairness of the proceedings (Walker, 2000; Froomkin, 2002; Chatterjee, 2006; Hörnle, 2009). In particular, the major flaw of the system is located in the fact that the UDRP does not provide any appeal process whatsoever. For instance, though the UDRP includes various clauses concerning procedural protection, such as fair hearing and the impartiality of the panel's members, there is no corresponding clause reacting to the case of breach of such rules. The same is true for appeals based on substantive matters, as there is no procedure to review the decision on the factual findings, and no appeal on points of law (Thornburg, 2002).

Additionally, legal certainty and consistency of the dispute decisions are not granted, given that UDRP does not implement a formal doctrine of *stare decisis*, meaning that the panel's members are not bound by precedents, though all the decisions are required to be published online by the dispute resolution service providers.[17] This can be justified by the expedited nature of the procedure, where the panel's members are required to reach decisions based on limited evidence within demanding time constraints, thus, a precedent doctrine cannot be feasible in this context. However, the fairness level could be improved if a more formal requirement of consistency were included within the UDRP, not merely limited to the willingness of the panel's members to cite previous decisions distinguishing the reasoning where different results are achieved (Lyndsay, 2007: 131).

3. THE CASE OF AUCTION PLATFORMS

The commercialization of the Internet network and the diffusion of the World Wide Web application paved the way for the creation and development of marketplaces for the exchange of goods and services online (Ramberg, 2002). So-called e-commerce offers any user the possibility of accessing resources from all over the world, together with an easy and rapid way to negotiate the bargain without moving from one's home. However, the electronic marketplace does not provide any of the traditional reference

---

16 See art. 4 (k).

17 See the archive of decisions and pending cases available at: http://www.icann.org/en/udrp/proceedings-archive-en.htm

points that buyers and sellers were accustomed to, such as the possibility of inspecting the goods to be purchased, or the assessment of the trustworthiness of the counterpart through direct contact, or the benefits that may be reaped from the experience of other buyers or sellers (Kaufmann-Kohler and Schulz, 2004: 76). This lack of reference points could be reflected in the lack of confidence in the electronic market.

However, technical features available on the Internet could solve this lack of confidence, for instance, trust-marks and identification systems can be used to increase the elements of accountability, at the same time defining a liaison with a particular community; reputation systems can strengthen the sense of community, for the reason that each member of a community may profit from the experience of others; finally, alternative dispute resolution systems can provide a faster, easier and less expensive way of solving disputes between users (Casarosa, 2009: 21).

Such features can be found in one of the most common and profitable selling methods available online, namely the auction sale model. Although this is an old trading mechanism, known since antiquity (Cassady, 1967; Riefa, 2009), the auction model received renewed attention with the increasing success of auction websites, such as eBay, Craigslist, PriceMinister, and the like.[18] Moreover, the manner in which digitalization affected this kind of negotiation process modified its traditional characteristics in order to adapt and reap the profits of the virtual environment. In order to provide an example of transnational private regimes available in the case of an online auction site, in this contribution I will refer to the eBay organization and management, whose business activity is not only carried out in transnational markets, from the US to Europe to Asia, but also presents an organizational structure which involves all the facets of a self-regulatory environment.

3.1 The Regulatory Function of eBay

eBay is a website founded in 1995 as an electronic platform where users can sell and buy any kind of goods through an auction process.

Any user who wishes to participate in the auction is asked to register on the website consenting to the user agreement and the related documents, after which (s)he can start her/his activity as buyer or seller. Thus, the standard setting function is carried out by eBay, as within the user agreement it defines not only the auction service and the ways in which it will be

---

[18] See the available online auction sites at: http://en.wikipedia.org/wiki/Online_auction_business_model

provided to users, but also the rules of behavior the user will have to comply with whenever (s)he participates as a buyer or as a seller. These rules are accompanied by a set of annexes concerning prohibited, questionable, and potentially infringing items, privacy policy, board usage by users, safe-harbor policy, etc.

When new goods are offered for sale, their presentation is included in the list of similar items so that any other user or visitor can browse the category and locate the particular offer. eBay auctions are organized as *English* auctions: sellers set a minimum price that serves as the starting bid and higher bids beat lower bids (Casarosa, 2009: 5). At the end of the predetermined period (3, 5, 7, or 10 days, 7 days by default), the highest bidder wins. After the auction, the buyer pays the seller, who ships the goods upon receipt of payment. Sellers pay a small insertion fee to eBay regardless of the sale, and in case of a sale, the seller also pays eBay a final value fee or commission.

eBay's role in the auction process is purposely limited, providing only a venue for sellers and buyers to meet, and a system through which to communicate and enforce its rules, without interfering in the negotiation process through provision of guarantees or authentication of goods. Thus, any claim concerning the behavior of the participants or the characteristics of the goods cannot be presented towards eBay. This is clearly stated in one of the clauses included in the user agreement:

> You will not hold eBay responsible for other users' actions or inactions, including things they post. You acknowledge that we are not a traditional auctioneer. Instead, the Sites are a venue to allow anyone to offer, sell, and buy just about anything, at anytime, from anywhere, in a variety of pricing formats and venues, such as stores, fixed price formats and auction-style formats. We are not involved in the actual transaction between buyers and sellers.[19]

However, in order to safeguard users' interests and to facilitate the transparency of negotiations, eBay appoints its own users to perform such monitoring activity. Each party is asked to post a feedback on the behavior of their counterpart as soon as the transaction is completed.[20] This feedback is quite simple as the format only allows for the outcome of the transaction to be described as positive or negative, with the possibility of adding a brief comment. Whenever the feedback is posted, it is stored in the negotiation history of either the seller or the buyer, thus building up their

---

[19] See at: http://pages.ebay.com/help/policies/user-agreement.html under the clause *Liability*.

[20] See at: http://pages.ebay.co.uk/help/feedback/evaluating-feedback.html

user profile and their corresponding rating. The whole history of any transaction can subsequently be browsed by other potential buyers or sellers; thus, a user who consults this reputational system before bidding in an auction can find out whether or not the counterpart has performed correctly in the transactions previously concluded (Gillette, 2001; Ramberg, 2002: 32).

The introduction of such a technical tool provides a twofold positive effect: on the one hand, each potential buyer or seller can profit from the preceding activity performed by other users in order to determine the credibility of the offer and of the seller (Katsh et al., 2000: 729); on the other hand, whenever a transaction is positively concluded, the reputation of the website itself increases owing to the fact that the participants indirectly attribute part of the successful outcome to the electronic platform itself, thus encouraging both the participation of more users and the correctness of their behavior in the performance of contracts (Grundmann and Kerber, 2001: 273).

However, the user agreement does not exclude the possibility of sanctions in the case of the breaching of one of the rules of the user agreement or the documents incorporated by reference, or in the case in which it is not possible to verify or authenticate any information provided by the user, or in the case in which the user's actions may cause financial loss or legal liability.

3.2 The Dispute Resolution System of eBay

As in any other marketplace, disputes can arise also within the framework of an eBay exchange, such as in the case of a failure to deliver an item whose payment was accepted or a request to erase the negative feedback received. In order to overcome these problems, eBay provides a set of mechanisms that can verify user behaviors, and, eventually, react with sanctions in case of a breach of the use agreement and related policies.

eBay provides two different mechanisms of control and enforcement. On the one hand, it can carry out an investigation into users' behaviors concerning possible violations, such as in cases of feedback violations (e.g. feedback extortion, or manipulation; inappropriate feedback comments; feedback removal), buying violations (e.g. transaction interference; offers to buy or sell outside eBay; invalid bid retraction; shill bidding), selling violations (e.g. seller performance standards violations; listing violations; avoiding eBay fees), and contact information and identity violations (e.g. misrepresentation of identity; false or missing contact information; invalid and dead email addresses; underage users).[21] In such cases, eBay would start an investigation upon report of any other user and eventually react to the existing violation. In these cases eBay can decide to limit the user's activity on the website, to suspend or terminate the user's registration or user's item listings, to remove any hosted content, or even to refuse to provide further service to the user without notification. However, eBay clarifies that:

> Because we respect the privacy of our members, we can't discuss the results of an investigation in detail. However, we might contact you to tell you that an investigation is complete.
>
> Before taking action against a member, we'll consider the circumstances of the violation and the member's buying and selling record. Our actions may include removing listings and range [sic] of other actions, including limiting buying and selling privileges and account suspension. Out of fairness to our members, if a complaint can't be proven, we won't take action.[22]

Thus, the investigation activity is under the closed control of eBay, with a very high level of discretion as to when and how to intervene and the sanctions to be imposed when a violation has been proved.

Alternatively, eBay provides an internal dispute resolution system in cases in which conflict arises between the buyer and the seller concerning one of the following issues: a failure to deliver an item whose payment was accepted; a significant misrepresentation of items (not meeting the terms and the description outlined in the listing); a refusal to accept payment for an item at the conclusion of a successful sale; a request to erase the negative feedback received. The solution provided by eBay is an online mediation process which puts the two parties in a position to communicate with each other to settle their dispute.[23] For instance, in the case of an unpaid item process,[24] when the seller reports that he has failed to receive payment for an item that has already been shipped, eBay gets in touch with the buyer through an email notification or a pop-up message at the user's next appearance on the website, reminding him that payment has not been received, and adding simple instructions on how to respond or how to pay for the item. If the buyer does not respond to the email or pop-up message within four days, the seller may file for a final value fee credit and the buyer receives an unpaid item strike in its feedback rating. If the buyer answers the seller, however, it is up to them to solve the dispute. In this case eBay

---

21 See at: http://pages.ebay.com/help/buy/report-trading.html
22 See at: http://pages.ebay.ca/help/buy/report-trading.html#results
23 See at: http://pages.ebay.com/help/buy/resolving-problems.html
24 See at: http://pages.ebay.co.uk/help/tp/unpaid-item-process.html

provides a message area where the buyer and the seller can communicate personally. Finally, the seller has other options in closing the dispute: the transaction may come to a positive completion, or the buyer and the seller may come to an agreement not to complete the transaction.[25]

The importance of the previous enforcement mechanisms can be appreciated also through research carried out by the Center for Information Technology and Dispute Resolution, of the University of Massachusetts, which was focused on eBay's dispute resolution system (Katsh et al., 2000). The study attempted to provide an evaluation of the legal constraints existing in the alternative dispute resolution system: although this method is employed to avoid existing legal rules, any negotiation, mediation or arbitration processes take place within a legal framework: the so-called 'shadow of the law', whose relevance is based on the parties' awareness of it and on their willingness to comply with it. The results show that the participants in the mediation process behave as if they were in the shadow of an 'eBay law', abiding by eBay rules in almost all cases. This fact can be explained if we assume the perspective of eBay users: the participants, in order to rely on the mediation system, had to internalize the rules of the website, and believe them to be binding. Moreover, the parties are aware that, whenever a dispute arises, their reputation will potentially suffer, and therefore they will feel concern about the possibility that future transactions on the website may be hampered.[26]

An additional mechanism should be included in this framework, which focuses on the specific claims concerning the copyright violations by eBay members, namely the Verified Rights Owner (VeRO) Program.[27] In this case, eBay implemented an enforcement mechanism that allows eBay to remove certain offers available on the auction platform where the items or the materials contained in the offer infringe intellectual property rights of third parties, whether or not the latter are members of the eBay community. eBay can, upon request of an identified copyright owner, remove an item offered if the latter is not an authentic product.

This system heavily relies on the monitoring activity of the copyright holders to identify and report the violations, while a limited role is played

[25] A dispute can only be open for 36 days after the transaction date (i.e. the date when the buyer commits him/herself to buying the item and the seller commits him/herself to selling it). If the seller has not closed the dispute within 36 days, it will be automatically closed. When this automatic closure takes place the seller does not receive a final value fee credit and the buyer does not receive an unpaid item strike.

[26] See more generally on the concept of shadow of the law, Cooter (1982).

[27] See at: http://pages.ebay.com/help/policies/programs-vero-ov.html

by eBay, which merely provides some technical tools to facilitate the possibility, for copyright owners, of verifying the presence of violations:

> eBay offers a feature called Favorite Searches to all users. As a rights owner, you can also set up your free eBay account to use Favorite Searches. With the Favorite Searches feature, you can conduct automatic searches for potentially infringing items. Our system will automatically notify you on a regular basis of any new listings posted which contain any terms in your selected searches.[28]

Although such an approach has been criticized, and in some cases sanctioned, by national courts,[29] the final conclusion in this case is that online auction sites cannot be held liable for trademark infringements caused by their users and that the burden for monitoring such sites rests with copyright owners (Rühmkorf, 2009; Stalla-Bourdillon, 2010).

4. ENFORCEMENT STRUCTURE AND MECHANISM IN INTERNET PRIVATE REGULATION

The previous analysis shows the set of differences between the available mechanisms of enforcement used in private regimes. Table 10.1 considers the most relevant elements that can be compared between the ICANN and the eBay system.

First of all it should be highlighted that a basic difference is the contractual framework that characterizes the ICANN enforcement system in comparison to the eBay one (see Table 10.1, points a. and b.). This difference affects some of the choices in the enforcement mechanisms available. In the former, the dispute resolution system is introduced within a chain of contracts that links ICANN with the registrars and their counterparts, namely the domain holders. In this case, a higher level of detail in the content of the dispute resolution rules is of utmost importance; registrars that do not want to apply the UDRP could still use the latter as a template to build up their own dispute resolution system thanks to clear and unambiguous criteria. The eBay enforcement mechanism, on the other hand, is mostly internally managed and resolved. The low level of detail in the procedures can be appreciated also by comparing the current system with the previously adopted one, which was based on a cooperation

[28] See at: http://pages.ebay.co.uk/vero/notice.htm

[29] See in particular the decision of the French Chambre de Commerce, *Parfums Christian Dior and others c/ eBay Inc, eBay International AG*, Tribunal de Commerce de Paris 1ère chambre B, Judgment of June 30, 2008; and the English case, *L'Oréal S.A., et al.* v *eBay International AG, et al.* [2009] EWHC 1094 (Ch).

Table 10.1 Comparison between enforcement mechanisms

	ICANN	eBay
a. *Type of enforcement*	Formal	Formal
b. *Level of detail of rules*	High	Low
c. *Type of enforcement*	Arbitration	Mediation
d. *Enforcer*	Accredited third party	Internal online system
e. *Type of sanctions*	Transfer or cancellation of domain name	Scale of sanctions from suspension of the offer to cancellation of the user from the system
f. *Effectiveness*	Self-enforcing	Self-enforcing
g. *Relationship with courts*	Possible stop if preemptive or subsequent claim in courts	No direct connection
h. *Appeal*	No	No
i. *Type of actors involved*	Third parties v regulatees	Regulatees v regulatees Third parties v regulatees

agreement between eBay and a third-party dispute resolution system, namely the Squaretrade website.[30] If an eBay member showed the trust-mark of Squaretrade, (s)he guaranteed that (s)he would comply with the code of conduct drafted by the provider (which was mostly replicating the rules defined by eBay). Moreover, the user bound him/herself to a clearly defined mediation process which Squaretrade provided in the case of a conflict with his/her counterpart, agreeing to any solution awarded by the provider (Hadfield, 2004). Furthermore, any non-cooperative behavior of one party in the mediation process could also result in a negative feedback in the eBay reputation system. In this case the rules concerning procedures and sanctions were more detailed in order to provide a reference for the third-party dispute resolution system, but when eBay changed its feedback

[30] See the information provided on the website: http://www.squaretrade.com/cnt/jsp/abt/aboutus.jsp

policy due to the increased number of negotiations through its platform, and introduced new looser rules to be applied in its own dispute resolution mechanism, Squaretrade stopped providing its services, as coordination was no longer possible between the two systems (Callies and Zumbansen, 2010: 159). This development in the enforcement mechanism of eBay shows that codification and clarity in rules are linked with a coordination role in the regulatory chain: the wider the distance between the standard-setter and the enforcer, the stronger the need for detailed rules.

Another element to be underlined is the choice of the enforcement mechanism: namely arbitration-like versus mediation (see Table 10.1, points c. and d.). This should be related, on the one hand, with the importance given to the willing participation of the parties to the dispute resolution system, and, on the other, with the third-party role that the private regulator would retain in the dispute resolution system. As a matter of fact, mediation is based on the participation of a third neutral party (eBay) with no or limited decision-making power, that tries to bring the parties to an agreement by using one of the styles developed for traditional mediation, for instance facilitative or evaluative mediation. Whereas, online arbitration provides for a third party chosen by the conflicting parties (within the list of ICANN accredited institutions), who should decide on the case after having heard the relevant arguments and seen the appropriate evidence (Schultz, 2002; Hörnle, 2003). Such difference can be related to the aforementioned eBay approach as a venue instead of an intermediary with regards to the auction model, a position adopted also in the management of the enforcement mechanism. This has as a consequence the exclusion of any liability on eBay, either as a standard-setter, given that it is not part of the exchange between the buyer and the seller, or as an enforcer, given that its role is a mere facilitator of the agreement between the conflicting parties. The same reasoning is not applicable to ICANN, given that the latter is more interested in improving its legitimacy as a standard-setter providing a reliable and coordinated dispute resolution system, though within the limited scope of trademarks infringements cases.

Concerning sanctions (see Table 10.1, points e. and f.), it should be noted that the technological framework in which the two private regimes are embedded allows for a high level of effectiveness of the sanctions imposed, given that in both cases the regulator can directly enforce the decisions: either they impose the transfer of the domain name or cancel the membership of the trader from the auction community. One element that characterizes both systems is the fact that no damages are awarded, and this is justified, in the ICANN case, by the fact that

> it seems appropriate that the remedies that could be awarded by the neutral decision-maker be limited to the status of the domain name registration itself and actions in respect of that registration. In other words, monetary damages to compensate for any loss or injury incurred by the owner of an intellectual property as a result of a domain name registration should not be available under the procedure. Such a restrictive approach to remedies would underline the nature of the procedure as an administrative one, directed at the efficient administration of the DNS, which is intended to be complementary to other existing mechanisms, whether arbitration or court procedures. The approach would also accommodate the preferences of a number of commentators for an ADR procedure that was compatible with available judicial remedies. (WIPO, 1999)

Looking at the relationship between private enforcement mechanisms and courts (Table 10.1, point g.), a difference arises: in the ICANN case the possibility for regulatees and third parties to initiate legal proceedings before a court is not only allowed but it is also included in the UDRP procedure, either before the end of the dispute resolution proceeding, stopping the latter, or when the decision is already taken, stopping the enforcement of the decision. On the contrary, no specific provision is included in the eBay system, implying the possibility for any regulatee or third party to claim before a court concerning the unlawful behavior of another regulatee (see Table 10.1, point i.). The different choices, however, are based on the same underlying rational not to limit access to justice. Moreover, in both cases the dispute resolution system does not award damages, nor does it provide an appeal to the decisions taken (Table 10.1, point h.); thus, court proceedings could be interpreted as a natural 'safety net' for the protection of the interests that were not taken into account within the dispute resolution systems.

5. CONCLUSIONS

This chapter has briefly outlined the regulatory systems and related enforcement mechanisms available in two Internet regulation regimes. On the one hand, the ICANN model is focused on the management of the technical architecture of the Internet network, providing a transnational private regime based on a chain of contracts that links ICANN with registries, registrars and domain name holders. The dispute resolution system in this case is an arbitration-like mechanism which relies on a detailed policy, but is limited to a set of cases involving the conflicts between trademark owners and domain name holders. On the other hand, the eBay model is focused on the regulation of commercial exchange through an online auction system. The management of this regulatory regime includes also monitoring tools, based on reputation mechanisms, and an internal dispute resolution system, based on mediation.

The analysis and the comparison between the two models highlights various differences, which are based on the regulatory strategies adopted in each case, on the regulatory objective taken by the private regulators, and the contractual model adopted by private regulators.

However, the current analysis provides only a general appraisal of just two of the models available in the online world. Differences could also be found in other regulatory systems existing in the same domain, such as regulation of virtual worlds, social networking websites, or labeling programs. The level of detail could be further improved, for example by an examination of the relationship between private regulation and courts' decisions regarding the legitimacy of private rules, or the possibility of conflicts with overlapping private regimes (e.g. in the case of auction websites, the potential conflicts with privacy rules), etc., but these matters are outside the scope of this chapter.

BIBLIOGRAPHY

Abbate, J. (1999), *Inventing the Internet*, MIT Press.

Benkler, Y. (2006), *The Wealth of Networks – How Social Production Transforms Markets and Freedom*, Yale University Press.

Botzem, S. and Hoffman, J. (2008), 'Transnational Institution Building as Public-Private Interaction – The Case of Standard Setting on the Internet and in Corporate Financial Reporting', LSE working paper.

Callies, G.-P. and Zumbansen, P. (2010), *Rough Consensus and Running Code: A Theory of Transnational Private Law*, Hart.

Casarosa, F. (2009), 'Online Auction Sites: An Example of Regulation in Electronic Communities?', *European Review of Private Law*, 1, 1–23.

Cassady, R. (1967), *Auctions and Auctioneering*, University of California Press.

ccNSO (country codes Name Supporting Organisation) (2006), *Guidelines for ccTLD managers Accountability Framework discussions with ICANN*, available at: http://ccnso.icann.org/node/25731

Chatterjee, N. (2006), 'Arbitration Proceedings Under ICANN's Uniform Domain Name Dispute Resolution Policy – Myth or Reality?', 10 *Vindobona J. of Int'l Com. L. & Arb.* 67.

Cooter, R. (1982), 'Bargaining in the Shadow of Law: A Testable Model of Strategic Behavior', *J. Legal Stud.*, 11(2), 225–51.

Deibert, R.J., Palfrey, J.G., Rohozinski, R. and Zittrain, J. (eds) (2008), *Access Denied – The Practice and Policy of Global Internet Filtering*, MIT Press.

Deibert, R.J., Palfrey, J.G., Rohozinski, R. and Zittrain, J. (eds) (2010), *Access Controlled – The Shaping of Power, Rights, and Rule in Cyberspace*, MIT Press.

Froomkin, M. (2002), 'ICANN's Uniform Dispute Resolution Policy – Causes and (Partial) Cures', 67 *Brook. L. Rev.* 605.

Gillette, C.P. (2001), 'Reputation and Intermediaries in Electronic Commerce, Essays in Honor of William D. Hawkland Unifying Commercial Law in the 20th Century: Understanding the Impulse and Assessing the Effort – A Symposium', 62 *La. L. Rev.* 1165.

Goldsmith, J. and Wu, T. (2006), *Who Controls the Internet? Illusions of a Borderless World*, Oxford University Press.

Grundmann, S. and Kerber, W. (2001), 'Information Intermediaries and Party Autonomy – The Example of Securities and Insurance Markets', in S. Grundmann, W. Kerber, and S. Weatherill, *Party Autonomy and the Role of Information in the Internal Market*, Walter de Gruyter.

Hadfield, G.K. (2002), 'Privatizing Commercial Law: Lessons from ICANN', *Journal of Small and Emerging Business Law*, 6, 257–88.

Hadfield, G.K. (2004), 'Delivering Legality on the Internet: Developing Principles for the Private Provision of Commercial Law', *American Law and Economics Review*, 6, 154–84.

Hörnle, J. (2003), 'Online Dispute Resolution – More Than The Emperor's New Clothes', Proceedings of the UNECE Forum on ODR 2003, available at: http://www.ombuds.org/unece2003/unece2003/

Hörnle, J. (2009), *Cross-border Internet Dispute Resolution*, Cambridge University Press.

Katsh, E., Rifkin, J. and Gaitenby, A. (2000), 'E-commerce, E-dispute, and E-dispute Resolution: In the Shadow of "eBay Law"', *Ohio State Journal on Dispute Resolution*, 15, 705–34.

Kaufmann-Kohler, G. and Schultz, T. (2004), *Online Dispute Resolution: Challenges for Contemporary Justice*, Kluwer.

Kesan, J.P. and Gallo, A. (2008), 'Pondering the Politics of Private Procedures: The Case of ICANN', Illinois Law & Economics Research Paper No. LE08–031, available at: http://ssrn.com/abstract=1120489

Koops, E.-J., Lips, M., Nouwt, S., Prins, C. and Schellekens, M. (2006), 'Should Self-Regulation be the Starting Point?', in E.-J. Koops, M. Lips, J.E.J. Prins and M. Schellekens, *Starting Points for ICT Regulation: Deconstructing Prevalent Policy One-Liners*, T.M.C. Asser Press, 109–49.

Leiner, B.M., Cerf, V.G., Clark, D.D., Kahn, R.E., Kleinrock, L., Lynch, D.C., Postel, J., Roberts, L.G. and Wolff, S. (2003), 'A Brief History of the Internet', available at: http://www.isoc.org/internet/history/brief.shtml

Lenard, T. and White, L. (2009), 'ICANN at a Crossroads: A Proposal for Better Governance and Performance', available at: http://ssrn.com/abstract=1434482

Lessig, L. (2006), *Code Version 2.0*, 2nd edn, Basic Books.

Lyndsay, D. (2007), *International Domain Name Law – ICANN and UDRP*, Hart.

Price, M.E. and Verhulst, S.G. (2005), *Self-regulation and the Internet*, Kluwer Law International.

Ramberg, C. (2002), *Internet Marketplace – The Law of Auctions and Exchanges Online*, Oxford University Press.

Riefa, C. (2009), 'A Dangerous Erosion of Consumer Rights: The Absence of a Right to Withdraw from Online Auctions', in G. Howells and R. Schultze (eds), *Modernising and Harmonising Consumer Contract Law*, Sellier European Law Publishers, 177–87.

Rühmkorf, A. (2009), 'eBay on the European Playing Field: A Comparative Case Analysis of *L'Oréal v eBay*', *SCRIPTed*, available at: http://www.law.ed.ac.uk/ahrc/script-ed/vol6–3/ruhmkorf.asp

Schultz, T. (2002), 'Online Dispute Resolution: An Overview and Selected Issues', Proceedings of the UNECE Forum on ODR 2002, available at: http://ssrn.com/abstract=898821

Schultz, T. (2007), 'Private Legal Systems: What Cyberspace Might Teach Legal Theorists', 10 *Yale Journal of Law & Technology* 151.

Solum, L. (2008), 'Models of Internet Governance', in University of Illinois, Public Law Research Paper n. 07–25, available at: http://ssrn.com/abstract=1136825

Stalla-Bourdillon, S. (2010), 'The Flip Side of ISP's Liability Regimes: The Ambiguous Protection of Fundamental Rights and Liberties in Private Digital Spaces', *Computer Law & Security Review*, 26(5), 492–501.

Strahilevitz, L.J. (2003), 'Charismatic Code, Social Norms, and the Emergence of Cooperation on the File-swapping Networks', in Chicago Working Paper series, available at: http://ssrn.com/abstract_id=329700

Thornburg, E. (2002), 'Fast, Cheap and Out of Control: Lessons from the ICANN Dispute Resolution System', *Journal of Small and Emerging Business Law*, 6, 191.

Walker, L. (2000), 'ICANN's Uniform Domain Name Dispute Resolution Policy', 15 *Berkeley Tech. L. J.* 289.

Weber, R. (2000), *Shaping Internet Governance: Regulatory Challenges*, Springer.

WIPO (World Intellectual Property Organization) (1999), 'The Management of Internet Names and Addresses: Intellectual Property Issues, Final Report', available at http://www.wipo.int/amc/en/docs/report-final1.pdf

11. Enforcement of transnational private regulation of advertising practices: decentralization, mechanisms and procedural fairness

Paul Verbruggen[1]

INTRODUCTION

The proliferation of transnational private regulation (TPR) has been viewed as a response to the absence or paucity of publicly established norms that govern cross-border business activities (Abbott and Snidal, 2009). The promulgation and functioning of TPR has received considerable attention in the literature recently, in particular in terms of legitimacy and accountability (Bernstein and Cashore, 2007; Black, 2008), whilst monitoring and enforcement of TPR have been addressed only sparingly. Enforcement is the Achilles heel of regulation and is an important means of giving credibility and authority to TPR regimes.

This chapter describes the operation of TPR in the particular domain of advertising. This has the purpose of analyzing the mechanisms through which TPR can be enforced. In addition, it discusses the concerns these mechanisms throw up in terms of procedural fairness. TPR of advertising practices is a somewhat idiosyncratic case, however. First, the enforcement takes place in relative openness, as exposure and publicity of sanctions is a fundamental part of the industry's approach to enforcement. While this enables relatively easy data collection, it is in stark contrast to the relative privacy and lack of transparency surrounding the enforcement of TPR in

[1] This chapter draws from the research undertaken in the case study on 'Transnational Private Regulation in Advertising' within the framework of the HiiL Research Project on 'Transnational Private Regulation: Constitutional Foundations and Governance Design'. More details on the case study and broader research project can be found on the project's website: www.privateregulation.eu

other policy domains.[2] Second, TPR in advertising presents an example in which the enforcement of TPR is strongly decentralized: while norms are adopted at the transnational level, their enforcement is administered by national private regimes.

This chapter starts by outlining the key characteristics of TPR in the advertising industry and goes on to analyze the decentralized character of the TPR enforcement, the design of national enforcement mechanisms, and the concerns these mechanisms raise in the light of procedural fairness standards.

TPR OF ADVERTISING PRACTICES

TPR of advertising practices has three main characteristics: it is multi-level, has been specified in relation to particular sectors, beneficiaries, marketing techniques and media, and forms an alternative to or complements public (trans)national rules governing advertising practices.

Multi-level Governance

TPR in the field of advertising operates across various levels of governance involving a range of different industry players. International trade organizations or business consortia have adopted codes of conduct governing advertising practices at a global or regional level. The general aim of these transnational standards is to ensure that advertising is legal, fair, not misleading, in good taste and socially responsible. The principle actor in this respect has conventionally been the International Chamber of Commerce (ICC). Since the mid-1930s, the ICC has played a key role in coordinating industry efforts to establish private regulatory systems for the control of advertising practices. Founded in 1919 as a global trade organization to promote the interests of international business, it soon recognized that the manifest differences among national regimes regulating advertising behaviour hindered the effective competition among businesses worldwide (Brandmair, 1978: 5). Therefore, the ICC spearheaded business initiatives to address these differences and the consequences thereof for international trade at an international level.

In 1937, it adopted the first piece of private advertising regulation established at the transnational level: The International Code of Advertising Practice. The specific purpose with which the ICC code has been adopted

---

[2] See also Colin Scott, Cynthia Estlund, Geoffrey Miller, and Federica Casarosa in this volume.

and amended over the years was to establish a number of general principles upon which systems of private regulation should be based (Boddewyn, 1992: 16). Although private systems had already been established in some countries before the first ICC code was adopted (Miracle and Nevett, 1987), the ICC codes provided a set of common principles to guide and spur national industries to create systems of their own. The same rationale can be found in the latest versions of the ICC code, the 'Consolidated ICC Code on Advertising and Marketing Communications Practices' (ICC, 2011). Article 25 of this code, which is entitled 'Implementation', stipulates in its first paragraph:

> The Code and the principles enshrined in it, should be adopted and implemented, nationally and internationally, by the relevant local, national or regional self-regulatory bodies. The Code should also be applied, where appropriate, by all organisations, companies and individuals involved and at all stages in the marketing communication process.

Despite the compelling wording of this provision, the ICC does not have any powers to require self-regulatory organizations (SROs), which are in charge of the administration of the national private regimes, to adopt or implement the ICC code in a uniform way. In fact, the way in which the ICC codes have been adopted at the national level is determined by local factors, such as different market structures and cultural, legal and commercial traditions. As a result, there are considerable differences between the way in which the national private regimes for the control of advertising practices have implemented the ICC codes. Three approaches might be distinguished. First, there are systems, such as in Sweden and Finland, which just apply the ICC codes. Second, there are regimes, like in France and Belgium, which apply the ICC standards as a general reference document and have adopted additional rules to deal with specific products (such as alcohol, cars, pharmaceuticals) or topics (such as portrayal of woman in advertising and food advertising to children). Finally, and this is the majority, there are regimes that have used the ICC codes, either explicitly or implicitly, as a broad guideline for the adoption of their own codes of conduct. Here, the individual codes use the same principles as outlined by the ICC, but have adopted their own wording and structure, and have gone beyond the standards expressed in the ICC codes.

At present, more than 50 countries around the world host private systems for the control of advertising practices that are based on the ICC codes. Private regulation is most developed in Europe, where 26 countries host private regimes. The European Advertising Standards Alliance (EASA) has deeply influenced this high state of development of private regulation. EASA was established as a network of SROs at the initiative of the European advertising industry in the early 1990s. Its creation followed after pressures by the European Commission to adopt legislative measures in order to overcome the difficulties the various national codes of advertising practice posed for the development of the Internal Market (Cunningham, 2000). Today, EASA's membership includes 32 national SROs from both European (25) and non-European (7) countries, and 15 European trade associations that represent the various segments of the European advertising industry (advertisers, advertising agencies and media owners) at the supranational level.

Unlike the ICC, EASA does not set out to adopt substantive standards for advertising practices. Rather, it helps to establish new private systems or improve the operation of existing systems by sharing best practices and by providing best practice guidance. Of particular interest in this respect is EASA's 'Best Practice Self-Regulation Model', which has been very influential in triggering institutional changes amongst EASA's SRO members. The model:

> describes the various component parts of the model self-regulatory systems which the EASA wishes to see in place in all existing EU member states and in Accession countries. It is designed to help the EASA and its members to evaluate, initiate and develop effective and efficient systems across Europe. It will also help identify areas where investment is needed to develop existing national arrangements in order to improve the provision and operation of self-regulation … (EASA, 2004)

The best practice model lays down operational standards for SROs as regards, inter alia, the adjudication of disputes, the remedies and sanctions available, and monitoring activities, and, as such, provides a common roadmap to the organization and functioning of European SROs. Accordingly, EASA, at least in Europe, plays a key role in downplaying the institutional differences between national SROs resulting from the free and unsupervised implementation of the ICC codes.

Recently, however, EASA has sought to extend its network beyond the borders of Europe. In 2008, it set up the EASA International Council, which has as its members SROs from Australia, Brazil, Canada, Chile, India, New Zealand, Peru and South Africa. For these countries, and other non-European countries wanting to establish a private system, it has developed an 'International Guide to Developing a Self-regulatory Organisation' (EASA, 2009).

With its membership including more and more non-European SROs, EASA's influence in the international domain steadily increases. Although EASA does not seek to undermine the authority of the ICC as a standard-setter, its importance as a forum to share, coordinate and learn from the various ways in which SROs design their national regimes has grown.

Contributing to EASA's increasingly global role is that EASA has become a member of the ICC and acquired a crucial position in the standard-setting process of the ICC advertising codes. In fact, EASA's Director General is a member of the ICC Commission on Marketing and Advertising, where he co-chairs the Commission's Code Revision Taskforce. This allows the SRO and industry members of EASA to have a direct say in the adoption of the ICC codes. EASA's operational standards consistently refer to the ICC codes as the common global standard for private regimes of advertising control. To further increase coordination between the two organizations, EASA has recently teamed up with the ICC to develop special training programs to promote responsible advertising among advertising professionals around the world (EASA, 2010: 48).

Specificity

The Consolidated ICC Code includes in its first part a number of rules generally applicable to advertising and other forms of marketing communications. These rules seek to ensure that the behavior of industry members is legal, decent, honest and truthful. However, these general principles have been specified in relation to different product sectors, beneficiaries, marketing techniques and media. At the European level, for example, the alcohol industry has been very active in adopting a number of codes of conduct on the responsible advertising of alcohol. Here, the European trade associations for spirits, beer, wine and cider have each established codes of conduct on, inter alia, the use of responsible drinking messages in advertising and the promotion of alcohol to minors (Brewers of Europe, 2003; CEEV, 2009; EFRD, 2008).

An example of a transnational advertising code adopted to benefit a particular group is the 'ICC Framework for Responsible Food and Beverage Communications' (ICC, 2006). This Framework seeks to further specify the general ICC standards on the advertising of food and beverages to children. The ICC Framework has been complemented by the 'Global Policy on Marketing and Advertising to Children', adopted in 2009 by the International Food and Beverage Alliance (IFBA). IFBA is a consortium of the world's leading food and beverage companies, which are committed to establishing company-specific voluntary measures in order to ensure that their products will not be advertised to children under 12 years, unless they fulfill nutritional criteria based on accepted scientific evidence and/or applicable national and international dietary guidelines (IFBA, 2009). This global initiative is the fruit of various local and regional initiatives and continues to create commitments in other countries around the world.

The growing importance of the Internet as a medium for advertising has recently led to the creation of transnational codes on privacy issues in this field. Internet technologies allow for advertising to be targeted to individual consumers (Evans, 2009). The general term under which this practice of matching advertising with individual consumer interests is discussed is 'behavioral targeting'. This specific marketing technique uses data about the web browsing behavior of individual Internet users collected over a certain period of time. This data can consist of, for example, the page views, page clicks, ad views, ad clicks and search terms entered. This data is then used to form an interest profile of the web user. Mathematical algorithms calculate, in real-time, which advertisements should be served to the individual web user so that the ad meets the profile of the user. The ability to convey information to a targeted audience has been said to be a distinguishing feature of the Internet: it creates important competitive advantages over traditional media (print, television and radio) in the market for advertising (Bergemann and Bonnatti, 2010). However, it has also raised concerns for consumers and governments in terms of the privacy and data protection rights that web users enjoy (Article 29 Data Protection Working Party, 2010; European Commission, 2010; Federal Trade Commission, 2009).

In response to these concerns, the trade associations of the companies involved in behavioral targeting activities, which include digital media owners such as leading search engines owned by Google, Yahoo! and Microsoft, are developing new codes of conduct. In the US such a code materialized in 2000 and was recently updated in 2009 (Interactive Advertising Bureau et al., 2009), whilst in Europe an industry framework was put in place only very recently (Interactive Advertising Bureau Europe, 2011) and will be implemented by the online advertising industry throughout 2012 (EASA, 2011a). Rather than regulating issues of advertising content, these codes address the privacy concerns of consumers and governments, and, as such, promote transparency about the fact that online behavioral advertising is taking place and requires firms involved in these practices to offer the consumer an opt-out of behavioral targeting. Nonetheless, these codes build on the conventional enforcement mechanisms used to deal with disputes over advertising content (see below).

Co-existence with Legal Standards

A third characteristic of TPR of advertising practices is that it co-exists with legal standards governing the control of advertising conduct. The Consolidated ICC Code defines the relationship between public and private advertising standards by stressing in the first article that advertising and all other marketing communications 'should be legal, decent, honest and truthful'. More specifically, the preamble to the ICC code holds that the code should be applied against the background of whatever legislation may be applicable (ICC, 2011: 4). Therefore, the private regimes governing the conduct of advertising professionals seek to complement applicable public rules (Boddewyn, 1986).

Indeed, most regimes of private regulation in the advertising industry, whether national or transnational, have been established or developed further due to pressures that governments or international government bodies would adopt legislative measures if the industry would not (Boddewyn, 1988; Miracle and Nevett, 1987). Where governments believe the private regimes of advertising control are sufficiently robust, they also, to some extent, institutionalize complementarities with private regimes. The European Unfair Commercial Practices Directive,[3] for example, explicitly acknowledges the role private regulation plays in the regulation of advertising conduct. Articles 10 and 11 of the Directive enable Member States to give to courts or public agencies the discretion to require prior recourse to private regimes to settle disputes over advertising practices before these public enforcers take action. Indeed, a number of Member States, including the United Kingdom (UK), Spain and the Netherlands, have given this discretion to public agencies, thereby designing the way in which public and private enforcement action should complement each other's enforcement activities, namely in a sequential fashion (Cafaggi, 2009). Moreover, Article 6 of the Directive finds a commercial practice like advertising misleading if an advertiser fails to comply with a code of conduct. The Directive thus promotes the breach of codes of conduct to an infringement of statutory law. Such a finding is, however, conditional on the facts that the commitment of the business to the code is 'not merely aspirational', but 'firm' and 'verifiable', and that 'the trader indicates in a commercial practice that he is bound by the code' (Howells, 2006).

[3] Directive 2005/29/EC of the European Parliament and of the Council of 11 May 2005 concerning unfair business-to-consumer commercial practices in the internal market and amending Council Directive 84/450/EEC, Directives 97/7/EC, 98/27/EC and 2002/65/EC of the European Parliament and of the Council and Regulation (EC) No 2006/2004 of the European Parliament and of the Council ('Unfair Commercial Practices Directive') (OJ L 149, 11.6.2005, p. 22).

ENFORCEMENT OF TPR: A DECENTRALIZED MODEL

The multi-level governance character of TPR of advertising practices has strong implications for the way in which its standards are monitored and enforced. Instead of adopting a centralized body responsible for monitoring and enforcement, the transnational codes of conduct of the ICC and other transnational trade organizations stress that their rules and principles should be adopted and applied by national regimes. Monitoring and enforcement activities are indeed carried out in a strongly decentralized fashion, typically under the auspices of the private bodies administrating the national regimes, namely the SROs. SROs generally comprise three separate bodies: a standard-setting body, an enforcement body and a secretariat. The *standard-setting body* usually represents the constituent parts of the national ad industry – advertisers, agencies and media – and is responsible for the adoption of codes of conduct, whilst the *enforcement body* – often called 'jury' – assumes the task of interpreting these codes, handling incoming complaints submitted by competitors, consumers, non-governmental organizations (NGOs) or public authorities about publicized advertising, and deciding whether the litigious advertising complies with the applicable codes. The *secretariat* employs personnel to administer the daily operation of the SRO and has the task of promoting the private regulatory system among industry members and to the wider public (EASA, 2007: 13).

Copy advice, pre-clearance and complaint handling are the main avenues of enforcing private standards. Data made available by EASA suggests that in Europe around 60 000 copy advices are offered annually, while over 75 000 advertisements are pre-cleared by SROs per year. In addition, some 50 000 complaints are filed with European SROs on a yearly basis, which corresponds to approximately 15 000 unique ads. Some 60 percent of the complaints concern issues of taste and decency, social responsibility, and health and safety, while deceptiveness accounts for approximately 35 percent of the total complaints submitted in Europe (EASA, 2011b).

While the bulk of these enforcement activities thus take place at the national level, there is a transnational dimension to monitoring and enforcement. When EASA was established in 1992, it set up a system for handling cross-border complaints about advertising in Europe. This system was to enable the quick transfer of complaints lodged before an SRO in one European country to the SRO in the country where the editorial decision to publicize the advertising was made. Indeed, EASA does not itself adjudicate on the complaint, but simply refers it from one SRO to the other. Since 1992, the system has processed over 2000 complaints (EASA, 2010: 52).

EASA has also assumed a pivotal role in conducting pan-European monitoring exercises. In relation to food and alcohol advertising, the European food and alcohol ad industries have entrusted EASA with the task of coordinating such monitoring activities. In carrying out this task, EASA requests a number of its national SRO members to assess the code compliance of advertisements that have been collected in a database by a commercial third party over a certain time period. The feedback given by the individual SRO member is then compiled by EASA in a monitoring report and made available on its website. In 2009, EASA also launched a cross-border copy-advice and pre-clearance service, which enables advertisers and agencies to obtain advice on code conformity of advertising copy from the SRO relevant to the local market. The format adopted is similar to the cross-border complaint handling system and EASA does not offer advice or pre-vet the ads itself but simply refers it to the relevant SRO member.

At the global level, the Consolidated ICC Code provides for the possibility of inquiring about the interpretation of the principles in the code at the ICC Interpretation Panel.[4] However, this panel does not rule on individual cases and there are no public records of the activities of this panel. Alternatively, competitors may bring their advertising disputes before the ICC's International Court of Arbitration and require it to rule on the matter on the basis of the ICC codes. Again, however, no data is available as to how often advertising cases are adjudicated. In the case of the aforementioned IFBA Global Policy on Marketing and Advertising to Children, the company-specific standards banning the advertising of fatty and sugar-rich foods and beverages to children under 12 years old are monitored centrally. Here, third-party auditors are paid to draw up compliance reports on the participating companies (Accenture, 2009). However, there are no mechanisms in place to enforce the standards on participating companies should they fail to comply with the standards. Arguably, this seriously undermines the credibility of the whole initiative.

Why do we observe this decentralized model of enforcement? The decentered model can be explained by reference to the local impact advertising practices tend to have. The way in which advertising conveys its message is inspired by the preferences of the target audience. It is at this local level that advertising has its commercial and normative impact and needs to deliver its message. It therefore plays on local sentiments and opinions by using language, humor and sentiments. Complaints about advertising will inevitably relate to these matters, and bodies that operate at

---

4 Article 25 of the Consolidated ICC Code on Advertising and Marketing Communications Practices, read in conjunction with the Annex of this code.

the same level as that on which the advertising is used are likely to best address the concerns of deception, offensiveness or responsibility underlying the complaints. Centralizing the enforcement of transnational private standards would run counter to considerable practical obstacles as well. A centralized body would have to deal with an enormous caseload (over 50 000 complaints a year), which would most likely cripple the speed with which complaints are now resolved. In Europe, about two-thirds of complaints are settled within one month of submission (EASA, 2011b: 23).

The consequences of the decentralized model are obvious. The disconnection between rule-making at the transnational level and the enforcement of those rules at the national level results in a loss of uniformity in the application of the rules. The question is whether this matters. While the ICC codes or other transnational private standards allow for diversity in application of the transnational norms, such diversity may induce regulatory obstacles for traders. Advertising campaigns have become increasingly international and target consumers in different regional markets through uniform formats (De Mooij, 2010; Walters et al., 2008). The costs prompted by the existence of multiple national private regulatory regimes could pose an obstacle to cross-border advertising, and it was exactly this concern that motivated the European Commission in the early 1990s to pressure the European ad industry to mitigate the differences in national private regimes. EASA was created to address this concern and maintains a close rapport with the Commission on its activities. Still today, the Commission keeps up a strong pressure on EASA to innovate and reduce divergence among the national regimes for the control of advertising practices (European Commission, 2006), in particular in the area of digital media advertising and behavioral targeting (European Commission, 2010).

VARIABLES IN DESIGNING NATIONAL ENFORCEMENT MECHANISMS

There are three key variables to the way in which private enforcement mechanisms are designed and operated by SROs at the national level. They concern: the timing of the enforcement activity; the participation of non-industry members in adjudication; and the remedies and sanctions available to promote and ensure compliance. These variables are discussed here with reference to the practice of several well-established European SROs.

Timing

SROs seek to ensure that advertising practices comply with the applicable codes of conduct both before (*ex ante*) and after (*ex post*) they are used in the public domain. The *ex post* control comprises the handling of complaints by a separate enforcement body of the SRO – the jury. The two principal mechanisms for the *ex ante* control of advertising practices, on the other hand, are the instruments of copy advice and pre-clearance. In these instances, advertisers or advertising agencies submit their advertising campaign to the SRO – either the SRO secretariat or a separate SRO – prior to its use in the public domain, in order to receive a preliminary indication on the compliance of the campaign with the private codes in force. In the case of copy advice this is done voluntarily, whilst pre-clearance implies a duty to submit copy to an inspection body prior to publication. This obligation can follow from statutory laws, broadcast licenses, contracts, or may be imposed as a sanction by the SRO jury. The importance of these *ex ante* compliance assessments should not be underestimated. All other things being equal, the use of copy advice and pre-clearance increases levels of code compliance of advertisements and reduces the need to take enforcement action *ex post*.

The extent to which the national regimes rely on the *ex ante* or *ex post* mechanisms of control varies greatly. For example, the French SRO, *l'Autorité de Regulation Professionnelle de la Publicité* (Authority for Professional Regulation of Advertising, ARPP), is characterized by its strong reliance on *ex ante* control mechanisms. Copy advice on advertising and pre-clearance of television commercials constitute the main activities of the SRO. In 2009, the SRO secretariat gave 15 196 non-binding advices on the compatibility of copy for radio, the Internet and printed advertising. The copy advice suggested in 9457 cases (62 percent) the amendment of the ad and in about 656 (4 percent) that the ad should not be published at all. As for the pre-clearance activities, 20 566 television advertisements were surveyed in 2009. Out of these 2407 (12 percent) were required to be modified. The *ex post* control activities the SRO jury pursues are much more limited. In 2008, only 518 consumer complaints were handled by the enforcement body (ARPP, 2009).

By contrast, the German and Dutch SROs have a much less strong reliance on *ex ante* control mechanisms. As a general rule, advertising is not pre-cleared in Germany, since this is historically associated with censorship. Further, the *Deutsche Werberat* (German Advertising Council), which is competent to address only issues of taste and decency in advertising, has, just recently, in 2009, started up a copy-advice service, which has handled only a few requests so far. Until recently, the Dutch SRO, *Stichting Reclame*

Code (Advertising Code Foundation, SRC), also relied completely on a complaint handling mechanism to secure compliance with private regulatory norms. However, in 2008 it established a new service that has slowly started taking on requests for copy advice. Pre-clearance is generally not required, except for the advertising of alcoholic beverages and non-prescription medicines and health products, which is carried out by industry-specific private pre-vetting bodies.

Outside Participation

Non-industry members have been included in the enforcement of codes of conduct in three particular ways. They may act: (i) as *complainants* by submitting complaints about advertising to the SRO; (ii) as a *litigator* by being a party to the dispute dealt with before the SRO jury; and (iii) as an *adjudicator* by being member of the SRO jury and deciding whether practices are compliant with the applicable codes. Complaints submitted by consumers constitute the principal source of complaints handled by SROs. Some 75 percent of the complaints come from consumers, while competitors (20 percent), NGOs (4 percent) and public authorities (1 percent) account for the rest (EASA, 2011b: 21).

The submission of complaints by consumers, consumer groups and NGOs may be said to serve three general aims. First, the submission of complaints by these third parties presents a cost-efficient alternative to monitoring policies. Complaint-handling mechanisms mean that, for consumers, the process of making a complaint is easy, fast, and incurs a low cost, if any at all. Where the SRO enjoys familiarity and reputation among these third parties, and these parties are willing to submit their complaints to the SRO, the SRO is assured of a constant feed of complaints from which it can distil the most pertinent cases which require adjudication before its jury. Second, complaint-handling mechanisms can be used as a proxy by the industry to test applicable codes against current social opinion. Trends in complaints feed standard-setting procedures and may lead to the enactment of new codes. Third, complaint-handling mechanisms also serve as a safety valve, allowing consumers to 'blow off steam' (Ramsay, 2007: 445). Advertising may at times be shocking and repulsive to some. Complaint mechanisms then help to ease such reactions and show that the industry is concerned about social values.

Second, non-industry members can be involved in SRO enforcement processes as party to the dispute, that is, as litigator. This possibility is, however, subject to the rules of procedure governing the complaint handling process. The British Advertising Standards Authority (ASA), for example, does not grant complainants standing in the procedure. In addition, no provision is made for oral hearings.[5] Instead, designated teams of the SRO assume responsibility over a complaint once it is filed, assess the complaint on its merits and collect necessary evidence to construct a reasoned draft recommendation on the complaint.[6] Much like a public prosecutor in the case of criminal proceedings, SRO staff prepare the case, do the fact-finding – even *ex officio*[7] – and determine the scope of the dispute. The SRO jury, the ASA Council, is there primarily to control the pre-trial investigation, and adjudicates on the basis of the draft recommendation.

In France and the Netherlands, by contrast, a more prominent role has been given to the complainant as litigant. Here, the complainant can present and argue its case before the SRO jury, thus allowing him or her to be actively involved in the dispute.[8] This seems most relevant in disputes between competitors, where the complaining competitor may want to bring scientific evidence rebutting the claims made by the advertiser. Accordingly, these procedures assume a more adversarial character.

Finally, non-industry members are also involved in enforcement processes as adjudicators. In Europe this practice became commonplace after the European Commission pressed the advertising industry to increase independence and impartiality in complaint adjudication (European Commission, 2006). Now, 21 of the 25 EASA SRO members include non-industry members in the composition of the juries presiding in first instance and in appeal (if available) (EASA, 2010: 237). These persons can be consumers, NGO representatives, lawyers, judges, academics, former public officials, laymen, etc. Government officials are not included in the jury composition. In several systems, the Chairperson of the jury is an honorable person who is not associated with the industry. In the United Kingdom, for example, this is a member of the Supreme Court, while in France

---

5 Paragraph 28, Non-Broadcast Complaint Handling Procedures (ASA, 2008) reads: 'The investigation executive will present the recommendation to the [jury], which adjudicates. No provision is made for oral hearings.'

6 Paragraph 26, Non-Broadcast Complaint Handling Procedures holds: 'On receipt of the response and any further written comments or clarification [of the industry member], the investigation executive will analyse the case and prepare a draft recommendation.'

7 Paragraph 11, Non-Broadcast Complaint Handling Procedures holds: '[the SRO] might itself initiate an investigation into what it believes are potential Code breaches …'.

8 Article 14, Règlement Intérieur Jury de Déontologie Publicitaire (ARPP, 2010) and Article 14(2), Reglement betreffende de Reclame Code Commissie en het College van Beroep (SRC, 2009).

it is a member of the *Conseil d'Etat* who chairs the SRO jury. In sharp contrast with common European practice sits the *Deutscher Werberat*, which is only composed of industry representatives and does not allow outsiders to participate.

The participation of non-industry members as adjudicators may help to inform decision-making and ensure that industry and non-industry concerns are balanced properly. It also signals to outsiders credibility and independence from the industry, in particular where a non-industry stakeholder chairs the jury. The signal of industry independence becomes even stronger where no industry representatives sit on the SRO jury, which is, for example, the case in France. Importantly, the participation of non-industry stakeholders as adjudicators might challenge the strong industry ownership of the rules. Where the jury is composed of a majority of non-industry persons, the final application and interpretation of the rules is no longer in the hands of industry. Indeed, where the SRO jury enjoys a large degree of independence, its rule-shaping activities may suggest a different scope or interpretation of the rules as originally meant by the standard setter. This may lead to concerns amongst the national industry members that the jury would 'walk away' with the rules.

The participation of non-industry stakeholders in adjudication is thus an important element in preventing regulatory capture of the SRO jury. The term 'capture' is conventionally used to suggest that a public regulator created to warrant public interests (e.g. environmental protection, food safety, or consumer protection) in a particular industry or sector does not fully ensure these interests, but instead pursues the interests of the industry that it was held to oversee. Private regulation implicitly suggests already a large degree of capture where the regulator coincides with the regulated. However, the inclusion of non-industry members is an important strategy to mitigate the risk of capture. Since capture may prevent any real enforcement action from happening, such inclusion is also crucial to the effectiveness of the enforcement activities overseen by the SROs.

Remedies and Sanctions

Once a complaint has been upheld in the adjudication before the SRO jury, it will seek to remedy the non-compliant situation or impose sanctions on the code offender. SROs do not provide for redress mechanisms. The industry views the decision that the ad cannot be used as a sufficiently strong deterrent since the investments made in the creation of the ad will be lost (EASA, 2010: 20). Claim substantiation has been described as an important alternative remedy to misleading advertising and is recognized by the Consolidated ICC Code (Article 8) and is also part of North

American and European commercial practices law (Maxeiner and Schotthöfer, 1999). Claim substantiation requires that advertisers support the claims made in the advertising by documentary proof. One obvious benefit is that it significantly reduces enforcement costs as it effectively reverses the burden of proof (Ramsay, 2007: 422). This evidently lowers the threshold for submitting complaints, in particular for consumers.

In addition to claim substantiation, SROs typically have the competence to order the advertiser, agency, or media involved to halt its campaign. Such decision has the same function as a cease-and-desist order. Alternatively, the SRO can require the advertiser to amend the advertisement in point so that it conforms to the code. In this case, the advertiser can continue to use the campaign, but has to modify the content or its manner of publication such that it meets the jury decision. In case of such affirmative injunctions the SRO secretariat might help the advertiser or agency to adjust the ad to achieve code compliance. The British and Irish SROs, for example, can even require that the advertiser submits all of its advertising copy to the SRO for prior vetting for a period of time. Occasionally, SROs may also be able to restrict the time for using an ad in broadcast media. Such a prohibitive injunction can imply, for example, that a TV commercial for an alcoholic beverage can only appear after 10 p.m. during weekdays, when the chances that children and minors are watching television are lower.

Further, the SROs impose sanctions on code violators. The sanctions typically at the disposal of the SROs include the denial of access to media, adverse publicity, 'ad alerts', and referral to public authorities. The denial of media access is the result of the participation of media owners in the private regimes. This involvement is a crucial element for the effective enforcement of codes of conduct. A substantial part of the advertising produced today requires a medium to target its audience. Television, radio, newspapers, magazines, postal services, Internet service providers, constitute a natural barrier to advertisers before they can reach potential customers. Given their intermediary role, media owners can act as gatekeepers and halt most of the non-compliant ads. When involved in the SRO structures, the media thus give teeth to the private regimes and can effectively prevent or stop the use of non-compliant advertising in a fast and inexpensive way. The involvement of media owners is therefore considered essential to establish an effective SRO (EASA, 2004).

Adverse publicity follows from the publication of each jury decision in the SRO monthly magazine and on its website. The naming and shaming this incites is viewed by the industry as a strong deterrent, but academics have viewed adverse publicity as a 'somewhat unreliable form of sanction', since SROs 'cannot control the incidence, amount, timing, location, editorial content etc of any such publicity' (Parry, 2000: 147). Moreover, such publicity is only likely to affect companies with strong consumer brands, which typically want to avoid reputational harm. So-called 'ad alerts' constitute a specific form of adverse publicity. In this case, a notification is sent to the press and other media warning the public about a specific advertisement or campaign. This happens only rarely and typically in cases where the advertiser is a repeat offender or simply does not intend to comply with the jury decision, or where the infringement is so severe that the chances of its affecting a large group of consumers are very high.

Further, the SROs may be able to refer cases they cannot settle of their own accord to administrative authorities, typically those that are competent in the area of fair competition, consumer protection law, broadcast media or data protection. However, such referrals are exceptional, and if they do happen, the referral is made at a very late stage. In the UK, for example, the low-cost airline Ryanair refused to comply with a number of SRO jury decisions that held its Internet advertising to offend standards of the British code of advertising practice prohibiting deceptive advertising over a period of two years. Eventually, the ASA referred the case to the Office of Fair Trading (OFT) in 2008, the previous case being in 2005 (ASA, 2009: 4). The OFT announced only in July 2009 that Ryanair had agreed to alter its ads (OFT, 2009). The fact that referrals are made only seldom and often at a rather late stage can be explained, on the one hand, by the reluctance of some SROs to report their own members to the public authorities, and, on the other, by the restrictive conditions that apply for referral. Public authorities, if in place, cannot and do not accept all cases that SROs report, mainly for two reasons. First, the competence of public authorities is typically restricted to deceptive and comparative advertising; issues of taste and decency fall outside the scope of their powers.[9] As noted above, these 'soft' issues account for the majority of complaints submitted in Europe. Further, the powers of public agencies may be restricted in their application to offences that harm the 'collective interests of consumers'.[10] Public authorities need to prioritize and carefully allocate their restricted enforcement budgets. Where the advertising does not constitute a grave infringement of consumer rights or does not greatly undermine the economic interests of consumers, they are unlikely to intervene.

In exceptional cases, private regimes can also impose fines or require them to make corrective statements, which is an obligation to publish a statement rectifying the initial false advertising. These sanctions are only administered on the basis of a contract between the private regime and a

---

9 Recital 7 and Article 5(2)(b), Directive 2005/29/EC.

10 See for the UK s.211(1)(c), Enterprise Act 2002.

trade organization. In Belgium and the Netherlands, for example, the SRO juries are allowed to impose a fine in the case of non-compliant ads for alcoholic beverages. Further, statutory law might give SROs the power to sue advertisers or agencies to protect industry or public interests. In extreme cases, SRO juries may decide to expel the industry member from the association. It will be the trade association that carries out that sanction of last resort.

The image that emerges is that while SRO juries have a substantive arsenal of remedies and sanctions at their disposal, they prefer to make use of only a few and will resort to more deterrent means only if the consensual approach has failed. Quantative data, although generally sparse, can be used to support this claim. Table 11.1 gives an overview of the decisions on unique advertisements by the jury of the SRO operating in Belgium, the *Jury d'Ethique Publicitaire* (JEP) in the period 2004–2009.

Table 11.1 Decisions by JEP

	2004	2005	2006	2007	2008	2009
No jurisdiction	0	2	1	2	6	4
Compliance	61	87	86	117	144	71
Opinion d'avis	12	14	12	10	14	3
Cease-and-desist order	33	58	57	67	218	93
Denial of media access	9	6	4	3	3	10
Other sanctions (referral, fine, compensatory damages, etc.)	1	0	0	0	0	0
Total	116	167	160	199	385	181

Sources: JEP, 2009; JEP, 2010.

Table 11.1 shows that the Belgian SRO was able to settle the bulk of the disputes by ordering the advertiser or agency to withdraw or amend the advertising in question. Where the advertiser or agency did not voluntarily comply with the decision of the jury, the jury turned to the media to stop the advertisement in question from reappearing. This proved necessary in only a limited number of cases. Only once in the period 2004–2009 was an advertiser required to offer compensation to the claimant. Since 2005, the JEP has concluded a covenant with the national alcohol industry allowing it to impose fines for non-compliance with the applicable sector-specific code. So far, however, the competence has never been used.

In the application of remedies and sanctions SRO juries have obvious preferences: cease-and-desist orders directed to advertisers and agencies are preferred over other means. SRO juries only impose other, more intrusive remedies or sanctions if this first approach does not have the desired effect, that is, rule-compliance. Accordingly, SROs use, either implicitly or explicitly, a sanction escalation policy to respond to non-compliance. This practice of graduated sanctions or enforcement pyramids has been observed in relation to other public and private regimes as well (Ostrom, 1990; Ayres and Braithwaite, 1992). Figure 11.1 offers an illustration of the policy that is typically applied by an SRO.

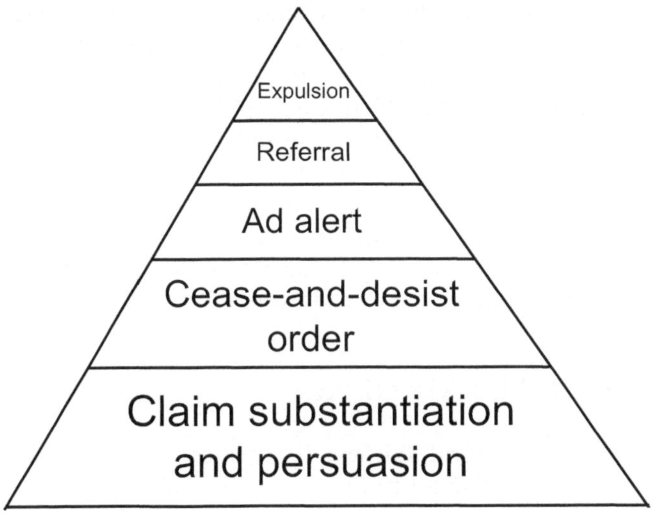

Source: Adapted from Ayres and Braithwaite (1992).

Figure 11.1 Example of an SRO sanction escalation policy

How can this particular approach to enforcement be explained? The objective of private regulation in the advertising industry seems crucial here. Its principal aim is to improve ethical standards amongst advertising practitioners by promoting advertising that is legal, fair, not misleading, in good taste and socially responsible (Boddewyn, 1989: 24). The enforcement activities undertaken by SROs follow this aim proactively by persuading the practitioners involved to amend or stop their irresponsible conduct and educating them to (better) comply with the rules in the future. The copy advice and pre-clearance facilities, as well as the pre-jury trial procedures, in which the advertisers and agencies can substantiate their claims and disputes are settled amicably, are particularly functional here. They facilitate a learning process and correct non-compliance at an early stage. The application of deterrent sanctions to violations of the codes of advertising practices does not fit neatly with the rationales of learning and prevention and would require codes of conduct to assume more law-like attributes, including punitive and deterrent sanctions and more precise wording.

Moreover, and as noted above, SROs are often concerned with issues that are considered by courts and public agencies as 'trivial' or 'soft' and outside their legal mandates. Here, the SROs fill an important gap left by more restrictive competencies of public enforcement institutions, which have, as a result of this, generally been very reluctant to address these matters. In fact, the lack of court jurisdiction to deal with issues of taste and decency, and non-discrimination motivated the establishment of SRO countries such as Germany (Reich and Micklitz, 1981: 75). Important to acknowledge, however, is that the issues of taste and decency do not lend themselves easily to be controlled through remedies and sanctions with compensatory or punitive rationales. These matters do not so much contradict legal standards on unfair competition or consumer protection, but standards of morality, integrity and ethics. Accordingly, different, more lenient approaches seem appropriate to address non-compliance.

PROCEDURAL FAIRNESS

Standards of procedural fairness (or justice) seek to ensure that the proceedings before dispute resolution bodies take place in an impartial fashion and that the parties to the dispute are treated on an equal basis. A general and widely accepted legal standard for procedural fairness is Article 6 of the European Convention on Human Rights (ECHR), which requires that in the determination of civil rights or obligations, or of any criminal charge, everyone is entitled to a fair and public hearing within a reasonable time before an independent and impartial tribunal established by law. Measured against this legal benchmark, the enforcement of private advertising standards by SRO juries raises a number of concerns. First, SRO adjudications are typically not open to the public and take place behind closed doors. Second, while juries usually include non-industry members, full impartiality from the industry is not guaranteed as industry representatives usually participate in the decision-making. Third, the right to defense is undermined by the fact that (oral) hearings are generally not provided for or even excluded in proceedings. Finally, while SROs often provide a possibility to appeal their jury decisions, the appeal does not usually take place before a different institution but generally amounts to a review procedure pursued before the same institution including the same decision-makers as at first instance.

In the face of these shortcomings the question emerges to what extent the adjudication procedures of the SROs can be considered in the light of standards of procedural fairness such as ECHR Article 6. Do these standards apply to SRO jury proceedings? The private enforcement activities can be deemed acceptable to the extent that they are fundamentally based on the notion that those submitted to the control of private enforcement regimes do so voluntarily. Indeed, private actors that want to waive their rights under ECHR Article 6 and subscribe to another enforcement regime can do so, provided that they unequivocally abandon these rights of their own accord (*Neumeister* v *Austria*, E.C.H.R, Series A, no. 17 (1974), 15–16 and *Colozza* v *Italy*, E.C.H.R., Series A, no. 89 (1985), 14).

This raises a subsequent question, namely just how voluntary are the private systems of enforcement? As a general approach, the SROs claim and assume to have jurisdiction over all advertising of which the editorial decision to use that advertising was made in their country. This implies that SROs cast judgments over the advertising practices of companies that have not explicitly subscribed to the private regime. Decisions by the SRO jury passed against such third parties can well lead to a block of the use of their advertising, as advertising agencies involved in the creation of the ad, or media that carry the ad, have subscribed to the private regime and are obliged to follow the SRO jury decisions on the basis of the SRO statute, rules of association or contract. In addition, statutory law or public agencies might require media owners to sign up to the private regulatory scheme, thus imposing membership on them.[11] In other instances, public authorities might delegate competences to the SRO, making it a semi-public institution exercising public powers.[12] As a consequence of the

[11] This is, for example, the case in the Netherlands, where the Media Law (*Mediawet*) obliges all broadcasters to be a member of the Dutch SRO. In the UK, on the other hand, the Office of Communications (OFCOM) has made compliance with the SRO enforcement decisions by media broadcasters a condition to obtain and extend licenses for their commercial activities, thereby effectively making adherence by broadcasters to SRO decisions legally binding.

[12] This is, for example, the case in the UK. Here, OFCOM has delegated its rule-making and enforcement powers as regards advertising to the British SRO via the Authorisation of the Contracting Out (Functions relating to Broadcasting Advertising) and Specification of Relevant Functions Order, SI 1975/2004.

enrollment of advertising agencies, and, in particular, media in the SRO structures, advertisers may see their ads stopped from (re)appearing much against their will. Third parties may therefore be directly affected by SRO-led enforcement activities without their consent.

The binding effect that the SRO enforcement activities might *de iure* or *de facto* have on third-party advertisers can thus be quite considerable. In the UK, the public function the SRO assumed in controlling advertising practices has triggered the application of ECHR Article 6, and jury decisions have been tested against this standard of procedural rights (*SmithKline Beecham PLC* v *Advertising Standards Authority*, 21 December 2000, [2000] EWHC Admin 442). Also other common standards of (administrative) procedural law, such as the duty to give reasons for decisions, consistency in the rulings and the use of precedent, and the standard of proof used in the SRO adjudication process might become relevant where private regimes assume a public function. Longitudinal research on the adjudication practice of the Dutch SRC, one of the best-established and funded SROs in Europe, reveals that such standards are not completely guaranteed (Venekatte, 2002). In particular, the analysis of the practice of the adjudicative bodies in the Dutch SRO shows that little use is made of expert reports and witnesses' hearings to prove assumptions made by the jurors. Also, it occurs rather frequently that jury decisions on disputes with a similar factual background have radically opposing outcomes and that no reasons are given in the decisions to explain such deviations (Venekatte, 2002: 576–80).

From a legal point of view, the situations in which private regimes can affect the conduct of industry members without their voluntary submission to the private regulatory regime should be viewed with a degree of suspicion (Widdershoven, 1999). The rules and procedures remain private in nature and only have legally binding effect *inter partes*. Where private regulatory regimes can nonetheless unilaterally exert influence on the practice of third parties, thereby restricting their rights, judicial review is considered a necessary mechanism to remedy this involuntary control (Black, 1998). In other words, the availability of judicial review is viewed as a crucial means to ensure the legitimacy and accountability of the private regime vis-à-vis third parties that are negatively affected by the enforcement activities of the SROs.

The availability of judicial review becomes even more crucial where the private regimes assume a public function or have been delegated specific tasks or legal powers. In these cases, the SROs can, either by their function or delegated competences, exert considerable influence on the exercise of the rights of individuals who did not explicitly consent to the applicable private law codes and procedures. However, in only a limited number of jurisdictions, such as the UK and New Zealand, have SRO decisions been held susceptible to judicial review (*Advertising Standards Authority Ltd v The Insurance Service Plc* (1989) ALR 77; *Electoral Commission v Cameron* [1997] 2 NZLR 421). In other countries, civil court proceedings based on negligence, libel or other types of non-contractual liability might offer affected third parties an alternative legal avenue to challenge allegedly wrongful SRO decisions and/or prevent the enforcement of those decisions (Verbruggen, forthcoming).

CONCLUSION

This chapter has sought to outline the key characteristics of the enforcement of TPR of advertising practices and highlight the type of concerns such enforcement throws up in terms of procedural fairness. Private standards governing the commercial practice of advertising are adopted at a transnational level but function primarily as an authoritative blueprint for national private regimes to adopt and adjust codes of conduct of their own. While transnational and national rule-making activities are thus conflated, the regulatory functions of monitoring and enforcement are even more decentralized, being carried out primarily at the local level. Here, national trade associations have established or mandated SROs to administer the application of codes of conduct, which might be either transnational or national in nature. In Europe, EASA has coordinated and managed the diversity between SRO code adoption and enforcement activities since the early 1990s, but has not engaged in monitoring or enforcement itself. Instead, it operates as a facilitator for cross-border monitoring or enforcement activities.

An initial assessment of the enforcement practices of the national SROs indicates that these practices may raise considerable concerns in the light of common standards of procedural fairness. Here, further research should develop a better understanding of the extent to which standards of fair procedures and general principles of administrative (procedural) law can be applied to SRO enforcement activities and the extent to which SRO decision-making practices comply with these standards and principles.

BIBLIOGRAPHY

Abbott, K.W. and D. Snidal (2009), 'Strengthening International Regulation through Transnational New Governance: Overcoming the Orchestration Deficit', *Vanderbilt Journal of Transnational Law*, **42** (2), 501–78.

Accenture (2009), 'Compliance Monitoring of Global Advertising for Television, Print, and Internet for the International Food & Beverage Alliance', available at: https://www.ifballiance.org/sites/default/files/IFBA%20Compliance%20Monitoring%20Report%2010%20Nov09.pdf (accessed 30 April 2011).

ARPP (2009), 'Activité 2008', available at: www.arpp-pub.org (accessed 30 April 2011).

ARPP (2010), 'Règlement Intérieur Jury de Déontologie Publicitaire', available at: www.jdp-pub.org (accessed 30 April 2011).

Article 29 Data Protection Working Party (2010), 'Opinion 2/2010 on online behavioural advertising' (Ref. 00909/10/EN WP 171, Brussels 2010), available at: http://ec.europa.eu/justice/policies/privacy/docs/wpdocs/2010/wp171_en.pdf (accessed 30 April 2011).

ASA (2008), 'Non-broadcast Complaint Handling Procedures', available at: www.asa.org.uk (accessed 30 April 2011).

ASA (2009), 'Annual Report 2008', available at: www.asa.org.uk (accessed 30 April 2011).

Ayres, Ian and John Braithwaite (1992), *Responsive Regulation: Transcending the Deregulation Debate* (Oxford Socio-Legal Studies), New York: Oxford University Press.

Bergemann, D. and A. Bonnatti (2010), 'Targeting in Advertising Markets: Implications for Offline v Online Media', Cowles Foundation for Research in Economics at Yale University Discussion Paper No. 1758, available at: http://ssrn.com/abstract=1577691 (accessed 30 April 2011).

Bernstein, S. and B. Cashore (2007), 'Can Non-state Global Governance be Legitimate? An Analytical Framework', *Regulation & Governance*, **1** (4), 347–71.

Black, J. (1998), 'Reviewing Regulatory Rules: Responsibility and Hybridisation', in Julia Black, Peter Muchlinski and Paul Walker (eds), *Commercial Regulation and Judicial Review*, Oxford, UK and Portland, OR: Hart Publishing, pp. 123–57.

Black, J. (2008), 'Constructing and Contesting Legitimacy and Accountability in Polycentric Regulatory Regimes', *Regulation & Governance*, **2** (2), 137–64.

Boddewyn, J.J. (1986), 'Advertising Self-Regulation: Organization Structures in Belgium, Canada, France and the United Kingdom', in W. Streeck and P. Schmitter (eds), *Private Interest Government*, London: Sage, pp. 30–43.

Boddewyn, Jean J. (1988), *Advertising Self-Regulation and Outside Participation: A Multinational Comparison*, New York: Quorum Books.

Boddewyn, Jean J. (1989), 'Advertising Self-regulation: True Purposes and Limits', *Journal of Advertising*, **18** (2), 19–27.

Boddewyn, Jean J. (1992), *Global Perspectives on Advertising Self-Regulation: Principles and Practices in Thirty-eight Countries*, Westport, CT and London: Quorum Books.

Brandmair, Lothar (1978), *Die freiwillige Selbstkontrolle der Werbung*, Cologne: Cad Heymanns.

Brewers of Europe (2003), 'Guidelines for Commercial Communications for Beer', available at: http://www.brewersofeurope.org/ (accessed 30 April 2011).
Cafaggi, F. (2009), 'The Great Transformation – Public and Private Enforcement in Consumer Protection: A Remedial Perspective', *Loyola Consumer Law Review*, **21** (4), 496–539.
CEEV (Comité Européen des Entreprises Vins) (2009), 'EU Wine Communication Standards', available at: http://www.ceev.be/ (accessed 30 April 2011).
Cunningham, Anne (2000), 'Advertising Self-regulation in a Broader Context: An Examination of the European Union's Regulatory Environment', *Journal of Promotion Management*, **5** (2), 61–83.
De Mooij, Marieke (2010), *Global Marketing and Advertising: Understanding Cultural Paradoxes*, 3rd edn, Thousand Oaks, CA: Sage.
EASA (2004), 'EASA Best Practice Self-Regulatory Model', available at: http://www.easa-alliance.org/ (accessed 30 April 2011).
EASA (2007), *Advertising Self-Regulation in Europe: An Analysis of Self-Regulatory Systems and Code of Advertising Practice*, 5th edn, Brussels: Poot Printers.
EASA (2009), 'International Guide to Developing a Self-regulatory Organization. Practical Advice on Setting Up and Consolidating an Advertising Self-regulatory System', available at: http://www.easa-alliance.org/ (accessed 30 April 2011).
EASA (2010), *Advertising Self-Regulation in Europe: An Analysis of Self-Regulatory Systems and Code of Advertising Practice*, 6th edn, Brussels: Poot Printers.
EASA (2011a), 'Best Practice Recommendation on Online Behavioural Advertising. Setting Out a European Advertising Industry-wide Self-regulatory Standard and Compliance Mechanism for Consumer Controls in Online Behavioural Advertising', available at: http://www.easa-alliance.org/binarydata.aspx?type=doc/EASA_BPR_OBA_12_APRIL_2011_CLEAN.pdf/download (accessed 30 April 2011).
EASA (2011b), 'European Trends in Advertising Complaints, Copy Advice and Pre-clearance', available at: http://www.easa-alliance.org/ (accessed 30 April 2011).
EFRD (European Forum for Responsible Drinking) (2008), 'Common Standards for Commercial Communications for Spirits', available at: http://www.efrd.org/ (accessed 30 April 2011).
European Commission (Directorate-General Health & Consumer Protection) (2006), 'Self-Regulation and the Advertising Sector: A Report of Some Discussion among Interested Parties', available at: http://ec.europa.eu/dgs/health_consumer/self_regulation/docs/report_advertising_en.pdf (accessed 30 April 2011).
European Commission (2010), 'Towards More Confidence and More Value for European Digital Citizens', Speech delivered by Neelie Kroes Vice-President of the European Commission responsible for the Digital Agenda at the European Roundtable on the Benefits of Online Advertising for Consumers, Brussels, 17 September 2010.
Evans, D.S. (2009), 'The Online Advertising Industry: Economics, Evolution, and Privacy', *Journal of Economic Perspectives*, **23** (3), 37–60.
Federal Trade Commission (2009), 'Self-Regulatory Principles for Online Behavioral Advertising', available at: http://www.ftc.gov/os/2009/02/P085400behavadreport.pdf (accessed 30 April 2011).

Howells, G. (2006), 'Codes of Conduct', in Geraint Howells, Hans-W. Micklitz and Thomas Wilhelmsson (eds), *European Fair Trading Law: The Unfair Commercial Practices Directive*, Aldershot: Ashgate, pp. 193–215.

ICC (2006), 'ICC Framework for Responsible Food and Beverage Communications', available at: http://www.iccwbo.org/ (accessed 30 September 2010).

ICC (2011), 'Consolidated ICC Code of Advertising and Marketing Communication Practice', available at: http://www.codescentre.com/ (accessed 30 April 2011).

IFBA (2009), 'Global Policy on Marketing and Advertising to Children', available at: https://www.ifballiance.org/ (accessed 30 April 2011).

Interactive Advertising Bureau, Council of Better Business Bureaus, the Direct Marketing Association, the American Association of Advertising Agencies, the Association of National Advertisers, and the Network Advertising Initiative (2009), 'Self-Regulatory Principles for Online Behavioral Advertising', http://www.iab.net/media/file/ven-principles-07–01–09.pdf (accessed 30 April 2011).

Interactive Advertising Bureau Europe (2011), 'European Self-regulation for Online Behavioural Advertising. Transparency and Control for Consumers', available at: http://www.iabeurope.eu/media/51925/iab%20europe%20oba%20framework_merged%20ii.pdf (accessed 30 April 2011).

JEP (2009), *Rapport d'Activites 2008*, available at: http://www.jep.be/ (accessed 30 April 2011).

JEP (2010), *Rapport d'Activites 2009*, available at: http://www.jep.be/ (accessed 30 April 2011).

Maxeiner, James R. and Peter Schotthöfer (eds) (1999), *Advertising Law in Europe and North America*, 2nd edn, The Hague, London and Boston: Kluwer Law International.

Miracle, G.E. and T.R. Nevett (1987), *Voluntary Regulation of Advertising: A Comparative Analysis of the United Kingdom and the United States*, Toronto: Lexington Books.

Office of Fair Trading (2009), 'Ryanair Improves the Clarity of its Website and Advertising' (press release), available at: http://www.oft.gov.uk/ (accessed 30 April 2011).

Ostrom, E. (1990), *Governing the Commons: The Evolution of Institutions for Collective Action*, Cambridge: Cambridge University Press.

Parry, Deborah L. (2000), 'The Future of Voluntary Regulation of Advertising', *Consumer Law Journal*, **8**, 137–59.

PriceWaterhouseCoopers (2010), 'IAB Internet Advertising Revenue Report', available at: http://www.iab.net/media/file/IAB-Ad-Revenue-Full-Year-2009.pdf (accessed 30 April 2011).

Ramsay, I. (2007), *Consumer Law and Policy: Text and Materials on Regulating Consumer Markets*, 2nd edn, Oxford and Portland, OR: Hart Publishing.

Reich, Norbert and H.-W. Micklitz (1981), *Consumer Legislation in the EC Countries: A Comparative Analysis*, New York: Van Nostrand Reinhold Co.

SRC (2009), 'Reglement betreffende de Reclame Code Commissie en het College van Beroep', available at: http://www.reclamecode.nl/ (accessed 30 April 2011).

Venekatte, Elizabeth (2002), 'Open Normen in de Reclame: Een Onderzoek naar de Uitspraken van de Reclame Code Commissie, haar College van Beroep en de Rechter in de Periode van 1982 tot 2000', PhD thesis, University of Twente, Enschede.

Walters, P.G.P., P. Whitla and H. Davies (2008), 'Global Strategy in the International Advertising Industry', *International Business Review*, **17** (3), 235–49.

WBZ (Wettbewerbszentrale) (2010), *Jahresbericht 2009*, available at: http://www.wettbewerbszentrale.de/ (accessed 30 April 2011).

Widdershoven, R. (1999), 'Enforcement of EC Regulation by Private Organisations: A Public Law Wolf in Private Law Sheep's Clothing?', in Jan Vervaele (ed.), *Enforcement and Compliance in EC Law*, The Hague: Kluwer Law International, pp. 235–46.

PART IV

Conclusion

12. The enforcement of transnational private regulation: a fictitious oxymoron

Sabino Cassese, Elisa D'Alterio and Maurizia De Bellis[1]

1. THE CONCEPT OF TPR: SOME CAVEATS

The concepts used when discussing TPR are ambiguous. Four caveats are necessary: (a) what TPR is, and, given that public–private distinction outside state regulation is very slippery, how private it is; (b) TRP enforcement terminology may be an oxymoron; (c) enforcement is a polysemous word; (d) enforcement is not a 'one-stop shopping' procedure.

(a) A definition of private regulation should be provided and just how private TPR is should be established. There can be three answers to these questions and all of them are featured in this book.

The first answer is the following: that TPR is fundamentally self-regulation. In other words, private regulation is non-State, market driven regulation.

A second answer assumes that TPR is private, but not as private as regulation inside the State is. It is private, but remote. It is far away from the regulatees, because the regulators are in other parts of the world, such as Geneva, or Washington, and the like.

The third answer is that TPR is not entirely private. The public–private distinction derives from categories traditional to State regulation of business, while TPR is mixed: different actors, for instance governments, NGOs

---

[1] This chapter is based on the conclusions of Professor Sabino Cassese presented at the Workshop 'Enforcement of Transnational Private Regulation', at the European University Institute, Fiesole (FI), May 14–15 2010. Elisa D'Alterio wrote Sections 4 and 5 while Maurizia De Bellis wrote Sections 2 and 3. The Introduction (Section 1) and Conclusions (Section 6) are the result of joint work.

and business, agree on common rules. It is not entirely private and can be better defined as hybrid regulation.[2]

(b) If one sticks to the first definition the consequence is that it is in the self-interest of the private community, of both regulator and regulatees, to ensure implementation. In this case, why should the enforcement of TPR be a problem? The answer implies that implementation is in principle voluntary, because TPR is based mainly on mutual consent. Following this reasoning, enforcement of TPR is an oxymoron: if it needs enforcement, it is not private, while if it is private it does not need a third party to be called to enforce the regulation.

But reality is more complex, as a growing number of hybrid, public–private regimes need to be enforced. In the following pages, several examples of hybrid, public–private, regulations will be discussed (Section 2). They raise a number of questions: is the distinction between public and private adequate, if we go beyond the State? If the State is not the main actor should this distinction be redesigned or even abandoned? What do we mean by 'public', outside the State? Inside the State, public is anything that has a connection with the State, a municipality, a local authority. What happens when we move to the global space where there is no one legal order and no State?

Strictly connected to the answer to the problem of the private–public divide in this area, is the question of the legitimacy of TPR. When there is a public authority imposing an obligation on private parties, the problem of legitimacy appears stronger.

(c) Enforcement is a polysemous word. It includes implementation, monitoring (as a form of overall control, or verification), review (which is usually done case by case), and dispute settlement arising from implementation (as a third party can claim in front of a national or global court a 'question of liability' arising from the standards established by that global authority). In the cases which will be examined in the following pages not

---

2 B. Kingsbury, N. Krisch and R. Stewart, The Emergence of Global Administrative Law, 68 *Law and Contemporary Problems*, nos. 3–4, 2005, at 22. There are several examples of hybrid regulations related to different sectors: the Internet, standardization, copyright protection, the environment, sport. As regards sport, for instance, a private regime has been recognized. It is composed of several regulatory organisms, some of which are private, others public: more exactly, the International Olympic Committee is an international corporation in which more than 205 national Olympic committees, 60 international sports federations, four associations of international federations, eight associations of Olympic committees, a number of multi-sport organizations and international organisms (such as the Court of Arbitration for Sport and the World Anti-doping Agency) participate. For more details, see L. Casini, *Il diritto globale dello sport*, Milano, Giuffrè, at 43ff.

all of these activities can be found in every sector. Moreover, even the use of terms is ambiguous: for example, the International Standardization Organization (ISO) uses 'certification' and 'registration' interchangeably.

(d) Enforcement often requires new negotiation, new agreements, and, many times, new decisions. It is not a one-stop shop. It is not a simple process: the decision is taken, and then is enforced. On the contrary, there is a long process from the decision to the enforcement.[3] It requires complex procedures. It is not uni-linear but multi-linear. There are many enforcement chains, in different directions: a decision can be enforced through a variety of means, procedures, measures and authorities. Finally, it is wrong to think that the enforcement process is not part of the decision-making process. It definitely is.

In examining these issues, this chapter focuses on ten examples: the International Bar Association (IBA); the Union Internationale des Architectes (UIA); the Forest Stewardship Council (FSC); the International Air Transport Association (IATA); the International Standardization Organization (ISO); the International Chamber of Commerce (ICC); the Internet Corporation for Assigned Names and Numbers (ICANN); the International Accounting Standard Board (IASB); the World Intellectual Property Organization (WIPO); and private food standards.

2. MULTIPLE MECHANISMS OF ENFORCEMENT

Enforcement of TPRs is channelled through a number of different mechanisms. The structure of these mechanisms is sometimes simple, depending on the private regulatory regime itself. In other cases, tools look increasingly complex, both because of their own functioning and because they involve different actors: private third parties, public authorities, intergovernmental organizations.

In some cases, standards are spontaneously applied. For example, market actors often comply with the ISO's technical standards – concerning the

[3] See J.L. Pressman and Aaron Wildavsky, *Implementation*, Berkeley, Los Angeles and London, University of California Press, 1984. See also the body of academic literature on comitology and implementation and enforcement in the EU: among the most recent works, C.F. Bergström, *Comitology: Delegation of Powers in the European Union and the Committee System*, New York, Oxford University Press, 2005, and T. Christiansen, J.M. Oettel and B. Vaccari (eds), *21st Century Comitology: Implementing Committees in the Enlarged European Union*, Maastricht, EIPA, 2009.

production of goods and services[4] – because they ensure interoperability and interconnectivity, so that their benefits increase as the number of users increase.[5] As will be shown in the following pages, though, this is far from being the only mechanism through which ISO standards are applied, and more specific and powerful tools to guarantee compliance are in place. Many companies apply spontaneously the standards drafted by the ICC, a global business organization founded in 1919, as they foster the harmonization of international trade.[6] In these cases, standards can be considered to be self-enforcing because of market dynamics.

More often, though, specific tools intended to enforce standards are in place. In professional organizations, the sanctions of the suspension or expulsion of members are typically found. Two cases in point are the IBA – bringing together bar associations, law societies and their members worldwide[7] – and the Union Internationale des Architectes (UIA) – the global professional organization for architects.[8] As both organizations set standards for the respective professions[9] and as such standards are taken into account when evaluating whether professional misconduct has occurred, the traditional sanction of expulsion indirectly enforces them.

---

[4] Since its constitution to the present day, the ISO has published more than 18 000 standards, in areas and sectors ranging from agriculture and construction, to mechanical engineering, to medical devices: see http://www.iso.org/iso/iso_catalogue.htm. About the ISO, see K.T. Hallström, *Organizing International Standardization: ISO and the IASC in Quest of Authority*, Cheltenham, UK and Northampton, MA, USA, Edward Elgar Publishing, 2004.

[5] See W. Mattli, The Politics and Economics of International Institutional Standards Setting: An Introduction, *Journal of European Public Policy*, 2001, Vol. 8, No. 3, 328ff., at 333.

[6] For more details about the ICC's history, see http://www.iccwbo.org/id93/index.html. For its structure, see the ICC Constitution, available at: http://www.iccwbo.org/uploadedFiles/ICC/ICC_Home_Page/pages/ICC_Constitution_EN_8_June_2009.pdf.

[7] It has a membership of more than 40 000 individual lawyers and 197 bar associations and law societies: see http://www.ibanet.org/About_the_IBA/About_the_IBA.aspx. It aims at promoting an exchange of information among legal practitioners and their associations and at advancing the science of jurisprudence. For the sanction of expulsion, see IBA Constitution, art. 3.20.2.2.

[8] The UIA dates back to the 1940s and aims at connecting architects worldwide and at representing the profession at the global level. For the sanction of expulsion, see UIA, Articles and bylaws, art. 20.3.

[9] See the IBA's *General Principles for the Legal Profession*, available at: http://www.ibanet.org/About_the_IBA/IBA_resolutions.aspx, and the UIA's *Recommended International Standards of Professionalism in Architectural Practices and Recommended Guidelines*, available at: http://www.uia-architectes.org/texte/england/Menu-7/3-bibliotheque.html

This type of sanction can also be found in professional organizations evolving into standard setters. The IATA, bringing together representatives of 230 airlines and adopting rules in specific fields, is a case in point.[10] The expansion in the organization's tasks, though, brings with it a development in the way the sanctions are administered, as the airline whose membership is terminated can seek arbitration under the IATA Arbitration Rules.[11]

Sanctions such as expulsion are frequent and very simple in their structure. Private global regulators, though, use a variety of tools to enforce their own standards, which do not correspond to a well-established typology. On the contrary, they seem to adapt to the specific features of a given sector. A first case can be found in the area of private[12] food standards, which are developed by a number of different actors: retailers (such as Marks and Spencer) and their trade associations (such as the British Retail Consortium (BRC) and the International Featured Standard (IFS)),[13] international coalitions of both retailers and producers/farmers (the Global Food Safety Initiative (GFSI)[14] and GlobalGAP (previously known as EurepGAP)),[15] and hybrid public–private organizations (the ISO

---

[10] IATA's mission is the one of representing and serving the airline industry: IATA Articles of Association, art. IV. About its membership, see http://www.iata.org/membership/Pages/Index.aspx. Among its rules, see the 'Multilateral Interline Traffic Agreements'; the 'Passenger and Cargo Services Conference Resolutions'; and the 'Passenger and Cargo Agency Agreements & Sales Agency Rules'.

[11] Membership can be suspended or terminated where a member no longer meets the criteria for membership or is in breach of any rules adopted by the IATA: IATA Articles of Association, art. V.5. and V.6.

[12] Public food standards, both global (established by the Codex Alimentarius Commission) and national (set by national governments or authorities), fall beyond the scope of this chapter.

[13] The BRC is the leading retail association in the UK: see http://www.brc.org.uk/. IFS is the result of a collaboration of three retail federations from Germany, France and Italy: see http://www.ifs-certification.com/

[14] Founded in 2000, the GFSI is a network of food safety experts from retailer, manufacturer and food service companies (even though the idea was first launched by a group of international retailer CEOs). GFSI does not intend to develop a code of its own, but aims to 'promote convergence among food safety standards through maintaining a benchmarking process', see GFSI, Joint UNCTAD/WTO Informal Information Session on Private Standards, available at http://www.unctad.org/trade_env/test1/meetings/wto1/swoffer_e.pdf

[15] Formed in 1997, Euro-Retailer Produce Working Group (Eurep) started as a uniquely retailer dominated network and later on evolved into a more collaborative one, in which producers' groups and consumers' associations could participate. In 1999, it established a standard of its own, the EurepGAP (Euro-Retailer Produce Working Group Good Agricultural Practices): OECD, *Final Report on Private Standards and the Shaping of the Agro-Food System*, 31 July 2006, AGR/CA/APM(2006)9/FINAL, at 16–9. As a number of producers and suppliers worldwide

has a specific standard for food safety).[16] Supermarket chains (such as Tesco) impose standards on suppliers, making them binding for producers willing to export their food products and hence excluding a number of products from being distributed (mostly from small-scale producers in developing countries). In this case, self-enforcement by a private standard setter of its own standards occurs, not only when a supermarket is imposing its firm's specific standard (like Tesco's Nature's Choice), but also when it is requiring compliance with a standard developed by an association in which it takes part (such as GlobalGap).[17]

A second case of sector-specific enforcement mechanisms put in place by private regulators can be found in the area of Internet regulation. The ICANN, the private entity responsible for the coordination of the sector, concludes contracts incorporating regulatory requirements with operators acting in the area of the 'top level domain systems' (TLDs):[18] as operators are obliged to do so, in this way 'non voluntary' contracts are put in place (*infra*, Section 5).[19]

Not all self-enforcement tools are based on the adaptation of private instruments such as contracts. On the contrary, they can be based on the constitution of specific bodies within the global private regulators. The WIPO – a specialized agency of the UN which can be considered to have a mixed, public–private, nature[20] – established the Advisory Committee on Enforcement (ACEA), aimed at assisting and coordinating stakeholders in

joined EuropGAP, in 2007 the name was changed to GlobalGAP: see http://www.globalgap.org/cms/front_content.php?idcat=19

[16] The ISO main standard for food is ISO 22000, relating to food safety management systems, deriving from ISO 9000, concerning quality management.

[17] Already in 2006, for example, EurepGAP was required in the majority of EU retailers, controlling 85 percent of the Western European fresh produce market: see G. Chia-Hui Lee, *Private Food Standards and their Impacts on Developing Countries*, European Commission DG Trade Unit G2 Brussels, 2006, at 13.

[18] ICANN plays a twofold role: as a standard setting body and a government entity. See J.G. Palfrey, The End of the Experiment: How ICANN's Foray into Global Internet Democracy Failed, *Harvard Journal of Law & Technology*, 2004, Vol. 17, No. 2, 410ff., at 426–9. ICANN sets standards for the assignment of domain names, IP addresses and Internet protocols, and supervises the entities (the registries and the registrars) who manage the domain names. Registries are entities accredited to manage top or generic level domain names (for example, '.com', '.org', '.edu'), while the registrars manage second level domain names.

[19] See S. Crawford, The ICANN Experiment, *Cardozo Journal of International and Comparative Law*, 2004, 409ff.

[20] The WIPO was established by the 'WIPO Convention' in 1967, with the aim of promoting IP throughout the world: see http://www.wipo.int/about-wipo/en/what_is_wipo.html. On its relevant 'private law profiles', see L.A. Cunningham,

the enforcement of intellectual property (IP) standards.[21] Similar to this is the case of ICC Commercial Crime Services, an internal division of ICC enforcing this organization's standards concerning commercial crime.[22]

Lastly, private (and hybrid) regulators tend to develop 'quasi-judicial' dispute settlement systems, which can be extremely sophisticated. For example, WIPO Arbitration and Mediation Center is competent for the resolution of international disputes between private parties involving intellectual property.[23] The ICC is perhaps the most striking example, putting in place a high number of quasi-judicial procedures:[24] the ICC International Court of Arbitration, the Alternative Dispute Resolutions (ADR), intended to ensure the amicable settlement of commercial disputes with the assistance of a neutral,[25] and the Dispute Boards (DBs), established at the outset of a contract and informally assisting the parties when disagreements arise, now a standard dispute resolution mechanism for contractual disputes arising in the course of mid- or long-term contracts.[26]

The mechanisms mentioned above have different natures, but are all put in place by the global private regulator itself. Other tools, though, involve different actors, private or public.

First, an increasingly used means of enforcement for TPR is certification by third parties.[27] Cases in point are the ISO standards for quality

---

Private Standards in Public Law: Copyright, Lawmaking and the Case of Accounting, 104 *Michigan Law Review*, 2005, 2–54, available at: http://papers.ssrn.com/sol3/papers.cfm?abstract_id=677647

21 See the Advisory Committee on Enforcement: http://www.wipo.int/enforcement/en/ace/

22 The ICC Commercial Crime Services, comprising three bureaux (the International Maritime Bureau, the Financial Investigation Bureau, and the Counterfeiting Intelligence Bureau) enforce standards concerning commercial crimes: see http://www.icc-ccs.org/about-us

23 See the 'WIPO Arbitration, Mediation, and Expert Determination Rules and Clauses': http://www.wipo.int/freepublications/en/arbitration/446/wipo_pub_446.pdf

24 For an overview of ICC Dispute Resolution Services, see http://www.iccwbo.org/court/

25 The ADR Rules were launched in 2001 to replace the 1988 Rules of Conciliation: see http://www.iccwbo.org/court/adr/id4447/index.html

26 See http://www.iccwbo.org/court/dispute_boards/id4527/index.html

27 See E. Meidinger, Private Import Safety Regulation and Transnational New Governance, in C. Coglianese, A. Finkel and D. Zaring (eds), *Import Safety: Regulatory Governance in the Global Economy*, 2009, Philadelphia, Philadelphia University Press, at 7 (arguing third-party monitoring has become a standard part of private regulation).

management and environmental management (the 9000 and 14000 series),[28] standards for forestry certification developed by the Forest Stewardship Council (FSC),[29] and private food standards (mentioned above). The standard setters do not themselves conduct certification; on the contrary, independent third-party organizations certify compliance with standards.[30] As certifiers are paid and selected by applicants, conflicts of interests can rise. In order to counterbalance such risk, certification bodies must be previously accredited. Control over certifiers is not purely *ex ante*: accreditation often involves an *ex post* monitoring over certifiers' activity. For example, Accreditation Services International (ASI),[31] competent for accreditation in a number of areas including forestry certification, monitors the certifiers' activity and reviews their decisions, suspending or terminating their accreditation in the event of a negative assessment.[32] This threat is not merely hypothetical, as some cases of suspension are documented.[33]

Not only is certification increasingly used in a number of areas: it also tends to follow a common model. From this point of view, the ISO plays a key role: one of its subcommittees, the CASCO, develops standards for conformity assessment activities[34] and principles and guidelines for certification in the forestry and food areas, widely based on ISO ones.[35]

---

[28] Currently, around 888 000 organizations in 161 countries are independently certified to these standards. See http://www.iso.org/iso/pressrelease.htm?refid=Ref1028

[29] Established in 1993, the FSC develops international standards for responsible forest management, including guidelines for certification, accreditation, trademark use, and governance: see FSC Bylaws, 2009, art. 1.

[30] For ISO, see: http://www.iso.org/iso/iso_catalogue/management_and_leadership_standards/certification/iso_does_not_carry_out_certification.htm. For FSC, see FSC Accredited Certification Bodies, November 2010. In the area of food standards, for example, GLOBALG.A.P. signs service agreements with independent Certified Bodies (CBs) which act as independent auditing companies: http://www.globalgap.org/cms/front_content.php?idcat=30

[31] ASI is an economically and legally independent body: see http://www.accreditation-services.com/

[32] See ASI Procedure for Extension, Reduction, Suspension and Termination.

[33] See E. Meidinger, The Administrative Law of Global Private–Public Regulation: the Case of Forestry, *European Journal of International Law*, 2006, Vol. 17, No. 1, 47–87, at 74.

[34] See ISO/IEC 17021:2006, *Conformity Assessment – Requirements for Bodies Providing Audit and Certification of Management Systems*.

[35] See ASI Accreditation Procedures, August 2010, available at http://www.accreditation-services.com/wp-content/uploads/downloads/2011/09/ASI-PRO-20–101-Accreditation_v3.0.pdf. The first page of the document includes a clear comparison with ISO rules.

Other means of enforcement involving private third parties are less uniform, but significantly widespread. When ICC advertising standards are used in national regimes, they end up being monitored and enforced by self-regulatory private organizations (SROs). SROs can order the advertiser or media involved to stop the non-compliant conduct (a measure equal to prohibitive injunctions) and impose sanctions such as adverse publicity and referral to public authorities.[36]

Other means of TPR enforcement do not involve third-party *private* actors, but *public* ones.

Sometimes, intergovernmental organizations enforce private rules. The most commonly involved one is the World Trade Organization (WTO). According to the Technical Barriers to Trade (TBT) Agreement, Member States shall use international technical standards (such as those of the ISO) as a *basis* for their domestic regulation.[37] This is not an obligation, but there are strong incentives for them to do so.[38] In this way, a public intergovernmental organization assisted by a quasi-judicial body – the WTO Appellate Body (AB) – enforces standards coming from a private regulator. As far as private food standards are concerned, the Sanitary and Phytosanitary Agreement (SPS) constitutes a very different hypothesis. SPS explicitly mentions public food standards (established by the Codex Commission). As the agreement was negotiated before private food standards became widespread, it did not regulate such phenomena. The issue of whether a WTO Member could be responsible for private actors in its territory, enforcing private food standards effectively and hence excluding some producers, has been raised before the SPS Committee.[39] Notwithstanding two years 'exploratory discussions' within this forum, a number of questions regarding the possibility of applying such a regime to private food standards are still open.[40] Another WTO agreement, on the Trade-Related Aspects of Intellectual Property (TRIPs), connects trade with WIPO standards. In turn, the latter organization's dispute settlement resolution body – the WIPO Arbitration and Mediation Center – is competent for

---

[36] See Paul Verbruggen in this volume.

[37] Art.2.4 TBT.

[38] See S. Battini, La globalizzazione del diritto pubblico, *Riv. Trim. Dir. Pubbl.*, 2006, 325ff., at 332.

[39] D. Prévost, Private Sector Food-safety Standards and the SPS Agreement: Challenges and Possibilities, *South African Yearbook of International Law*, 2008, Vol. 33, 1–37, at 16 and 34–6.

[40] D. Casey, Private Food Safety and Quality Standards and The WTO, *University College Dublin Law Review*, 2007, Vol. 65, No. 7, 65ff., at 66 and 88.

Internet disputes according to ICANN's Uniform Dispute Resolution Policy (UDRP).[41]

Linkages do not involve only intergovernmental organizations, but also transnational networks and the International Financial Institutions (IFIs). The Financial Stability Board (FSB)[42] endorsed IASB standards within its *Compendium of Standards*.[43] Moreover, the IMF and the World Bank check compliance with such rules through the Reports on the Observance of Standards and Codes (ROSCs).[44] In this way, not only do global public regulators exercise a soft power of persuasion towards the adoption of private standards through their incorporation in the Compendium, but two of them (the IMF and the World Bank) actively monitor their compliance.

Linkages among global regulatory regimes can result in several types of enforcement, the differences among which will be further discussed below (Section 4).

Not only global public regulators enforce private standards, but also regional and domestic ones. From this point of view, the EU appears extremely active, especially in the areas of air transport, Internet regulation, food standards and accounting. Yet, the conditions and scope of the EU's enforcement of private standards vary across the sectors, and they will

---

[41] According to the Uniform Dispute Resolution Policy (UDRP), para. 4, dispute settlement resolution is administered by accredited administrative dispute resolution (ADR) service providers: see ICANN, List of Approved Dispute Resolution Service Providers, available at: http://www.icann.org/en/dndr/udrp/approved-providers.htm, and WIPO, *Guide to the Uniform Domain Name Dispute Resolution Policy* (UDRP), available at: http://www.wipo.int/amc/en/domains/guide/index.html. Among these providers, the WIPO Arbitration and Mediation Center is the most relevant. For a comment on the selection and composition of the Tribunal, see M. Froomkin, ICANN's 'Uniform Dispute Resolution Policy' – Causes and (Partial) Cures, 67 *Brooklyn Law Review* 605 (2002), at 671–4.

[42] Bringing together representatives of domestic financial authorities from the G20 countries, together with intergovernmental international organizations (the International Monetary Fund (IMF) and World Bank, in particular) and transgovernmental regulatory networks for banking, securities and insurance (the Basel Committee on Banking Supervision (BCBS), the International Organization of Securities Commissioners (IOSCO), the International Association of Insurance Supervisors (IAIS)).

[43] Highlighting 12 key standards deemed essential for sound financial systems: see http://www.financialstabilityboard.org/cos/index.htm

[44] ROSCs are reports on countries' degree of compliance, with some global financial standards wholly corresponding to the Compendium's 12 Key Standards, among which there are IASB standards: see http://www.imf.org/external/NP/rosc/rosc.aspx

be examined in depth when looking at the interactions among public and private in the enforcement of TPR (Section 3).

The means of enforcement discussed above do not mutually exclude one another; on the contrary, they often combine, reinforcing each other. For example, in the case of IATA two private means of enforcement – the sanctions of suspension, exclusion and certification mechanisms[45] – are coupled with enforcement coming from a public body (the EU). In the area of Internet regulation, the aforementioned peculiar use of contracts – ending up in being binding – combines with a 'quasi-judicial' enforcement (through the WIPO Arbitration and Mediation Center). In the case of ISO standards, not only voluntary compliance and certification for management standards take place, but also enforcement by an intergovernmental organization, because of the functioning of TBT. In the enforcement of international accounting standards five means of enforcement can be recalled, going from the traditional sanction of expulsion,[46] to monitoring on compliance (from international organizations, such as the IMF and World Bank), to informal endorsement (because of the inclusion in the FSB Compendium), to incorporation in a binding regulation subject to the control of a judicial body.

The cases examined above show that the multiple types of enforcement do not come only from the private regulator itself or from a third-party private actor: they involve public actors, resulting in a hybridization of TPR enforcement (Section 3), through a number of different linkages

---

[45] In the area of transport, the most important certification mechanism is based on the IATA Operational Safety Audit (IOSA), the standard for airlines' safety management. As IOSA registration is necessary to maintain IATA membership, such a standard is now mandatory for the organization's members: see http://www.iata.org/ps/certification/iosa/Pages/Registry.aspx. Assessment of compliance is conducted by the IOSA Audit Organizations (AOs), third-party accredited private entities: see http://www.iata.org/ps/certification/iosa/Pages/audit-organizations.aspx. The other main auditing program is the IATA Safety Audit of Ground Operations (ISAGO), modeled on the IOSA framework: see http://www.iata.org/ps/certification/isago/Pages/index.aspx. Here, though, instead of a third-party certification, a form of self-certification – conducted by the ISAGO Audit Pool – occurs.

[46] Art. 2.6 of the IASCF Constitution provides that '*any member may be suspended or expelled in case of non compliance with the obligations of membership*'. This sanction of the suspension or the expulsion of the member appears to be an inheritance from the standard setter's structure before its reorganization in the 2001. Being at the time an organization representative of the accountancy profession, the sanction typical of associations of professionals was the most natural and immediate one. With the evolution into a standard setter with a more complex membership, including all the actors with an interest in accounting, so also the means of enforcement proliferated and became more evolved.

(Section 4). Because of the different combination of these tools, the efficacy of the enforcement varies significantly (Section 5).

3. PUBLIC AND PRIVATE IN TPR ENFORCEMENT

The analysis above shows that complexity in the means of enforcement tends to go hand in hand with the hybrid, public–private nature, of the enforcement process itself.

Private regulatory regimes are seldom self-contained. Only a few cases (such as the IBA and UIA) support the thesis according to which private regimes are 'complete': that is, they may set standards, monitor for compliance, and carry out enforcement without the need for intervention from public bodies.[47] Even in these cases, though, the picture could change rapidly because of the implementation of the General Agreement on Trade in Services (GATS).[48] Another example in which standards enforcement appears to be exclusively private is that of the FSC, as accredited private actors manage certification. Yet, two trends show a more complex picture. First, some observers point to the increasing relevance of public actors within the global regulator for forestry.[49] Until now, though, the admission of government officials among FSC Assembly economic members appears to be more theoretical than actually enacted.[50] Second, FSC standards are used as a basis for public mandatory regulations in some countries, such as Eastern European ones (Poland and Latvia are two cases in point):[51] in this

---

[47] See C. Scott, Private Regulation of the Public Sector: A Neglected Facet of Contemporary Governance, *Journal of Law and Society*, 2002, Vol. 29, 56ff., at 58.

[48] The scope of one of the WTO agreements, the General Agreements on Trade in Services (GATS), covers professional services. According to Article VI, 5(a), to determine whether a State is respecting its GATS obligations, account must be taken of that State's application of international standards. This is a transitory rule, to be applied until the Council for Trade in Services (CTS) establishes specific disciplines for domestic regulation. Until now, only disciplines for accounting have been approved, and both the IBA and the UIA have been consulted with the view to adapting the disciplines to the legal and architectural professions. See Laurel S. Terry, Lawyers, GATS, and the WTO Accountancy Disciplines: The History of the WTO's Consultation, the IBA GATS Forum and the September 2003 IBA Resolutions, 22 *Penn State Int'l L. Rev* 695 (2004)

[49] See E. Meidinger, The Administrative Law of Global Private–Public Regulation: the Case of Forestry, *supra* note 33, at 59.

[50] See FSC Membership List 2010.

[51] See P. Paschalis Jacubowicz, Forest Certification in Poland, 2004, paper presented at the Symposium Forest Certification in Developing and Transitional Societies: Social, Economical and Ecological Effects, Yale Law School, June 10–11

hypothesis, a second type of enforcement, entirely public and passing through the traditional legislative process, parallel to the private voluntary certification one, takes place.

In the majority of the cases mentioned above, public actors are involved in TPR enforcement, and increasingly so. A mixture of private and public is a general tendency within global governance. Some authors point to the emergence of 'hybrids': a term used to reflect the opacity of the means involved.[52] Others have suggested a number of different taxonomies (for example, distinguishing between co-optation, co-regulation, and private self-regulation in the shadow of hierarchy and State adoption of privately negotiated regimes).[53] The relationship between public actors and private entities is evolving: the first no longer delegate their power to the latter; but rather they tend to co-exist.[54] There is a 'tacit alliance' between private and public,[55] which tends towards them combining and reinforcing one other. Hence, one of the key questions is what the role of public actors in such a new context is. The type of intervention of public actors within TPR enforcement provides some significant insights.

The EU's enforcement of private standards enacts three different models. First, in the area of food regulation, the EU – more than playing an active role in the enforcement of private standards – shows a neutral approach towards market operators' choice among public or private rules.[56] A second hypothesis occurs in the regulation of air transport and the Internet, where

---

2004, available at: http://www.yale.edu/forestcertification/symposium/eastern europe.html#poland

[52] J.-C. Graz, Beware of Hybrids: Power Devolution in Globalisation, paper for Pekea 2005 Conference, Rennes, November 3–6 2005, available at: http://fr.pekea-fr.org/Rennes/T-Graz.pdf

[53] See, *ex multis*, T.A. Börzel and T. Risse, Public–Private Partnerships: Effective and Legitimate Tools of International Governance?, in E. Grande and L.W. Pauly (eds) *Complex Sovereignty: Reconstituting Political Authority in the Twenty-first Century*, 2005, Toronto, University of Toronto Press, 195–216.

[54] See Meidinger, Private Import Safety Regulation, *supra* note 27, at 7.

[55] D. Casey, Private Food Safety and Quality Standards and the WTO, *supra* note 40, at 68.

[56] According to EU Regulation (EC) no. 852/2004 of the European Parliament and of the Council of 29 April 2004, on the hygiene of foodstuffs, art. 5, food business operators shall put in place quality management systems based on the Hazard Analysis Critical Control Point (HACCP) principles. Various standards based on such principles exist (such as BRC and IFS), and all of them can be used for purposes of compliance with the Regulation (even though the drafting of ISO 22000 aims precisely at providing a common harmonized standard for food safety management). See F. Wendler, The Public–Private Regulation of Food Safety through HACCP: What does it mean for the Governance Capacity of Public and

the EU enforces a set of specific standards established by global private regulators (IATA's blacklist[57] and standards relating to the .eu top level domain name, respectively).[58] A third and more complex hypothesis is the model enacted for accounting. Regulation CE n. 1606/2002 (so-called IAS Regulation) requires all publicly traded EU companies to prepare their consolidated accounts using IFRS as *endorsed* in the EU.[59] This means the IAS Regulation foresaw a systematic endorsement of *all* IASB standards in the EU. At the same time, no automatic incorporation is in place; on the contrary, the European Commission – assisted by two committees – is entitled to decide on the applicability of IAS/IFRS.[60] Moreover, the EU aims at influencing the global private standard setter's decision-making process.[61]

Private Actors?, in E. Vos (ed.), *European Risk Governance: Its Science, its Inclusiveness and its Effectiveness*, CONNEX Report Series Nr 06, ISSN 1864–1539/6, available at: http://www.connex-network.org/series, 223ff., at 239–42.

[57] The EU used IATA's blacklist for purposes of its own transport regulation. More than enforcing a private regulator's standards, in this case the EU is strengthening a private regulator's sanction concerning compliance with its standards.

[58] EU law enforces Internet standards through EU regulations (EC) 733/2002 and 874/2004, concerning the implementation of the .eu top level domain name, provides for revocation of the website in case of breach of the main terms of registration and establishes an alternative dispute resolution procedure. Regulation (EC) 733/2002 of 22 April 2002 on the implementation of the '.eu Top Level Domain' and Regulation (EC) 874/2004 of 28 April 2004, lay down public policy rules concerning the implementation and functions of the '.eu Top Level Domain' and the principles governing registration. See also the recent Regulation (EC) 560/2009 of 26 June 2009 amending Regulation (EC) No 874/2004 laying down public policy rules concerning the implementation and functions of the '.eu Top Level Domain' and the principles governing registration.

[59] Regulation (EC) No 1606/2002 of the European Parliament and of the Council of 19 July 2002 on the application of international accounting standards.

[60] Since 2003, more than 40 endorsement regulations have been approved: see http://ec.europa.eu/internal_market/accounting/legal_framework/regulations_adopting_ias_text_en.htm. The most recent consolidated version is Regulation (EC) 1126/2008 of 3 November 2008 adopting certain international accounting standards in accordance with Regulation (EC) 1606/2002 of the European Parliament and of the Council.

[61] See Communication from the Commission to the Council and the European Parliament, *Accounting Harmonisation: A New Strategy vis-à-vis International Harmonisation*, COM 95(508) of November 1995, available at: http://ec.europa.eu/internal_market/accounting/docs/com-95–508/com-95–508_en.pdf, para. 5.4: 'in order to ensure an appropriate European input into the continuing work of the IASC, the Contact committee will examine and seek to establish an agreed position

The example concerning food standards can be considered a first step by the EU in the area of private standards for such a sector, but not enacting a specific strategy yet. Hence, it could be inferred that there are essentially two tracks in the EU's enforcement of TPR: a purely *ex post* and case by case one, in which the EU chooses whether or not to lend its binding legal force to a specific set of private standards, and a more systematic strategy, aimed at endorsing the standard setting activity of a specific private actor as a whole. Even in this second case, the EU tries to retain the power of deciding on the applicability of each standard within its legal order. The most significant difference, though, lies in the EU's efforts to influence the global private standard setter, the IASB (it must be borne in mind that such an effort would have faced more difficulties in the Internet area, given ICANN's persistent ties with the US government).

Similar patterns can be found in the involvement of global public regulators in TPR enforcement.

The WTO TBT Committee elaborated the decision in its 'Principles for the Development of International Standards, Guides and Recommendations',[62] aimed at influencing international standard setters (mostly the ISO and the IEC) whose standards are relevant for the application of TBT. In this case, as in the accounting one, the global public regulator tries to influence the standard setting process of the private regulator to whose activity its agreement refers.

In the accounting area, a Monitoring Board (MB) has recently been established, intended to ensure the public accountability of the IASB. It is made up of representatives of the IOSCO, the Financial Services Agency of Japan (JFSA), the US Securities and Exchange Commission (SEC) and the EU Commission: hence, some, but not all, of the bodies constituting the FSB – which, as mentioned above, recommends compliance with IASB standards through recognition in its Compendium – are taking part in. Even though there is not a perfect correspondence among the members of the FSB (whose membership is wider) and those represented in the MB, the establishment of the latter can be seen as an attempt to match *ex post*

---

on future Exposure Drafts ... This will allow the Union progressively to gain a position of greater influence on the IASC's work, including the determination of its agenda, so that its output will increasingly reflect the EU viewpoint.' In the last decade, the EU participated extensively in IASB work.

[62] Decision of the Committee on Principles for the Development of International Standards, Guides and Recommendations with relation to Articles 2, 5 and Annex 3 of the Agreement, Annex 4 to the Second Triennial Review of the Operation and Implementation of the Agreement on Technical Barriers to Trade, the Committee on Technical Barriers to Trade, G/TBT/9, 13 November 2000.

endorsement of private standards with public actors' influence over the private regulator. In this case, instead of procedural means, this attempt is based on the use of a structural means, through the establishment of a monitoring body.

Public actors' role in TPR enforcement is not simply that of incorporating standards and lending their binding legal force to voluntary regimes. More often, public actors do not simply recognize private rules, but try to influence the private regulators' activity, especially through imposing procedural requirements.

However, it must be borne in mind that the mixture of public and private does not take place only at the level of the implementation, but also within the structure of the regulators. ICANN is generally considered to be the most illustrative example of the increasing hybridization of a private regulator.[63] With reform in 2002, the powers of the Governmental Advisory Committee (GAC), in which national governments participate, was reinforced. Yet, the type of public bodies influencing ICANN are diverse, and do not identify with the EU.[64] The ISO, which defines itself as a 'non-governmental organization that forms a bridge between the public and private sectors',[65] can be described more accurately as a hybrid organization than a private one, as many of the domestic standard setters composing it are connected to (or mandated by) national governments.[66] The WIPO incorporates an opposite trend, with the increasing privatization of an international organization.[67]

---

63 See J. Zittrain, ICANN: Between the Public and Private – Comments before Congress, 14 *Berkeley Technology Law Journal*, 1077 (1999).

64 See GAC members: https://gacweb.icann.org/display/gacweb/GAC+Representatives

65 See http://www.iso.org/iso/about.htm

66 Even though some of the national standardization bodies taking part in it have their origins exclusively in the private sector, being the result of national partnerships of industry associations, others are part of the governmental structure of their countries or are mandated by their government: hence, the variety of the domestic standardization bodies is mirrored in the global standard setter and affects its nature. See E. Shamir-Borer, The Evolution of Administrative-Law Norms and Mechanisms in the International Organization for Standardization (ISO), paper presented to the second GAL Seminar, June 2006, Viterbo, at p. 9 (pointing out over 70 percent of the national standardization bodies taking part in the ISO have a governmental nature). Moreover, only one standardization body per country is admitted: a feature showing a tendency to take into account the connection with national governments.

67 Private law profiles of the WIPO concern its membership, finances, nature of the standards and collaborations. Some 250 NGOs and IGOs currently have official

But how exactly do linkages among regulatory regimes work? The following section will examine this issue more deeply.

4. MULTIFARIOUS LINKAGES

Almost all the above mentioned global regulators can be defined as linking regimes.[68] The idea of the 'linking regime' may be considered the opposite of the 'self-contained regime' definition. The latter, in fact, is a system that operates 'in complete isolation from international law' and from the other global regimes.[69] The global space is characterized by several linkages among the regulatory systems, and only seldom it is possible to recognize 'self-contained regimes'.[70] Hence, some authors uphold that 'the chimera of "self-contained regime" remains a phantom with no legal basis in international law, a notion which, despite its persistent appearance in jurisprudential debate, is best confined to the lively world of myth and fable'.[71]

Linkages between regimes can take different forms: specific issue, substantive, strategic, borrowing, sanction,[72] hierarchical, membership, incorporation, interpretive, participatory, permissive unilateral.[73] Therefore, 'borrowing regimes' are a specific type of linkage, insofar as they are 'a

---

observer status at WIPO meetings. Furthermore, the organization is largely self-financing through the earnings from the services that WIPO provides to the private users of the international registration system; other earnings derive from WIPO's Arbitration and Mediation services and sales of publications. Moreover, many of the standards that the WIPO enforces are first set by global private regulators (as is the case of ICANN standards about IP).

[68] See D.W. Leebron, Linkages, 96 *American Journal of International Law*, 5ff. (2002).

[69] A. Lindroos and M. Mehling, Dispelling the Chimera of Self-Contained Regimes: International Law and the WTO, 16 *The European Journal of International Law*, 5, 858 (2006).

[70] IBA and UIA may be considered self-contained regimes insofar as they are 'complete', although they have been consulted for the application of GATS rules. See Section 3.

[71] A. Lindroos and M. Mehling, Dispelling the Chimera of Self-Contained Regimes, *supra* note 69, at 877.

[72] The sanction linkage would be a specific type of 'borrowing regime', insofar as 'the sanction claim for linkage is a specific example of a more general type of linkage benefit, namely regime borrowing. That is, linkage may be sought to obtain the institutional and procedural benefits of an existing regime, when similar arrangements cannot be independently negotiated for the issues sought to be linked' (D.W. Leebron, Linkages, *supra* note 68, at 14).

[73] The taxonomy is drawn from D.W. Leebron, Linkages, *supra* note 68.

source of linkage claims where one of the issue areas, but not the other, is characterized by well-developed institutional structures':[74] in other words, the less developed regime borrows the structures from the more developed regime. This taxonomy may be useful to the analysis of the following examples.

(i) A 'specific issue linkage' characterizes the relationship between some ISO standards and food standards. It is the simplest form of linkage, referring to a linking between narrow questions that can be regulated by different regimes. This type of linkage may become stronger when it is based either on some relationships between norms of the two regimes, or on the consequences of norms of one regime for the goals of the other (so called 'substantive linkage'), or on negotiation strategies and outcomes (so-called 'strategic linkage').[75] In these cases, the linking regimes may share the same mechanism of standards enforcement.

Hence, the relationship between some ISO standards and food standards is a 'specific issue linkage', because both types of standard are related to the food safety issue, and regulate risk management procedures, performance indicators, safety programs, etc. In particular, the ISO[76] elaborates certain standards, for instance, ISO 22000:2005, related to food safety procedures, risk management and the implementation of the prerequisites programs (PRP), and ISO 9001:2000, concerning quality management, performance indicators, system planning, 'quality manuals', and codes of conduct. Conversely, global food standards are set and enforced by several regulators:[77] private associations, cooperatives or supermarkets (CIES, IFS, Federalimentari, Certiquality, British Retail Consortium-BRC, Tesco, etc.),[78]

---

[74] D.W. Leebron, Linkages, *supra* note 68, at 15.

[75] More exactly, the substantive linkage is a type of relation between systems based 'on the consequences of the norms of one regime for the goals of the other', insofar as the implementation of the norms of the former regime aims at achieving the goals of the latter. The strategic linkage, instead, is based on 'negotiation strategies and outcomes' in the enforcement process of the norms belonging to the different regimes (D.W. Leebron, Linkages, *supra* note 68, at 11ff.).

[76] On the ISO case, see K.T. Hallström, *Organizing International Standardization: ISO and the IASC in Quest of Authority*, *supra* note 4, at 4–7.

[77] On food standard setting, see T. Havinga, Private Regulation of Food Safety by Supermarkets, *Law & Policy*, 2006, Vol. 28, No. 4, 515–33.

[78] For example, the CIES (Food Business Forum), the world's most powerful association of major food retailers, established the Global Food Safety Initiative (GFSI), to 'promote convergence among food safety standards through maintaining a benchmarking process for food safety management schemes' (Food Business Forum 2009). For more details, see Section 2.

certification companies, ultra-state networks (Infood-network), governmental organizations (Codex Alimentarius Commission), global organisms (IFS Food, Global Gap,[79] etc.), European institutions,[80] national agencies, accreditation bodies (Accredia, UKAS, Cofrac, etc.), and local administrations (local health authorities, etc.).[81] As with ISO standards, these standards also regulate food safety, management quality, performance indicators, etc.,[82] and can be used within self-control systems (Hazard Analysis Critical Control Point (HACCP) systems),[83] provided by the 'European food law'.[84] In order to implement the HACCP system, an

---

79 As regards Global Gap, see Section 2.

80 In the European Union, food safety is regulated by a group of rules, called 'Hygiene Packet' (Reg. EC no. 178/2002; Reg. EC no. 852/2004; Reg. EC no. 853/2004; Reg. EC no. 854/2004; Dir. 2002/99/EC; Dir. 2004/41/EC; Reg. EC no. 183/2005; Reg. EC no. 882/2004; Reg. EC no. 2073/2005; Reg. EC no. 2074/2005; Reg. EC no. 2075/2005; Reg. EC no. 2076/2005), which were transposed by many Member States (relating to the application in Italy, see legislative decrees no. 190/2006 and no. 193/2007).

81 See M. Hendrickson, J. Wilkinson, W.D. Heffernan and R. Gronski, The Global Food System and Nodes of Power, 2 August 2008, available at: http://papers.ssrn.com/sol3/papers.cfm?abstract_id=1337273. In this composite system, 'private regulation complements public regulation at the transnational level in relation to standard setting, monitoring and enforcement'. See F. Cafaggi, Private Regulation, Supply Chain and Contractual Networks: The Case of Food Safety, RSCAS 2010/10 (Robert Schuman Centre for Advanced Studies – Private Regulation Series), available at: http://papers.ssrn.com/sol3/papers.cfm?abstract_id=1554329. National authorities, regional administrations and local health authorities, within their powers, are responsible for the implementation of the 'Hygiene Packet'.

82 Just to mention some examples: the 'British Retail Consortium-BRC' (a private suite of four industries) sets 'Global Standards' designed to implement HACCP, and to satisfy the general requirements established by the EU 'General Product Safety Directive' (2005) and the EU Regulations no. 178/2002 and no. 852/2004. The 'IFS', instead, sets the 'International Food Standard', designed to enable a uniform check of the quality systems, and to comply with the legal requirements on food safety. This standard is, in particular, applied to all processes related to agricultural production in which food is processed.

83 'HACCP systems involve proactively searching for and analyzing safety hazards, identifying critical control points where the hazards can be managed or eliminated, establishing preventive measures with critical limits for each control point, monitoring the control points, taking corrective actions where critical limits are exceeded, keeping good records, and regularly verifying that the system is working properly' (E. Meidinger, Private Import Safety Regulation and Transnational New Governance, Legal Studies Research Paper Series, Paper no. 2009–13, available at: http://papers.ssrn.com/sol3/papers.cfm?abstract_id=1416758, at 9).

84 The Regulation (EC) no. 2073/2005 envisages the adoption of self-control systems entrusted to the private operator's initiative and management. The operator

operator may, in fact, choose the standard that he considers the most appropriate among those offered by several food standard setters (ISO 22000:2005–9001:2000 standards included).[85] ISO and food standards are, therefore, enforced through the same mechanism, based on both accreditation and certification procedures,[86] and the national authorities' surveillance of the implementation of the HACCP systems and measures.

(ii) A 'specific issue linkage' also characterizes the relationship between (private) food standards and standards set by the Codex Alimentarius Commission ('codex standards'),[87] which are in turn related to the parameters established by the WTO agreements. The codex standards are, in fact, considered the benchmarks against which national food measures and regulations are evaluated within the legal parameters of the WTO Agreements (SPS and TBT Agreements).[88] Accordingly, the relation is based on the consequences of norms of one regime (Codex Alimentarius Commission) for the goals of the other (WTO), and it could be therefore defined as a 'substantive linkage'.

From this standpoint, there may be chains linking different global regimes based on a common issue of regulation:[89] certain links of the chain correspond to 'specific issue linkages' (see the relations among private food standards setters, ISO, Codex Alimentarius Commission), others to 'substantive linkages' (see the relation between the Codex Alimentarius Commission and WTO).

---

is responsible for the application and the documentation of the systems for the risk analysis and critical control points. In this sense, the whole regulation is inspired by a 'principle of flexibility', allowing operators to adopt systems and quality standards that they consider the most appropriate, within the general readings of the European and national rules.

[85] On the websites of some standard setters, there are specific sections dedicated to the 'reasons to choose' the standard offered by the company. Special courses on 'how to orient the choice of standards' are organized by several food standard associations.

[86] See Section 2.

[87] The Codex Alimentarius Commission is a 'second-level' organization, founded by two intergovernmental organizations (the World Health Organization and the Food and Agricultural Organization of the United Nations). It is, therefore, a public organism appointed to elaborate food standards and codes of practice, and generate reputable texts for the management of food safety and consumer protection based on the work of the best-informed individuals and organizations concerned with food.

[88] See D. Prevost, Private Sector Food Safety Standards and the SPS Agreement: Challenges and Possibilities, 33 *South African Yearbook of International Law*, 1–37 (2008) and D.K. Casey, Private Food Safety and Quality Standards and the WTO, *supra* note 40.

[89] See Section 1.

(iii) 'Substantive linkages' are recognizable also in relations between IATA and ICAO (International Civil Aviation Organization) in the air transport sector. In fact, IATA provides input to the work of ICAO, which coordinates regional air navigation and support for airports and operational aids in countries which could not themselves afford such services. The application of IATA standards contributes to the achievement of the goals of ICAO,[90] for instance by ensuring the financial transactions between the world's airlines and airline-associated companies, by ruling the activities of different subjects operating in the airline industry sector (consumers, airlines, cargo agents, industry suppliers, services providers, etc.), by assigning 'airlines codes' to the world's airlines,[91] and by providing for a collaboration with national governments.

(iv) In some cases, the connection between systems is simply based on the adoption of similar enforcement mechanisms. It is not, therefore, a 'linkage', but rather an 'analogy' between regimes.[92] The enforcement of both food and forestry standards,[93] for instance, is characterized by the application of similar procedures for accreditation and certification.[94] The accredited certification schemes, in turn, must be in accordance with the

---

90 Article 5 of the 'IATA Bylaws' defines its mission and aims as to: '... 1. Promote safe, reliable and secure air services for the benefit of the peoples of the world; 2. Provide means of collaboration among airlines engaged directly or indirectly in international air transport; 3. Cooperate with the International Civil Aviation Organization and other relevant international organizations'. The Preamble of the ICAO Status (Chicago Convention) refers to the promotion of 'cooperation between nations', to the application of principles 'in order that civil international aviation may be developed in a safe and orderly manner'.

91 These standards are described in IATA's twice-annual publication ('Standard Schedules Information Manual'). Since 1967, ICAO has also issued airline identification codes.

92 The figure of 'analogy' is relevant insofar as it indicates the existence of enforcement systems very similar to each other, despite the diversity of standards taken into consideration.

93 We recall that important forestry standards are set by the FSC (see Section 2). In the FSC case, see E. Meidinger, The Administrative Law of Global Private–Public Regulation: the Case of Forestry, *supra* note 33, at 47ff. and J. McNichol, Transnational NGO Certification Programs as New Regulatory Forms: Lessons from the Forestry Sector, in M.-L. Djelic and K. Sahlin-Andersson (eds), *Transnational Governance*, 2009, Cambridge, Cambridge University Press, 349ff.

94 Standards set by private organisms must be certified by 'independent certification bodies' (also called 'Third Party Certification'), that are qualified and licensed to issue a certificate. 'Certification Bodies' may themselves be assessed by an 'Accreditation Body' against an internationally defined standard to an accredited certification scheme. The Accreditation Body is a national or supranational authority (in the food standards sector, there are the Italian 'Accredia', the British 'UKAS'

requirements of specific ISO standards.[95] Also, in this case, a chain of different kinds of relations among regulatory regimes takes place: while the relationship between food and forestry standards is based on an 'analogy', the relation between these two standard systems and ISO may be defined as a 'regime borrowing linkage'. Food and FSC systems, in fact, borrow parameters from ISO for the application of accreditation and certification procedures.[96]

(v) Other interesting examples of linkages concern financial regulation. The FSB, in which – as highlighted in Section 2 – representatives of many organizations participate (IMF, the World Bank, BCBS, IOSCO, IAIS), endorses IASB standards in its 'Compendium of Standards'.[97] The compliance with these rules is checked by the IMF and the World Bank.[98]

In this sector, four types of linkage may be identified: an 'incorporation linkage' corresponding to the endorsement of IASB standards in FSB's Compendium; a 'regime borrowing linkage' insofar as the FSB borrows standards from another regime (IASB); a 'participatory linkage' because of the participation of several regimes in the FSB; and a 'substantive linkage' insofar as IMF, the World Bank and 'e-Standard Forum' check the achievement of the IASB's goals.

(vi) In copyright regulation[99] a 'mutual regime borrowing linkage' between ICANN and WIPO takes place.[100] The breach of ICANN[101]

---

and the French 'Cofrac'; on FSC standards, see 'ASI Accreditation Procedures', August 2010, available at http://www.accreditation-services.com/) that carries out an independent verification of the Certification Bodies for the way in which they manage the audit processes and make decisions on whether to issue certificates. At the European level, the Regulation (EC) no. 765/2008 sets the requirements for accreditation and market surveillance relating to the marketing of some products (including food products). See also Section 2.

95 The Accredited Certification schemes must be in accordance with the requirements of the internationally recognized accreditation standard ISO Guide 65 (EN 45000). See also ISO/IEC 17021:2006, *Conformity Assessment – Requirements for Bodies Providing Audit and Certification of Management Systems*.

96 See Section 2.

97 See http://www.financialstabilityboard.org/cos/index.htm

98 The findings are published in specific reports (ROSCs). For more details, see Section 2.

99 See L.A. Cunningham, Private Standards in Public Law: Copyright, Lawmaking and the Case of Accounting, *supra* note 20.

100 See M.D. Fan, Governing Copyright in Cyberspace: the Penalty Default Problem with State-Centric Sovereignty, 43 *Jurimetrics* (2003) available at: http://papers.ssrn.com/sol3/papers.cfm?abstract_id=1157899

101 On the role of ICANN, see, in particular, B. Carotti, L'ICANN e la governance di Internet, 3 *Rivista trimestrale di diritto pubblico*, 681ff. (2007). From a more general perspective, see also M. Mueller, *Ruling the Root: Internet Governance and the*

standards, related to the intellectual property issues involved in the introduction of 'gTLDs', can be submitted to the 'WIPO Arbitration and Mediation Center'.[102] At the same time, the breach of WIPO standards[103] related to domain name rights can be enforced through the use of the ICANN Domain Name Dispute Resolution system (UDRP).[104]

(vii) Finally, many linkages among global regimes involve the WTO. Although it has been noted that 'few would nowadays claim that the World Trade Organization (WTO) – being a prime example for such "special regimes" – is entirely self-contained, existing in isolation from international law' and from other global regimes,[105] this organization borrows standards, structures, assistance, indications from several global regulators.

Three examples are highlighted here. First, WTO may borrow standards from ISO. In fact, the TBT Agreement imposes the application of the notice and comment procedure and other obligations where Member States' regulation 'is not in accordance with the technical content of relevant international standards', including most ISO parameters.[106] It is simply an example of 'borrowing regime linkage'.

Taming of Cyberspace, Cambridge, MA, MIT Press, 2002; and more recently, E. Brousseau, M. Marzouki and C. Meadel (eds), *Governance, Regulations and Powers on the Internet*, Cambridge, Cambridge University Press, 2009; L.B. Solum, Models of Internet Governance, Illinois Public Law Research Paper no. 07–25 (2008), available at http://papers.ssrn.com/sol3/papers.cfm?abstract_id=1136825

[102] We recall that for those who conclude a contract with ICANN there is no duty to participate in the WIPO Dispute Resolutions system.

[103] Note that WIPO, moreover, administers 24 international treaties (16 on industrial property; seven on copyright; as well as the Convention establishing WIPO) and collaborates with more than 33 organizations.

[104] See also the relationship with ICANN and ISO: the classification of the top level domains relies on an ISO standard, which provides for the definition of the geographical areas using two-letter codes, recognized and applied worldwide. See RFC 1591, of March 1994, one of the most important standards and still in use: it is available at: http://www.rfc-editor.org/cgi-bin/rfcdoctype.pl?loc=RFC&letsgo=1591&type=ftp&file_format=txt. See also P.K. Yu, The Origins of ccTLD Policymaking, 12 *Cardozo Journal of International and Comparative Law*, 387 (2004).

[105] It is defined also as a 'closed legal system'. See A. Lindroos and M. Mehling, Dispelling the Chimera of Self-Contained Regimes, *supra* note 69, at 858. Even these authors conclude that the WTO isn't a self-contained regime (876).

[106] Art. 2.9 – from 2.9.1. to 2.9.4 – TBT and Annex B. These provisions involve 'cases of competing standards'; in fact, 'the TBT thereby allows for recognition of standards adopted not only by international organizations but also by hybrid or private bodies, such as the International Standards Organization (ISO) and NGOs that adopt standards on subjects such as sustainable forestry and fishing methods. This arrangement creates the possibility of requiring WTO authorities to choose among competing standards issued by different organizations in new or rapidly changing fields of regulation … where a variety of private or hybrid public-private

Second, WTO borrows structures and assistance from WIPO. According to an agreement signed in 1995,[107] the WIPO Secretariat received a mandate from the WIPO General Assembly to assist both its own Member States and WTO Members in implementing their obligations under the TRIPs Agreement. Thus, WIPO's advice focuses on ensuring that national legislation would be in compliance with those obligations, and, mostly since 2000, WIPO Member States have increasingly sought assistance and advice in exploiting the flexibility under international treaties in implementing their obligations.[108] Therefore, the relationship between WIPO and WTO is a perfect example of 'mutual borrowing regimes', even a kind of 'incorporation'.[109]

Lastly, the WTO receives recommendations from the ICC[110] on several issues related to international trade.[111] In this case, there is only a

---

standard-setting organizations compete'. See R.B. Stewart and M. Ratton Sanchez Badin, The World Trade Organization and Global Administrative Law, IILJ Working Paper 2009/7, 21.

[107] The agreement is available at: www.wipo.int/export/sites/www/treaties/en/agreement/pdf/trtdocs_wo030.pdf

[108] The relation between these organizations is based on 'a mutually supportive relationship … and a view to establishing appropriate arrangements for cooperation'; therefore, the WIPO 'International Bureau shall make available to developing country WTO Members which are not Member States of WIPO the same legal technical assistance relating to the TRIPs Agreement as it makes available to Member States of WIPO which are developing countries. The WTO Secretariat shall make available to Member States of WIPO which are developing countries and are not WTO Members the same technical cooperation relating to the TRIPs Agreement as it makes available to developing country WTO Members …' (art. 4 of the WIPO–WTO Agreement). Article 4 also provides for the cooperation and exchange of information between the WIPO International Bureau and WTO Secretariat.

[109] 'The Uruguay Round Agreement on Trade-Related Aspects of Intellectual Property Rights (TRIPs) represents a more limited form of incorporation. In that case, many of the norms of an existing regime, that is, the various agreements concluded under the auspices of the World Intellectual Property Organization (WIPO), were incorporated directly into the WTO TRIPs Agreement …' (D.W. Leebron, Linkages, *supra* note 68, at 19).

[110] The ICC sets several types of standards: see, for instance, Incoterms, which have the general aim of helping traders avoid costly misunderstandings by clarifying the tasks, costs and risks involved in the delivery of goods from sellers to buyers. Incoterms are also recognized by UNCITRAL as the global standard for the interpretation of the most common terms in foreign trade. The latest version of these standards is 'Incoterms 2010', which went into effect on1 January 2011. See also Section 2.

[111] On the major aims of ICC, as defined by the preamble of the ICC Constitution, see Section 2.

'substantive linkage', although there are proposals for the evolution of this relation in a stronger linkage.[112] Also the collaboration between ICC and other organisms – for instance, the UN[113] and a number of non-governmental organizations (ISO, ICANN, WIPO, etc.) – could be defined as a kind of 'substantive linkage'.

5. EFFECTIVENESS

The mechanisms of standards enforcement may be classified on the basis of their different degree of effectiveness,[114] depending on many parameters related to the existence of administrative monitoring, judicial remedies, economic incentives, and public measures for the implementation of global standards. Using these parameters, it is possible to identify at least three levels of effectiveness.

First, a 'soft effectiveness' characterizes the enforcement mechanisms based on the monitoring of administrative bodies inside the private regulators. This type of standards enforcement, which is used by many regulatory regimes (IATA, ISO, ICANN, IASB, WIPO and ICC), may be defined as a 'soft mechanism' because of its non-binding effects and internal application. In fact, administrative bodies can merely take note of the implementation of standards, by drawing up specific reports or documents that may be, only sometimes, advertised globally.[115]

---

[112] See the ICC recommendation, 'ICC's Expectations Regarding a WTO Investment Agreement', prepared by the Commission on Trade and Investment Policy (7 March 2003): '... in order to provide effective protection of investor rights, the agreement should include a binding investor-to-state dispute settlement mechanism, in addition to and separate from the WTO "state-to-state" dispute settlement procedure ... Under such an investor-to-state mechanism, investors should be free to choose between resort to arbitration or going to the courts, this choice however having to be fixed at a given time. In the case of arbitration, a WTO investment agreement should include a provision stating that WTO members agree to submit themselves to arbitral proceedings, which the investor may put in motion. While the investor and the host government should be free to select the arbitration rules and forum, a WTO investment agreement should nevertheless foresee a choice of competent authorities in case no selection was previously made, namely ICSID, UNCITRAL, or the ICC International Court of Arbitration.'

[113] Note that the ICC is the main business partner of the UN and its agencies.

[114] The term 'effectiveness' refers to levels of functioning, incisiveness, efficacy, strength, practicality and appropriateness of the mechanisms that ensure implementation of standards.

[115] The expression 'administrative enforcement' would indicate the implementing and monitoring activities performed by specific bodies or committees inside the

Three examples show this: the 'IATA Safety Audit for Ground Operations – ISAGO' is an administrative body which improves safety and reduces costs in the environmental sector.[116] This body is active in standards development and maintenance: the standards are reviewed and updated as necessary.[117] Nevertheless, these standards have no binding effects on non Members and they are applied only within the Association.

A second example is the enforcement of ICC standards. There are many administrative institutions responsible for promoting and monitoring the implementation of these rules. The International Bureau of Chambers of Commerce (IBCC) (now called the World Chamber Federation – WCF) promotes cooperation between chambers of commerce in developing and industrial countries, and administers the 'ATA Carnet system' for temporary duty-free imports; the Institute for World Business Law is responsible mostly for studying legal issues relating to the application of standards in international business. Also, specific national committees promote 'the adoption and implementation of the policies advocated by ICC by the governmental authorities, administrative agencies and other institutions with a view to their implementation in [their countries]' (Article 3 of ICC Constitution). Lastly, the Secretary General has the general responsibility for developing and implementing ICC standards (Article 6 of ICC Constitution).[118] Therefore, all these administrative bodies carry out research, promotion and monitoring of standards, without, however, exercising powers of intervention or applying sanctions when standards are infringed.

The third example concerns WIPO standards. The 'Advisory Committee on Enforcement',[119] created after the WIPO Consultation Meeting on Enforcement (September 2002), offers technical assistance and coordination with certain private sectors to combat counterfeiting and piracy

---

regulatory regime. Therefore, this type of enforcement differs from the (quasi) jurisdictional enforcement performed by courts, panels and arbitral tribunals.

116 ISAGO is based on the 'IATA Operational Safety Audit' (IOSA) framework and aims at implementing a formal, systematic process to manage operational risk and safety, reducing accidents, incidents and injuries. See also Section 2.

117 For more details, see www.iata.org/workgroups/Pages/isago.aspx

118 Note that there is a specific enforcement mechanism of standards relating to the fight against commercial crimes. In the 1980s, ICC set up three services to fight commercial crime, corresponding to the 'International Maritime Bureau', the 'Counterfeiting Intelligence Bureau' and the 'Financial Investigation Bureau'. There is also a bureau responsible for the enforcement of the standards relating to cybercrimes. The 'ICC Commercial Crime Services' coordinates the activities of the specialized anti-crime services. These bodies, mostly, exercise prevention and monitoring functions, and are considered 'watchdogs for international trade'.

119 See http://www.wipo.int/enforcement/en/ace/

activities; furthermore, it provides for the exchange of information on enforcement issues through the establishment of an Electronic Forum. However, the general mandate of the Committee is assisting Member States in strengthening their systems and infrastructures for effective enforcement of IP rights.[120] Consequently, the implementation of standards requires cooperation between the global regulator and national authorities.

Also economic incentives – see, for instance, IATA and IASB cases – may be considered a 'soft enforcement mechanism' insofar as such measures may constitute a persuasion tactic. In the former case, the compliance with IOSA opens up market incentives for carriers, by including code-sharing, wet lease, and aircraft leasing opportunities. In the latter, the publication of data by the e-Standard Forum may be a market incentive to the implementation of IASB standards.[121]

Second, arbitration and quasi-judicial remedies envisaged by some regulatory regimes correspond to enforcement mechanisms with a 'medium effectiveness'.

In particular, Article 6 of the 'IATA Bylaws' establishes the right to be heard and to arbitration.[122] There are specific 'Arbitration Rules',[123] that provide for recourse to arbitration between parties, who agree to settle their disputes under these rules, through the conclusion of a 'standard

---

[120] The 'WIPO Program & Budget 2006–2007' indicates many possible activities: 'providing, upon request, legal and technical assistance to Member States in relation to the development and establishment of effective IPR enforcement mechanisms; operating the IPEIS as a forum for parties involved in the enforcement of IP rights to share their experiences and information; collecting, and providing upon request, information on good practices, including cost-effective measures for the enforcement of IP rights; undertaking consultations and studies on specific issues pertaining to the enforcement of IP rights; coordinating activities within WIPO regarding enforcement; developing projects and information material for use in activities to enhance public awareness in the fight against counterfeit, piracy and other IPR infringements' (http://www.wipo.int/enforcement/en/activities/). The implementation of these activities is based on the strong cooperation especially with non-governmental organizations. Periodical reports on the 'WIPO Enforcement Related Training and Awareness Raising Activities and Cooperation with Intergovernmental and Non Governmental Organizations' are published on the WIPO website (http://www.wipo.int/enforcement/en/activities).

[121] See Section 2.

[122] This article states that '... a Member ... may seek arbitration under IATA Arbitration Rules. Invocation of this procedure shall suspend the effective date of the termination, pending the results of the arbitration. The decision of the arbitration tribunal shall be final and binding.'

[123] These rules are published at: http://www.iata.org/whatwedo/Documents/IATA_Arbitration_Rules.pdf

arbitration agreement'.[124] Also the ICANN 'Uniform Dispute Resolution Policy' (UDRP)[125] is a quasi-judicial remedy.[126] The procedure is mandatory only to the registries and registrars that have concluded agreements with ICANN (relating to gTLDs); in other cases (ccTLDs), the procedure is voluntary.[127] This mechanism is 'interchangeable'[128] with the WIPO quasi-judicial system (WIPO Arbitration and Mediation Center),[129] which includes procedures of mediation, arbitration, expedited arbitration, and expert determination. Another important example is the ICC International Court of Arbitration.[130] It is considered the world's leading institution for resolving international commercial and business disputes, and constitutes one of the most important services offered by ICC.[131] The procedure is regulated by specific 'ICC Rules of Arbitration':[132] the parties can agree to

---

124 Article 2 of the 'Arbitration Rules' establishes that 'where parties have agreed by means of an arbitration clause in an agreement that any dispute arising between them concerning the agreement shall be settled under IATA Arbitration Rules, any party may initiate arbitration proceedings by submitting a Request in writing to the Director General of IATA'. Any dispute may be settled by a sole arbitrator or by three arbitrators (arbitral tribunal).

125 On UDRP, see, in particular, M.J.G. White, ICANN'S Uniform Domain Name Dispute Resolution Policy in Action, 16 *Berkeley Technology Law Journal* 229 (2001); L.M. Froomkin, *ICANN's* 'Uniform Dispute Resolution Policy' – Causes and (Partial) Cures, 67 *Brooklyn Law Review* 605 (2002); L.R. Helfer, Whither the UDRP: Autonomous, Americanized, or Cosmopolitan?, 12 *Cardozo Journal of International and Comparative Law* 493 (2004). Note that the review can also be provided by other mechanisms, such as the Reconsideration Committee, the Independent Review Panel (IRP) and the Ombudsman.

126 It was set up in 1999 on the proposal of WIPO itself. The proposal was adopted following a recommendation by the 'Domain Name System Operation', with WIPO itself and the US National Arbitration Forum (NAF) being approved as the first dispute resolution service providers under the UDRP. In 2000, e-Resolution and CPR were approved as UDRP arbitrators; e-Resolution later withdrew and was replaced in 2002 by the Hong Kong-based Asian Domain Name Dispute Resolution Centre.

127 The procedure will be included in the contracts of users applying for the registration of new domain names; it will be applied once a new dispute is settled.

128 See Section 4.

129 We refer to the 'WIPO Arbitration, Mediation, and Expert Determination Rules and Clauses' (http://www.wipo.int/freepublications/en/arbitration/446/wipo_pub_446.pdf).

130 See Section 2.

131 The total number of cases handled by the Court since it was founded is more than 16 000. In 2009 alone, 817 cases were filed, involving 2095 parties from 128 countries.

132 See http://www.iccwbo.org/uploadedFiles/Court/Arbitration/other/rules_arb_english.pdf

submit to arbitration under the Rules, adding a standard ICC arbitration clause to the contract, or concluding a written ICC agreement to arbitrate.[133] The ICC also provides other dispute resolution services,[134] corresponding to the pre-arbitral referee procedure, the ADR-Alternative Dispute Resolutions, the Disputes Boards, and the ICC Expertise proceedings.[135] Moreover, the parties can request ad hoc proceedings from the ICC.[136] All these procedures ensure the application of the rule of law guarantees. Lastly, the 2006 ICC Code establishes the possibility of inquiring about the interpretation of ICC advertising standards to the 'ICC Interpretation Panel', which can be defined as a sectional judicial body of the ICC.[137]

In all the above mentioned cases, decisions adopted by the quasi-judicial bodies are generally not self-executing in national systems, mainly because of their private nature.[138] Accordingly, these enforcement mechanisms are less effective than cases in which the breach of standards may be invoked before national or European judicial bodies (see food, forestry and IASB standards).[139] In these cases, standards are, in fact, endorsed in national or European rules, the breach of which, consequently, can be submitted to

---

133 For more details, see http://www.iccwbo.org/court/arbitration/id4399/index.html

134 In these cases, the parties have to include 'combining clauses' in the contract, which allow use of the different services. See also Section 2 above.

135 There is an 'ICC Commission on Arbitration', which constitutes (with specific task forces and groups) a forum for experts to pool ideas and impact new policy on practical issues relating to international arbitration, the settlement of international business disputes and the legal and procedural aspects of arbitration.

136 ICC standards are applied in all these cases. The standards can have regard to both the solution of the dispute, and the procedure, or only the procedure, parties decide to use different rules on the merit. On international trade arbitration, see P. Bernardini, *L'arbitrato commerciale internazionale*, Milano, Giuffrè, 2000, 122ff.

137 On this point, see Paul Verbruggen's chapter in this volume.

138 Note that also the self-executing nature of the decisions of intergovernmental judicial bodies is often questioned, as emerged in the *Medellín* case related to the execution of the ICJ's decision in the USA (US Supreme Court, *Medellín* v *Texas*, 552 U.S. (2008) (No. 06–984)).

139 See also the case of ICANN, where national courts may implement a judicial review of ICANN standards. In certain cases, in fact, national courts have declared their jurisdiction, even if a UDRP procedure had already taken place. On this last point, see the case '*barcelona.com*', where the first decision was given by the WIPO Arbitration and Mediation Center, UDRP – Domain Name Dispute Resolution, Administrative Panel Decision. The case is available at http://arbiter.wipo.int/domains/decisions/html/2000/d2000–0505.html; while the second decision was given by the United States Court of Appeals for the Fourth Circuit (available at: http://www.case.info/domain/barcelona2.pdf).

domestic or supranational courts. In this sense, a national or supranational 'indirect check' of TPRs enforcement takes place.

Third, the enforcement mechanisms involving public authorities are characterized by a high degree of effectiveness or, in other words, a 'hard effectiveness'. As already noted,[140] the participation of public authorities in the implementation of TPRs may take different forms: (i) the accreditation procedures in food standards[141] and ISO cases;[142] (ii) the application of sanctions by national authorities, for instance providing for the breach of some food and WIPO standards;[143] (iii) the decentralized model related to the implementation of ICC standards in advertising and consumer protection (2006 ICC Code), entrusted to national and supranational organisms;[144] (iv) the registration mechanism, which characterizes the implementation of ICANN standards;[145] and (v) the endorsement of

---

[140] See Section 3.

[141] The accreditation is a quality infrastructure tool which supports the credibility and value of the work carried out by conformity assessment bodies and thus of the corresponding attestations issued by them (inspection reports, certifications, etc.). Point no. 8, EC Regulation no. 765/2008, for instance, states that 'accreditation is part of an overall system, including the conformity assessment and market surveillance, designed to assess and ensure compliance with applicable standards'. See also the document of the European Commission, *State of the Implementation of the New Legislative Framework (NLF)*, September 14, 2010 (available at: http://ec.europa.eu/enterprise/policies/single-market-goods/files/new-legislative-framework/nlf_implementation_report_en.pdf).

[142] See Sections 2 and 4.

[143] In Italy, the legislative decrees no. 190/2006 and no. 193/2007 introduce a series of sanctions, relating to the breach of the European Food Law. They provide for a special administrative penalty for the failure by the food business to prepare for self-control procedures, such as those based on the HACCP principles, or even those on food chain information. The copyright enforcement system (see part III of the TRIPs Agreement), instead, provides for criminal procedures and penalties to be applied at least in cases of wilful trademark counterfeiting or copyright piracy on a commercial scale; the Members may provide for criminal procedures and penalties in other cases of infringement of intellectual property rights. The remedies shall include imprisonment and/or monetary fines. On this last point, see I.D. Manta, The Puzzle of Criminal Sanctions for Intellectual Property Infringement, 24 *Harvard Journal of Law and Technology* 2 (2011), available at: http://papers.ssrn.com/sol3/papers.cfm?abstract_id=1675206; W.A. Adams, Intellectual Property Infringement in Global Networks: the Implications of Protection Ahead of the Curve, 10 *International Journal of Law & Information Technology* 1 (2002), available at: http://papers.ssrn.com/sol3/papers.cfm?abstract_id=306879

[144] For more details, see Paul Verbruggen's chapter in this volume.

[145] We recall that the registries, in certain cases, may be national or supranational public bodies with the delegation of particular top or generic level domain names (e.g. '.com', '.org', '.it', '.fr', '.es' or '.eu'); while the registrars deal with

global standards in national or supranational rules, as in the cases of food standards,[146] FSC,[147] ICANN[148] and IASB.[149]

A very particular example concerns the formulation and the application of the IATA blacklists, which can be set up by national or supranational subjects.[150] IATA can provide for action to suspend carriers from the acceding country/territory to the Billing and Settlement Plan (BSP)[151] in the event a government added a carrier to the blacklist and, consequently, placed an operating ban on it.[152] From this standpoint, the 'blacklists mechanism' works like an 'elevator': the process starts at the second floor (the global regulator sets safety standards); then, goes down to the first floor (national and supranational authorities ensure the application of standards, by adding to the blacklist carriers who infringe rules); and finally, it comes back to the second floor (the global regulator takes action to suspend carriers appearing in the blacklist). The blacklist is a strong

requests for second level domain names registrations. The system creates a form of 'distributed administration'. See also Section 2.

146 Note that the European Food Law is defined a 'pre-empting public regulation with private food quality standards'. J.J. McCluskey and J.A. Winfree, Pre-empting Public Regulation with Private Food Quality Standards, *European Review of Agricultural Economics*, 2009, Vol. 36, No. 4, 525–39 (available at http://papers.ssrn.com/sol3/papers.cfm?abstract_id=1551704).

147 On the FSC case, see E. Meidinger, The Administrative Law of Global Private–Public Regulation: The Case of Forestry, *supra* note 33, at 47.

148 We refer to Regulation (EC) 733/2002 of 22 April 2002 on the implementation of the '.eu Top Level Domain' and Regulation (EC) 874/2004 of 28 April 2004, laying down public policy rules concerning the implementation and functions of the '.eu Top Level Domain' and the principles governing registration. See also the recent Regulation (EC) 560/2009 of 26 June 2009 amending Regulation (EC) No 874/2004 laying down public policy rules concerning the implementation and functions of the '.eu Top Level Domain' and the principles governing registration.

149 On IASB standards, see, in particular, Regulation CE n. 1606/2002 (the so-called IAS Regulation) and the following Regulation (EC) 1126/2008.

150 The European Union adopted the so-called 'Blacklist Regulation', establishing the European list of air carriers which are subject to an operating ban within the Union (Commission Regulation (EC) No. 474/2006, amended by several following regulations).

151 The BSP is a system designed to facilitate and simplify the selling, reporting and remitting procedures of IATA Accredited Passenger Sales Agents, as well as to improve financial control and cash flow for BSP airlines.

152 The 'suspension action' is regulated by IATA Resolution 850, Attachment F. The IATA provisions state that 'where a BSP Airline is subject to blacklisting by a government regulator for reasons of safety and security … the International Space Station shall take action to suspend the BSP Airline only from the country/territory's BSP …'. This text was amended with formal corrections in May 2010.

enforcement instrument: in fact, the addition of a carrier to the list yields negative publicity;[153] moreover, IATA's suspension action may severely affect the carrier's finances, by threatening their commercial operations.

Although it may be viewed as a paradox, the 'self-enforcing' or 'de facto mechanisms' are also highly effective, because in these cases the application of private standards is an essential condition for the protection or exercise of certain rights and interests.

'Self-enforcing mechanisms' may characterize some ISO, ICC and ICANN standards. Market actors, for instance, spontaneously comply with ISO 9000 and ISO 14000[154] because of a series of benefits deriving from their implementation. A similar logic may underlie the ICC standards enforcement. Many companies voluntarily adopt these rules, by including them in binding contracts. In this light, ICC standards could be considered 'internationally agreed rules' that recall the medieval idea of '*lex mercatoria*'.[155] Their application, in fact, ensures the uniformity and the harmonization of international trading and produces not only a very positive input to the development of the global economy, but also relevant benefits to the companies. Hence, it is possible to recognize a kind of 'spontaneous enforcement' in both cases.[156]

As regards the ICANN standards enforcement, access to the 'top level domains system' is ensured only to those who conclude the contract with ICANN. Furthermore, the regulator imposes fees on registries and registrars,[157] and can declare the contract terminated when the net operators do not pay the fees. In this way, the operator is de facto obliged to observe not only ICANN standards, but also the fees. This mechanism constitutes a very effective standards enforcement: in fact, no operator could operate with a domain name without an established arrangement with ICANN.[158] It would be technically possible to create an independent system, but, as

153 For this reason, many carriers proposed to change the term 'blacklist', used in the IATA Resolution, to a softer and more specific term.

154 See Section 2.

155 F. Galgano, *Lex mercatoria*, Bologna, Il Mulino, 2001.

156 See G. Teubner, Global Private Regimes: Neo-Spontaneous Law and Dual Constitution of Autonomous Sectors?, in Karl-Hainz Ladeur (ed.), *Public Governance in the Age of Globalization*, Aldershot, Ashgate, 2004, 71–87 (http://papers.ssrn.com/sol3/papers.cfm?abstract_id=894423).

157 Note that it is the major source of income for ICANN.

158 In other words, if the management of a TLD is denied to a particular company, it will have no possibility of working in the sector. Moreover, a failure to comply by the operator implies the termination of the agreement (note that the ICANN bylaws provide an independent review panel to evaluate the opportunities for terminating the contract).

some scholars highlighted, 'users will tend to aggregate to the more suitable system, the one most used that provides more possibilities of interaction with others'.[159] From this standpoint, the relationship between ICANN and the operators is based on 'non voluntary contracts'.[160] Therefore, it is a peculiar kind of 'self-enforcing mechanism': in fact, while in the cases of ISO and ICC this terminology – 'self-enforcing' – would indicate the spontaneous or voluntary compliance with the parameters, with the aim of achieving certain economic benefits, in the ICANN case the implementation of standards is not really spontaneous, since it arises from the need for a service, which is otherwise inaccessible.[161] In this sense, 'self-enforcement' is based on a de facto obligation or, more exactly, a burden. More interesting conclusions may be drawn if one considers Internet access – and the use of domain names – as a fundamental right:[162] from this perspective, compliance with ICANN standards may be defined as an anomalous limit to the exercise of a fundamental right, what's more, one not envisaged by the law.

This analysis suggests at least two final remarks. First, the strength of enforcement mechanisms does not always depend on the complexity of systems: for example, the enforcement of ICC standards is more complex than that of food standards, because the former can be implemented by different mechanisms (quasi-judicial, contractual, administrative, etc.), while the latter is, mostly, entrusted to national procedures or to private entities (the certification bodies or, for instance, the supermarket chains); nonetheless, the enforcement of food standards is more incisive than that of

---

[159] B. Carotti, *L'ICANN e la governance di Internet*, *supra* note 101, 691–2. Moreover, this does not happen for what has been recognized as a 'network externality' (M. Mueller, *Ruling the Root*, *supra* note 105, at 52). See W.H. Page and J.E. Lopatka, Network Externalities, in B. Bouckaert and G. De Geest (eds), *Encyclopedia of Law and Economics*, Cheltenham, UK and Northampton, MA, USA, Edward Elgar Publishing, 2000, vol. I, at 952ff.

[160] This 'oxymoron' is drawn from S. Crawford, The ICANN Experiment, *Cardozo Journal of International and Comparative Law*, 2004, 442. See also Section 2.

[161] We specify that the implementation of ICANN standards does not affect the material access to the World Wide Web, but it conditions the possibility of operating in the network, exchanging data, communication, etc. These activities are possible, in fact, only through the tool of domain names set by this global organism.

[162] For instance, the French Constitutional Council, with a controversial decision taken on 10 June 2009, has defined Internet access as a fundamental right, ruling that the 'Internet is a component of the freedom of information'.

ICC standards, because sanctions and public measures can be applied in the first case which are not provided in the second case.[163]

Second, the existence of due process guarantees (see the cases of FSC, IATA, ISO, ICANN, IASB, WIPO and ICC) only partially affects the effectiveness of enforcement mechanisms. These guarantees, in fact, either relate to standard setting procedures, and not implementation mechanisms (see FSC, ISO, ICANN and IASB),[164] or are provided only within arbitration procedures (see IATA, ICANN, WIPO and IASB).[165]

6. CONCLUDING REMARKS

At the beginning of this analysis, we raised the question of whether the enforcement of TPR is an oxymoron or not. Our examination shows private standards are often implemented spontaneously, in the self-interest of the community involved. Yet, voluntary compliance is increasingly coupled with other types of enforcement. For example, ISO standards are voluntarily used because they guarantee interoperability. At the same time, ISO standards about quality management are certified; moreover, ISO standards are enforced through the WTO TBT Agreement. Self-enforcement is not excluded, but it is more and more one among a number of ways of enforcement.[166]

Enforcement of TPR does not look like an oxymoron for a second reason. Complexity in the means of enforcement goes hand in hand not

---

163 Similar considerations concern the relationship between IASB or ICANN standards and ICC standards.

164 For instance, the 'ICANN Bylaws' incorporate a complete code of administrative procedure, which is the equivalent of the US Administrative Procedure Act. Therefore, the application of ICANN standards can be strengthened by administrative guarantees, such as the private parties' participation in the standard setting procedure, transparency, etc. Also in the FSC case there is a 'Code of Good Practice for Setting Social and Environmental Standards', set by ISEAL (an umbrella organization which brings together, along with the FSC, other certification bodies) (2010: available at http://www.isealalliance.org/resources/p005-iseal-code-good-practice-setting-social-and-environmental-standards-v50), that requires the standard setter to follow notice and comment procedures and to consult with stakeholders (arts 4.2.2–4.2.3; 5.3.1–5.3.3).

165 To mention one example: IATA Arbitration Rules establish that the parties have the right to be heard, to receive reasonable notice, and to fixed procedural time limits.

166 On this point, see the seminal work of J. Braithwaite, Enforced Self-Regulation: A New Strategy for Corporate Crime Control, *Mich. L. Rev.*, 1981–1982, Vol. 80, 1466ff.

only with a mixture of public and private in the enforcement process, but also with the hybrid nature of the standard setters themselves.

Hence, enforcement of transnational private regulation is not an oxymoron: first, it is not always self-enforcement, but often third-party (public or private) enforcement; second, it is not always private, but increasingly hybrid, regulation.

Section 2 showed a very composite patchwork. There exist, in fact, multifarious mechanisms of TPR enforcement with heterogeneous features. First of all, we noted that standards are implemented in very different ways: from the suspension or expulsion from the system (IBA, UIA), to the certification and accreditation procedures (forest, food and ISO standards); from the provision of quasi-judicial remedies (ICANN, IASB, IATA, WIPO, ICC), to the existence of administrative bodies and measures for monitoring the implementation of standards (IASB, IATA, WIPO, ICC); from the conclusion of private contracts (ICANN), to the application of sanctions (food standards, WIPO); just to mention some examples.

This heterogeneity also distinguishes public authorities' involvement in the enforcement process, as well as the architecture of each mechanism. In relation to the latter point, in only a few cases there exist simple mechanisms, within which standards enforcement is totally entrusted to the same standards setter (IBA, UIA). Conversely, in a large number of cases the enforcement mechanism is highly composite at the structural and procedural levels (IASB, WIPO, ICC). Moreover, some enforcement systems are based on the transposition of standards in national or supranational law, entrusting, consequently, the monitoring of compliance with these parameters to States or supranational organizations (food and forestry standards, IASB, ICANN). The complexity of the examined mechanisms shows a lack of flexibility and simplicity characterizing the enforcement of TPRs. It could be considered a paradox insofar as the private nature of the regulators should usually be coupled with a higher flexibility of standards implementation. Therefore, it challenges the myth according to which public regulation is more complex than private regulation.

The complexity in the ways standards are enforced matches the increasing mixture of public and private in the enforcement process (Section 3). Private regulatory regimes are seldom self-contained.[167] Very often, public regulators take part in TPR enforcement. The cases examined above show

[167] A. Lindroos and M. Mehling, Dispelling the Chimera of Self-Contained Regimes, *supra* note 69.

how public actors can play different roles. Two models of public intervention in enforcement are particularly recurrent and need to be clearly distinguished.

In some cases, public authorities enforce a *set* of specific standards established by global private regulators (EU regulation incorporating IATA's blacklist and EU regulation relating to the '.eu' top level domain name are two cases in point). In other cases, public actors refer to an unspecified number of standards (potentially, all the standards established by a private regulator). The EU IAS Regulation and TBT reference to international standards are two such examples. While in the first hypothesis public authorities' roles identify with their lending their binding legal force to a specific set of private standards, selected on a case-by-case basis, in the second case, given the broad reference to the standard setting activity of private regulators, public authorities try to go one step further: they try to influence the private actors.

Instruments used for this purpose can vary. Very often they are procedural ones. The EU tries to make its voice heard within IASB due process. The WTO TBT Committee's 'Decision on Principles for the Development of International Standards, Guides and Recommendations' tries to influence international standard setters (mostly the ISO and the IEC) relevant for TBT application.[168] Yet, there exist also tools affecting the structure of private regulators. The Monitoring Board – aimed at ensuring the public accountability of the IASB and bringing together representatives of a transnational network such as the IOSCO and of domestic regulatory authorities (the JFSA, the SEC and the EU Commission) – is a case in point.

About the increasing hybridization of TPR, two last points must be noted. First, the mixture of public and private is not exclusive to the implementation, but is a feature of the very structure of the regulators (the ICANN and the ISO are two cases in point). Even though there are several examples of an increasing hybridization of private actors, also the opposite trend, that is, the increasing privatization of an international organization, can be observed (the WIPO). Second, public authorities connecting with

---

[168] On this point, see R. Howse, A New Device for Creating International Legal Normativity: the WTO Technical Barriers to Trade Agreement and International Standards, paper for the NYU Law School 'Global Administrative Law Conference', 22–23 April 2005, available at: http://iilj.org/global_adlaw/documents/HowsePaper.pdf

private ones can be found at all levels (domestic, regional, global). However, the EU appears particularly active, often connecting with private actors for regulatory purposes.[169]

Several enforcement mechanisms operate on the basis of linkages between different regulatory regimes, as examined in Section 4. More than a dozen types of linkages characterize the relations between enforcement mechanisms, making the TPR enforcement process even more complicated. This phenomenon raises some questions: why does ICANN standards enforcement – to mention a significant case – need recourse to WIPO structures? Why are there several cases in which governmental organizations, such as the WTO, are involved in the enforcement process of global private standards set by different regulators? In other words, what are the reasons for the linking regimes phenomenon? There are at least four possible answers.

First, linkages allow for a better operation of the enforcement mechanism, mostly in the case of borrowing regimes. The standards implementation, for instance, is more reliable when one can make use of (quasi-)judicial remedies provided by more global regulators (as in the case of ICANN and WIPO standards). In this way, in fact, there is a greater possibility of enforcing the standard when it is infringed or not applied. In other cases, a linkage may ensure a better operation of enforcement mechanisms insofar as it provides a means of harmonization. Accreditation or certification schemes related to food and forestry standards, for instance, must be in accordance with specific ISO standards. This leads to the uniformity and standardization of enforcement mechanisms.

Second, linkages avoid or solve problems of overlap between regimes regulating the same areas or similar issues. The exercise of security functions in the air transport sector at the global level, for instance, requires coordination between IATA and ICAO, which takes the form of a substantive linkage. In this case, it is recognizable as an example of 'positive comity' insofar as the conflicts of competence are avoided or solved in a cooperative manner, in the absence of parameters regulating this relationship.[170]

---

[169] A. Nolke and J-C. Graz, Conclusion: the Limits of Transnational Private Governance, in J-C. Graz and A. Nolke, *Transnational Private Governance and its Limits*, New York, Routledge, 2008, 225ff., at 234 (arguing that the EU 'has come out as a major driving force behind the spread of transnational private governance').

[170] On 'comity mechanism', see R. Paul, Comity in International Law, 32 *Harvard International Law Journal*, 1 ff. (1991); id., The Transformation of International Comity, 71 *Law and Contemporary Problems*, no. 3 (2008).

Third, linkages may be 'de facto situations', when different global regulators set standards related to the same issues (see the food standards case). In these cases, so-called specific issue linkages,[171] enforcement mechanisms are interchangeable, and the implementation of a standard may be replaced by a different enforcement mechanism (see the relation between some food and ISO standards).

Lastly, 'unity is strength'. In other words, the linkage between different regulatory regimes may improve the effectiveness of enforcement mechanisms and the achievement of targets set by the global regulator. It occurs in financial regulation, within which incorporation, borrowing, and participatory and substantive linkages improve the IASB standards enforcement. Also linkages involving the participation of the WTO are very emblematic. We recall that the WTO can borrow standards from the ISO, receive assistance and establish forms of cooperation with WIPO, and accept recommendations from the ICC. In these cases, the enforcement of WTO rules, as well as the achievement of the organization's goals, are improved by the linkages with the different private regulators. A remarkable paradox takes place: the public regulator uses enforcement instruments set by private entities to make its implementation mechanisms more effective. The paradox is recognizable insofar as the opposite situation, usually, occurs (see all those cases in which private standards enforcement requires the involvement of national or supranational authorities).[172] In fact, it is more reasonable to think that private regulators need the assistance of the public authority, since they cannot provide coercive measures for the implementation of standards. However, as noted, it is a 'mutual need'. This phenomenon shows that not only may TPR enforcement mechanisms have an efficacy comparable to that characterizing the public instruments, but also interchangeability between public and private mechanisms takes place. The permeability of public–private[173] at the global level, therefore, becomes ever stronger.

Section 5 identified three levels of effectiveness, distinguishing soft, medium and hard enforcement mechanisms on the basis of specific parameters. It is not a rigorous classification; on the contrary, there are several areas of '*chiaroscuro*' characterizing the TPR scenario. The enforcement mechanisms of ICC and ICANN standards are significant examples. In both cases, the standards implementation can be entrusted directly to

---

171 D.W. Leebron, Linkages, *supra* note 68, 5ff.

172 See Section 3.

173 See J. McLean, Divergent Legal Conceptions of the State: Implications for Global Administrative Law, 68 *Law and Contemporary Problems*, no. 3–4, at 183 (2005).

private entities. In this perspective, they are similar mechanisms, attributable, on the basis of the above mentioned taxonomy, to the 'hard', 'self-enforcing' level of effectiveness. Different degrees of 'self-enforcing', nevertheless, may be in turn identified. As underscored in Section 5, the 'self-enforcement', in fact, may be more or less incisive according to the existence of a de facto obligation (ICANN) or a mere condition (ICC). A similar assumption also concerns the other levels of the above mentioned classification (medium and soft degrees) in relation to, respectively, the different efficacy of each (quasi-)judicial remedy and the peculiarities of administrative monitoring measures.

This analysis leads us to a relevant conclusion. TPR enforcement mechanisms may be very effective, bypassing national governments and legal orders. In fact, they are directly applicable to civil society, although public authorities, in several cases, play a key role in their enforcement process. These standards may compete with national rules in numerous fields: food safety, environment, finance, copyright protection, trade, just to recall some examined examples. In these cases, some scholars recognize a challenge to state sovereignty:[174] TPRs are 'not directly subject to control by national governments or domestic legal systems or, in the case of treaty-based regimes, the states party to the treaty'. Furthermore, 'these regulatory decisions may be implemented directly against private parties by the global regime or, more commonly, through implementing measures at the national level'.[175] Private regulatory regimes, therefore, pose a much more difficult challenge to state sovereignty than public regulatory regimes (as international governmental organizations, transnational network administrations, distributed administrations). In the latter case, regulatory regimes are usually established by States, and their regulatory power is delegated by national governments. From this perspective, they could be considered 'global outsourcing cases', in which the States outsource some regulatory

---

174 On this point, see, in particular, S. Cassese, *La crisi dello Stato*, Roma-Bari, Laterza, 2002, 14ff.; id., Global Administrative Law: an Introduction, 37 *Journal of International Law and Politics*, 4, Summer 2005, 663–94 (available at: http://www.iilj.org/GAL/documents/Cassesepaper.pdf). See also C. Scott, Regulating in Global Regimes, UDC Working Papers in Law, Criminology & Socio-Legal Studies Research Paper no. 25/2010 (available at http://papers.ssrn.com/sol3/papers.cfm?abstract_id=1598262); K.A.D. Camara, Costs of Sovereignty, 107 *West Virginia Law Review*, 385 (2005) (available at http://papers.ssrn.com/sol3/papers.cfm?abstract_id=554963).

175 B. Kingsbury, N. Krish and R. Stewart, The Emergence of Global Administrative Law, *supra* note 2, at 5.

functions at the global level.[176] As regards private regulatory regimes, they are hybrid intergovernmental–private administrations (as ICANN, WIPO, etc.) or totally private bodies (as ISO, IATA, ICC, etc.)[177] that do not exercise powers delegated by States, but have independent regulatory functions.[178] Some interesting questions concern the reasons why global private entities perform public regulatory functions: they could be mere economic reasons, as in the food standards case where private regulators sell standards to market operators; or the more noble purpose of 'better regulation'.[179] According to the latter interpretation, sectors related to the safeguarding of global interests (environment, Internet, trade, etc.) would be more efficiently regulated by private and independent entities, which are not affected by governmental interests and political dynamics. In this sense, concerns about the TPRs' democratic legitimacy[180] would be somehow counterbalanced by the benefits deriving from the independence of these organisms.

The problem of the legitimacy of global private regulation is highly debated.[181] If legitimacy concerns are weaker when a purely voluntary implementation of private standards is in place (Section 1), they look particularly timely when standards are third-party enforced. The high number and variety of tools for enforcement (Section 2) and their multifarious linkages (Section 4) make private standards extremely effective (Section

---

[176] In this case, the term 'outsourcing' has a meaning similar to that of 'delegation'. The object of outsourcing, therefore, is a traditional state function, whose 'ownership' remains in the hands of the States that, when setting up a global body (by treaty, etc.), sell a portion of their sovereignty.

[177] See A.G. Scherer, G. Palazzo and D. Baumann, Global Rules and Private Actors – Towards a New Role of the Transnational Corporation in Global Governance, 16 *Business Ethics Quarterly*, 505–32 (2006) (available at http://papers.ssrn.com/sol3/papers.cfm?abstract_id=959416); C.M. Bruner, States, Markets, and Gatekeepers: Public-Private Regulatory Regimes in an Era of Economic Globalization, 30 *Michigan Journal of International Law*, 1 (2008) (available at: http://papers.ssrn.com/sol3/papers.cfm?abstract_id=1152307), and more recently, T.M. Roberts, Innovations in Governance: a Functional Typology of Private Governance Institutions, 10 October 2010, *Duke Environmental Law & Policy Forum*, forthcoming (available at http://papers.ssrn.com/sol3/papers.cfm?abstract_id=1690831).

[178] In this case, there is no form of 'delegation' or 'outsourcing', because the body has not been created by the State.

[179] Here, the expression is used with the meaning of 'more efficient regulation'.

[180] On this point, see E. Benvenisti and G.W. Downs, National Court Review of Transnational Private Regulation, 2011, available at http://papers.ssrn.com/sol3/papers.cfm?abstract_id=1742452.

[181] For a general overview of the debate, see A. Nölke and J-C. Graz (eds), *Transnational Private Governance and its Limits*, Abingdon, Routledge, 2007.

5). Moreover, when public actors enforce these standards, they can become legally binding (this is the case when the EU comes into the picture, for example when using IATA's blacklist or when endorsing international accounting standards: Section 3). The combination and effectiveness of the enforcement tools make legitimacy concerns even more complex to cope with.

Some of the developments examined above show the tendency of public actors systematically enforcing private standards to (try to) impose participatory requirements (the TBT Decision, the EU's efforts to influence the IASB) on private standard setters, or to establish new bodies with the task of ensuring these private regulators' accountability (the Monitoring Board controlling IASB's actions). But are these tools effective? How far do instruments coming from the domestic administrative law tradition (such as participatory rights, due process and duty to give reasons), used at the global level, go in fostering the legitimacy of private regulators? How can the Global Administrative Law perspective be used in order to frame such a pressing problem? This chapter has highlighted the areas where legitimacy concerns are stronger – where linkages are stricter and public authorities are more involved – thus identifying the areas where further research is most needed.

Index